A Minority of One

WO2 Payne W. RMP, AIB, LS&GC, GSM, scorer of important goals, cricketing sensation, squash player extraordinaire, all round nice guy, GCEs in Maths, Science, English, Human Biology, French and German, A Levels in German and Geography, Leicester City supporter, Member of Leicestershire CCC, Member of Newfoundpool Working Men's Club etc.etc.

This is the second volume of *A Monkey's Tale*.

Full title of the first volume:

Wally by Name : A Monkey's Tale
ISBN: 0-595-34650-2. Published by iUniverse Inc, 2005.

For further information on Volume One, see
www.diadembooks.com/payne.htm
For further information on Volume Two, see
www.diadembooks.com/wally.htm

A Minority of One

A Monkey's Tale Continued

(Volume Two)

Wally Payne

iUniverse, Inc.
New York Lincoln Shanghai

A Minority of One
A Monkey's Tale Continued

Copyright © 2005 by Wally Payne

All rights reserved. No part of this book may be used or reproduced by any means, graphic, electronic, or mechanical, including photocopying, recording, taping or by any information storage retrieval system without the written permission of the publisher except in the case of brief quotations embodied in critical articles and reviews.

iUniverse books may be ordered through booksellers or by contacting:

iUniverse
2021 Pine Lake Road, Suite 100
Lincoln, NE 68512
www.iuniverse.com
1-800-Authors (1-800-288-4677)

ISBN-13: 978-0-595-35110-7 (pbk)
ISBN-13: 978-0-595-79812-4 (ebk)
ISBN-10: 0-595-35110-7 (pbk)
ISBN-10: 0-595-79812-8 (ebk)

Printed in the United States of America

DEDICATION

To Bob—a friend indeed

Contents

Military Postings ix

CHAPTER 1 1

CHAPTER 2 13

CHAPTER 3 31

CHAPTER 4 39

CHAPTER 5 54

CHAPTER 6 80

CHAPTER 7 98

CHAPTER 8 125

CHAPTER 9 142

CHAPTER 10 159

CHAPTER 11 172

CHAPTER 12 186

CHAPTER 13 196

CHAPTER 14 215

CHAPTER 15 234

CHAPTER 16 242

CHAPTER 17 259

CHAPTER 18 274

CHAPTER 19 286

CHAPTER 20 305
CHAPTER 21 317

Military Postings

The Author's Military Postings in this Volume:

LOCATION	DATES	CHAPTERS
CYPRUS	1976–78	1–4
WERL, WEST GERMANY	1978–81	5–7
HOHNE, WEST GERMANY	1981–82	8–9
NORTHERN IRELAND	1983–84	10–12
COLCHESTER	1984–86	13–15
EDINBURGH	1986–88	16–18
HOHNE, WEST GERMANY	1988–89	19
DETMOLD, WEST GERMANY	1989–90	20
HONG KONG	1990–91	21

1

It was a dramatic transition, from peering through a portacabin window over-looking a rainswept runway at Aldergrove airport, to a mess with a well-tended garden and a panoramic view of the blue Mediterranean…The Greek who drove the NAAFI tea and sandwich truck around Episkopi summed up my feelings with the only three words of English that he knew: 'Welcome to Cyprus!'

Everything in the military seemed to move at a snail's pace here, compared to the hurly burly of Northern Ireland, my last posting. Work started at the ungodly hour of 0700 hrs admittedly, but by 1300 hrs everyone had finished for the day and had gone home for a siesta, or headed for the beach, or gone down to Happy Valley to play sport. Those on police duties worked around the clock of course—even sleepy Cyprus had its criminals. Our unit lines were situated at the junction of the main road that ran through the Western Sover-eign Base Area and the road that led into the garrison itself. It was a modern, airy building and a pleasant place to work from. I was a section commander, which meant I had a mere four guys under my command. I was content to ease my way slowly into the job and enjoy what appeared to be the ultimate place for a lazy, sunshine posting. The Officer Commanding, however, had other ideas about me sitting on my backside in the sun.

Resplendent in my new lightweight suit, I was marched in to see Major Stansfeld for my initial interview. Initial interviews only last for a couple of minutes, during which time the OC will attempt to ascertain whether you have both arms and legs, whether you are daft, deaf or in debt and, if he is the sporting type, whether you play any blood sports.

"Welcome to Cyprus, Sergeant Payne," he said. "Been here before? I understand you are a sportsman of some renown? Care to join a climbing expedition in the south of France?" He was clearly in a rush to get onto something more important than my interview.

"Thank you, sir." I qualified my reply: "Yes, in 1972. Yes, and no thank you, I don't care for sheer heights."

"Well, it isn't mountain climbing per se, more mountain walking really, all on defined paths," he said, proving that he could be sparing with the truth when trying to recruit an expedition member at the eleventh hour.

"In that case count me in. When do we leave?"

"Tomorrow evening's flight to the UK. It will cost you sixty quid Cypriot. See Corporal McTavish—he has all the details."

I was ushered out of the office by a highly disgruntled CSM, who had just seen his long awaited sergeant replacement stolen away for a month before he had even unpacked his suitcase.

Major Stansfeld was the RMP version of Blashford-Snell and was infamous for organising expeditions that seldom went to plan and rarely reached their objective. The reason for my swift recruitment was the fact that he couldn't browbeat anyone else into joining the jaunt; stories of how he had almost lost a team member down a crevasse in Canada the previous year were still doing the rounds. Payne had been conned. Next morning I met up with my old pal McTavish, the pride of Galashiels. A more unlikely mountaineer than the Glayva swigging Borderer would be hard to find. If he could survive a month in the mountains, then I certainly could. The fact that Cyprus only has one mountain worthy of the name might explain why the corporal at the RAF mountaineering stores, where I had gone to cadge whatever kit they could spare, was so pleased to see me. He really couldn't have had too many customers and I wondered if his stores might have prospered from a move to an alternative location—one with mountains! Mustn't knock them, though; prior to visiting his store my entire hill climbing gear consisted of a pair of hand knitted socks. Some of the stuff the storeman gave me proved invaluable—crampons, snow gaiters and snow goggles, for example. He also gave me some stuff that I would certainly have been better off without. My 'French cut' walking breeches that fitted where they touched were particularly nasty; they had enough room in the arse to store a stone of potatoes as well as my backside. It beggars belief that they were actually designed with the human form in mind—pity the poor soul that they fitted. My ice axe was the world's worst. It only ever stuck in the ice once, but fortunately for me, this was at a time when I needed it most and it saved my life. More about that later! The storeman produced a pair of walking boots that may well have been on the inventory since he was a lad. Constructed by a manic cobbler, they were size twelve, tawny coloured (to clash nicely with my grey Charlie Chaplin trousers) and constructed of super porous leather.

"The very thing for walking in the snow," claimed the lying storeman.

Glad of anything, I signed for the kit and hurriedly packed it in readiness for our evening departure. It was only when they had me captive on the plane, flying from Akrotiri to Brize Norton, that the true aim of the expedition was revealed. The seven of us were bound for Chamonix in the High Savoy, the town that lies at the foot of the 18,000-foot Mt. Blanc. So much for the major's 'mountain walking' and 'defined paths' propaganda! Out of the team of seven, only three had experience of climbing anything steeper than a flight of stairs; the rest of us were novices in the purest sense of the word. Somehow, I had volunteered to climb the highest mountain in Europe. We finally reached Duesseldorf, where we met up with the eighth member of the team, Sammy Gromzik. Sammy had been on the previous year's expedition and yet had still volunteered for a second helping. That spoke volumes for his mental state.

The RMP Adventurous Training Stores were kept in Duesseldorf—and a pitiful collection of kit it turned out to be. We took a few ropes and a couple of rucksacks and left the remainder of the rubbish to rot for a further year. Included on the store's inventory was the only canary yellow Landrover in Europe and this was to be our means of transportation for the long ride down to Chamonix. We packed the kit and ourselves into the rear of the ancient machine and set off for France in the pouring rain. It piddled down throughout the entire, uncomfortable journey, during which we were treated to Jimmy McTavish's cavalier driving. He put it all down to loose steering, although that failed to convince me, having experienced his individualistic driving style many times throughout the years. He may have been a fellow Borderer, but there was definitely no bloodline between Jimmy and Jackie Stewart. We made it to Chamonix and pitched camp in a public campsite. It wasn't exactly Chris Bonnington stuff, but until the rain abated, it gave us a chance to live comfortably, given that the camp was equipped with toilets, washrooms—and a bar.

By the third morning the weather had changed and we had clear blue skies and warm sunshine. Mt. Blanc was visible from the site and looked very big. We now had the chance to get onto the snow and build up some fitness in readiness for an assault on the monster. Before setting off on the first morning's effort, the major called us together for a conference. His plan was that we should train for two weeks on the snow and ice lower down the mountain, before making our attempt on the summit. The original idea had been to hire a guide to lead us to the summit and the major had ventured down into Chamonix for the purpose of finding someone suitable. Once he had discovered that the fees were beyond the expedition's limited financial resources, the unilateral decision maker dispensed with the idea of a guide. There were those among us who were unhappy at this decision and would have been more than willing to put our hands in our pockets to augment funds. Instead of spending the money frivolously on a Frog with a feather in his hat, a man that would know the mountain like the back of his hand and who would guarantee the team's safety, the major elected to use our money more wisely. He purchased several cases of decent wine and bought an Ordnance Survey map of the High Savoy region. At least Mt. Blanc was on the map. Again, there were several of us who were less than impressed by our leader's show of irresponsibility, but he wasn't the kind of man to submit to an inquisition and, in any event, the damage had already been done.

Led by Major Eddy Stansfeld, the man with the map, we set off towards Mt. Blanc looking anything but professional. Getting onto the lower glacier from our campsite was simplicity itself. It involved walking along a tarmac road for a mile, turning left over a wooden bridge, right along a track for a hundred yards and then taking a final left up another track. After a few hours of hard graft, that would bring us to the terminal moraine at the foot of the glacier. By the time we had crossed the wooden bridge over a fast flowing glacial stream, Steady Eddy stopped, scratched his head and called for a second opinion about our position. This was indicative of the doubtful leadership he was to display throughout the expedition. Fortunately, we had a cavalry officer in the team, a climber who had been on Mt. Everest with the British Army Expedition. He knew what he was doing and was able to advise Eddy quietly, but positively. He would undoubtedly have made a better leader, but Eddy's arrogance would never allow him to relinquish the role, even for the good of the rest of us. We made it to the glacier by lunchtime and after eating some hard tack biscuits and jam, something I'd usually have fed to the camp dog but which tasted remarkably good at this altitude, we embarked on some elementary crampon work. This would allow us novices to get some idea of walking and climbing on ice. Eddy's first period of instruction was dedicated to 'front pointing' and proved most elucidating. He demonstrated the method of climbing up a sheer ice wall, by alternatively kicking the foremost points of the crampon into the ice and at the same time, smacking your axe into the ice above your head to gain leverage. It was surprisingly simple once you had become accustomed to the idea of all your weight being taken by a couple of spikes attached to the end of your boot. Eddy performed most impressively as he progressed up the forty-foot ice wall, commenting on his every move as he did so. We novices were mightily impressed—until he reached the top, that is.

"And when you reach to top, you disengage your ice axe and put your favoured leg up until you...*Aaaaaaaaaaagh!*"

He tumbled down to the bottom rather more quickly than he had climbed up, ripping the elbows out of his pullover and the knees out of his breeches at the same time. He was bleeding nicely and was undoubtedly in considerable pain; the embarrassment must have been killing him, too, but being a proper officer, he promptly climbed back up the wall. What were our chances of climbing Mt. Blanc when our leader fell off after only forty feet?

We spent a lot of time on that glacier and the glacier further up, attempting to master skills that might prove invaluable once we were on the mountain proper. Actually, climbing up mountains in Europe is a pretty pointless pursuit, given that most of them have a train or cable car running all the way to the top. Mt. Blanc has a cable car and train that go part of the way up, but doesn't have anything that goes anywhere near the summit. Having spent the whole of one training day inching our way up a glacier, I turned a corner to discover a crowd of old ladies from the Alsace Lorraine Darby and Joan Club. They were watching our pathetic progress from the security of a footpath, having come up by 'glacier train' from Chamonix in half an hour. One old biddy called me over to deliver a lecture, first in French and then in German, about the folly of risking one's life on a mountainside. She actually offered to pay my train fare back down to Chamonix, but I wasn't too keen to be seen wearing these trousers in public and declined her kind offer.

Following two weeks of hard training, Eddy announced that we would attempt the summit next day—without a guide, naturally. As quartermaster, which really meant that I was responsible for the pile of rubbish we called stores and for the food, I was required to prepare three day's rations. We celebrated the news of the attempt by downing a few bottles of Eddy's wine, which proved very drinkable.

On the big day, we took the cable car up as far as it went and legged it from there. Purists might frown on the use of the cable car and consider it cheating, but as there was nothing pure about our little band, we considered it to be well within the rules. From the cable car terminal, we followed a small track and were soon onto an ice field that stretched for miles. I was immediately struck by the vastness of the mountain, by how big some lumps of ice can be, how noisy creaking ice sounds and how scary it is to jump over a seemingly bottomless crevasse.

It was too warm. The snow was wet and the ice melting rapidly. These were absolutely the worst conditions for climbing in snow and ice, apparently, not that I knew anything about the subject. We pressed on regardless and after a few hours we were faced with a difficult decision. The most direct route upwards took us over an ice bridge that spanned an enormous crevasse. The ice was still melting and although the bridge looked solid, the question of whether it would take our weight was debatable. The alternative route was to skirt around a recent icefall to our right and thereby reach a position above the ice bridge. Eddy, the born leader of men, put the decision to the vote and we elected to try our luck by trekking up to the icefall. It took ages to reach the enormous blocks of ice, which lay at the top of a steep incline covered in waist deep snow. We took it in turns to lead and trample a path for the others. This was exhausting work and I was suffering from my first experience of making a strenuous effort at altitude. We weren't that high, around 10, 000 feet, but it was certainly enough to make you puff and blow a bit. We finally reached the icefall, where Major Eddy made one of his poorer decisions. Rather than struggle all the way round the vast icefall, he decided that we would go through it. First we had a fifty-foot ice wall to contend with, but that was easy meat following Eddy's front pointing lesson and most of us made it up smartly. Once we were all inside the icefall, we were faced with another mighty decision. The whole area was dripping with melting ice and it was creaking and groaning horribly, as if about to tumble further down the mountainside at any moment. It was also full of snow-covered crevasses that needed to be located and negotiated. Progress was almost impossible. I will admit to a certain amount of misapprehension about the wisdom of carrying on and was on the point of panic. Some of the others had already panicked and the vote as to whether we carried on, or returned to base and forgot about the whole ascent attempt, was a close run thing. Sammy Gromzik brought us all back to our senses, by misquoting a bit of Monty Python in his broad Yorkshire accent.

"When I were a lad, I used to dream of being killed in an icefall like this," he said.

It made us all laugh instead of shouting at each other and so we carried on. We were forced to move painfully slowly, since the place was full of hidden crevasses and every inch required prodding with a pole, to establish what was lurking beneath the snow. When it became obvious that at our puny rate of progress we would still be in the icefall come Christmas, Sammy came up with an innovative plan. We still had a hundred yards to cover before we reached a massive ice wall that marked the boundary of the icefall and Sammy, either as mad as a hatter or brave beyond compare, volunteered to be roped up and to jump along the remaining distance. That way, we would quickly know if there were any crevasses lurking underneath, because Sammy would disappear. He did go through a couple of times, but he was firmly held by the rest of us. We were at the ice wall in minutes rather than hours. Now we needed to edge our way around to the back of the wall and along its base for about twenty yards, to reach the comparative safety of a large snow covered area.

With the ice wall to our right and a bank of snow to our left lying at an angle of 45 degrees, we needed to inch our way along the base of the ice wall, using our crampons and ice axes. We were all roped together and my position was number six of eight. The first three had already made it to the safety of the snowfield by the time it was my turn to make a forward move. Eddy was directly in front of me and when he was half way along, he slipped from the base of the ice wall and down towards the snow slope. Fortunately, he managed to smash his ice axe into the wall and save himself from tumbling and quickly recovered his position. What he had done though, was to reveal that the snow bank was supported by nothing more than a few spars of ice and that we were directly above a crevasse of immense proportions. There was no option but to go on, so on Eddy's advice, I edged my way down the snow bank and attempted to stride from one spar of ice to the next.

What happened next is unclear. Presumably an ice spar gave way, because I was hanging down the crevasse and being held by the rest of the team, with Eddy screaming at them to belay. I hung there waiting for my life to flash in front of my eyes and feeling reasonably calm, all things considered. My left crampon came off and tinkled as it fell, but it didn't appear to hit the bottom. Looking down when you are in difficulties isn't recommended, but I couldn't resist a little peep. Surely the hole wasn't deep enough for my crampon to have dropped out of earshot? It was! That crevasse was big—it was greenish blue in colour, it appeared bottomless, and I wanted my Mam.

The sound of Eddy's voice concentrated my mind. He was shouting over the top of my hole to the Himalayan climber, who was last man on the rope. Their discussion centred on whether they could pull me out without endangering everyone else, or whether they would need to cut me down. I wasted no time in giving them the benefit of my opinion and the Himalayan agreed with my sentiments. By this time, my head was below the level of the snow and ice, but a rescue plan was swiftly put into action. My mates began to swing me inwards, until I was able to make one almighty effort and smash my ice axe into the wall. Adrenaline allowed me to find strength that I didn't know I possessed and my axe went in with such force that it wouldn't come out again. It was the first time the bloody thing had stuck in properly on the whole expedition and now it was being left behind. Then I leant back, until my legs were above my head and my remaining crampon firmly in the ice of the wall. This allowed the others to heave me up and out. Once I was out and had reached Eddy, the relief was such that I burst out crying uncontrollably, rather like a sobbing toddler. He had held me single handed for a considerable period immediately after the fall and had taken all my weight for so long that he had wrenched his back badly. With that immense effort he had probably saved us all, for had I gone down the crevasse, the others might well have been dragged down too. Suddenly I regretted my rude comments about Warwickshire CCC.

The volume of noise coming from behind me soon bettered that of my sobbing. Jimmy McTavish's cries of abject fear at the prospect of being the next to negotiate the crevasse echoed down the valley. My tears soon turned to laughter when he threatened to kill anyone who attempted to move him before he declared himself ready to do so. In the end, he decided that he would stay on the ice wall until he died of old age and he might well have been there to this day, but for our leader's order to pull. Jimmy stumbled a little, but made it in one piece. Then we all watched in admiration as the Himalayan cut a path for himself high up on the ice wall and made it over, as easy as you like. We pulled ourselves together and set off for the manned refuge hut that was located a couple of thousand feet further up. I managed to dangle my feet into a second crevasse on the way, but this time scrambled out unaided. We made it to the refuge hut just as the sun was setting, but not before we saw a descending team following our tracks into the icefall where we had so nearly come to grief. We blew our whistles to warn them, but they were too far away to hear us and they blundered on. Perhaps they were more experienced than us and made it through without any bother, or perhaps they are lying preserved by the cold at the bottom of that crevasse.

We stayed for two nights in that hut, drinking gallons of tea and contemplating the prospect of moving on. The odd climbers coming down from the summit warned us that the warm weather wasn't making things easy further up and the decision was made to return to base. This pleased Jimmy and myself, who had resolved to go no further in any case. We had even considered asking the custodian if it were practical to hire a helicopter to bring the cowardly pair of us down. We descended with considerable speed and had made it to within two hundred yards of the end of the snowfield, when disaster nearly struck again. This time it was Jimmy's turn. The path we were following had been made by the tracks of descending skiers and was far from easy to walk on. Every few steps we would fall through the snow, often up to our waists, although there was no real danger. Jimmy saw it differently. He was mightily unnerved and far from keen to carry on, but had no option but to proceed. At one point, a stream of melt water was cascading down the slope. It hit the track and went under the ice for about ten yards, before shooting up to the surface once again. Somehow, Jimmy managed to slip at the precise moment he was crossing the stream and was dragged under the ice by the force of the water. He was stuck on his back, a mere half an inch under the ice, but quite incapable of doing anything other than drown. It all looked so comical, to everyone but Jimmy that is, and we all howled with laughter as we rushed to his aid. The dour Scot was not amused, not least by our show of mirth and it took the coaxing of the combined team to persuade him to move on.

We reached the descending cable car at the same time as a group of Japanese tourists, all of whom were done up in their Sunday best. We had been up on the mountain for days and must have looked and smelt awful. I swore to assault the first one that looked at my breeches with anything that approached a look of superiority, but they were all perfectly friendly. They applauded enthusiastically when I treated them to two of the words from my four-word Japanese vocabulary, 'Yashika' and 'Seiko'. The other two, 'Hiroshima' and 'Nagasaki', didn't seem appropriate. We arrived back at camp and drank a few beers to unwind. These had been days that ace mountaineers Sir Edmund McTavish and Sherpa Payne were unlikely to forget.

We made a few more forays onto the glacier in the days that followed, in preparation for what would be the second and final attempt on the summit. I was having severe problems with my lips, suffering from a condition known as bark lip. It's caused by sunburn at high altitude and is easily prevented by wearing lipstick or lip salve, both of which I had considered too effeminate to apply to my masculine visage. On the night of the Queen's Birthday we went down to Chamonix to celebrate. My lips were looking like the trunk of an oak tree by this time and were hurting like hell. The pain was such that it prevented me from participating in the Loyal Toast in the conventional style and I needed to drink to our Monarch's health through a straw stuck into the side of my mouth. It was during this little get-together that I fell out irreparably with Major Eddy. A locally purchased copy of the *Daily Express* carried a story of an Irish tinker with eighteen kids, who was sponging from the Welfare State and living in regal fashion on the British taxpayer. This started a discussion about the Welfare State that became animated. My dying father was in receipt of a small benefit that I considered his right, considering his war service and the fact that he had never taken a day off work in his life. I maintained that there was no comparison between a person like my father and the tinker. Major Eddy, a man born with a silver spoon in his mouth, disagreed. He maintained that the entire Welfare State system should be scrapped, leaving those unable to fend for themselves to die. Perhaps he had drunk too much wine, perhaps he was trying to wind me up, but his comments were not appreciated and he will never know how close he came to receiving a crack on the jaw that evening. Rather than smite an officer, I left my drink and my straw, and took a taxi back to the campsite. Determined not to stay in this arrogant man's mountaineering team a moment longer than necessary, I packed my gear and prepared to leave. When he returned from Chamonix, he made a half-hearted attempt at an apology, by asking me to prepare the rations for the next day's assault on the mountain. He was told precisely what he could do with his expedition and exactly where he could shove his hard tack biscuits. All of a sudden it was 'sergeant' and 'sir' again, as he barked out various orders. His orders were ignored. Early next morning, I took a train into Switzerland and made my way back to the unit in Cyprus under my own steam.

I had been back on Aphrodite's Island for a week before Major Stansfield returned and it was another week before he deemed to speak to me. He had me marched into his office by the CSM and ordered me to apologise for the remarks that I had made to him in Chamonix. After three days of being marched in and out of his office, he realised that the prospects of eliciting an apology from me were slim in the extreme and he gave up. We avoided the subject of Mt. Blanc thereafter and the matter died a death, until it was time for my annual confidential report, many months later. My alleged failings at Chamonix were well documented in the pen picture and that wasn't on. We met many times across his table in an effort to negotiate the content of that report. When he had deleted all reference to the expedition, we managed to agree on a pen picture that made fair comment on my ability as a military policeman.

Having returned from the mountaineering fiasco, it didn't take me long to settle into the mess and the easygoing way of life that the military personnel enjoyed in Cyprus. Sport took up a great deal of my time and saw me involved in something almost every day. The Garrison's Happy Valley complex was marvellous and there were facilities for almost every sport in this lush oasis. I tried my hand at archery, cricket, golf, hockey, netball, polo (only treading down the divots), riding (only looking at the girls on the horses), rugby, soccer and swimming. Inside the camp were a dry ski slope, tennis courts, a gym and a squash complex. The place was tailor made for me. Why did I go and spoil it all then?

I was perfectly content to remain a bachelor for the rest of my life—it suited my selfish nature. My life involved spending all of my money on myself, paying court to a lady when the mood took me, getting pissed sometimes and doing exactly what I wanted to do. It was just that now, with me being in my mid-thirties, people were beginning to wonder about me. Invitations invariably requested the attendance of Sergeant and Mrs Payne at a function and people simply assumed that, at my age, I ought to be wed. It was food for thought. What harm would there be if, instead of running away at top speed whenever a woman expressed her affection for me, I should tarry awhile and see what transpired? A couple of weeks after contemplating my future attitude towards women, fate saw fit to have me wander up to the sergeant's mess for coffee rather than suffering the dubious brew back in the office. This was my first NAAFI break in the mess at Episkopi and I was surprised to see that, apart from a woman sergeant, there was no one else present. It transpired that she was only there because it was her first day in Cyprus and she was waiting for her boss to arrive. Not being a lad to hang around, I arranged to meet her that evening and most evenings thereafter.

I'll fast-forward twelve months at this juncture.

A year later, having 'let it happen', I was about to be married. Whatever possessed me to drift into marriage in this fashion is beyond me! A few days before making the irrevocable decision, something told me it was all a big mistake, but like so many reluctant men who have found themselves in the same position, I did sweet bugger all about it. Her parents arrived from Scotland two days before the event and, in all honesty, the looks and demeanour of her mother ought to have warned me about the folly of my impending action. What a cow *she* turned out to be! She really was an appalling woman and it was a case of hate at first sight between us. Her father was rather more to my liking; he got off the plane with more than a few complimentary drinks in the bank and greeted me like a long lost brother. He declared that he had two questions to ask before he would give his unequivocal blessing to our union: "You're nae a catholic, are you?" and "Dae ye tak' a dram?" I was able to satisfy him on both counts. Arriving home from the airport at 0500 hrs, John produced a bottle of the Glemnorangie and we set about it. Fortunately, he fell asleep very quickly and so never heard me when I brought my share up—all over the bondhu.

The big day arrived and, despite my absolute conviction that I was doing the wrong thing, I foolishly went through with the wedding. To compound my misery her mother decided to stay on for a further week, I became a year older that Tuesday, and Elvis died the same day.

2

An individual squash league comprising ten divisions, with six players in each, was in operation in Episkopi. You played each person in your own division once during the course of a month, with the top two being promoted and the bottom two relegated at the end of the period. I managed to remain in division one the whole time, but sometimes only by the skin of my teeth.

My first match at the start of a new month's fixtures was against a recent arrival, a chief technician in the RAF, who had won the previous period's second division. I had seen this guy around the camp and, like most others, had taken a profound dislike to the boastful, body beautiful, Brylcreem boy. His torso was undeniably well developed, but this poser felt compelled to accentuate the fact by wearing the tightest singlet that Marks and Spencer produced and shorts so snug that one was left in no doubt as to which side he dressed. He bought all this arrogance with him into the squash court for our first encounter. Parking his considerable frame in the middle of the court from the outset, he refused to budge or to give me a fair view of the ball, refusing all my calls for a point or even for a let. On the occasions when he was not blocking my view, he was parked so close to my rear that his breath was discernible on the back of my neck. He argued the toss over every point and was making the match something an ordeal. I had played and beaten plenty of guys of his ilk—a hard drive into the middle of the back, or an exaggerated follow through with the racket usually doing the trick. Having put several round bruises onto his back and rear end, he had taken the hint and was now playing more of the game from the back of the court. Struggling to hang on during one rally, he was right up my bum as I played a backhand shot. Perhaps the shot was played with a little more back swing than was really necessary, but the tactic worked and he failed to return the ball. In fact, he didn't return any more balls at all that day, since he left the court for some rather urgent medical treatment. He was cut beautifully, right above the right eye and needed five sutures to close the wound. Once he felt up to a rematch, he called me again. The game was a duplicate of the first, except that a single stitch was required in his left eye this time.

You had to hand it to the chief technician, he was game and we squared up for a third time in an effort to establish who was the better man. This time I managed to avoid his eyes, but the match didn't last any longer than the previous two. With him standing in the middle of the court and making no attempt to get out of the way, I played the ball between his legs, missed and hit him in the balls with my racket. His testicles were tweaked several inches further forward than they were designed to go and he fell groaning in a heap on the floor. He scorned my suggestion that he should put his head between his legs and even refused to accept my tongue in cheek apology. What a bad sport! Once he had recovered sufficiently to walk, he hobbled to the score sheet and marked me down for a 5-0 victory. We were paired in the same league regularly after that, but never played each other again. As soon as the sheets were pinned up on the court notice board at the beginning of the month, he would hurry down to pencil me in for a 5-0 victory.

It was my intention to carry on playing blood sports until my legs packed in. The unit second-in-command, my namesake, Captain Ron Payne, had other plans for me, however. Intent on preparing me for my imminent physical decline, the path down which he had embarked upon many years previously, he decided that a man with my sporting prowess would undoubtedly make a decent golfer. How wrong he was. For the princely sum of five pounds, the world's tattiest golf bag, several ancient clubs and dozens of old balls became mine. He press-ganged me into joining the Episkopi Golf Club and, just a week later, I was standing on the first tee in a competition. It was a 'Four Ball Better Ball played under Stableford Rules', which meant as little to me then as it does now. My golfing experience up to that point consisted of two rounds of pitch and putt at Seaburn. Why did I allow myself to be talked into playing in that dreadful match? Captain Ron's insistence and the fact that he was the person who would be writing my annual report may have had some bearing.

My partner was a Royal Signals sergeant with a low handicap, and our opponents a colonel who played off six and a schoolteacher who was no slouch either. They drove off at the first and both balls landed on the brown. (Browns replace greens in Cyprus, because decent grass doesn't grow at all well. A mixture of sand and oil rolled onto a concrete base gives a putting surface remarkably similar to damp grass.) My partner also found the brown first whack, leaving me to make a fool of myself by slicing both of my first two shots into the very same bush. We played with his ball and lost the hole. There was worse to come. The second tee was raised high above a fairway that stretched for miles into the distance. They all hit their balls a good way and straight down the middle. My two efforts found the bushes at the base of the plinth on which the tee was housed and my partner suggested we play with his ball again. We came second on that hole too. Hole three was very short, but again it was my partner who played the better ball, as I failed to reach the brown with my tee shot. I caused a minor sensation by holing a fifteen-foot putt for a birdie and was given the condescending praise of those unlucky enough to be burdened with my presence. My success was short lived and things went badly wrong for me on the fourth. My driver had a loose plate at the bottom and the clicking noise it made each time it was grounded was putting me off a bit. I gave the ball an almighty smack off the tee and it soared for a magnificent fifty yards, before disappearing into the bushes. I hacked my way along the bushes and emerged triumphantly at the hole a quarter of a mile away, only to discover that the others had finished the hole without me.

Hole five was another long one with a raised tee, which had a fairway, a row of bushes, the beach and the sea all running parallel. My driver clinked as I grounded it and prayed for a decent effort. My swing lacked everything but raw power, but I connected with a decent thump. The ball sailed away, down the middle initially, before developing the most remarkable swerve to the right—that's a slice in golfing parlance, I believe. It cleared the bushes and the beach and finally plopped into the sea. As if that wasn't bad enough, the club slipped out of my sweaty palms and flew fully eighty yards straight down the middle, coming to rest on the fairway. The embarrassment was intense and I sank to my knees, begging the Lord to take me there and then.

"Having a bad day, old chap?" asked the colonel.

"Actually, I've never played before," I admitted, looking for sympathy.

My partners would only have been mildly surprised to hear me confess that; it couldn't have been every day that someone as inept as me was to be found playing in a competition. I soldiered on, much relieved at having cleansed my golfing soul by confession. My game actually improved a little and, wonder of wonders, at the seventh, my drive actually went further than my partner's did. Only twelve holes are played in Cyprus during the summer months—it's just too hot for any more, and it was a relieved novice golfer who returned to the clubhouse for a beer and to hide his face. The tale of my infamous round had somehow beaten me back to the nineteenth, or should that be the thirteenth, and the captain collared me at the bar. Without waiting for a committee decision, he banned me from playing in any more competitions until I had a handicap.

"Just put in two cards under a hundred, old bean, and Bob's your uncle," he said.

That was easy enough for him to say. It took me eight bloody years to break a hundred! My golf may not have been up to much that day, but I did at least record an ornithological first at the eighth. The Episkopi course lies at the foot of a three hundred-foot cliff, which has a huge up draught caused by the sea breezes that rise as they hit it. The area is the haunt of griffon vultures that spend their days circling on the thermals above the cliff. These big birds never need to flap their wings thanks to the up draught, the merest twitch of a tail or wingtip feather being sufficient to adjust their flight path. My slice at the eighth was really savage, even for me. Not only did the ball go off almost at right angles, but it also rose steeply, clattered off the rock face and rebounded, missing the beak of a passing griffon by inches. The alarmed creature flapped its wings furiously to escape the possibility of a second missile, but it needn't have worried as my three off the tee actually landed on the fairway.

Severe hangovers and cricket don't really mix, but this was the day of the match against the RAF police, the archenemy. It was the nearest thing there was to a grudge match on the peaceful island and my presence was mandatory, hangover or not. Thanks to the previous evening's overdose of kokkinelli I felt particularly vile, but made it down to Happy Valley by start of play. As well as opening the bowling and the batting for our modest unit side, the burden of skippering the team was mine too. I duly lost the toss—only to be expected, really, for nothing was going to go right today. Every ball I bowled hurt my head and every delivery caused me to wince with pain. My head ached, my eyes ached and I wanted to be sick. In such dire circumstances, it would be reasonable to assume that your bowling would get tanked all around the ground, but not today. For some inexplicable reason, my line and length were immaculate and my reactions even better. I took three catches off my own bowling, one of them described by our cricket playing major as 'the best caught and bowled I have ever seen', and four other wickets to boot. We had the RAFP out for a modest score, which enabled me to put myself much further down the batting order than normal, confident that it wouldn't be necessary for me to wield the willow. As the others took tea, I slipped quietly away and sat in my car for a much-needed snooze, waking only when Taffy came across and told me we had won by nine wickets. Playing cricket with a stinker may well have been the answer to my sometimes-wayward line and length, but despite my success on this occasion, I had no desire for a repeat performance.

During my second cricket season in Cyprus, we found it impossible to raise a unit side and so threw in our lot with the garrison team. I was fortunate enough to be selected for the opening match and our composite side took the field against a team representing the Episkopi based infantry battalion. Our skipper was a major from the HQ who, despite his girth, was a splendid all round player. We won the toss and the major elected to bat. He opened himself, along with a Pay Corps sergeant who was also a player of renown. Because I was only batting fifth wicket down and since the Army matches seldom have independent umpires, I was standing. The opening partnership was approaching a hundred, when the major scored the runs that took his personal tally over the fifty mark. There was some deserved applause from the pavilion and the sergeant walked down the wicket to add his congratulations.

"Well batted Charles," he said genuinely, offering his hand.

"I beg your pardon sergeant! How dare you address me by my Christian name? To you sergeant, it is either major or sir. Don't you ever forget that!" shouted the skipper.

"We're playing a cricket match, Charles, and I don't consider that rank should be a consideration," he replied in his defence.

"Well I do, sergeant—remember your station," replied the major, sounding as if he were Head Boy of Charterhouse during the 1920s.

The pair of them batted through the innings and amassed an unbeatable score. The skipper wasn't content just the same and at tea, he took the sergeant to one side to reiterate his feelings about being called by his Christian name. He then sloped off to eat his sandwiches on his own. This was just the stuff to engender team spirit in a newly formed side and, following the match, the eight non-officers in the team went into emergency session to decide whether or not we wanted to play our cricket under these circumstances. We elected to inform the major that none of us would play for him if he were to persist with his unacceptable style of leadership. It was indicative of the man that he refused even to discuss the matter and consequently the team folded after one match and one victory. We then entered the league as Episkopi Rebels, whereas the major cobbled together a side to represent the officer's mess. It was a pleasure to play in the side that thrashed the officers' eleven—although the victory was tarnished since the mad major declared himself diplomatically indisposed on the day. We went on to win the league.

There were no grass surfaces in Cyprus to compare with those of the football pitches down in Happy Valley. Not even the professional teams could boast turf as lush, but then they didn't water theirs with genuine British effluent the way we did. Effluent may not be good for much, but combined with constant sunshine, it doesn't half make grass grow. The football teams in the Cyprus lower divisions all played on dirt pitches and they were delighted to receive a challenge from our RMP side—not just for the chance to play of the valley turf, but in the knowledge that they would be provided with beer and a buffet following the match. It was my way of fostering Anglo-Cypriot relations and to see if they had brought any decent looking ladies with them. Christagi Neophytides was my good friend and also the guy who arranged the fixtures against Greek sides. He was a Sovereign Base Area policeman—a former professional with EPA Larnaca, and a man well connected in local football circles. Chris fixed matches against sides of all standards and we won the majority of our games. What always surprised me, though, was the fact that we did so well against the Cypriot first division sides that he matched us against. We took on the likes of Aris, AEL and Appollon, all top Cypriot sides, and yet never lost by more than the odd goal; sometimes we even scraped a draw. Considering that these guys were full-time professionals, who rubbed shoulders with the best in European competition, perhaps we were a better side than I had ever imagined. What I didn't know until many years later was that Chris only agreed to let these sides play us on the valley on the strict understanding that they didn't win by more than one goal. So we played a series of fixed matches over two years, with me believing the whole time that we were giving them a good run for their money.

Against the lesser sides the results were definitely not contrived, and some of them were bitterly contested. A couple of games never even made it through the ninety minutes. The first such match was against Grindlay's Bank, a fixture arranged by me without consulting Chris. Who would have imagined that a game against a group of bank clerks could turn out to be so bloody? The match started off as a hard contest, became increasingly dirty and was abandoned by the referee in the second half, when full-scale fighting broke out. The bank team was promptly struck off both our Christmas card and fixture lists. The most peculiar finish to a game came in the match against the staff of the Amatheus Beach Hotel—a team presided over by hotel resident Sam Longson, the former Derby County Chairman. During the first half it began to rain heavily and, largely because Greeks have an aversion to playing in the rain, we had built up a commanding lead by half time. They failed to appear at all for the second half. The pitches at Happy Valley could take any amount of water and so it wasn't the state of the surface that bothered them, it was simply that they didn't like getting their hair wet. After waiting more than twenty minutes for them to appear, I marched across to the changing rooms and gave them an ultimatum. Either they returned to the pitch, or they could kiss goodbye to ever playing on the hallowed turf again. They trudged back onto the field with the greatest reluctance and allowed us to score five soft goals within fifteen minutes of the restart. Their skipper then approached me, to ask if we had scored enough goals to allow them all to go home without any hard feelings. There was no point in continuing with this farce and they were told to bugger off and never to darken our valley again.

Billy McFlou was a rarity in military circles. Whereas it's common enough for warrant officers and senior NCOs to continue their service beyond the twenty-two year point, Billy was almost unique in being a long service corporal. He was employed as the assistant to the sergeant's mess manager and performed all the tasks that were deemed beneath the dignity of the staff sergeant. Everyone liked little Billy, for whom nothing was too much trouble. His simple requirements in life were a bed, the odd meal and lots of beer at night. His ambitions were equally modest. On completion of his military service he wanted to return to his native Sunderland and become a steward at his local workingmen's club.

Our Sunday social soccer team was about to depart for the pitches at Happy Valley to take on the might of the 15/19 Hussars alcoholic eleven when, with only fifteen minutes to kick off, our goalkeeper saw fit to inform me of his unavailability. I was furious and never picked the ginger haired bastard again. Still cursing, I stormed into the mess, wondering who I could pressgang into pulling on the green jersey. Billy saw me spitting blood.

"What the hell's the matter with you?"

"Bloody goalie's let me down at the last minute, Billy."

"Do you want me to turn out?"

"Can you play?" I asked, surprised that he of all people should claim to be a footballer.

"Used to be the regimental keeper for years, man," he replied confidently.

I had no option but to give Billy a try, although to say that our team members were surprised to see the diminutive figure of Billy McFlou between the sticks would be an understatement to say the least. Nevertheless, Billy was a sensation and caused everyone who had muttered comments about his suitability to eat their words. He was by any standards a handy keeper and at his prime, he might well have been very good indeed. He became our regular choice keeper after that and was thrilled at the idea of playing for us. For the first time in years he belonged to something, instead of being a shy loner. As the season wore on Billy was starting to play really well and we conceded very few goals.

We had an important match coming up and, as was my wont on such occasions, I drafted in a few guest players. One of them was a Cypriot, who had actually played for the Zimbabwean national side. Don't ask me how he qualified. He had a ferocious shot in either foot and during the kick in, he let rip with a scorcher that Billy parried and promptly fell to the ground clutching his arm. He called me over.

"That bugger's just broken my arm," he said quietly.

"Don't be a silly, Billy," I replied.

"I'm not kidding marra, get me up to the medical centre will you?"

He *had* broken his arm and so, for several weeks, we were without our star keeper. His recovery was swift and within a week of having the plaster removed, he was pestering me for a game. His comeback match was arranged and during the kick in we treated the returning hero gently. He handled everything with consummate ease; it was as if he had never been away. We were winning the match comfortably when, during the second half, their centre forward broke away for a rare assault on our goal. I set off in pursuit and just as he pulled his foot back to shoot for goal, I slid in from behind and poked the ball back to Billy. It was a brilliant piece of defending, even if I do say so myself. Billy watched the ball bobble back towards him, bent down to retrieve it and promptly let it through his legs and into the net. I had just sprinted sixty yards to make the defensive tackle of the season, only to watch Billy let the ball through his legs! As the skipper it was my duty to have a few words with him about his concentration, which was precisely the wrong thing to do. We went on to record an easy victory, as Billy went from bad to worse. After the match, he handed me his gloves and declared that he didn't want to play any more. His confidence had gone. He never did turn out for us again, despite the pleas of the whole team. He graced the touchline on occasions, but it was the end of the line for Billy McFlou, goalkeeper extraordinaire.

Sides from both major and minor formations contested a single Army Football League, with the bigger units having an obvious advantage. Tiny outfits like ours were bound to prop up the league and the RMP had in fact finished seventeenth out of seventeen the season before I arrived. The ignominy of the wooden spoon stiffened our resolve to do much better this time around. A few decent players had been posted in during the summer, but not enough for us to have a realistic chance of winning the competition. This being the case, I resorted to an alternative method of obtaining the results we needed and cheated. Against the better sides, we seldom fielded more than four or five bona fide players, the remainder of the team being made up of 'ringers'. Our pool of ringers included several Cypriot first division professionals posing as SBA policemen, a Zimbabwean international, the goalkeeper who had played for Cyprus against England and several tasty British and Danish players from the UN. We won every single match that season. The warrant officer who organised the league knew full well that RMP had cheated unreservedly and he made his feelings known at the trophy presentation. It was his entire fault, anyway; he had omitted to include the requirement for team sheets in his league rules and that was inviting chicanery. The great Jonah Barrington maintained that, 'The game is nothing, winning is everything'—and I concur.

That season's classic match was against the Mayor of Limassol's eleven, played at Happy Valley for a trophy donated by the mayor himself. Since the press and TV cameras were there, I selected my strongest team and just as well. Their side didn't appear to be much at first glance, until Christagi pointed out that the mayor was a football fanatic who only employed ex-professionals on his staff. We had a match on our hands. The game was a joy to play in and the result was a 4-4 draw. Nothing for it, declared the mayor, but to replay the game a week hence on his pitch. His pitch turned out to be the Tsirion Stadium; home to the three Limassol based first division sides and an international venue. We didn't quite fill the 35,000 capacity arena; in truth, only a hundred or so came along to watch, but it was another cracking game. We cheated even more than usual this time, by including two stars borrowed from the Royal Anglians, both of whom had been on Leicester City's books. It almost did the trick, but from leading 4-3 with only minutes left to play, we contrived to snatch defeat from the jaws of victory and lost by the odd goal in nine.

There is a damp postscript to this event. During the formal post match presentations, both teams lined up in the middle of the pitch facing each other as the mayor and an assortment of hangers on filed down the middle shaking hands. Suddenly the sprinklers activated and everyone was soaked to the skin before we could run for cover.

When not playing or organising sporting activities, another of my passions is hill walking and Cyprus lends itself perfectly to this pursuit. I had planned the walk from Episkopi village in Paphos District, to Episkopi village in Limassol District during the summer. The villages lay some forty miles apart by typical winding Cypriot road and track, but only twenty-five miles as the crow flies. The chance to do the walk fell one Saturday and my companions were Taffy Clay, Stu Ritchie and Dave Bowen. A week prior to the walk I had run into a local car dealer, to whom I had mentioned our forthcoming jaunt. He appeared excited at my story and I presumed that he wanted to walk with us, but his enthusiasm was restricted to the fact that Episkopi in Paphos was his home village and the very mention of the place filled him with pride. He wrote a note in Greek and instructed me to hand it to the owner of the village coffee shop on the morning of our walk.

It had rained heavily for two days and it showed no sign of abating on Saturday morning. The Garrison RQMS, a celebrated tippler, volunteered to drive us to the start point and at 0800 hrs we departed through the wind and rain. One wonders whether the RQMS had wind of a potential drinking session, otherwise there didn't appear to be any sound reason why he would have volunteered his services for such a mundane task. Episkopi in Paphos lay at the end of a serpentine road that stopped abruptly at the village square and went no further. We located Georgios' coffee shop, ordered five cups of the local brew and handed him the note written by car man. He read it, brought our drinks and then disappeared. We sipped our coffees and waited. Georgios remained conspicuous by his absence and my presumption was that Charlie's note had merely instructed the innkeeper to serve us coffees without poison, on the house. We prepared to leave, but were prevented from getting up by Georgios, who reappeared with another round of coffee with brandy chasers. Within ten minutes, we were tucking into a full Cypriot meze, which included beers, brandy and all the food we could handle. It was a very decent gesture, but hardly what we needed immediately prior to sallying forth on a long hike. Having finally convinced Georgios that it was imperative that we depart before we drank too much brandy, the larger part of the village population that had gathered to watch the chimpanzee's tea party bade us a hearty farewell. The RQMS was happy to stay and, as we left, he was still locked in conversation with the village drunk. The good wishes of the villagers turned to cries of disbelief as we turned left outside the taverna and headed down the hill towards the dry riverbed.

"Oxi, Oxi!" they cried, indicating that we should walk in the opposite direction.

This was my expedition and the route recce had been well done, so what was the cause of their concern? As we reached the bottom of the hill, the reason became apparent. What was a dry riverbed for most of the year was now a raging torrent, swollen by three days of constant rain.

"No probs lads, it's only shallow. We can wade it easily," I said unconvincingly.

"There is one prob mighty sergeant," said Dave Bowen. "I can't swim."

That wasn't the sort of comment an expedition leader wanted to hear, so I ignored it and led the way through ten yards of raging foam. It was rather deeper than it appeared at first glance and there was the added hazard of submerged rocks that were being swept along the riverbed at speed. Despite the hidden perils, the three swimmers reached the opposite bank without major incident; it was now Dave's turn. Because he couldn't swim, we took the precaution of tying a rope around his middle—and it was just as well that we did. Halfway across, he was knocked off his feet by a fast moving rock and carried away downstream. It would have been reasonable to expect a non-swimmer to panic, but Dave remained remarkably calm in the circumstances. The rope had probably given him confidence, or then again, he might have been paralysed by fear? The moist Mancunian was none the worse for wear once we'd pulled him out and was able to continue almost immediately. Sadly, the march proved just a bit too much for a couple of the team and we needed to abort mission, still five miles short of our objective.

Some people never learn and both Stu and Dave elected to accompany me on my next adventure, to one of the remoter parts of the island. Starting at Kykko Monastery, the burial place of Archbishop Makarios the Third, the plan was to walk across some fairly difficult terrain for a dozen miles or so, until we reached the convergence of two forest tracks. Once the track junction was achieved, it was only a matter of a two-mile walk along a path to a streambed, then a further couple of miles along the streambed to a bridge. At the bridge, my wife would be waiting with the transport and refreshments. That was the plan, anyway.

The first few miles were easy enough, but then we ran out of paths. Following goat tracks, we struggled through an undulating, thorn infested area, until we reached the base of a steep hill. Convinced that we were still on course, I announced that the path that we needed lay at the top of the hill. By this time, the other two were suffering from the heat and I wasn't feeling too frisky myself. Our problems were exacerbated by the fact that my companions had insufficient food or water and mine had to be shared three ways. Our water ration was patently inadequate and Cyprus has precious little running water, especially in the summer. Struggling to the top of the hill, we saw the track as I had predicted. Confidence soared and thirsts were temporarily forgotten. All we needed to do now was to bear right, walk as far as the track junction and we were as good as home. After an hour, we still hadn't reached the junction. Surely it couldn't be much further? Stu and Dave were all in by now and needed to rest in the shade of a tree, so I pressed on alone. Before long it dawned on me that I had buggered up the map reading and that I was heading in exactly the opposite direction to that required. When you are lost, though, it's simplicity itself to look at the map and convince yourself that you are going the right way. Scrutinising the map one more time, I had to accept that this track was taking me back towards our start point. There was nothing for it but to turn around and set off back up the hill. When I reached the lads they were still under their tree, too hungry, thirsty and knackered to continue, so they stayed put as the gallant leader trudged on to find the elusive track junction. It took me twenty minutes. Had we turned left instead of right when we first reached the crest of the hill, it would have been plain sailing. I jogged down an incline to the streambed. The stream contained a couple of algae covered pools of water, so I unashamedly scooped the green stuff off the top and drank deeply, without giving a thought to sterilising tablets. Refreshed somewhat, I found the energy to run the last couple of miles to our RV at the bridge.

We should have been there three hours previously and it came as no surprise to discover that my wife had given up the ghost. Ten minutes later, though, as if in answer to my prayers, she reappeared. She had been patrolling the road in the car in an attempt to locate us. She produced an enormous flask of orange juice from the boot and I downed it in a Cypriot All-Comer's record time. Then, having discussed the predicament that the others were in, we decided to drive back to pick them up by using an alternative route. Slamming the boot lid down, we jumped into the car and she prepared to drive us off on our mission of mercy.

"Where are the car keys?" she asked.

"You were driving the car, where did you put them?"

For once in her life she was stuck for words, but finally whispered that she had left them in the boot. I was furious, but at least she had the good sense to keep her mouth shut. It was impossible to prise the boot open so, in desperation, I tried to yank the back seat out and get into the boot that way. That proved impossible too. There was no way in, other than with the key or a pair of bolt cutters and they were in my toolbox in the boot. Stu and Dave were a serious concern and something had to be done. This was a largely unpopulated part of the island and one seldom saw another person, let alone a vehicle. My map showed a small hamlet only a couple of miles away, but a thousand feet up. My tired legs could have done without the climb, but the village finally came into view. In the square was a small taverna. I made straight for the place and ordered a large beer. The owner was a pleasant old guy who spoke reasonable English and before I could ask for help, he came across and engaged me in small talk.

"Where are you from?"

"Episkopi."

"No, no. Where do you live in England?"

"The big 'L'—Leicester."

"Leicester!" he said excitedly. "I was stationed at Melton Mowbray during the war, at the RAVC Depot. Do you ever watch Leicester City? I used to watch them regularly."

Would you believe it, a fellow Blues supporter in this unlikely spot? I slipped the names of a few wartime players into the conversation, just to please the old boy and almost succeeded in reducing him to tears. It earned me a beer on the house. But I was on an important mission and really didn't have time for all this small talk, not even to discuss the Blues. Once my predicament was revealed to him, the old soldier proved himself a real star. He went off and found a vehicle for me to drive down to Episkopi and pick up my spare car keys. The only transport available turned out to be the lorry that the villagers used to transport the contents of their earthen toilets to the fields and it smelt like it. It was a cumbersome old lorry, but believing that my walking companions might be in a desperate condition by now, I drove down the windy roads at record speed.

I had almost completed the return journey and was negotiating the final steep descent towards the bridge where my car was parked, when another vehicle came up the hill. In the rear seats sat two contented looking guys that closely resembled Stu and Dave. A goatherd had found the pair lying underneath the tree and had led them to a tap located at a church that was under construction not a hundred yards away from where they were lying, dying of thirst. The goatherd had then taken them to his village, where they had eaten their fill and supped a bottle of brandy, before agreeing to drive them home. I carried on down to the stream and put my wife out of her misery, before returning the shit wagon back to its rightful owner. After paying our car hire charges and supping some celebratory ale in the village taverna, we returned to Episkopi, where my wife prepared a pleasant meal by way of penance. We had all learned a lesson or two this day.

Twice in two walks Dave Bowen had almost come to grief, enough to put anyone off Wally Payne's walks for life, you would imagine. Not the pugnacious Manchester lad! He was made of sterner stuff and he rashly volunteered for the next adventure. This one fixed him, though; it was a long trek, through the middle of the island, on a baking hot day. Four miles from the finish Dave fell and couldn't regain his feet. He had heat stroke. He recovered quickly, but was never to be seen on any of my walks after that.

The Cyprus Walkabout sounds as if it ought to be a jolly jaunt across the beautiful island, but nothing could have been further from the truth. It was a serious examination of a three-man team's stamina and map reading ability. The event was scheduled for late summer and set over a meandering and undulating sixty-mile course, designed to take an average team twenty hours to complete. Twelve hours was the maximum allotted time to complete the 5,500-foot ascent of Mt. Olympus on the first day, with the descent on the second day needing to be completed by sunset.

The OC, Len Rudd and myself were to represent the unit in the event and we had trained hard for six weeks during the height if the Cypriot summer. We were confident that we would be able to finish the course, but harboured no illusions about being one of the first teams home. Then the major dropped a bombshell. Halfway through our three months of training, he announced that he was defecting to the officer's mess team. In fairness to him, I'm sure he would have preferred to remain with us, but the colonel had made him an offer that he would have been foolhardy to refuse. Just the same, Lenny and myself weren't best pleased. Where were we going to find anyone with enough stamina to join us at this late juncture? High summer in Cyprus is hardly an ideal time to be looking for volunteers that are fit enough, and daft enough, to start running up and down steep hills. Several plucky guys tried, but none of them were anywhere near strong enough. With only five weeks left to the big event, we were still searching for someone who could struggle up to the top of Olympus in ten hours and make the return trip next day in the same time.

Wally Pate came down from Dhekelia for a trial; he would be our last hope, five weeks being the absolute minimum period of time he would require to get enough strength into his legs. Wally was a fit, sinewy sort of man and if he had the stamina and will, then perhaps he would be our third man. After ten of the twenty-five miles we intended to cover on his first walk, he needed to drop out. Ten miles wasn't a bad effort; most of the other aspirants had thrown in the towel before that. We had christened a tree five miles out from our start point 'Cowell's Oak' in deference to one would-be team member who had all but expired under its shady boughs. It wasn't an oak tree at all, but Cowell's Oak sounds altogether more poetic than Cowell's Carob. We put Wally aboard the Landrover that met us at prearranged points along the route; the driver could take him back to camp and then meet us further up the hill. It looked as if Lenny and I would be competing as individuals after all. We battled on through the searing heat as far as the village of Lophos, where the Landrover was waiting for us, along with Wally Pate! As whacked as he was, he badly wanted to be the third member of our team and he proved his guts by walking the next section with us. He didn't make it all the way that day, but he proved that he was our man. Thereafter, he travelled down three times a week from Dhekelia for a full day's walking and was soon able to last the pace. Wally reached peak fitness a few days before the event, whereas Lenny and I had probably peaked a couple of weeks too early if the fact be known and were not to be absolutely 100% on the day. We had agreed that Army boots were the ideal form of footwear for the Walkabout, although the infantry teams who ran the course all wore trainers and would no doubt argue the point. We only ever intended to walk the course and therefore the ankle support afforded by the boots was important. There was a late panic, when Len's right boot split away from the sole along a three-inch length during a training walk. I was far more worried about it than he appeared to be, but would have been most unhappy had the boot given way on the day and ruined our chances. He was convinced that it would hold out and was proved right.

The big day dawned and, along with seventy-nine other teams, we reported to the administration area early in the morning, weighed down with loads of kit that it was mandatory to carry. The list included some perfectly silly items that would have proved a boon in the case of earthquake, volcanic eruption, typhoon or snowstorm, but which were in reality an encumbrance. Start numbers were drawn and teams soon began to leave at two-minute intervals. We had drawn number forty-two and had ample time to chat to the encouragingly large number of supporters who had gathered to see us on our way. Three tents marked the start point. In the first our identities were checked and maps issued. In the second, our kit was checked to ensure that we were carrying all the crap that the organisers considered so important. The third tent contained the master map from which we could plot our route, having first studied a printed sheet with checkpoint locations and clues listed on it. Once you were outside this tent, the clock was running and you could take as long as you wanted to plan the ascent. We didn't need long. As team leader I was delighted to see that, apart from the first checkpoint in each direction, we had physically walked every inch of the route. We wouldn't have any problems.

The prize for the team winning the Walkabout was a perfectly tasteless trophy, an old Army boot that had been dipped in silver paint and mounted on a plinth. Even if we had been good enough to win, which we weren't, the thing wouldn't have been given houseroom. The rules specified that any team winning the trophy for a third time would be given the dubious honour of taking permanent possession of the awful thing. The winners in both 1972 and 1973 had been the King's Regiment, and the Royal Anglians, who had taken over from them as resident infantry battalion, had been successful in 1974 and 1975. The Anglians, determined to make it three in a row, had written men off for months prior to the event in order to prepare them fully, which was hardly within the spirit of the original idea of a stroll up the mountain. They ran up on Mondays and Thursdays, down on Tuesdays and Fridays, and rested the remainder of the week. The Kings weren't about to lie down without a scrap either and they trained up three Army cross-country runners in the Brecon Beacons for several months prior to flying them out to Cyprus. All this for a DMS boot, painted silver!

The Kings were super fit and super confident and they just happened to be the team setting off immediately in front of us. Rabbie Burns remarked that, 'The best laid schemes of mice and men gan oft a gley' and, in the case of the Kings, their scheme couldn't have gone more badly 'a gley'. Their star runner, preoccupied with reading his map, managed to trip over the guy rope of the last tent and snapped his ankle as clean as a whistle. The other members of his team showed an understandable lack of sympathy.

The previous year's Walkabout had proved something of a disaster. The route up the mountain had been far too severe in view of the exceedingly hot weather and as a result, only eleven teams out of eighty had completed the event. By way of compensation, this year's route up the mountain was set at only twenty-five miles in length and three quarters of the teams made it to Troodos. Even the twenty-five miles were sufficient for me, especially as I'd managed to pick up a rotten cold only days prior to the off. We arrived in Troodos to a heartening reception from a dozen or more of our unit supporters who had journeyed up to welcome us. They had come by car, naturally. There was no chance to socialise, though, as we were whisked away to our overnight accommodation at the Troodos Hotel, where I slept particularly soundly.

Having confirmed with Len and Wally that they were happy with my intended route down, we set off in good heart on the thirty-five mile descent. My good humour soon evaporated, as it became obvious that we were hopelessly lost in a forest at the back of Mount Troodos. I didn't say anything to the other two, but Wally Pate was beginning to mumble as we blundered on through a succession of dense woods, bramble thickets and thorns that all tore at the legs. It was obvious that my leadership was in question when the normally docile Len asked for a look at the map. When all appeared lost, we stumbled out of yet another bramble thicket and on to a track. To my total amazement and considerable relief, fifty yards along the track stood an Army tent and a Landrover. It was the first checkpoint! Len and Wally were never made aware of the fact that, for a considerable period of time, I had been clueless about our position and of the location of the checkpoint. They averted their eyes when they were given my, 'You bastards didn't trust me, did you?' look.

As we continued downwards and with around ten miles still to cover, we began to overtake a succession of teams that were nearing the end of their tethers. One participant we overtook had frothy blood squirting out of the lace holes of his boots and I rather hope he limped on to the end. This was no time for sympathy, however—we were preoccupied with getting ourselves over the finish line. We knew this section of the terrain particularly well and we watched with incredulity as two tired teams stumbled off in quite the wrong direction. The light was beginning to fade as we reached the last checkpoint, located at the edge of Episkopi Camp. We all shook hands; there was only a mile of tarmac road to negotiate now. It wasn't until we started walking along that tarmac road that our aching feet began to hurt, but the finish was in view and so pain was irrelevant. A loudspeaker announced that the next team to finish would be the threesome representing the RMP and a loud cheer greeted the news. A better captain than me would have stood back at this point, to allow Len and Wally to cross the line first, but my competitive spirit got the better of me and I led the way in myself. We had done it, in twenty hours and a few seconds.

Having rested for twenty minutes, I stood up to discover that my legs no longer worked. Wally Pate helped me to my car and we all went to my place for a well-needed shower and a bite to eat. A celebratory party had been arranged in the corporal's mess, but fatigue suddenly overtook me. Considering that an hour's kip might put me right, I retired to bed with the instruction to my wife that she should wake me at 2000 hrs. It was at noon the next day when I finally stirred. The party had gone on without me.

3

Life wasn't dedicated entirely to sport—there was a little police work that needed attending to as well. Work needed to be kept in perspective, naturally, and I can recall an occasion when the three of us on duty played in a football match at Happy Valley, with the radio turned up full in case the girl in the duty room needed to call us. She didn't and we won 5-0.

Taffy Salter was a gentle giant. On the rugby field he was formidable, on the soccer pitch a veritable rock in defence, but otherwise he was just a big, amiable Welshman who never seemed to lose his temper. The pair of us had been called down to Steve's Hamburger Heaven on Archbishop Makarios the Third Avenue, where a couple of squaddies were causing bother. It appeared that two guys from the Royal Anglians had ordered hamburgers to take away, but were reluctant to pay for them. Steve Stylianakis, on the other hand, was determined that they cross his palm with coin of the realm before they sampled the delights of his griddle and a bit of 'argy bargy' had ensued. Taffy and I were able to convince the pair that their best interests would be served by paying up and scoffing their burgers on the way back to camp. On leaving the restaurant, however, Private Chaucer couldn't let things be and he smote the long-suffering Steve Stylianakis a mighty blow on the nose. Taffy promptly arrested him and I took hold of his mouthy mate, to prevent him from getting in on the act. The amount of abuse to which these two men then subjected us would have filled a book, and since they were adamant that we weren't men enough to take them in, we did precisely that. We only had a patrol car that evening, rather than the usual mini bus, and shoving two reluctant squaddies into the back of a small car isn't easy, unless you knock the stuffing out of them first. So we knocked the stuffing out of them first and they fitted in just right. Even though they were beaten men, the threats and insults continued from the cheap seats at the back. It was when the insults turned anti-Welsh that Taffy decided he had heard enough. I do believe that he was losing his temper. Without consulting me, he drove to a secluded street in Limassol and allowed the two soldiers to climb out.

"OK boyos," he said, "you've been full of threats these last fifteen minutes, isn't it? Now let me see what the two of you are made of."

They thought better of it when they saw Taffy squaring up to them and climbed into the car for the drive back to barracks of their own volition. Once they were locked up for the night and our reports compiled, the matter should have been concluded, but it wasn't. Our OC received a letter from a colour sergeant in the Royal Anglians, a person who had witnessed the arrest of Private Chaucer and his chum. Accompanying the letter was a splendid drawing of two red-hatted thugs throwing two innocent, God fearing soldiers into a car. The letter itself suggested that the demeanour of the military policemen had been menacing and aggressive. Really!

The OC called me in and asked me to do a job for him.

"Sergeant Payne, could you could investigate a complaint for me? It appears that a couple of our chaps may have been a trifle over zealous in affecting an arrest on Saturday evening. Would you take a look at it?" He handed me a sheaf of Basildon Bond notepaper upon which the complaint had been documented.

"Can't do that sir," I replied.

"And why not?"

"I'm one of the guys in the drawing."

He put the complaint in the bin.

Prior to arriving in Cyprus, a single British soldier might be excused for assuming that the Island of Aphrodite overflowed with love and getting your leg over. This wasn't the case. Local girls didn't throw it around by any means and in most cases, you needed to pledge your troth before you dipped your wick. Once a lady had an engagement ring on her finger, though, it was a different matter. It was then accepted that she slept with her fiancé, although once she had been bedded, woe betide any man who changed his mind.

One of the lance corporals in the tank squadron was engaged to a local Cypriot girl and fully intended to marry her. His Officer Commanding, however, refused him permission to take Miss Andropolous as his lawfully wedded wife. So intent was the OC to prevent the union from taking place, that he took the radical step of posting his man back to the UK. Having claimed the girl's virginity, however, you could be equally certain that her family would do its utmost to ensure that the tankie walked her down the aisle. The logic behind the officer's decision was difficult to fathom; the soldier wanted to marry the girl, the girl wanted to marry the soldier, so where was the problem?

The lance corporal's solution to the dilemma was to go absent and despite a full-scale squadron hue and cry, he couldn't be located. After a week, the RMP were called in to track him down and, because I knew the guy, the OC gave me the task of finding him and returning him to his unit. It took me a whole hour. Since the family Andropolous lived up in the mountains, that seemed a logical place to start looking and I was bumping up the winding track that led up to their remote village, when the twice-weekly bus to Limassol came down the other way. There, on the front seat, sat my man. I turned my vehicle around and chased after the bus, stopped it and arrested the fugitive. His unit had never considered visiting the village in the whole week they had been looking for him! The poor guy had the book thrown at him. He was busted and sent back to the UK under escort on the next available plane, without marrying or even having the opportunity to explain his predicament to his fiancée. The story does have a happy ending, however. On the pretext of visiting the toilet at the UK airport, he slipped his escort and disappeared. He was never found.

One of our Corps' real characters had been critically injured in a traffic accident in the UK and was lying in a coma from which he would never recover. As was the norm in such tragic circumstances, the RMP found a way of raising a little cash to help the bereaved family and our Training Centre organised a worldwide raffle for the family's caravan. In the assumption that everyone in the Corps would buy at least one ticket, a tidy sum could be realised to assist the grieving family. My section's requirement was to buy ten tickets at a pound a throw. Since this guy was a friend, I bought six shares and expected the other four guys to wade in with a ticket apiece. To my great annoyance, one member of my section flatly refused to put his hand in his pocket and no amount of coercion could convince him to do the right thing. He went down mightily in my estimation from that day on. His wife was also serving in the unit and she had a cushy number up in the orderly room. Our female chief clerk asked her to buy a ticket, but having been briefed by her husband, she too refused to open her purse. What a pair! The chief clerk was made of sterner stuff than I was apparently and threatened dire consequences should the young lady not display the more charitable side of her nature. With the utmost reluctance and with her arm twisted up her back, she stumped up a quid.

Sod's Law struck at the draw to decide who should be the new owner of the caravan. Those mean buggers from Cyprus won it and, unlike any other members of the Corps who would have promptly returned the thing back to the wife, they kept it. The man in this case went on to become a respected RSM in the RMP, a respect that didn't extend to me.

In addition to having the RMP as custodians of the law, the good citizens of the Sovereign Base Areas had the dubious pleasure of a second police authority to keep them out of harm's way. The Sovereign Base Area Police were locally recruited policemen, under the command of a retired senior British police officer. Originally formed in 1960 and made up equally of Greeks and Turks, the coup of 1974 had really put a spanner in the works. Now, in 1976, the Greeks were stationed exclusively in the Episkopi area and the Turks at the other end of the island, in Dhekelia. They carried out their duties in English and all their charges and reports were written in the same language. Not surprisingly, this was where they fell down. Whereas many of them spoke reasonable English, they simply couldn't unravel the dialects. These comments are based on my experience with the Greek element, as I never actually met any Turks, but almost did. A Grand Police Ball had been arranged, at which all the RMP, SBAP and Army Depot Police of all persuasions would get together socially for the first time since the coup. Then, two days before the event, Archbishop Makarios was called to meet his Maker. The whole of the Greek part of the Island was plunged into a lengthy period of mourning, the party was cancelled and several hundredweight of barbecue meat went rotten in our storeroom.

Most of the military police NCOs had little time for the SBAP and the feeling was clearly mutual. The fact that they insisted on flying the RAF flag above their HQ, for no logical reason that we could ascertain, did little to endear them to us either. It was largely the question of jurisdiction that drove the wedge between us so bitterly. There existed a couple pages of legal instruction that was supposed to specify exactly who was to do what, but the document was couched in such vague political language that it was possible to argue that it gave either, neither or both police forces the right to carry out primary investigations. Despite hours of argument and debate, the question of jurisdiction remained unresolved and so, the first patrol on the scene of an incident became the ones who got the job. It was all nonsense, of course, since we couldn't speak Greek and needed them to assist us, whereas they were helpless with the Geordie and Scottish dialects that were unintelligible to them. We really ought to have been able to work together, but seldom did. It usually stopped short of fisticuffs at the scene of an incident, but if looks could have killed...

Taking statements under caution was particularly difficult for the local police. How could they take a verbatim statement under caution at a soldier's dictation, when the guy talked in a distinct regional dialect and the policeman had only a rudimentary grasp of the English language? How did they ever win a court case in these circumstances? Things hadn't been problematic when the resident infantry battalion was full of men from the south of England, who spoke something akin to the Queen's English. Now a unit of six hundred Lancastrians that had a squadron of Geordie tankies in support had replaced them and life was no longer straightforward. The SBAP were in trouble and we became a little more popular. A case occurred where they were really found wanting and it illustrates the necessity of understanding a language fully in order to produce a statement under caution that is acceptable in a court of law.

A drunken Geordie was wandering his way towards the main gate at RAF Akrotiri, when he espied a scantily clad maiden in the open window of a married quarter. The randy soldier went to the door of the house and, discovering it unlocked, made his way inside. He backed the frightened woman into a bedroom, pushed her down onto a bed and was about to force his attentions on her, when the enormity of what he was doing registered through the intoxication. He apologised profusely to the lady for his unwarranted actions and left the house. This case was dealt with by the SBAP, who took a statement under caution from the soldier at his dictation. Now the accused was not a particularly bright individual and he spoke with the thickest of Wearside accents. What he had said during his confession was something along the lines of the following.

"So aa pushed hor on tiv the bed and thowt aad hev misell a bit, but aa thowt aad best hang on, it cud hev landed wa in bother."

When the case went to court, the SBA policeman responsible for taking his statement maintained that what the barely literate soldier had said was: "So I pushed her onto the bed intent on obtaining sexual gratification, until I realised that the enormity of my actions could lead to serious charges being brought against me."

Needless to say, the defence had a field day in the light of such a glaring concoction of evidence and the judge stopped the case.

Outside of the Sovereign Base Areas, the Cypriot police had jurisdiction and we were seldom called to assist them. There was a sensational happening one Friday night when they did require our assistance just the same. The incident happened in one of the seedy bars that proliferated in the badly run down Heros Square red light district of Limassol, when a sixty-five year old homosexual was discovered lying stiff and still on the floor of the bar at closing time. A post-mortem ascertained that he had succumbed to a blow on the back of the head and the pathologist suggested murder. Although none of the bar customers could recall having seen the deceased involved in a fight, or even an altercation, one witness could remember seeing the man talking to a person who was not Greek and possibly British. Other than that, there was nothing to go on.

The newspapers on Saturday and Sunday were full of the story and police action was frantic. Without a half decent description and with no leads whatsoever, the task of finding the person responsible for the old man's death wasn't going to be easy. Over the course of the weekend, every soldier who had booked out to Limassol on Friday evening was interviewed, but there was still no progress in the case. With a co-ordinating conference of all police agencies due to assemble in Limassol at 1000 hrs on Monday, I had the pleasure of an unexpected visitor in the duty room around 0930 hrs. He was a corporal in the Royal Engineers, a man in his mid twenties, who was in Cyprus for a six-week exercise with his UK based unit. He explained that he had arrived in the area on Friday and, being an old Cyprus hand, had travelled down to Limassol for a few beers the same evening. Whilst drinking in one of his old haunts in Heros Square, an old homosexual had begun pestering him. Despite changing seats a couple of times to avoid his advances, the corporal had found himself trapped in a corner by the old pervert. He had pushed the man away, finished his drink and left to continue his evening's entertainment in another bar. Totally unaware that the old man had sustained fatal injuries from the fall that he had caused, the corporal had drunk a few more beers and then returned to camp. He had been oblivious to the furore that had ensued and it was only when he read a newspaper on Monday morning that he realised he was probably the most wanted man in Cyprus. Desperate to clear his name, he had come directly to the RMP. Since the death had occurred in the republic, the Limassol CID investigated and the corporal was duly charged with murder. He was remanded in custody for several weeks before the charge was reduced to one of common assault. He ought never to have been subjected to such a long period on remand, but this wasn't the UK, this was Cyprus and the game was played to their rules. In court, he pleaded guilty to the charge and was fined forty pounds.

Over a period of several weeks, there had been numerous reports of prowlers in and around the Episkopi Married Quarters. We responded by giving the area more attention and it was during one such patrol that I noticed a Greek guy sitting in a car, by the telephone box at the end of Londonderry Lane. I lived in this street and was aware that the call box had been out of order for months, so he wasn't sitting there waiting for a call. We turned our patrol car around and went to check him out. Once he became aware we were interested in him, he started up his car and sped away in the direction of Paphos. I went after him as quickly as my low powered Ford Escort would allow and we hurtled down the winding road that leads to Happy Valley. This guy was certainly in a hurry and such was his desire to leave us behind that he took the most awful risks on that dangerous section of road. It would have been no surprise to see him crash down into the valley below, or collide with something coming the other way, but he managed to keep his car on four wheels. We followed him up the other side of the valley and on towards Pissouri. My partner called our control in order to have the Greek police stop this madman at one of the villages further along. The Greek police were their usual inefficient selves, however, and we saw neither hide nor hair of them as we went through the villages at high speed. This guy was no slouch as a driver, but despite my car's lack of cubic capacity, I managed to tail him all the way to Paphos. We had been behind him for twenty-five miles, but once we reached the town he quickly lost us in the side streets that make up the old Turkish quarter of the town. The best we could do was to report the matter to the local police in Paphos. Given a full description of the driver and the colour, make and registration number of the vehicle, not even the Cypriot police could fail to locate the driver. He turned out to be well known to the police and a stalwart of the local community. Through an interpreter, he gave a perfectly plausible reason for his presence in married quarter area and maintained that he had never noticed us pursuing him during the crazy race. He was a fibber of the highest order and I didn't trust him. More importantly, his friends in the constabulary did and that was all that mattered. Once the interpreter had passed on our adversary's profound apologies for causing us any unnecessary trouble, he shook my hand limply, thanked me in almost flawless English for my understanding and pressed his business card into my hand.

"Give me a call if ever I can be of assistance. You can be assured of quality service and a good discount," he said as we parted.

I took a look at his card; it read: 'Spiros Prodromou—Funeral Director.'

There was precious little to do on day mobile patrols and driving the fifteen miles down to Limassol to look at the girls was a normal pursuit. The United Nations had a military police detachment located in a large house on the far side of the town and if we were really bored, we would make that our target and call in for a natter and a drink. The detachment was made up of Danes, Swedes and Finns, as well as a couple of Brits, both of whom were Scousers. English was the lingua franca, so it was easy to understand all of them, with the exception of the Scousers.

On this particular visit, the UN guys were having a lunchtime celebration and we were offered a drink to complement the smorgasbord. Considering the heat in Cyprus, most of us had no qualms about downing a pint of Carlsberg to quench the thirst whilst on duty. By 1700 hrs, though, I had consumed enough Carlsberg to make standing a problem and the driver was in a worse state than I was. He could neither walk or talk and it took three of us to carry him out to the Landrover. I reversed out onto the main road, causing a passing Morris Minor driver to make a splendid emergency stop, and drove off in the direction of Episkopi. I drove for two hundred yards before stopping and admitting to myself that the prospects of me making it back to base without coming to grief were remote. My partner in drink chose that moment to resurrect from the dead; he put a cigarette into his mouth and then dropped his very last match onto the floor of the vehicle. The match fell through a hole in the floor panel, where a securing screw had fallen out, and down onto the roadway. We clambered out of the truck and began a search for the errant Swan Vesta. What an impressive sight we must have made, crawling around and under the vehicle on all fours like a couple of drunks, which of course we were. My mate needed his cigarette badly and the decision was made to return to the UN to get a box of matches for him and a replacement driver for me. Mercifully, the other road users were alert enough to avoid the erratically reversing Landrover and we made it back in one piece. The guys on the night shift fell for the old chestnut about both of us having gastro enteritis as a result of eating some dodgy kebabs and they sent a driver down to rescue us. Whilst waiting for him to arrive, we took in another couple of Carlsbergs, just to stave off any dehydration.

4

There were members of my Initial Training Squad at the Depot who served a full twenty-two years, but whose paths never crossed mine again. On the other hand there was Jimmy McTavish, the pride of Galashiels, who appeared at some time or another in almost every unit that I ever served in. Jimmy was a classic complainer who was never happy in the place he was serving, until he had left, that is, whereupon he would sing its praises to anyone who would listen. This was the fourth unit we had served in simultaneously and he moaned and groaned about Cyprus as if it were the worst place on God's earth. Despite his gruff exterior and testy nature, he was a big-hearted individual and a unit was generally a better place for his presence.

Jimmy was proud of his latest acquisition. He had forsaken the modest saloon cars that had always been his preference before and gone seriously up market. His new wheels were attached to nothing less than a Ferrari, a Ferrari with an automatic choke. It wasn't the latest model; in fact, it was a fairly aged machine, but there was no arguing with the rampant horse badge that adorned the front grill. During my first few months in Episkopi, he honoured me with several invitations to accompany him for a drive in his sporty two-seater, a car with character and, if the truth were known, a rather jerky pull away from a standing start. The canny Scot was delighted with his car, albeit a little perturbed about the amount of fuel it guzzled.

His latest pastime was fishing. As with everything he undertook, he threw himself wholeheartedly into his new pursuit and, despite his reluctance to part with money, he had all the kit. He probably pictured himself as a salmon fisherman, standing up to his middle in the icy waters of a stream in his native Scotland. Here in Cyprus, he had to make do with the man-made Yermasoya Reservoir. Jimmy spent most of his waking hours at the lakeside now that the fishing bug had bitten him and, because we worked on the same shift, I sometimes accompanied him there on a day off. Fishing was never a favourite activity of mine; the feel of a wriggling fish makes me feel queasy, but I went with him because it was sublimely peaceful on the lakeshore. Even with my half-hearted approach, my catch was invariable bigger than Jimmy's was and, being such an expert, this irked the Scot considerably. He put my success down to beginner's luck, although it seemed to me that catching fish at Yermasoya was ridiculously simple; the water was teeming with numerous varieties that seemed only too happy to give themselves up. At my insistence, all my fish were returned directly to the water, but Jimmy would keep his in a net and kill all the poor little dace before we finished and take them back with him. Dace are tiny little creatures and it would take an awful lot of them to make a meal, but master angler McTavish insisted that his friends just couldn't wait for him to bring them a bagful. I'm sure that people only accepted the fish to keep Jimmy happy and I have a sneaky suspicion that most of the unfortunate creatures were consigned to the dustbin the moment his back was turned. Those poor old dace died in vain, although some of them took posthumous revenge on their assassin.

Many days after his last fishing trip Jimmy opened the boot of his car to retrieve a pair of shoes, only to discover two forgotten plastic bags full of undelivered dace. It had been blisteringly hot and the rotting fish had caused the plastic bags to distend until they were like large balloons. The very act of picking up the bags meant that they burst, leaving Jimmy covered in the most disgusting liquid that smelled so vile, you could almost see it. The experience had a definite effect on him and he was not seen dangling his line in the reservoir nearly as often after that. He needed to continue with the fishing competition that he had press-ganged everyone into entering just the same. This was an event that he was desperate to win and, because he had fished Yermasoya so often, he believed that he knew the best pitch. He arranged for himself to be positioned in his favourite spot on the day of the Grand Match. It was a splendidly organised day out and Jimmy should be given due credit. It was, alas, also the last time he ever dipped maggot into water, for his retirement from the sport followed immediately after the prize giving. Confident of victory and with one hand already on the winner's trophy, Jimmy confidently cast his line that day. Sadly, Lady Luck chose to spurn him for, not only did he fail to lift the champion's prize, but had to suffer the ignominy of going forward to receive a special prize—for the competitor who failed to catch a single fish! Poor Jimmy.

Things didn't always run smoothly when McTavish was the organiser of an event. You could be certain that he would put his heart and soul into trying to make the party go with a swing, but misfortune and Jimmy worked hand in hand. He had volunteered to be the President of the Mess Committee of the corporal's mess and was still holding the position when the Summer Ball was held. As usual, he had put in a tremendous amount of work to ensure that everything was ready for the big night and as the guests began to arrive, he took up his position by the entrance. Each guest received a glass of sherry as they came in, served by the fair hand of Jimmy himself, who then passed them on to another member of his committee to be seated. All appeared to be functioning smoothly although, in retrospect, putting him so close to an unlimited supply of free drink was tempting fate. Before long, he had developed a system that suited him admirably. For every sherry that he dispensed, he drank one himself, and by the time all the guests were at their tables and his official duties completed, he was very much the worse for wear. He spent the next hour circulating, being obnoxious as an opportunity presented itself and growing louder by the minute. Finally, he was heard to say something disparaging about the brigadier, within earshot of the important man and our OC. The major ordered him to be removed from the mess, but none of the corporals fancied the task. The borderer could be a handful when in drink. It befell two of us sergeants to eject him, but not before he had cursed us roundly and banned us from ever entering his mess again. We took him to his room and tried to talk some sense into his befuddled brain, but he was in no mood to allow reason to cloud his thinking. Half and hour after we had thrown him out, he was back again. He called for silence and, surprisingly, got it. He then embarked on a barrage of insults directed at the brigadier, the OC, the bastards who had thrown him out of his own mess and the world in general. The bastards who had thrown him out the first time threw him out again, this time for good. Despite Jimmy's outrageous behaviour, the merrymaking went off splendidly and the brigadier stayed to the bitter end. Such was the quality of this fine officer that he asked that Jimmy be commended for his efforts and that no action should be taken against him for his verbal excesses. Jimmy had survived again.

The time came when Jimmy accepted the fact that his car was beyond his means; fuel and service costs were keeping him a poor man. He advertised in the papers and soon had potential purchasers calling to view the machine. It was a Ferrari collector who finally bought it. The expert jumped into the driver's seat to give the car the once over and turned the ignition key. The engine spluttered to life in its normal sluggish fashion, as Jimmy squirmed with embarrassment.

"The chokes out," said the Ferrari man knowledgeably and before Jimmy could show his ignorance, he reached under the dash and pushed the choke button in.

The car sounded much better after that. Jimmy was struck dumb because for eighteen months he had told everyone that his Ferrari had an automatic choke, when in reality he had been driving around with the thing out the whole time.

Once work had been done and sport played, there was nothing for it but to throw yourself wholeheartedly into the social scene. Food and drink were cheap and you could find a party somewhere any night of the week. Some Cypriot wines needed to be treated with caution just the same, especially as the stuff was so reasonably priced that the decision to buy a second bottle need never be tempered by cost. In many tavernas they actually gave the wine away free, provided you bought a meal. This free wine was usually the dreaded kok-kinelli—a dark red beverage produced from the fifth pressing of the grape mixed with an undisclosed quantity of embalming fluid. Served in a hollowed out gourd, it is guaranteed to induce a hangover of the utmost severity and ought never to be drunk by anyone who hasn't undergone the Army's 'Kokki-nelli Survivors Course'. The following are a series of tales involving the consumption of alcohol to varying degrees.

A popular watering hole for the RMP was the Evdhimou Taverna, a taverna located, not surprisingly, in the small village of Evdhimou. One of the regulars in the bar was Gregory, the Evdhimou police sergeant with a soft spot for anything British, particularly young white girls and immediate post-war music. We seldom had reason to call in on him on a professional basis, but socially we knew him well. On the anniversary of nothing in particular, Gregory announced that he was holding a party at his police station. He left it to me to invite a dozen of my contemporaries, with the proviso that some of them would be female. Our stunning WRAC girl Marge Nichols was his real target, just as she was the target of the majority of the male population of Episkopi, but at fifty, balding and portly, his chances were not good. Marge agreed to come along nevertheless, just to please him.

A dozen of us assembled in the corporal's mess, where we drank a couple of brandies apiece and headed for Evdhimou police station. The station was a converted medical centre that was painted throughout in the brightest white paint that Dulux ever manufactured, and except for a few tables and chairs, contained no furniture. Two dozen assorted Greeks and British sat down to eat and drink in this huge white room, which was also devoid of all decoration except for the obligatory framed photograph of Makarios. It struck me as being a perfect setting for a Monty Python sketch. Once the food was eaten and the booze flowing, Gregory announced that it was time for the singing competition. He and I would nominate three participants, each of whom would perform one song, the winners being decided by the applause recorded on the clapometer. Knowing full well that he had a fine singing voice, Gregory led off for his team with a passable rendition of 'Bluebells over the White Cliffs of Dover'. Yes, I know it should be 'bluebirds', but Gregory sang 'bluebells'. The applause was warm and he sat down a contented man. He indicated that I should nominate our opening singer and so I elected to play my trump card first. We had Taffy Clay, the Ivor Emmanuel of Llantrysant, in our ranks. Taffy had been a member of the world renowned Triorchy Male Voice Choir before joining the Army and possessed one of the most beautiful tenor voices imaginable. His forte was singing unaccompanied, in Welsh. He would open the batting for our side. Taffy rose to his feet, demanded hush and gave us 'Men of Harlech'. It was awe-inspiring to hear such a beautiful voice and it brought tears to more than one drunken eye. I wondered, not for the first time, what on earth possessed a man with such talent to pursue a career in the RMP. He was wasted. A stupendous performance was rewarded with stupendous applause. When it had died down, Gregory rose and addressed the audience.

"The contest, I think, it is finished. How can anyone follow singing like that?"

He was right, so we accepted his capitulation and celebrated our victory with more brandy.

At this juncture I think I'll add a few words about two of the characters in that last story, Taffy Clay and Marge.

Taffy was destined to make it to the top in the RMP, but with promotion to the rank of sergeant virtually assured before the end of the year, he surprised everyone by applying to join the SAS. Following some rigorous training in Cyprus, he packed his rucksack and headed for Hereford. Despite the fact that most aspirants use the return portion of the rail tickets rather more quickly than they expect, most of us considered it unlikely that we would ever see Taffy again. When he was only days away from winning the coveted beret, however, he fell during training and broke his arm. Unable to finish the course, he was forced to return to Cyprus. He had obviously created the right kind of impression during his stay in Hereford, because they offered him a place on a subsequent course. In August, he declared, he would try again.

In June, Taffy went back to Wales to marry his lovely fiancée. The wedding went as planned, as did the honeymoon by all accounts; and then, for no accountable reason, Taffy disappeared. Numerous efforts were made to contact him in order to ascertain the reason for his failure to return to the unit, but he had gone to ground. Eventually, the inevitable became unavoidable and the unit posted him AWOL. What drove him to take such an uncharacteristic action was beyond those who knew him. The police in the UK and the RMP from London went through the motions of trying to find him, but living in a remote part of Wales as he did, evading the pursuing lawmen would have been a simple exercise. Not another word was heard about Taffy, until he arrived back in Cyprus fully seven months after disappearing.

Directly after the New Year, he had simply surrendered himself at the Training Centre in Chichester and he had now been returned to his unit for disciplinary action. There would, of course, have to be a court martial. It takes forever and a day to arrange these things and Taffy had become a respected and popular member of the company once again by the time his hearing was held. He pleaded guilty naturally and, considering the length of time he had been on the run, the court was most lenient in their punishment. He was merely reduced to the ranks and he walked out of the court as a private soldier. Since the lowest rank in the RMP is lance corporal, this effectively meant his discharge from the Army. No other unit would be likely to accept a de-frocked military policeman, even someone with the talent and fine tenor voice of Taffy Clay. Our OC made an impassioned appeal to the Provost Marshal on his behalf, pleading for another chance for the likeable Welshman. The PM wouldn't hear of it and the Corps lost another good man.

Had Marge been German and twenty-two years old in 1939, instead of 1977, Adolf Hitler would have had her posted directly to the camp where they were breeding the master race. She was a stunningly attractive young lady; tall, blonde, beautiful and blessed with a figure that compared favourably with that of the Venus de Milo, except that Marge had arms. An Army uniform has never contained such a heavenly form and she certainly turned heads in the garrison. In town, the Greeks positively drooled over the delicious creature and she could have made a fortune had she been that way inclined. Luckily, Marge was a member of my section and I often had the pleasure of patrolling with her. Alas, even the delectable Marge had flaws that detracted from her allure. Her shrill voice, dreadful Brighton accent and vocabulary of rude words (bad enough to make a navvy blush), indicated that she had never been to finishing school. I was walking through the garrison with her one afternoon, when four squaddies came walking past the other way. As they turned to take in the view, she turned too and put her hands on her childbearing hips.

"What's the matter with you fucking lot? Got your fucking eyes full?" she screeched.

They died of embarrassment and probably never looked at another pretty girl again—well, not for several minutes, anyway. The constant attention, although flattering, must have been very wearing for her. I know that I sometimes get tired of women ogling me!

It wasn't only the soldiers and airmen of Episkopi who were enamoured by our pretty WRAC girl; the commander himself found her particularly easy on the eye. Whenever I was on duty and the commander's car passed the duty room, he would have his driver stop the vehicle and call out to enquire whether Marge was on duty or not. If the answer was in the affirmative, it was not beyond him to come in for a private chat. I often wondered if they ever met elsewhere, but a brigadier would never risk his career for a bit on the side, no matter how attractive the bait, would he? Despite the stories that proliferated about her (and pretty damning some of them were too), I knew no one in the Corps who could put his hand on his heart and say that he had bedded her. She left Cyprus before me, fell in love on her next posting and married a guy from one of those funny regiments. Marriage may have been just what she needed. And so, back to the alcohol related stories.

One of the sergeants living in the mess was a chap who had been in Iserlohn at the same time as myself. He had transferred from the Dental Corps to the Intelligence Corps since those days and now worked at something that was far too sneaky to tell me about. He was about to leave Cyprus on posting, but promised to show me around his favourite haunts before he left. One of our first ports of call was the bar at the Amathus Beach Hotel, where he introduced me to Peter, the Head Barman. It had always been his habit to slip Peter the odd bottle of duty free whisky and, in return, Peter sometimes became forgetful when it came to presenting the bill. When my chum from the Intelligence Corps finally caught the plane home, I continued to frequent the Amathus regularly, never imagining that he had used the bar as anything other than a pleasant watering hole. Tucking into my second brandy one evening and shovelling down some of the wonderful, low calorie peanuts that they served in the bar, a swarthy looking guy slithered onto the barstool next to mine. Without looking at me, or moving his lips, he started to whisper.

"The Gulgarian is the gan sitting with his gack to the grungger," he said with all the expertise of a workingmen's club ventriloquist and promptly disappeared.

I looked over towards the band and actually saw the man that was sitting with his back to the drummer, but didn't really care whether he was Gulgarian, Grittish or Grazilian. On my next visit, another guy sidled up to tell me something about a Czechoslovakian, before melting into the night. Peter was aware that information was being passed to me and so I called him to a conference.

"Look Peter, I've no idea what my mate was up to here, but I'm just a friendly military policeman having a quiet drink."

Peter winked a couple of times.

"Yes, that's what they all say," he suggested.

I stopped using the place.

The latest addition to the Cardigan family had Cypriot godparents, which meant that the christening celebrations went on for weeks. Then, once the Greeks had finished their effort, the lads decided that one final celebratory function should be held in the corporal's mess. It was to be the 'Mother of all Christening Parties'. The organising committee agreed that the buffet ought to include a spit roast animal of some kind; a sheep or goat would be the best bet, this being Cyprus. Although the cost of an animal would be well within our financial means, two of the unit members thought that our funds would be more prudently spent on the purchase of a couple of barrels of beer. They undertook to deliver a beast for roasting on the night, free of charge. Taffy Clay was a multi-talented man, although his penchant for poaching sheep was a talent to which only his closest Welsh friends had hitherto been privy. Stu Richards, on the other hand, was known to have been a master butcher in Civvy Street. If this pair couldn't produce an animal, then there was no hope for mankind.

Perhaps there was something wrong with Taffy's night vision on the evening that they went stalking their prey, for instead of a sheep or a goat, it was a pig that appeared on the spit. Stu maintained that this was quite the noisiest pig that he had ever slaughtered and that the animal's squealing had alerted the villagers from where they had acquired it, almost causing them to be discovered. It was a splendid function, with a roast pork buffet worthy of the risks taken by our resident poachers.

Although officially the corporal's mess, the establishment was used by all ranks and all unit members were at liberty to come and go as they pleased. Married men needed to be cautious when using the place in the evenings, however, for this was the domain of the most militant single men in the RMP. It is with pride that I confess to being one of those who formed a society to positively discriminate against married pads. It was our way of redressing some of the injustices heaped on the single man in the Army. The League against Married Pads, or LAMP for short, was formed during my first year in Cyprus and the honour of being elected as its first Grand Wizard fell to me. We organised private functions to which married pads were cordially invited, but only provided that they purchased two tickets for the buffet, one for them and one for their spouse. It was at the buffet table that we really made our statement, you see. None of us had any objection to a lady going to the table before the gentlemen; we wouldn't have had it any other way at normal functions. Our gripe was that, with the collusion of the wives, the married men had the girls bring back their buffet too. By the time the long-suffering singlies made it to the front of the queue, there was usually only the most meagre fare remaining. To see piles of food lying unwanted on plates, but taken out of sheer gluttony, made the hackles rise. At LAMP functions, therefore, we made a great ceremony out of announcing the buffet and always finished with a call of, "Single men to the buffet first please!" This was always greeted with roars of approval from the singlies and perhaps even the good-humoured acknowledgement from the pads that the tables had been turned.

Subscriptions were taken and from these funds, bottles of rum were purchased and placed behind the bar for the consumption of members at their leisure. Quite why this particular spirit was selected as the single man's tipple is shrouded in mystery, but the LAMP rum bottle became a feature of the Episkopi bar. Each Sunday, an informal meeting of the league would be held, during which any matters of a 'single' nature could be raised and breeches of LAMP rules brought to the attention of the committee. Each Sunday invariably saw the trial of one or more of our esteemed membership, individuals who were to be charged with offences as serious as accepting an invitation to dinner at a pad's house, or having been seen in the company of a lady. More serious charges, such as 'having been seen looking in a jeweller's shop window whilst in the presence of a female' or, even worse, 'promising to buy a woman a ring' might be heard. Members were required to take an oath vowing to tell the truth in court, although evidence was largely irrelevant, since the verdict never varied. Guilty as charged. Minor offenders were required to purchase a bottle of rum for the good and benefit of LAMP members; misdemeanants had to buy two bottles and felons three. The real weight of LAMP law was reserved for those knaves found guilty of the despicable crime of pledging their troth. They were excommunicated!

It was during my second year in office that I committed the unpardonable sins of simultaneously announcing my engagement and my wedding date. The fact that the grand wizard had committed such acts of heresy rocked LAMP to its foundations and members were numbed with shock. Notwithstanding my high office, the members were forced to convene a hearing, for there could be no mercy. I was found guilty as charged and sentenced to the harshest punishment ever meted out to a member. I was excommunicated, ordered to purchase four bottles of rum and sent to Coventry for twenty minutes. LAMP continued without me of course and although I was invited to all subsequent functions, they subjected me to the ignominy of waiting at the back of the buffet queue at all times, just like the other pads. The shame was hard to bear.

Nowhere in the world could have suited me better than Cyprus; I was playing all the sport I wanted and enjoying life to the full. Physically I hadn't been in such good shape since playing in the first division in Hong Kong and the medical centre didn't know me from Adam. But things were to change.

On duty at the arrivals lounge at RAF Akrotiri one afternoon, I suddenly collapsed. Despite being back on my feet only seconds later and none the worse for the experience, this was the first of a series of times that I was to hit the deck for no apparent reason. Worse than the total loss of balance that preceded each collapse was the most awful feeling that it brought upon me, that of the absolute conviction of impending death. On other occasions I would have the sensation that, whilst part of a group, I was somehow detached from the others and watching from afar. It was all very worrying and after hitting the floor for the tenth time, my friends convinced me that a visit to the MO was overdue. He told me that my symptoms were consistent with overdoing things and suggested that I took things easy for a while, so I went directly from his surgery to rugby training and took things easy on the wing.

A couple of weeks later, I was summoned to attend a medical examination at the RAF Hospital at Akrotiri. My MO had referred my case down to them and when a wing commander specialist came over from the UK, to give the hopeless cases the once over, Sergeant Payne was his first customer. I chatted with the pleasant Welshman for a while and gave him the rundown on my problems. He made some notes and put his pen down before addressing me.

"Well, I don't think you're bonkers boyo," he said.

"Bonkers, sir? I'm not bonkers."

"Your MO thinks you are."

It transpired that the wing commander was the psychiatrist at RAF Wroughton and although he had pronounced me sane, he decided that I should return to the UK for some tests just the same. I ended up in Millbank Army Hospital, in a ward full of really sick people. My fellow invalids were cancer patients, heart attack victims and guys that had suffered strokes. What the hell was a perfectly healthy chap like me doing here? I saw doctors, psychiatrists, psychologists and a neurologist, as well as undergoing an electro encephalograph and a brain scan. After two weeks in the place, they sent me home for ten days' leave and then brought me back for more tests. My condition was so severe that I went into London every night, to the pictures, the pub, or to the greyhound racing and awoke most mornings with a hangover. On a night out in London with my old mate Super Dooper Hooper, we arrested a villain who was trying to rob the Hertz Rent-a-Car office, just as we were returning Dave's car. Next morning I gave evidence at the magistrate's court. Yes, I was really ill!

Professor Bonham-Carter, the Queen's neurologist, was the last of the eminent physicians to see me. He declared that they had been unable to find a single thing wrong with me and that I was to return to my unit. First, though, they gave me another fortnight's sick leave.

Having been back in Cyprus for only a week, I started to fall over again, so it was back to the medical centre. This time Major Singh, a TA doctor over in Cyprus for his annual two-week camp, listened to my tale of woe as he thumbed through my notes.

"Tell me, sergeant, you have been prodded and poked around by a series of notable personages in the course of the last two months. Did any of them look into your ears?" he enquired.

The answer was no.

"Well, my dear fellow, I need look no further into your notes—I know exactly what is wrong with you. You are suffering from Menieures' Syndrome, a problem of the inner ear."

All that time and money spent sending me to the UK, the immense sums paid out in hiring civvy doctors and brain scan machines, and a TA doctor recognises my complaint in a trice! I still don't know if he was right in his diagnosis, because the problem never did reoccur.

Whilst in Northern Ireland, my company's task had been to support the RUC at various police stations throughout Belfast. With our unsociable working hours and the fact that we were so widely dispersed, the provision of food became a problem. For once, the shiny arses that sat in the safety and comfort of the HQ came up with a sensible solution to a problem and arranged for us to use the twenty-four hour restaurant facilities at a city centre hospital. We were paid a meal allowance for each shift we worked as part of our salary, regardless of whether we ate or not and, at the hospital, we merely wrote our details on a sheet and the pay office debited our accounts accordingly. It occurred to me that this system was ripe for a fiddle. Using a fictitious name was out of the question because the pay office would rumble that, but what if you used someone else's number, rank and name? Now a soldier never forgets his own number, but rarely does he remember anyone else's, unless it's as full of zeros as the number belonging to Geraint Hughes. With a name like that he ought really to have come from the valleys, but he was in fact a native of Stoke-on-Trent. I ate heartily on the man from the Potteries for a year or so and drew my full whack for meals at the same time.

I never saw Geraint again until he showed up in Cyprus, resplendent in his light blue UN beret. We celebrated our chance encounter in the Kyrenia Bar and my hangover next day was of such severity that it rates the number two position in my 'Top Ten Hangovers of all Time' list. Our evening together was given over to telling 'fuck all' stories, tales that are sometimes slightly embroidered, that one relates to friends and which one fully expects to be treated with an amount of scepticism. On completion of your story, the listener will say, "That's fuck all!" and proceed to tell an even taller tale. It was during one of Hughes' fuck all stories that the subject of meals at the Belfast hospital arose.

"Do you recall how we used to sign for our meals," I said, fishing to see whether he was aware that he had subsidised me for so long.

"Do I remember?" he said. "I'll say I bloody remember. Do you know that some dirty sod used my number, rank and name to have free nosebags on me? I allegedly ate meals at that hospital when I was back home on leave and on one occasion, I supposedly ate lunch there when I was actually in Torremolenos on my holidays! If I'd ever found out who that dirty bastard was!"

"Have another drink Geraint. Do you fancy a bite to eat? It's all on me. How about some decent brandy or a cigar?"

"That's very decent of you, Wal," said Geraint.

"It's my pleasure 23900002 Corporal Hughes, Geraint," I replied.

"You bastard, Wal!"

Cyprus boasts dozens of archaeological sites and if their Museum's Authority had the mind to excavate them properly, they would doubtless discover masses of hidden treasure just below the surface. Despite the fact that they are reluctant to organise official digs, amateur digging is strictly forbidden, as is the importation of metal detectors. I knew one guy who, armed with an illegally obtained metal detector and a reasonable knowledge of Cypriot history, had discovered a large horde of Roman silver coins. The fact that he had been able to sell them for a considerable sum of money whetted my appetite, not as an archaeologist, but as a prospector. I had visions of finding a leather bag tied with a thong and with the Greek or Latin for gold written on the side. My interest was aroused even more by my chance find of a Roman coin whilst out walking in the Akamas training area. It was in excellent condition and I sent it to Leicester Museum for their appraisal. They sent me a most informative letter giving me the history of the coin, but declined my offer to keep it for display purposes as they already had several similar coins. A London dealer offered me a measly three quid for it, but rather than sell it for that price, I gave it to a young lad who was a collector. The find made me all the more determined to get a metal detector, particularly as my time on the island was coming to an end. I wanted to strike it rich before departing. One of the lads sneaked one in for me on an RAF flight.

On my first night duty as a metal detector owner, I drove down to the ruins of the Temple of Apollo Hylates. With my patrol partner keeping watch, I crept into the site and set to work on the edge of a previously excavated area. Within seconds the gentle humming of the machine was replaced by a high-pitched scream. The Roman loom weight that I subsequently dug up now stands in a showcase at the Episkopi museum. Flushed with success, I scoured the map for areas where bags of gold might be hidden and set out next morning for a cliff face that had several catacombs along its base. The catacombs were almost hidden by mounds of earth with nettles growing on them, but I cleared away some soil in front of the largest of the ancient graves and thrust my metal detector inside. The thing screamed right away—there was metal in there for sure. I shone my torch into the hole, but there was nothing to be seen. More earth was scraped away with a trowel before a second attempt. The detector screamed again; there was definitely something in there, just under the surface. By lying full length and allowing the nettles to do their worst, I was able to scrape away the remaining covering of earth and prise some metal to the surface. By shining my torch in again it was possible to see the piece of metal. It was a thin disc, about four inches across and it was gold in colour. Gold, I was rich! I picked it up between my thumb and forefinger, nettling myself badly into the bargain and finally managed to bring my find out into the daylight. Perhaps this was the first time that the piece had seen the light of day for thousands of years? I examined the object that was about to make me rich beyond compare. It was gold coloured, it was circular and had serrated edges. One side was plain, but on the other side in bold black letters were printed the words 'Sausage and Beans—16 oz'. It was the top of an Army ration can that had been discarded by some bloody squaddie. How dare he use my secret catacomb as a rubbish bin? My keenness for archaeology never recovered from this cruel disappointment. I would have to find another way to make my fortune.

I have no objection to anyone's creed, provided that the devotees don't attempt to force their particular beliefs onto me. When that happens, then I'm liable to show my feelings. The annual RMP sponsored church service was held at the end of Corps Week, a week of fun and sport that used to be celebrated in all units, before the increase in the workload and the decrease in manpower forced its abandonment. The service was traditionally held in a Free Church, to minimise any ill feeling amongst the religious zealots. I have even seen the service held out of doors when the weather permitted, so the denomination of the church in which it takes place was by no means critical, provided it didn't offend anyone. It's doubtful for example whether the service would ever be held in a synagogue, mosque or 7th Day Adventist's church. To my mind, Cyprus would have been the ideal spot to have an open-air service, but the CSM nominated a committee to decide upon the venue of the service instead. A committee whose membership of five included the OC, the CSM and a sergeant, all of whom were card carrying members of the local Roman Catholic Church. To the surprise of no one, it was decided that the service would be held in the Garrison's Pope Pius 23rd Church. As a died in the wool Methodist, I lodged the strongest objection to this choice of venue, one of my prime objections being that the incense might adversely affect the lungs of my football team. The CSM stood his ground, however, and decreed that the service would be held at the Roman Church. No one was going to throw Catholicism at me and I was adamant that I wouldn't enter a catholic church under any circumstances. Furthermore, I vowed to make every effort to dissuade other protestant members of the company from attending. The CSM put paid to that ploy, by making the event a parade and ordering every one to attend in uniform. As I understood things, although we were duty bound to parade as detailed, it was no longer possible in the Army to order a person to attend a church service. By the morning of the event the dissenters numbered twelve, all of whom declared their solidarity with my views. We agreed that we would attend the parade, but refuse to enter the church. Once again, the CSM proved too wily for me and he got at my objectors, informing them that their careers would be adversely affected should they fail to enter the nominated place of worship. After the parade we were given the order to fall out and everyone filed obediently into Pope Pius 23rd Church—everyone with the exception of me, that is. I simply walked off home. The CSM never mentioned my absence. I was the manager, coach, captain and selector of the company's soccer team and it would have adversely affected his career as our midfield schemer if he had.

During my entire two and a half-year tour in Cyprus, not one decent police investigation had come my way. With no cases outstanding and this being my last tour of duty on the island, I stood myself down at midnight to make sure that I witnessed nothing that might require me to come all the way back for a court case. I went home to bed, but Sod's Law manifest itself at 0200 hrs and I had to return to the duty room to sort out a case of drunken driving. So my last couple of days in Cyprus before flying off to Germany weren't to be my last on the beautiful island after all. Four months later I returned to give evidence.

5

Returning to Werl as a sergeant, I was mortified to discover that not only was Inky Davis a staff sergeant, but that he was to be my platoon commander. There have been many howlers committed by promotion boards over the years, but elevating Inky to the rank of staff sergeant topped the lot. My pleas to the RSM that he should allow me to serve elsewhere fell on deaf ears. It was not by accident that I had been allocated to 29 Platoon, it seems.

"I've put you in that platoon so that you can keep an eye on him Wally," the RSM said. "And smack him around the ear whenever necessary."

In that case, methinks I should have been the staff sergeant. Inky had christened his charges Penal Platoon, which I considered a rather witty double entendre. Then I remembered his lavatorial sense of humour and concluded that the reference to prisons would have been accidental. The blokes were all strangers to me, but with a Ukrainian, two Poles, a Welshman, an Irishman and three Geordies in its complement; it had a certain cosmopolitan feel to it. In order to show me around, Inky deemed to grace my first night shift with his presence. Perhaps the fact that I had already served for five years in this very area had slipped his mind. In the early hours of the morning on this my first night shift with 29 Platoon, a badly injured young man was helped into the duty room by two caring Germans. It transpired that he was one of our guys, who had been enjoying a night off by supping a few beers in the nearby village of Wickede. He had taken a real pasting and was in no fit state to explain just how he had come by his injuries. Fortunately, the locals turned out to be excellent witnesses as well as good Samaritans. They explained that he had been assaulted for no good reason by three soldiers and that, by chance, these men were now walking up the road towards the barracks. We thanked them for their benevolence, dispatched our fellow platoon member to medical centre and prepared to put the 'Inky Davis plan for apprehending errant soldiers' into action.

We went outside the barracks and lay in wait for the squaddies at the side of the pitch-black road. The first audible comment came from a Londoner and was so damning that it might have come straight from a police duties training film.

"Did you see the way that monkey went down when I nutted him?" said an anonymous voice.

At that, Inky stood up and uttered those never to be forgotten words.

"I am Staff Sergeant Ian Norbert Kitson Davis of the Royal Military Police. Stay where you are—you are all under arrest."

To my considerable surprise, two of them did stay put. The third, however, turned on his heels and scarpered, hotly pursued by Inky, Corporal Krzeszewski and me. The Pole collared him first and held onto him long enough for Inky to arrive and confuse matters. The squaddie was proving a handful. Our Pole was barely holding onto his man and poor Inky was being kicked firmly on the shins each time he attempted a handhold. After a couple of minutes of watching them making a real pig's ear of the arrest, I moved in to deal with him in my own style. I punched him squarely in the kisser, grabbed him around the neck and dragged him back to barracks. Easy!

Inky was well proportioned for a man of 5 feet 10 inches, but unfortunately he stood 6 feet 8 in his stocking feet! With legs that wouldn't have disgraced Wilt the Stilt Chamberlain, he was one of the tallest men ever to join the RMP. It was this extreme elevation above sea level that was the root cause of many of his problems. Inky hated being so tall and, as almost everyone with whom he entered into a conversation felt duty bound to make some reference to his height, he suffered miserably whenever meeting people. There was nothing he could do about it of course, other than having his legs amputated, but he allowed the references to his length irritate him so severely that his whole life was affected. Loose false teeth that hissed and clicked whenever he spoke only served to compound his misery and lower his self-esteem even more. He may well have been the most inept MP of all time and his catalogue of disasters and failed schemes would fill a book. If only he had stopped for a moment to think a plan through, or considered the possible pitfalls of an undertaking before throwing himself wholeheartedly into it, he may conceivably have been more successful. As well as his chronic impetuosity, Inky was blighted with ill fortune and his sheer bad luck transcended any law of averages. If he were to arrange a barbecue in the middle of the Kalahari Desert, he would almost certainly select the only day in ten years when it rained.

On the second night in my new quarter in Werl, I was surprised to find a young girl standing at the door.

"Are you Uncle Wally?" she asked innocently.

"Yes darling, I'm Uncle Wally. Who are you?"

"I'm Susie and Daddy says 'How are you bollocks for spots' and will you come round for a drink at eight o' clock?"

"Tell your Daddy that I'll be there at eight darling."

It wasn't necessary to ask where she lived—this just *had* to be Inky's daughter. I arrived at his place ten minutes after the prescribed hour and was surprised when Susie opened the door.

"Where are your Mummy and Daddy, Susie?"

"They're in the bedroom. I'll give them a shout."

Perhaps I'd misunderstood Susie and arrived too early, or had she given me the wrong time? Inky appeared a few seconds later, all legs and dressing gown.

"When you weren't here by eight, me and the missus thought we might as well have a shag," he said by way of explanation.

Wanda, Inky's wife, wasn't over endowed with brains. Anyone with a modicum of the grey matter would never have married him in the first place. She nodded her head when she talked to you, rather like one of those dogs that people keep on the back shelf of their car. Their three children were at various stages of imbecility, driven that way by the outrageous antics of their father and the total passivity of the mother. Inky wasn't bright enough to have heard of Professor Pavlov, but he and the Russian had many things in common. His two boys were certainly a few pfennigs short of a Deutschmark and they were terrified of him. Given the task of cleaning the car one evening, they returned to the flat within a couple of minutes.

"What's the matter with you useless sods? Give me the fucking keys and I'll do it myself!" he screamed.

"We can't Dad, they're in the car."

"Don't leave them in the bloody car, fetch them now!"

"We can't Dad," they pleaded, but Inky wasn't listening.

"Get the bloody keys now!"

They knew that to attempt an explanation was futile. The fact that they had inadvertently locked the keys into the car and that they had come back for the spares wouldn't interest Inky when he was in this frame of mind. The two boys took a hammer, broke the driver's side window and retrieved the keys.

Inky was satisfied that his order had been obeyed and then decided against cleaning the car after all. The fact that his window was broken didn't dawn on him until he drove to work next morning. It had poured down during the night.

Another Inky classic was the case of the missing toys. He had shown a typical display of temper when he returned home from work to discover all the kid's toys lying strewn around the living room carpet. He prepared to take punitive action, blithely unaware of the fact that the children's bedrooms had been painted that day.

"Where shall we put them Dad?" they asked, presuming that their father knew that the bedrooms were out of bounds.

"Put the fucking things in the dustbins for all I care, just move them now!"

It was in the early hours of the morning that Wanda's brain cell activated and she told Inky that the children were sleeping with neighbours until the bedroom paint dried. It then occurred to Inky that if the toys were no longer on the living room floor and were obviously not in the bedrooms, then they might just conceivably be where he had told the children to put them. The military police received several calls from concerned citizens during the course of the night; all regarding the antics of a tall man dressed in a tracksuit that was rummaging through the waste bins in the area.

The fear with which he ruled inside his home was not restricted to human beings. Inky once put the family parakeet out on the third floor balcony to get some air. He inadvertently left the cage door ajar and the bird, incapable of flight but still possessed of sound mind and body, seized the opportunity to end its years of misery as the Davis family pet. It walked calmly off the overhang to its doom. That bird's demise was preferable to the way in which its replacement met its end. The Davis family was leaving for a camping holiday in Austria and, having been unable to find a bird sitter, they decided to take the creature with them. Their Volkswagen bus, however, was packed to the gunwales and the cage simply wouldn't fit in. Inky jettisoned the cage, tied the parakeet's leg to the rear of the van with a piece of string, and sallied forth, driving slowly, so that the bird could keep up. At the first stop for fuel, Inky went to the rear of the van to check on the bird. He was genuinely surprised to find that the parakeet had vanished, leaving only its left leg behind.

This was the man with whom I had to work for the foreseeable future. In theory at least, he would actually be responsible for compiling my annual report. Heaven forbid! Fortunately, the majority of my first three months in the company would be spent in the field, where my section would be located far away from the main HQ, where Inky regularly wrought havoc.

Although every quartermaster of whom I have enquired has strenuously denied the assertion, it has long been my contention that the standard British combat uniform is impregnated with a chemical designed to have a certain effect on the wearer. Whether the chemical is applied at some stage of manufacture, or sprayed on by some treasonous sod in the stores, I'm not certain, but the fact remains that once a soldier dons this ill fitting garb, a metamorphosis occurs. Instantaneously, the wearer becomes hungry, horny and is bursting for a shit! These conditions are not attributable to the contents of his stomach, prostate gland or bowel and the phenomenon occurs regardless of whether the soldier actually deploys, or remains in barracks. The reaction ceases once he is divested of the garment, which proves my point. Someone ought to look into it!

One of the marvellous things about summers in northern Europe is early sunrises and those peaceful hours of daylight available to the early riser. My stag on this particular morning of the exercise was from 0300-0500 hrs and there I was, on the road outside the slumbering HQ location, telling myself just how good life was in the British Army. It was already pleasantly warm and I felt at ease with the world, even if I was on sodding exercise. I appeared to be the only soul around and there was not even a single Volkswagen on the road to taint the scented air with its exhaust fumes. After some time, I became aware of a slight movement in the distance. Something was coming in my direction along the road that stretched away for a couple of miles to my left. It wasn't a vehicle—it wasn't moving quickly enough—and it wasn't a person on foot—it was too slow for that. After several minutes of squinting, staring and fanciful speculation as to what the advancing object might be, it came close enough to be recognised. It was a group of twenty cyclists out enjoying the early morning air.

These were no ordinary cyclists, however. They were a group of young girls aged between eighteen and twenty, not one of whom was dressed in anything more substantial than her undergarments. It made a most pleasing interlude, given that the majority of them were very easy on the eye. I gave them a cheery wave and a sound ogling as they rode by. Sadly, they disappeared again all too quickly. The trouble was that there was no one else present to confirm the sighting of those lovely bosoms and bottoms and my story was received with a mixture of incredulity and scorn when I related it over breakfast. Those sceptics variously accused me of lying, smoking pot and needing to sew my oats at the first opportunity. It wasn't a mirage though, no matter how amazing a sight it may have been.

The Division was exercising in the north of Germany and had cleverly chosen the town of Freden an der Leine as its HQ location. Not that there was anything wrong with this little town or its citizens. It was just that it lay on the main north-south railway line of the German Bundesbahn. Consequently, the level crossing gates on the edge of town opened and closed every couple of minutes, to allow the fast moving trains to speed through on their way to and from Hamburg. This made the movement of heavy vehicular traffic across the line a less than simple task for the RMP escorts. Our small detachment was encamped near to the crossing and we spent the majority of our working hours hurrying to get tanks from one side of the lines to the other, before the level crossing barriers came down again. A speeding train colliding with sixty tons of Chobham armour didn't bear thinking about.

Something peculiar happened during my first off-duty period of this exercise, the sort of thing that one only reads about in *Playboy* magazine, or imagines in moments of sexual fantasy.

I was standing alone in our control tent, when the flap was lifted and in walked a young German girl. There was nothing peculiar in that—we often had inquisitive locals calling in for a look around, not that we had much to show them. During my brief conversation with this girl I ascertained that she was sixteen years of age, that she lived with her parents in the next village and that she was probably the randiest little thing in the whole of Niedersachsen. This brazen little Lolita told me of a secluded spot in some nearby woods and explained that if I were to meet her there twenty minutes hence, she would be happy to take her knickers off and display herself for my approval. I considered that a pretty fair offer, although quite what a pretty teenager, complete with white ankle socks, saw in a grey haired squaddie who hadn't changed his combat kit for a week, is beyond me. Twenty minutes later I met the little temptress in a forest glade, where I unashamedly took advantage of her. Not that I wasn't smitten with feelings of guilt for having perpetrated such a dastardly deed, because I was—for several seconds, in fact. We enjoyed several other clandestine meetings in between my route signing and tank escort duties, and I found it difficult to believe my good fortune. A few days later we pulled out from Freden an der Leine in the early hours of the morning and I never had the opportunity to say thank you or goodbye.

One Sunday evening, many years later, I was driving through her village at the head of a column of vehicles when, lo and behold, there she was coming out of church. Unfortunately, I couldn't even stop to see whether she had time for a quickie. Shame.

After a military exercise the race back to camp resembles the Wacky Races. Right at the back of the convoy you will find a REME recovery vehicle, an ambulance and an RMP vehicle. Tail end Charlie was never a popular job. It usually meant work and you invariable arrived back at camp hours after the others. This had been an uneventful drive so far, nothing had gone wrong and the final armoured personnel carrier was coming to the point where the convoy left the autobahn. I was close behind this last APC and saw it indicating its intention to take the autobahn fly-off less than two hundred yards further on. Then, for some inexplicable reason, it suddenly left the tarmac and drifted onto the muddy, downward sloping embankment on the right. Its weight caused it to sink into the mud and, at the same time, slide very slowly down the slight incline. There was certainly plenty of time for the two guys sitting on the top to jump to safety. Had they known that the mud building up at the side of the vehicle was going to cause it to tip over, they surely would have. Perhaps they were asleep because, despite the almost leisurely way the thing overturned, they didn't appear to make an effort to get off. I watched the APC as it rolled over through 360 degrees and finished up back on its tracks again. Closely followed by the ambulance, we drove off the autobahn and down to the APC, but there was nothing that could be done for the two guys who had been sitting aloft. Both their heads had been squashed by eighteen tons of armour. We merely covered them up and waited for the German ambulance to come and take them to the nearest morgue. The other three crewmembers were shaken, naturally, but otherwise uninjured. They were taken away to the military hospital as a precautionary measure and we were left to pick up their kit and throw it into the back of the APC. A pair of earphones, with the remains of some poor sod's brains left inside, is my abiding memory of the event.

For reasons quite beyond my comprehension, it was always deemed necessary to clean vehicles and equipment before standing down after an exercise. The blokes were always knackered and in an almighty hurry to have a bath, eat something not out of a tin, drink a beer and to copulate, not necessarily in that order. Therefore, the task of cleaning up was never done properly and it all had to be done again on the next working day. I had sworn years before that in the unlikely event of my promotion, my platoon would not conform to this stupid ritual. So 29 Platoon dumped everything into the stores and garages the minute we arrived back and sorted it out properly after the stand down period. Our platoon stores in Werl were really rather grand. Purpose built, they were a vast improvement on the waterlogged cellars or attics that normally had to suffice as storerooms. Ours even had sufficient radiators to dry our kit out instead of leaving it to mildew and rot, a rarity indeed. Mind you, regulations stipulated that heating only came on between the first of October and the first of April, so for half the year our kit rotted anyway.

Following another blindingly boring exercise, we had thrown all of our stuff into the stores as usual and I was about to lock up with what I erroneously believed to be the only set off keys, when Myron approached. Corporal Myron Demitriuk, the bane of my life, produced a brace of pheasants that he claimed had miraculously appeared in the back of his Landrover on the last day of the exercise.

"Can I hang these in the stores until Tuesday, our kid?" asked the Ukranian.

Despite my threats to do him physical damage, he persisted in referring to me as 'our kid'. One day I'd kill him. I wasn't keen on having a couple of flea-ridden birds in the stores, but reluctantly agreed because of my rush to get home. He hung them on a wire above the window. We returned on Tuesday morning and trooped over to the stores to attack the piles of grotty kit. I opened up and walked in, only to exit at a far swifter pace. The stench in the storeroom was overwhelming. Thinking quickly, I put on my respirator and returned to investigate the cause of such an appalling smell. Had I inadvertently locked one of the lads in over the long weekend? The answer, of course, was Demitriuk's pheasants. Having hung them in the window over the radiators, the heating had switched on automatically over the weekend and rotted the birds to a tee. I came back out of the stores and gave one of the very few direct orders that I ever needed to give in the Army.

"Demitriuk! Get in there and get rid of those fucking birds."

If it were humanly possible, then Myron Demitriuk would find a power source on exercise. If he couldn't steal electricity from an unguarded socket in a farmyard to power his electric kettle, heater and waffle iron, then he would trade something for a supply. The Bardic Lamp was a popular acquisition for the rural Germans; it was better and more robust than any torch and squaddies always had an abundance of batteries to give away. Myron caused me to write more reports about allegedly stolen and lost Bardics than all the rest of my men put together. On the positive side, at least you could be assured of all the creature comforts when he was around; so I turned a blind eye to his entrepreneurial exploits and simply spun the QM a load of codswallop when we returned. It was by no means unusual to see at least one wire leading from the RMP tent and through a window or door and into a farmer's house. Myron personally took charge of the wiring and he was always quick to tell the farmer whenever we were leaving, in order to settle his account in one way or the other. He was caught on the hop, however, when the brigadier ordered a crash out at four o'clock one morning. Packed up and ready to move, except for two power cables leading through a window into the farmer's house, no amount of door banging could awaken the slumbering man of the soil. Under no circumstances would the shifty Myron consider cutting the cables, as that would have cost him money. Having made one last, futile attempt to wake the farmer, he decided that he would simply drive away and see what happened. Securing the cables to the back of the Landrover, he drove gingerly away until something gave. The plugs came away from the sockets and burst through the slightly open window, breaking the glass and wrecking a window frame at the same time. It was down to the imagination what havoc the flying cables may have caused to the ornaments in the front room of the farmhouse. Myron stopped his vehicle, wound in his cable and drove off with a shrug of the shoulders. Forced to return to that location later in the exercise, Myron kept an unusually low profile.

It wasn't advisable to leave any items of your platoon stores lying around in Werl, otherwise they would quickly find their way into someone else's Aladdin's cave. One particular staff sergeant, a Scot, not surprisingly, had made it his life's ambition to gather every item of kit issued to the company's six platoons into his own store. He had elevated the stealing of momentarily unguarded pieces of equipment to an art form and, by the time he was posted, he had almost achieved his aim. Most stuff could be replaced by simply indenting for more from the QM; the more expensive or more collectable 'starred' items were more difficult to replace. With them, it was necessary to submit a report regarding the circumstances surrounding the loss before the QM would entertain an application for a replacement. Alarmed by Jock's dexterity, the platoon commanders decided upon marking kit with a strategically placed dab of paint. This simple idea would save some of the pathetic squabbles that erupted the moment a screwdriver was misplaced and cut down considerably on the bloodletting that occurred when a direct accusation of theft was made. Scarlet was the colour decided upon by 29 Platoon, not for any deep-seated socialist reasons, but because a tin of paint of that hue was discovered lying around the barracks one day, without its owner. Among my motley crew was a former painter and decorator of Polish decent and he was volunteered to put his experience to good use. Krzeszewski was a thoroughly disreputable man and he was instructed to put a discreet dab of red gloss on all our kit, as a punishment for a string of recent misdemeanours. I was about to disappear on leave and left the instruction that he should paint everything red by the time I returned.

Arriving back in good form three weeks later, I decided that a glass or two of Iserlohner Pilsener wouldn't go amiss before facing the realities of life next morning. The RSM was putting in one of his rare appearances in the mess that evening and appeared to be in uncharacteristically good humour. As if his bonhomie wasn't enough, he surprised me further by reaching into his pocket to buy me a drink. I smelt a rat.

"Have you been in your stores yet, Wally?" he asked all casually.

"No, not yet sir, I've just arrived back off leave."

"I think you ought to go and take a look. Now."

I couldn't really have given a shit if the stores had burnt to the ground since I'd been away, but the RSM insisted. He accompanied me across the parade square to the block where the stores were located. They hadn't burnt down, but it occurred to me that there must be something seriously afoot for the RSM to want to be in on the kill. Opening the doors and, switching on the lights, I was greeted by a truly astonishing sight. *Everything* had been painted red! Army equipment is predominantly green, sometimes brown, or black, or grey, but generally a drab colour. My stuff was all scarlet. I closed the door and returned to the mess to endure the ritual taunting and to drink a few more Iserlohners. The Polish painter would feel my wrath on the morrow.

Next day I went over for another look, to make sure that it hadn't been a terrible dream. It hadn't, Krzeszewski had painted everything red. Mine were the Army's only red Jerry cans; not even the Russians had red Jerry cans! Lights, lamps and torches were all red, tyre pressure gauges, first aid kits, vehicle jacks and tow chains—all red. A burst of panic hit me. What about the vehicles, surely he hadn't painted them red as well? I sprinted over to the garages and was mightily relieved to discover that they were still indistinguishable from any others. Krzeszewski must have got word that his arse was on the line, as he proved most elusive. It wasn't until next morning that he felt my fingers around his throat. He maintained that I had told him to paint everything red and that he had merely complied with my order. It took him weeks to scrape all the paint off—in his own time, naturally.

Back from exercise for a while, I was lying on the sofa with a cushion under my head and vaguely aware of that hissing, pulsating noise that results from having your head at a certain angle. Suddenly, my heart missed a beat! I'd supped a load of beer the previous night, but surely not enough to affect my heart? I listened more intently. Sure enough, every dozen beats or so my heart was missing one. Panic set in and I sat up to take my pulse. That confirmed it. My ticker was definitely missing a beat. Would I survive until morning? It proved to be a long night and I was first in the queue to see the MO. He gave me the once over and explained that my heart wasn't actually missing a beat, but performing a double beat.

"Nothing to worry about," he said.

That was easy for him to say—it wasn't his heart that was out of synch.

I wanted a second opinion, so he sent me down to the military hospital in Iserlohn for an electrocardiograph. It was an unpleasant experience, especially when they made me breathe in and out rapidly for a whole minute. The test only served to confirm my double beat.

"Nothing to worry about," said the nurse. "Your MO will give you the results once the consultant has read your printout. About a week."

A week! I might well be dead by then. Ten days went by and there wasn't a squeak out of the medical centre. They were functioning with their normal efficiency. After two weeks without a call, I took the initiative and called them. The receptionist had the vague recollection of seeing something about my result, she maintained, but couldn't put her finger on it. Next day she called me. Some scribbled notes regarding my case had been found on the back of an old envelope, next to a recipe for Dundee Cake and an order for Bratwurst. She read out the brief forensic findings.

"The considered opinion of the cardiologist is that you are either eating or drinking too much," she declared.

After all that time and worry, a man who had never clapped eyes on me had reached this unsatisfactory conclusion. Worse still was the fact that the information had been passed on to me via the back of a manila envelope! I had expected a rather more precise diagnosis and a rather more professional attitude from my medical centre. My anger was such that I was still cursing and swearing when I went into the HQ to pick up my mail. My fit of pique was overheard by the OC who, I learnt, harboured a long-standing hatred for the MO. This resulted from an occasion when the doctor had refused to come out in the middle of the night to visit the major's sick child. The kiddie had subsequently taken a turn for the worse and needed to be rushed to the German hospital for emergency treatment.

"How's this for a plan, sarge? You attend sick parade in the morning and if you don't get absolute satisfaction from that oaf, I'll be on hand to jail the bastard."

I wasn't sure what grounds there would be for actually jailing the MO, but the major was at the medical centre next morning, resplendent in his service dress, armband and medals. He was serious. Perhaps the doctor had seen the major spitting fire and venom in the waiting room and realised that there was mischief afoot, because when he saw me, he was embarrassingly polite and helpful. He gave me a comprehensive rundown on my problem and put me at ease for the first time in weeks. He even offered an apology for the half-hearted performance of his receptionist.

"She needs the sack in my opinion," I remarked.

"Actually sergeant, she's my wife."

"I couldn't give a shit whose wife she is, she's inefficient," I said.

He didn't reply. I left the surgery as the victor and travelled back up to camp with the OC, who was genuinely disappointed that the MO hadn't stepped out of line.

This exercise season was almost over—only the big one left to do. The gods were being particularly kind to me at this time too, Inky was to be detached to Cyprus for a tour with the UN, and I was to assume control of the platoon in his absence. Unbeknown to me, the promotion board had pre-selected me for promotion to staff sergeant anyway and unless I cocked up in a big way, I'd reach the dizzy heights once we returned from the field. My chances for promotion were by no means diminished by the fact that I took six wickets for the company side in the semi-final of the Divisional Cricket Knock Out Cup Match. Our OC was skipper of our cricket eleven.

The platoon was renamed Tiger Platoon the moment Inky departed, mainly because the old name exposed me and my men to ridicule, but also in deference to the fact that there were now three Leicester blokes in our ranks. Meanwhile, I prepared to play a blinder on the FTX. Our first location was in a farmyard that had a conveniently situated guesthouse only a stone's throw away. We were too busy to use the place during the first five days of the exercise, but with the weekend stand down looming, all eyes turned towards the pub. The RSM called us to Friday evening prayers.

"That guesthouse remains out of bounds this weekend," he declared.

Minutes later he departed from the exercise location to spend the weekend back in Werl with his wife and family. It was all right for him, he'd get all the good food and drink he wanted tonight and a bit of something else too, no doubt. The rest of us were to stay behind in a farmyard that was luxurious by exercise standards, but to deny us access to the welcoming hostelry was a bit cruel. Once the sound of his vehicle exhaust had died away, the braver ones among us decided to risk big Brian's wrath and headed straight for the guesthouse anyway. With my promotion imminent, it was probably a little foolhardy to risk my crown for the sake of a few sherberts, but the flesh was weak and I joined the first wave of pioneers. Our efforts to remain reasonably sober were scotched by the over friendly locals and we all drank far too much. Shortly before last orders, I left the guesthouse with Ginge Stringer, who was in possession of an Army torch containing the weakest batteries in the world. The bulb glowed a dull red and proved an impediment, rather than an aid, to lighting our way back to the barn. We were about to head in a vaguely westerly direction, when one of the locals called out.

"*Nein, nein, da drueben gibt's eine Kurzung,*" he said, indicating a shortcut that lay directly ahead.

We thanked him for imparting this snippet of information and, assisted in no way by Ginge's torch, made our way along a particularly narrow path that formed the shortcut. The moon broke through the clouds momentarily and quickly disappeared again, its light giving me just enough time to see that our narrow path actually ran alongside a road.

"Why are we stumbling along this path, Ginge? There's a road running alongside," I said drunkenly, simultaneously stepping onto the newly discovered thoroughfare.

It wasn't a road. It was a trout hatchery. Up to my neck in trout and muddy water, I couldn't climb out for laughing and Ginge proved to be no friend in need. He was too consumed with drunken mirth to offer even token assistance and it was several minutes before our combined efforts succeeded in extracting me from a potentially watery grave. We made the decision to return to the guesthouse for a nightcap, agreeing that the sudden immersion in water may well have given me a chill. One more glass of schnapps was enough. We finally made it to the barn, this time taking the scenic route rather than the shortcut and were just about to go to bed, when the OC hove into view.

"Where the hell have you been, Sergeant Payne?" he enquired.

"Actually, I've been in a trout farm."

"Send your men to bed, sergeant," he ordered.

I could only see Ginge and, strictly speaking, he didn't qualify as 'men'. I was about to pick the major up on the point, but noticed a rather serious look in his eye. In any case he was sober. I certainly wasn't.

"Go to bed, you men," I said.

Ginge dutifully disappeared, leaving the major to deliver the standard military bollocking that went in one ear and straight out of the other. Remonstration over, I simply couldn't resist getting in the final word, a lifelong failing.

"Many thanks for the bollocking, sir, which was magnificently delivered if I may be bold enough to suggest. May I now have your kind permission to squelch away to my bed?" I said insolently, before lumbering away in the direction of my sleeping bag.

I was awoken next morning by the bass baritone tones of the RSM. It was Big Brian, back already! He must have had a row with the missus.

"Have a good time last night did we Wally?" he was charitable enough to enquire.

"Yes, thank you kindly sir," I replied, at the same time estimating that my hangover measured in the region of an eight on the Richter scale.

"Up, wash, shave, shit, shampoo and report to me in ten minutes."

By omitting the shit and the shampoo, neither of which were really necessary, I managed to make the deadline.

"Do you want the good news or the bad news?" he asked.

This was his standard opening gambit. I never found it funny, but he did and since I wasn't holding a very good hand, it was wise to play along.

"I'll have the good news please."

"There isn't any."

"Can I have the bad news then please, sir?"

"The bad news, Wally, is that you will forfeit your day off and perform a tank route recce for me. Get the details from the CSM and report back to me by last light."

Last light! It was going to be an all day recce with a massive hangover. Oh joy! A tank route recce consisted basically of ascertaining whether the roads on a planned route were wide enough and had bridges that were strong enough to take a sixty ton tracked vehicle. It was usually a pleasant task, but not with a stinking hangover. I had completed several miles without a hitch and had just concluded that a junction was wide enough to accommodate a right turn by an Abram's tank. Noting the fact on my map, I put my Landrover in reverse and backed straight into the Renault that had pulled up behind me. The shunt didn't damage my truck, but it dented the French car rather badly. To make things worse, the other driver turned out to be none other the Freiherr von Plotho, one of the German landed gentry and a man who was probably related to the Queen. If you are going to have an accident, then have it in decent company I always say. With Army regulations stipulating that a driver may not drive within twenty-four hours of an accident, I returned to the farmyard to break the news to the RSM.

"Oh dear, Wally. Having a particularly bad day aren't we? Take Lampton along as your driver. I'll leave it to you to explain why he has lost his day off."

We finished the task and devoured a couple of German sausages apiece, before setting off on the return leg with steady Colin at the wheel. Almost immediately we came upon a T-junction, at which we were required to halt. We both looked left and right, but it appears that it was only me who saw the Audi saloon indicating its intention to turn. This vehicle had almost completed its left turn, when Colin suddenly shot forward and rammed into the German car. I alighted and was surprised to see an old lady sitting in the back seat of the Audi, admiring an unrestricted view of the town centre. Almost like a sardine can, the car had lost its entire left-hand side! I returned to the truck to fetch the necessary paperwork and found Colin still sitting transfixed in the driver's seat. He was white with shock; even his lips were white. He recovered after another sausage and our dented machine was driven carefully back to base.

"Oh dear, Wally," said Big Brian. "Better take an early night, tomorrow must be an improvement on today. Couldn't be much worse, eh?"

After the exercise I kept a fairly low profile; perhaps the OC would overlook my exercise cock-ups and give me my promotion anyway. I was off duty on the day that my elevation was due, but during the course of the afternoon I was summoned to parade at the RSM's office.

"Afternoon, Wally."

"Afternoon, sir."

"Good news or the bad news, lad?"

"Bad news first I think, sir."

"There isn't any," he replied with a smirk.

I could never fathom out just why he found this charade so rib-tickling funny.

"Can I have the good news then, sir?"

"You are promoted to staff sergeant. Congratulations."

He offered me his ham-sized fist and I shook his hand. I'd made it, no thanks to Dortmunder Union Brewery, Freiherr von Plotho or Colin Lampton's driving.

Taking over as platoon commander was a double-edged sword. Sure, it was great to be a staff sergeant and there was always the extra money, but 29 Platoon was designated as the exercise platoon. That meant we would spend a large proportion of the next exercise season out in the field. I never liked being in the field, even in the old days when exercises were held during the warmer summer months. Now that they were scheduled for the coldest part of the year, I positively hated them. Fiscal restraints had forced the Army's hand. The amount of damage caused to growing crops, farm tracks and fields meant that the cost of compensation was taking a large slice of the ever-shrinking exercise budget. The answer was to hold exercises in winter, when the crops had been harvested and the ground was frozen solid. The guy that came up with that masterstroke was probably awarded the MBE, but I'll bet he never wore a combat kit in his life. Here are some reminiscences of the miserable times I endured out in the field as 29 Platoon Commander.

For the entire sixteen-day duration of the exercise the temperature never rose above freezing point and it was very much colder most of the time. Everyone participating in Exercise Far Fling could think of a million places they would have rather been than in Landkreis Detmold, and the mood of the troops wasn't improved by the knowledge that several guys had copped their lot during these manoeuvres. No training exercise is worth the death of a soldier. As military policemen, one of our tasks was to erect an information post at the edge of a village, or forest in which the HQ was located. The reason for sighting our tent on the most exposed ridge in the whole of North Rhein Westfalia on this particular night, however, was something known only to the imbecile recce officer. It had been twelve days since we came out, we were wet, freezing cold and exceedingly pissed off as we put the info post up at three in the bloody morning. As soon as the tent was erected, the heater was lit and we all attempted to de-thaw a little. Some poor soul would have to brave the elements one more time though, to put out the signs. It always seemed a little incongruous to me that thousands of man-hours were spent expertly camouflaging a location in order to make it undetectable, only for the RMP to erect signs at the side of the road announcing its whereabouts. To show the young guys that despite the greying temples, staff still had what it takes, I donned my parka and braved the Arctic conditions to erect the signs.

"I'm just going outside and I may be some time," I said, wondering just how desperate Laurence Oates must have been when he uttered those words.

Unoriginal it might have been, prophetic it most certainly was. Knocking the stakes that support the signs into the trackside proved a major undertaking; the ground had been hardened by weeks of sub-zero temperatures and was like concrete. With considerable huffing, puffing and noise, I finally reached the furthermost point from the HQ. Having hammered the last stake home and erected the sign that read, 'INFO POST 300 M', I was preparing to return to the tent, when a punch to the side of the head knocked me to the ground. Jumping to my feet after the walloping, I became aware of five or six shadows around me. Ignorant of the fact that these guys were merely the exercise enemy, I was convinced they were about to do me in, so waded into the nearest one and put him on the deck. Another whack on the head put me down again. Believing that I was fighting for my life, I got up for another go, before a rifle butt put me down for keeps. I was convinced that my end was about to come when a Cockney voice rose above the others.

"Take it easy squire, it's only a bleeding exercise!"

This group was merely an exercise raiding party intent on taking a prisoner. Had I known of the existence of an 'enemy', there certainly wouldn't have been so much melodrama or bravado from me.

"Why don't you just give in and come with us, mate?" said another voice. "We're billeted in a village hall that's got a great heater. You can thaw out."

The exercise was in its second week and, despite attending two briefings every day, the fact that there was a live enemy participating had never been mentioned. Since the IRA and other idealistic zealots were particularly active in BAOR at this time, the failure to give out this information was criminal.

There was no need for me to ponder such a sound proposition. I gave them my gun and submitted to the childish application of a blindfold, before being led away to a waiting vehicle. After a short drive, we arrived at a village hall that had what appeared to be a jet engine mounted into one wall. It acted as a giant-sized heater. It was wonderfully warm in the building and my captors gave me some food and a stretcher to sleep on. This was sheer bliss after suffering so many days of bitter cold. After two days in this holiday camp my gaolers, whose unit I never did ascertain, informed me that they were about to leave the location. Despite my protests and the suggestion that they just leave me here on my own, they were unsporting enough to insist that I be passed on to another enemy unit. It's difficult to understand why they took so much trouble; there was no intelligence to be tortured out of me. I knew bugger all. My new captors were a Royal Signals unit that was perched on the top of a windswept hill a few miles away. My presence was neither required, nor appreciated, and following a day and a half of sitting contentedly at the side of the cookhouse burner, their OC demanded my presence. He gave me a map, told me my present location and pointed out the last known location of the formation from where I had been so ingloriously snatched. Then he told me to sod off. It took me most of the day to walk back to the wood where the Divisional HQ had been located, as there were several guesthouses on the way. Finally, I plodded up the forest track that led to the location and discovered that everyone was still there. The info post tent was frozen solid and my men were inside, huddled together for warmth. They were so pissed off that my return did little to enthuse them. I went to find the recce officer, to report my valiant escape from the clutches of the enemy. He wasn't a happy man.

"Where the fuck have you been, staff? We've spent days trying to find you."

"I was taken prisoner," I replied, "by an enemy that you didn't even tell us about. That's were I've fucking well been!"

"Yes, it was remiss of me, I suppose. Anyway, I'm too cold and pissed off to care. It's Endex in an hour, so who gives a shit."

"Not me, that's for sure,' I replied and hurried back to break the glad tidings to the boys.

Another exercise, more Arctic conditions! At the start of this one, a troop of signallers preparing the communication wiring had managed to overturn one of their paraffin burners and destroy a Dutch barn. Shortly afterwards, some engineers had burnt down another barn, resulting in costs running into tens of thousands of pounds. The colonel declared that the next person in his command to start a fire would be for the high jump and banned the use of all burners forthwith. It was all right for him, of course; generator powered electric heaters warmed the officer's mess and his personal caravan. Our archaic paraffin heaters were hopelessly inefficient and gave off scarcely enough heat to warm a badger's bum. At the same time they emitted the most appalling stink of burning paraffin, unless you knew how to trim the wick just so. With the temperature dropping to new lows, there were those who would have been willing to brave a few fumes, provided it thawed out the freezing extremities. The order from HQ forbidding their use was quite specific, however.

With the possible exception of the infantry, RMP spent more time out in the elements than anyone and, considering that my guys were freezing their bollocks off, I gave the instruction to light the burners in our tents. I would simply gamble on the fact that none of our lot was stupid enough to start a fire. The threat of a court martial and a beating from me would surely be enough to ensure that every precaution was taken. I was wrong. Within half an hour of lighting the bloody thing, our new Welshman almost killed himself and the four other guys huddled with him around the burner. With fuel running low, Taffy was remiss enough to fill the reservoir of the heater with petrol rather than the paraffin. In the Army, petrol comes in a Jerry can marked with a red plate, paraffin a blue plate, and diesel yellow, and I vowed to send the Welshman for a colour blindness test the moment he returned to camp. It was at the moment of ignition that the boys had reason to be grateful for the extreme cold. When the thing exploded, the flames kept very low and they were able to throw it outside before any serious damage was done. It burnt itself out without even singeing the sides of the tent, although we weren't out of the woods yet. The incident had come to the notice of a passing snitch and he wet his pants in his haste to report the fact that the nasty RMP had caused a fire. I was ordered to report to the colonel with a full explanation. Taffy and me were in the mire, or were we?

It was Myron who spotted the miracle first. The outside of the petrol can that Taffy had used to fill the heater had been slightly burnt, turning the red indicator plate light blue. The plate, which was clearly marked 'petrol', was now exactly the same colour as a paraffin plate. What a stroke of luck, we had a defence. I marched into the colonel's caravan armed with the jerry can and a cock and bull story as to why it had been absolutely imperative to test our burner. Instead of cowering and waiting to be questioned on my decision, I launched into an attack against the Ordnance Corps for issuing cans marked with the wrong colour indicator plates and thereby putting our lives at risk. Not only did my performance save Taffy and myself from the direst consequences, but I also left his caravan with the words 'very well done' ringing in my ears.

Throughout the miserable winter season, we froze and shivered as the temperature stubbornly refused to rise above zero for weeks on end. The most miserable aspect of it all wasn't the cold, but the fact that we had wet feet most of the time. Cold feet are bad enough, but cold and wet plates of meat really are the pits. We all had two pairs of boots, but even if you did find some method of drying them out, they were sodden again within a few minutes of tramping out in the snow and slush. The fact is, the DMS boot was not up to the job, although it took hundreds of cases of trench foot and the Falklands War to convince the powers that be that they were crap. The answer, of course, was to wear a pair of Wellingtons; at least they kept your feet dry when you ventured out into the snow. Wellies were on issue in limited supplies and when you wore them under your combat trousers, it took an observant man to notice the difference between them and boots, especially when you were plodging around in a foot of snow and mud.

By the time the next exercise came around, most of the senior ranks in our division had managed to beg, steal or borrow a pair of Army issue black Wellingtons. We all had reasonably dry feet and we were happy. That wouldn't do for the Chief of Staff, however.

"Quite unacceptable for a soldier to wear gum boots," he declared.

So, with wellies summarily forbidden, we all changed back into our sodden boots.

He wore rubber boots, of course, but not those vulgar Army issue things—his were green. Although green wellies were most definitely not on issue, they do form part of an officer's wardrobe. Green gumboots, you see, go so splendidly with the Dunn's hat, Barbour jacket and Dalmatian at the polo match. (In some commands a Labrador is acceptable in lieu of a Dalmatian, incidentally.) For the remainder of that miserable exercise we went wet footed, whilst that arrogant Scottish bastard swaggered around in his green wellies, the ones with a string around the top. There was a lot of muttering in the ranks, but because soldiers function best when they have someone to despise, the job was done properly.

Don't mention Marienmuenster to Colin Lampton. On Exercise First Fling it was desperately cold all the time and during the early hours of the morning, it sometimes fell to minus twenty-five Centigrade. I spent the entire two weeks with Colin, who was perhaps the only person in the whole British Army who hated living in the field more than I did. He had been posted into my platoon as an eighteen year old, already going on thirty-five and was mature way beyond his years. This premature ageing could be put down to the fact that his father cruelly forced him to watch Newcastle United during his formative years, when there was a perfectly decent side who played in red and white only a few miles down the road. The week we spent in Marienmuenster is etched, or rather carved, into my memory. When we first arrived, Colin had refused to enter the Hammer House of Horror complex until I had found him a crucifix and a clove of garlic. Along with Badger, our third team member, we controlled access to this Transylvanian style farm complex from a dilapidated, unheated, unlit hut situated just inside the farmyard walls. For the whole period our boots were frozen solid, our kit was frozen solid and our minds were numbed with cold. Why the hell were we out here? Why does the Army need to practice being uncomfortable? It doesn't matter how many times you practice in the cold; it doesn't get any easier, or warmer.

The boredom on this exercise was overwhelming and we needed to devise methods of keeping sane, no matter how disreputable they might appear now. We ran a sweepstake on who would be brave enough to venture to the toilet most often in the Arctic conditions. I won the event, but was accused of duplicity, as I claimed two visits to the lavatory whilst spending a few hours back in camp one evening. Colin paid up with exceedingly bad grace and declared that comfy shits would be excluded from future competition. Marienmuenster really was a bloody awful spot. I recall standing at the entrance early one morning, unable to sleep for the intense cold and taking in a deep breath of super cooled air. I experienced a most peculiar sensation, something like having a chopstick shoved up each nostril, as the mucus froze all the way up to my brain.

Apart from our set up in the HQ, we had three MPs at each of two other locations. As the platoon commander, at least I had the opportunity of driving out occasionally to visit the others, on the pretext of giving them some information critical to the war effort. In reality, I was sneaking a few minutes out in my Landrover. It had a heater as useless as those fitted to every other vehicle of this make, but it gave me a modicum of relief from the icy blast. On the twelfth day of misery, a Friday as I recall, I called to see the crew at 'Step up'. They were in a state of extreme agitation. Apparently the formation commander had told them that, with my permission, they could return to camp.

"Fuck off as fast as you can then, you jammy bastards," I advised.

Moving on to the next location I was met by Myron. He had already packed up and was about to depart for Werl.

"Been told we can bugger off our kid, we're just on our way," he said.

Myron wouldn't have waited for my permission; another five minutes and I would have missed him altogether. Only Badger, Colin and myself were left behind to suffer. I was aware that the exercise proper was over, but that the

Signals and the Brigade HQ were being inspected in the field on Monday. It didn't involve the RMP in any way, but a pound to a pinch of shit we would be required to stay out, just in case we were needed. I arrived back and asked Badger whether there was any news, half hoping we might have been told to bugger off too. No such luck.

"Major Disaster called in though, he wants you to go and see him."

In the absence of an RMP officer in the field, Major Disaster was our boss and a proverbial pain in the backside. He would probably want to brief me on our tasks for the weekend. I slouched over to the HQ without much enthusiasm.

"Ah, staff," he said, the plum in his mouth unaffected by the extreme cold, "we're having our ARU in the field on Monday as you probably know, but there's no need for you chaps to stay out, unless you particularly want to."

I had not run so fast since an angry ram chased me across a field in Derbyshire in 1968. We struck camp and packed just as quickly as our frozen fingers would permit and were on the road back in record time. It was the only time in my career that I ever had to hammer a tent flat with a mallet; the frozen rain had made it as solid as a rock. The boys hung on like grim death as I sped away at breakneck speed, just in case Major Disaster should have a change of mind. Once we were clear of the immediate area, we stopped to repack before making our way home at a more leisurely pace. The worst exercise I had ever endured had come to a mercifully premature finish.

As everything was functioning perfectly well, HQ invented something new to complicate matters again. Instead of logging vehicle movements by radio as we had done for years, a new system of reporting by telephone had been devised. With the agreement of the German telephone authority, small black boxes mysteriously appeared at specific locations dotted around the countryside. The concept was simple, we were to connect the wires of our field telephones to the connections on the magic black box and then you could call any number you wished. It was strictly controlled, though, so no prospect of calling one's Aunty Lil in Australia. Prior to the exercise on which the new system would be tested for the first time, we were called together for a period of instruction. A Royal Signals sergeant baffled us with technical details and then, amid great pomp and ceremony, the secret grid location of each traffic post's telephone connection was divulged.

We arrived at the place where we performed our tedious traffic control task, both at the beginning and the end of every exercise and I checked the map reference of the location for the first time. Would you believe it, it was exactly the same as the secret map reference for our black box. And there it was at the side of the track, except that it wasn't black but green, and it wasn't open as promised, but firmly locked. We waited for several hours in the vain hope that a man from the telephone company would appear with a key, but when the first convoys started to appear, I decided that the box had to be opened at all costs. This was a metal construction of uncommon strength and no amount of hammering and levering would give us access. By now it was crucial that we contact our HQ and I ordered more positive action. A passing REME vehicle was flagged down and to the glee of the mechanics, we asked them to open the box by any means at their disposal. No task is insurmountable when you have the right equipment, and the craftsmen had the lid off the box in a couple of minutes. It was at this juncture that I realised my error. This wasn't the telephone connection point at all, but an electricity master fuse box. We had come close to blacking out large parts of Paderborn. I scratched my head in Stan Laurel fashion and took another look at those grid references. Oh dear, they weren't quite the same after all; our black box was actually two hundred metres away. Armed with a handset and a roll of telephone wire, I set off towards the middle of an adjacent field where, attached to a telegraph pole and wide open, was the black box. It took half a minute to make contact with some idiot at control, who accepted my bullshit about defective telephone handsets and we were out of the mire.

Thanks to an arrangement with the RSM of the Royal Signals, a man about whom I knew a thing or two that he wouldn't want publicising, my platoon were permitted to travel up to the Brigade Headquarters on the morning that an exercise began. That was far preferable to spending the night before on the barracks square with the rest of the rabble. It meant a very early start, but it also meant an extra night in our own beds before enduring the misery of days, or even weeks, in the field. Our presence at the time of the initial movement was crucial and our absence would have caused much anger and the immediate withdrawal of the privilege. Hating exercises with a passion so all consuming that I'd do anything for an extra night in my own bed, the boys knew that my ire would be considerable should they ever be late. It had all worked perfectly for eighteen months and our early morning arrival was accepted as the norm, until the day that Gary decided he didn't want to play at soldiers any more. There was no replacement for Gary—he was our signaller and he simply had to be there. On this occasion, though, he failed to appear at the prescribed hour, he didn't phone in and wouldn't answer his private phone in his quarter. There had been no reports of traffic accidents and so I presumed he had simply slept in. Two vehicles were sent off to Soest, whilst Colin and I loaded all of Gary's stuff for him and set off to pick him up at his married quarter down in Werl. Several rings on the doorbell finally stirred Gary's pretty wife, the delicious Gudrun, who came to the door wearing a fetching line in night attire.

"Where's Gary, Gudrun?"

"He is in the bed and is telling me that he is not to the exercise going."

"Why isn't he to the exercise going?"

"We have a disagreement and that is why he goes not."

"Gudrun, go and tell Gary that if he's not here in two minutes, I'll come in and drag him out by the hair."

She disappeared and returned a couple of minutes later, without the reluctant signaller.

"He is saying that he is too upset to be coming," said Gudrun.

I dispensed with her services as an intermediary and stormed into his bedroom.

"Right pal," I said. "You have precisely five minutes to be up, dressed and in the back of the Landrover, otherwise I'll come back and break your fucking nose. Do you understand?"

I find that a little gentle persuasion works sometimes and within the prescribed time limit, we were racing towards Soest with Gary aboard, but minus his weapon. Only a person to whom a weapon is allocated may withdraw it from the armoury and we didn't have the time to go back. Gary would be in the mire when we returned from the exercise. We were late, of course, and in future would be required to spend the night before the exercise on the square with all the rest of the grunters. That really pissed me off and it was all because Gary 'did not to the exercise want to go'. In all my years in the Army, you could count the number of times I charged a guy on the fingers of one hand, but I made sure Gary copped for this one.

For the entire six weeks of Exercise Crusader, I was to be found either down in a cellar where the Safety Cell was doing its business, or asleep in the tent I shared with Boozy Hughsie. This was the biggest military invasion of Germany since the real one back in the forties and tens of thousands of troops from many lands were taking part. Our function was to ensure that they all returned home alive and, in that aim, we were brilliantly successful. One solitary fatality was recorded and that was the result of a traffic accident in Holland, before the exercise began. That figure must have exceeded the most optimistic projections of the organisers. It was rumoured that the Ordnance Corps had enough coffins in the field to accommodate several dozen customers, but they took them all back home with them. The local population didn't fare nearly as well and a dozen Germans died in traffic accidents. Sitting behind the wheel of their Mercedes or BMW, all Germans consider themselves to be both expert drivers and impervious to injury. They never seem to learn that when there are battle tanks in the vicinity, travelling at 90 mph isn't conducive to longevity.

Two things stick in my mind about that dreadful cellar. One was the vast amount of Milde Sorte filter coffee that we consumed, so much in my case that I had caffeine withdrawal symptoms for a week after returning to barracks. The other was the larger than life Texan, our American MP representative, who chewed tobacco constantly and spat the excess goo into an empty Coke can. How gross!

Towards the end of the exercise, the BBC descended on the location and selected certain members of the HQ staff to be interviewed for a radio programme. Seldom stuck for words, I was nominated to appear on behalf of our little organisation. This was to be my first radio interview and it was only when the tape recorder was switched on and the microphone pushed under my nose that I realised that I suffer from stage fright. My stuttering, blundering effort was pitiful.

"Well staff, I understand that traffic accidents on the exercise have been remarkably few in number. Can this be attributed to the work of the Safety Cell?"

"Yes-it-can-be-attributed-to-the-work-of-the-Safety-Cell."

"That's intriguing. Now, do you think that the troops have been heeding the good advice that you have been putting out on the radio?"

"Yes-I-think-that-they-are-heeding-the-good-advice-we-have-been-putting-out-on-the-radio."

It was pathetic and I felt sorry for the poor interviewer. It speaks volumes for the man that, by the time the interview was broadcast, he had managed to transform my garbage into something that sounded really quite good. My next interview was with Anne Armstrong, the professional do-gooder for the soldier and his family. It came as a mighty relief to see that she was armed with just a notebook and pencil. My confidence returned immediately and she left with enough crap to fill a dozen programmes. She finished by asking if I had a record request for the folks at home. I felt like a national serviceman marooned on Christmas Island back in the fifties. Didn't she know that even we common other ranks had access to STD now and that most of us phoned home whenever the mood struck us? Just the same, I selected a record for my mum back in far away Leicester.

"Shirley Bassey singing 'The Laughing Policeman', please Anne," I requested.

The silly old sausage actually apologised on the air for not being able to find Shirley Bassey's version. Well, there's a surprise! Instead, she played me the scratchy old 78rpm version by Charles Penrose, the long forgotten music hall artist.

6

Shortly after my promotion to staff sergeant, my wife decided to return to Scotland and start her life anew. I hadn't made much of an effort to hang on to our eighteen-month-old marriage when things were going awry and twice drove her to the airport following arguments—just to show her how easy it was to leave. She finally took the hint and boarded a plane for Edinburgh. A little later I pondered the wisdom of my actions and made a reasonably serious attempt to win her back, by travelling to Scotland to see her. I drove all the way from Werl to Kincardine Bridge, only to be repulsed. She told me to bugger off, maintaining that she would be better off without me. Well crivvens, jings, help ma Boab!

In order to drive up to Scotland, I had done something exceedingly stupid, even by my high standards of outrageous behaviour. It was during my attendance at an All Arms Firearms Course at Sennelager that it had occurred to me to make one final attempt to repair our marriage and I had absented myself without permission. I did call in and see my padre and our second-in-command before disappearing, but not the OC or RSM, the very men I ought to have consulted. The venture had been to no avail and now that I was back, there would be all hell to pay. A masterful Payne performance would be required to talk my way out of this one; otherwise I might well finish up as a corporal, or in jail. Knowing that the RSM took breakfast very early, I made sure that I was in the dining room before he came in for his Rice Krispies. I bade him a cheery good morning and waited for the flak.

"Well Wally?" he demanded.

He listened patiently to the whole sorry saga and once my tale of woe had been told, I awaited his pronouncement. He couldn't have been more understanding. He explained that he was already on his third marriage and knew how painful a break up could be. To my amazement he was willing to forget the whole matter, his only stipulation being that I should call in on the OC and apologise. What an escape!

I'm not sure whether etiquette demands that you should inform your best man once your marriage is over, especially when he happens to be a Greek Cypriot. I wrote and told Christagi Neophytides anyway and was surprised to receive a letter by return of post, him being a notoriously reluctant penman. It was not only the speed of his reply that surprised me, but also the letter's content. He explained that he had found the most marvellous girl, who was not only beautiful, but rich too. My heart went out to Chris' wife Nitsa, a wonderful lady, who was being ditched for a younger model. Reading on, however, I was much relieved to discover that he wasn't two timing Nitsa at all—the lovely girl he had found was for *me*. In his capacity as best man, he had felt obliged to find me a replacement wife. It's part of Greek tradition presumably? He closed his letter by urging me to travel to Cyprus with all haste in order to meet the girl. Not being one to let the grass grow under my feet, I took some overdue leave and set off by car to drive down to Athens. The plan went awry in Austria, where the snow fell with a vengeance and closed all the Alpine passes. I was forced to return home to contemplate my navel. I decided to fly over to Cyprus to meet Thalia Hadjiiannou.

Chris and Nitsa picked me up from Larnaca airport and that first evening we all went out for the oddest of dinner parties. On my side of the table in the restaurant were Chris, Nitsa and myself. On the other side, in the red corner, sat Thalia Hadjiiannou, her sister and her brother-in-law, Achilles. We ate dinner, during which the conversation was stilted to say the least, but at least the food was good and someone else picked up the tab. Once we had finished eating, we all went home and that was that. If this was the way one paid court to a Cypriot lady, then it was novel to say the least.

Next day, Chris and I took in a soccer match at the stadium on the sea front in Limassol. All the spectators were accommodated in a stand that ran the length of one side of the pitch and Chris and I were right in the middle of thousands of fans. The skipper of the home side, New Century, turned out to be none other than Achilles, Thalia's sponsor. Before the match kicked off, he brought his entire team over to wave a greeting to me. Fifteen hundred faces on either side turned inwards to take a look at the personality—they must have been gravely disappointed. It was a lousy match, but New Century achieved the draw that they required too keep them in the top flight the following season. Chris assured me that the match had been fixed.

That evening I was invited to the team's celebration dinner, along with Chris and Nitsa. How did they know that they could arrange a celebration dinner if the result hadn't been negotiated beforehand? Among the guests was Thalia, who just happened to be sitting next to me. She turned out to be a most agreeable lady. As a recent divorcee, a lady of considerable means and belonging to a respected Cypriot family, she may have made a decent catch. Tradition dictated that she took an acceptable husband at the earliest opportunity and I was being lined up as a candidate. Perhaps I had led Chris to believe that I was already divorced, which wasn't the case. I wasn't in a position to marry this woman, even if the idea had appealed to me. After dinner we went to a disco, whereupon everyone with exception of me took to the dance floor. I hate dancing and take to the floor only when drunk, or under extreme duress. Achilles tried his damnedest to urge me to dance with his sister-in-law, but I remained resolute. He finally accepted that I wasn't going to dance, so he joined me at the bar. I was aware that he was the official matchmaker, but wasn't really prepared for his next plan of attack.

"Well Wally, what is your answer?"

"My answer to what?"

"Do you wish to marry Thalia or not?"

"My answer is no," I said with conviction.

"Okay, my friend, no problem."

And that was it. He had shown me the goods; I had looked at them, but decided not to buy. It was as simple as that.

I stayed on to enjoy my holiday, there was no ill feeling at all and Thalia was officially on the market again. Six weeks after returning to Germany, the news reached me that Thalia had married a sea captain. I hope that they made a happy couple. I need rather longer than twenty-four hours to make a decision of such magnitude and, even then, I'm prone to the most serious misjudgements.

My wife had been gone for a considerable time, but I was having difficulty getting her off my mind. On reflection, I was probably wallowing in self-pity rather than suffering from a broken heart, but decided that a holiday would prove beneficial. And where's the best place to go for a wife-forgetting holiday? To the very place where you met, married and lived together for a year with her, that's where. Cyprus it was, then, and my good chum, the incredibly thin Bones Kitchenbrand, decided to come along to keep me out of harm's way. We travelled all the way down to Piraeus in Greece in his trusty Volkswagen, sailed over on the boat to Limassol and then came all the way back again. The only bloody tape in his car was 'The Best of Olivier Newton-John' and I've been word perfect on her songs ever since. It was a good holiday, though, and it served to lay the ghost of my wife. Bones proved to be a true friend and I will be eternally grateful to him for giving me a shoulder to cry on. He listened patiently as the boring story of my marriage was told and retold to numerous Cypriot friends. The long trip back was made at record speed and despite the fact that Bones had shouldered most of the driving, it was me who needed a nightcap to bring me down to earth when we finally arrived in Werl. Although it was only a couple of hundred yards from the camp, I had never ventured down to the Dandy Bar before. I ordered a glass of the amber fluid and sat quietly in a corner, happy with my own company, when the prettiest young lady approached.

"Are you Staff Payne?" she enquired in a cultured accent.

"The very same," I replied, giving her the once over.

She was lovely, beautifully dressed and only about twenty years of age.

"These young guys are getting on my nerves! May I sit with you?"

Laura was a nineteen-year-old stunner who had been posted into our unit during my holiday in the Mediterranean and, from that night on, we had a marvellous relationship. She wanted an older man and I needed a shot in the arm like Laura to help me recover from my recent trauma. If ever a lady was heaven sent, it was she. I made something of a fool of myself, by falling for her, but she was lovely and I didn't much care what people were saying behind my back. It was a marvellous boost for me, and for her, a period of infatuation for an older man perhaps.

At a Saturday night party a couple of months later, she asked me outside for a quiet word. There was no need; I knew instinctively that it was all over. She had found a younger suitor, one that enjoyed dancing probably, and she wanted to give him a try. It hurt for a while, but then another WRAC girl came along. She wasn't as attractive as Laura, but she served her purpose too. I always knew that female soldiers had to be good for something.

It was probably a subconscious reaction to having been sacked as a husband, but I seemed to be getting more than my fair share of the other. On one occasion, however, I came precariously close to burning my fingers.

The happy couple had been engaged for several months, although their betrothal hadn't stopped my clandestine visits to her room on moonless nights. The groom approached me one day, near to the garages where he worked as a mechanic. He was carrying the largest, heaviest spanner I had ever seen. My immediate thought was that he had discovered my little secret and that this was the showdown.

"Excuse me staff, may I ask you a question?"

This was it, get ready to defend yourself, Wally!

"Sure BT, what is it?" I replied, as nonchalantly as I could manage.

"You know that Cynthia and I are to be married next month?"

"And so would you kindly stop shagging her before I put this spanner around you ears?" was what I expected to hear, but he was clearly oblivious of my nocturnal misdemeanours.

"And we wondered if you would do us the honour of being best man?"

"Well, of course, I'd be delighted, honoured," I replied, wondering if he could detect the sense of relief in my voice.

"That's great news. Would you care to join us for dinner tonight at the Italian? We can discuss some details."

To be honest, the groom would have been hard pressed to find a more unsuitable person than me to act as best man at his forthcoming marriage. Had he known of my association with his bride to be, I fancy he might have asked someone else to perform the duty. It turned out to be a very enjoyable meal, as it happened, but I couldn't help wondering how Cynthia felt. The choice of me as best man was hardly likely to have been her idea. Quite why BT decided to ask me still remains a mystery, as we were hardly bosom buddies.

In fact, it was just as well that he did choose someone with a little experience in these matters, because he had done precious little in the way of organising things for the big day. Everything was left to me and a couple of willing helpers. I performed my duties with extreme diligence, as a sort of penance for being so naughty with Cynthia. BT tried my patience just the same; his naive assumption that everything would turn out all right without any input from him was irritating. On the morning of the wedding, for example, he was overcome by nerves and disappeared for a spin on a motorbike, returning only an hour before the ceremony.

At the service, presided over by the Black Watch padre, the bride looked radiant, the groom smart and the best man immaculate. Everything went well, both at the service and at the reception, vindicating BT's carefree approach to the whole affair perhaps. The highlight of the reception was the best man's speech. I poked some gentle fun at the groom and the vicar, but let Cynthia off the hook. There had been enough poking in that area already. During my gentle knock at the padre, I made reference to a piece of graffiti that had appeared on the wall of an American Theological College in St. Paul's Minneapolis. The graffiti was in the form of a parody on a piece from the Gospel.

Jesus said to them, "Who do you say that I am?" They replied, "You are the eschatological manifestation of the ground of our being, the kerygma of which we find the ultimate meaning in our interpersonal relationships." And Jesus said, "What?"

This was particularly well received and no one laughed louder than the minister did.

"Where did you get that from Wally?" asked the man of the cloth.

Was he about to excommunicate me from his Kirk for heresy? I explained its origins and gave him my copy.

"This is my sermon for tomorrow."

"But it's ten o'clock on Saturday night; surely you've prepared tomorrow's effort already?"

"Yes, I have, but I'm changing it."

I was at the Kirk next morning, with a fuzzy head from the previous night admittedly. The Gospel reading ought to have given it away, I suppose, but all readings sound the same when delivered in a Fife accent. Then the sermon began.

"I was at a great wedding yesterday. The priest was brilliant. Mind you, self-praise is no recommendation. The best man's speech was a cracker too—let me quote."

He went on to read my piece of graffiti, which the congregation appeared to enjoy as much as the audience had the previous night. Then he pointed me out and I had a hot flush of embarrassment, or was it the effect of the champagne? I vowed not to take the vicar on again, as he went on to make another of his telling sermons based on that little piece of graffiti.

The Black Watch were fortunate indeed to have a padre of the calibre of the Reverend Norman. He transformed what had been a lacklustre church into a place that was fun to go to on Sunday mornings. His preaching was inspirational and his leadership dynamic, but despite this, he remained a humble and approachable man. His ability to reach out to all the men in his battalion was illustrated by the fact that he had turned a meagrely attended church into a place where you couldn't get a seat, unless you arrived fifteen minutes before the service began.

This was the Army's Year of NBC and we were supposed to give nuclear, biological and chemical matters utmost priority during training. The fact that

Army shortages were most critical in the NBC equipment area didn't make this an easy aim. The order to concentrate on NBC matters hadn't been lost on our good padre who, for reasons best known to the HQ, actually sat on the NBC committee.

Sitting on the left-hand side of the church on the Sunday morning immediately following an exercise, I caught site of the elder carrying the bible down the aisle prior to the start of the service. Following close behind the elder, dressed in his robes of office but wearing a respirator, was the good reverend.

"Good morning and welcome to the Kirk of the Black Watch," said a voice distorted by the gas mask. "Just a wee minute while I take this thing off," continued the Scottish version of David Frost. "I was at a great party last night and Billy MacKintosh, who is sitting at the back of the Kirk, incidentally..." Everybody turned around and had a wee keek at Billy. "Billy bet me fifty marks for charity that I wouldn't dare to wear my gas mask in the Kirk. Stick it in the plate when it comes round, Billy."

This was just an example of the spontaneity and fun that endeared him to so many. Reverend Norman then invited the congregation to bow their heads for Prayers of Intercession.

"Let us pray," he intoned. "Let us pray for Adam Smith's wee lassie Fiona, who is so very ill back in Auchtermuchty. She's not on the mend yet, but she's no worse. May the Lord be praised for that?"

Several other worthy prayers were offered before he came towards the end.

"Let us also give thanks that Andrew Gardiner has pulled through from his operation. May the Lord be praised for that? Finally, but by no means any less important for that, yesterday at Murrayfield, Scotland beat Wales and that means that Wales cannae win the Triple Crown. Oh, may the Lord be praised for that?"

Some vicar!

I have made several references to Myron Demitriuk already, but this amazing man deserves a few pages of his very own.

It's improbable that there was ever a better example of a fish out of water in a chosen career than Myron Demitriuk as a military policeman. There was no doubting the fact that the Ukranian was academically bright, that he had certain talents, that he was linguistically talented, and that he could sell a refrigerator to an Eskimo. Despite these positive characteristics, which ought to have propelled him rapidly through the ranks, he possessed an even greater talent that served to hold him back. That was the uncanny ability to infuriate the person responsible for writing his annual confidential report. Furthermore, Myron had not a modicum of respect for anyone; his barefaced cheek was legendary and his presumptuousness infuriating. Apart from that, he was a good lad.

Within a few days of taking over command of my new platoon, I had developed certain misgivings about some of its members. Not only did I have Myron to contend with, but what about Corporals Krzeszewski and Wierzuchowski? Which Army was I in, for goodness sake? It had already been reported to me that Myron was a notorious character and he confirmed his status on only my second night on duty. He approached me midway through the shift.

"I don't think you understand the system, our kid."

"What system is that, Corporal Demitriuk?"

"You haven't been filling the entries in on my board."

"What board?"

He went into the interpreter's office at the rear of the duty room complex and returned with a homemade board covered in plastic, to which a Chinagraph pencil was attached by a length of string.

"Whenever an enquiry comes in about a removal and I'm on patrol, you simply write the details on my enquiry board."

"Removals! What bloody removals?"

"I help to run a furniture removal firm in my spare time and I use the duty room as my contact point. When a call comes in and Myron isn't, put it on the board. It's that simple."

"Corporal Demitriuk. Perhaps you used to run a removal business from the duty room—from now on you don't."

He took the news rather badly. It transpired that 25% of all calls that came into the unit were either enquiries, or bookings, for Myron's Removals. What if a serious caller was unable to get through to the RMP because Myron was taking a booking for the removal of someone's three-piece suite? The business stopped there and then.

Actually, the demise of the removal business was only partially attributable to me, as Myron's partner did a moonlight flit with all the funds shortly afterwards. The Ukranian merely diversified and became a motor dealer. The term 'Would you buy a used car from this man?' might have been coined especially for him. One of his sales resulted in him becoming the most wanted man in Werl, amongst the Turkish community anyway. He sold a large, blue van to a Turk. It was a decent machine and the purchaser was satisfied with the deal—it was just that Myron couldn't produce any papers for the vehicle. He had the papers all right and the transaction was all above board. It was just that the documents were locked in a safe and the only person with the key had taken it on holiday with him to Italy. Despite numerous visits to the duty room, the Turk still hadn't been able to elicit the vehicle papers from Myron who, to his credit, had tried every conceivable way of opening the safe. Myron set a date a few days hence, by which time he positively guaranteed his customer's satisfaction and promptly went on leave himself. He was less than popular in absentia and his Turkish customers besieged the barracks for three weeks. The arrival of the bronzed Myron for his first duty after leave coincided perfectly with the appearance of three Turkish thugs. They were determined to leave the barracks with the vehicle papers, or his gizzard. They pinned him against the duty room wall and appeared set to summarily execute him, until I presented the assailants with the paperwork that had been retrieved from the safe earlier. A major Anglo-Turkish conflict had been narrowly averted and, to his credit, Myron took the hint by retiring from that line of enterprise too. I doubt if he ever made much money from his ventures; at least he rarely ever put his hand in his pocket. He will be long remembered for his most famous con trick, for which we all fell at one time or the other. The famous 'I'll park the Landrover up our kid, you get the bratties and the beer' ploy was a Demitriuk classic.

As difficult as it was to believe, Myron had attended a seminary in Rome as a youth and had studied for the priesthood in the Greek Catholic Church. In addition to English and his native tongue, he spoke reasonable French, German and Italian, and purported to be fluent in Latin and Byzantine as well. He could also get by in Russian.

During one of the colder periods of the Cold War, the military command in Germany required soldiers to report the sighting of any Eastern Block vehicle seen off the autobahn directly to the RMP. During the course of a busy week, we might receive ten reports, most of which were impossible to confirm or to follow up. We simply passed the information on to the Intelligence Corps, who would then do something terribly secret with the report and not tell a soul. I was on duty one Sunday afternoon when the Black Watch guard commander reported that a Russian lorry had just passed their barracks. As their camp was adjacent to ours, we were able to walk out and watch the lorry as it struggled up the hill towards the village of Wickede.

"Leave this to me our kid," said Myron.

He ran over to a minibus and sped off in pursuit of the lorry. Ten minutes later he came up on the radio.

"No problems here our kid. I've had a good chat with the driver; he's from Moscow and he's delivering sand to a foundry in Wickede."

He insisted on giving me the details over the radio and finished off by saying that he had invited the Russian back to the mess for a drink. That was a decent gesture, but not one that the Intelligence Corps would have taken kindly to. I had Myron withdraw the invitation.

You would think that a bloke with his experience would be able to deal with an incident without any undue hassle. Actually, he was a perfectly competent investigator, although you could be sure he would pass on the chore of writing a report to one of his juniors.

"Just giving him the chance to learn, our kid."

The trouble with him was that whenever he did deal with an incident, something would invariably go wrong. I learnt to expect the worst. Even the most straightforward job would turn horribly complex the moment he arrived on the scene. A case in point was the time when a bar owner in Menden called to ask for assistance. A soldier had wandered into his premises, consumed a few beers, refused to pay for them and had thrown a glass of Iserlohner Pilsener over the bar owner's accounting books. Absolutely standard British squaddie stuff, what could conceivably go wrong? I foolishly detailed Myron to deal with the case.

"No problem our kid," he said, as he sped off for Menden.

Half an hour later he called me from the bar.

"Slight problem here, the squaddie isn't a squaddie at all, he's an officer. Can you call his unit and have the adjutant meet us at the guardroom?"

This was the normal procedure whenever officers were involved in an incident. The adjutant rather than the guard commander was required to take responsibility for the alleged offender. It wasn't possible to contact the adjutant or the duty officer on this occasion, but as luck would have it, the commanding officer of the regiment happened to be in the guardroom as Myron arrived. He declared that he would deal personally with the errant officer.

Myron called me from the guardroom.

"No problems here, I've handed him over to the CO. We'll just have a cup of coffee and head back in. Do you want the details?"

Incidents involving officers needed reporting to the HQ with all haste, so he began to relay the details. Half way through he stopped.

"I'll have to call you back our kid, there's a bloke just died in the Guard-room."

He put the phone down. A bloke had just died in the guardroom! Why did I send him out there in the first place? He called back to explain the latest part of the escalating drama. It appeared that one of the prisoners was polishing a floor, when he had suddenly collapsed and stopped breathing. Our gallant Ukrainian had performed mouth-to-mouth resuscitation and heart massage and had successfully brought the guy back from the brink. He had then called the ambulance and sent the soldier on his way to hospital. Myron Demitriuk had saved a man's life. He was a hero. He returned to the duty room and produced all the facts, whereupon I stood him down from duty. There had been enough of his complications for one night. I penned the report myself and made a big deal of his prompt and calm action in saving a person's life. The colonel of the regiment also commended Myron and our OC put him up for a medal. He was subsequently given the GOC's Commendation, a twopenny-halfpenny award and far less than he deserved.

The last time that I saw him in the Army, he was working as a storeman in Northern Ireland, a gopher in other words. It was a dead-end job, he was still a corporal and he hadn't a hope in hell of ever being promoted. He was still wheeling and dealing and upsetting all the people that mattered. Myron sensibly called it a day at the twelve-year point of his service and left the RMP. I was destined to see him again, though.

Living in splendid isolation in the Edinburgh Castle Officer's Mess many years later, I was sitting in the TV lounge one evening when I was suddenly aware of footsteps coming from the direction of the kitchen. Myron appeared in the doorway.

"All right our kid?"

"How the hell did you get in here, you old rogue?"

"I used to be stationed in Edinburgh and they never used to lock the kitchen door to this place. They still don't. Just climb over the back wall and you're in," he explained.

So much for security in Edinburgh Castle! It was clear that he hadn't changed a great deal, despite the passing of the years and he filled me in on his latest get rich quick scheme. He was repossessing cars for a Japanese company, although you could be sure that he would have someone else to handle the rough stuff. It came as no surprise to discover that he had a second string to his bow. He had always been involved with the Ukrainian community in his native Nottingham and had even taken me to their club on a couple of occasions. So, as well as repossessing Japanese cars, he was also the tour manager for a Ukrainian song and dance troop. I was invited to watch them perform at the Carnegie Hall the following evening; entrance was free of charge. That wasn't the Carnegie Hall in New York, I should point out; this was the Carnegie Hall in Dunfermline, an altogether less eminent venue. Only fifty people turned up to watch the performance, which was a pity, as they were really quite good. Myron didn't care how many people turned up.

"We're paid by the Art's Council our kid, so it doesn't matter a shit if no bugger turns up."

We shook hands after the show and he and his gallant troop headed south. Our paths haven't crossed again, but it wouldn't surprise me to hear him at the other end of the phone one fine day.

Serving in the unit at this time was a unique character, a rum person in some people's reckoning, but a former Iserlohn stalwart and therefore a pal of mine. Oliver McClelland had changed a great deal over the years; he had put on at least five stones in weight for starters and had achieved his long cherished ambition of becoming a sergeant. God knows it had taken him long enough. His fabled stinginess was still apparent, along with his Achilles' Heel, his overwhelming persecution complex. When the decision was made to open a new police post in Iserlohn, Ollie was the obvious choice for village bobby. He was pleased with his selection and set about building his little empire with commendable zeal. He had the place looking professional in no time at all and was particularly proud of his latest acquisition, an enormous fish tank. He had cadged the tank from the previous occupant of his office, who had also bequeathed Ollie a pair of fish to stimulate his interest. The huge tank contained nothing in the way of aquatic adornments, but Ollie assured me that if I would contribute to his newly formed fish fund, the matter would be rectified by the next time I visited.

"What kind of fish are they anyway, Ollie?" I enquired.

"Dinnae ken," was the unhelpful reply.

I saw him a week later at the Company HQ. He was sporting a smart line in snow-white slings, in which his heavily bandaged right hand was resting.

"What happened Ollie?"

"Dinnae ask! Yon ungrateful bastards," he wailed, ever the master of the confusing reply.

"Which ungrateful bastards are they then?"

"Those bloody fish," he said, clarifying precisely nothing.

"What happened? Did the fish tank fall and trap your hand?"

"You mind ma fish didn'ae hae onything in their tank but water? Well, I went to the aquarium place and bought some weed and a couple o' wee castles. Bought, mind you! Well, I put the weed in and one o' the castles, nae bother, then, when I was putting the second castle in, one o' the bastards tried tae bite ma bloody knuckle aff."

It transpired that the two fish were piranha and that one of them had attached itself to Ollie's finger, with no intention of ever letting go. Even when he had pulled his hand out of the tank, the piranha had clung stubbornly on. It remained firmly attached to Ollie's finger until he hit it a firm blow on the head with a handily placed ruler. He needed several stitches to repair the damage, whereas the piranha, apart from having a nasty bump on its head, returned to the tank to swim around as if nothing had happened. The bump on its head never did go down and a year later it was still swimming contentedly around, despite the swelling.

Lance Corporal Sidney Swallow was the latest addition to Tiger Platoon. One of the boys was quick to point out that in his part of Manchester there lived a man by the name of Sid Swallow, who sold surgical goods. Our new guy became Surgical Sid ever thereafter. Sid, the pride of Grotton Hollow, turned out to be selectively dyslexic, if such a condition exists. His spelling was perfectly normal, except in two particular situations. Whenever two different vowels appeared together in a word, he would always get them the wrong way round, and whenever the same two consonants appeared consecutively in a word, he would unerringly omit one of them. To Sid, therefore, an 'Alleged Assault' became an 'Aleged Asualt', whereas captains and majors were 'Comisoined Oficers'. It was all rather distressing for Sid and a real pain in the arse for the person who had to correct his statements and reports. I developed a system that went a good way to curing his problem, although I doubt whether the British Medical Council would have approved. He was beaten soundly around the ears whenever he made an error, until he became too scared to make a mistake.

Surgical Sid sticks in my mind as the stereotype north country Brit, the sort who would wear a knotted handkerchief (knoted handkercheif) on Blackpool beach. As my leave dates and his once coincided, I made the mistake of inviting him to accompany me on a holiday to Cyprus. After three days of me showing him all the sights by day and treating him to the best of Cypriot cuisine by night, he came up with a classic suggestion for day four. Instead of eating in a taverna, his plan for a gastronomic treat was to drive up to the Army camp in Episkopi and eat some real food in the NAAFI. I didn't enjoy my double cheeseburger, double egg and chips, although Sid apparently did. He took a taxi up to Episkopi every evening after that, to take in the film showing at the Army cinema, before tucking into a NAAFI fry up. What a waste of a holiday to Aphrodite's Island. But that was Surgical Sid, the man who couldn't be bothered to open his eyes to look at Belgrade as we went through on the bus and who considered the walk up to the Parthenon in Athens too much trouble.

The journey back from what had been a nightmare holiday proved an even bigger nightmare. As the plane hurtled along the runway at Larnaca, I was overwhelmed with the certain knowledge that the thing was going to crash. There was no logical reason for my fear, but I pressed the button to summon a stewardess anyway. Once we were airborne, a gorgeous creature with 'Olympic Airways' emblazoned across her bosom answered my call. She told me that my request to get off the plane was impracticable, since it was well on its way to 30,000 feet, but that she would bring me something to calm my nerves. I expected a dose of Valium, or an injection of something to make me drowsy, but she returned with a bottle of Schweppes lemonade instead. I wasn't aware until then that Schweppes lemonade has sedative qualities, but it does when a big-breasted Greek bird serves it. The ninety minutes to Athens were sheer misery just the same and after alighting with shaky legs in the Greek capital, I vowed never to fly again.

Our bus tickets back were only good from Thessalonica and so we made the trip up from Athens on a rickety old bus that stopped at every village on the way. Then disaster struck in the northern Greek city. Because we hadn't confirmed our tickets, we didn't have any seats. As luck would have it, though, I had over tipped the driver on the way down and he was driving the coach back up north. We got the two seats he had been saving to sell at the right price, right in the middle of the back row. As if being on seats directly over the engine wasn't bad enough, a freak of design meant that our seats sloped downwards rather than backwards. After three days of adjusting my rump every five minutes to prevent me from sliding onto the floor, I had a backside like one of those baboons that you see on natural history programmes, the ones with the bright red backsides. I vowed never to travel by bus again either.

Sid made the national newspapers some years later, after he approached the NAAFI Financial Services for funds to buy a horse. The organisation had provided funds for tens of thousands of cars, caravans and boats over the years, but Sid's was the first horse. He got the cash.

Those of us gathered in the corporal's mess had seen in the New Year with style and the feeling of goodwill towards men abounded, until an Irishman chose an inopportune moment to open his big mouth.

"Let's raise our glasses to good old Ireland," he suggested in a moment of alcohol induced, nationalistic fervour.

That didn't go down too well with some people, several of whom held firm views about Irish nationalism following many tours in Northern Ireland. He was one of Tiger Platoon's sergeants and, leaving his nationality aside, I really couldn't stand the shallow, devious, untrustworthy individual. With my judgement that night also impaired from a surfeit of good cheer, I concluded that this would be a good time to give him an overdue punch on the nose. So I did. Not being a lad who was lacking in pluck, he bounced back up just before the count of ten and raced in for a second helping. My educated left ensured that this time he stayed down for good.

If you should ever feel inclined to smite one of your sergeants, then don't do it in the corporal's mess. There's always a sneak lurking in some dark corner who will delight in telling the tale to the RSM. A report of my misdeed did reach his ears, along with the tale of another staff sergeant in our unit, who had also involved himself in fisticuffs on New Year's Eve. He had whacked a private soldier at a drunken party in the married quarters down in Werl. We were both charged with a catalogue of offences and required to answer for our crimes in front of the OC early in the New Year. My mate was marched in first; emerging ten minutes later with a white face and trembling lip. He was bursting with rage and clearly very upset.

"Three hundred and fifty quid and a severe dig," was all he would say.

That seemed a bit harsh to me, but it set me thinking. If whacking a private soldier cost that much, what would thumping a sergeant set me back? I had made up my mind to plead guilty, because I was guilty and saw no point in prolonging the agony. The major read the charges and asked me to make my plea.

"Guilty sir," I replied.

The OC liked me, that much I knew. He despised the Hibernian, I knew that too. Paddy had not endeared himself to the major, by driving back pissed from the brothel in Hamm one evening and straight into a German police checkpoint. To compound the crime of drunken driving, he had also caught a dose in the whorehouse. In the major's view, he had let the side down rather badly. But back to the assizes!

"You are my best platoon commander staff," said the OC, merely confirming what I already knew, "and this action is completely out of character. Surely there must have been some extenuating circumstances?"

"Only one sir."

"What was that?"

"He was Irish, sir."

"Perfectly good reason for hitting a man. I find you not guilty."

"But the man pleaded guilty sir!" said the perplexed RSM.

"And I find him not guilty. March him out, RSM."

Here was a legal anomaly if ever there was one.

Vittoria and Albuhera Barracks lay side by side, although the occupants could scarcely have been more different. We were in Vittoria, the Black Watch in Albuhera. The two sergeant's messes were rather different, too; the Jocks had more than a hundred members with a couple of dozen livers-in, whereas we boasted only twenty-two members, with only the RSM, Bones Kitchenbrand and myself of single status. The Black Watch lacked little when it came to hospitality and at their regular livers-in dinners, a place was invariably set for us paupers. Resplendent in our formal mess kit, here we were once again, being plied with drink before being summoned to dinner by the sound of the pipes. No matter how speedily one drank, these hospitable Jocks never allowed you to see the bottom of your glass, and buying a drink was out of the question. Guests were forbidden to approach the bar at all, in actual fact. The pipes swirled, we went in and a fine dinner began. As each course was presented, a piper would tune up outside and burst into the dining room to circumnavigate the dining table whilst playing a stirring melody. The piper followed this procedure during every course, before making one final entry, which was altogether different. This time he piped an unrecognisable dirge, which went on for an inordinate length of time. After five circuits of the table and with the food stone cold, there was still no sign of the piper weakening. I turned towards Bones, who was bored rigid.

"If he goes around one more time, I think I'll scream," I whispered in a barely audible voice.

The piper eventually finished his musicianship and the diners tucked into cold rump steak, which was followed by a pudding of indeterminate provenance. Once we had toasted our Monarch, there was nothing for it but to head for the bar and continue the motion. It promised to be a memorable evening, until the President of the Mess took me to one side.

"I want a word in your ear outside my mess please staff."

I accompanied him to an anteroom, blithely unaware of the reason for our exit.

"Man!" he snarled. "You talked during the piobreoch."

"Was there a course during which we weren't allowed to talk?" I enquired.

"Man! Are you ignorant, or what?"

"I think I must be ignorant sir."

"The piobreoch was the beautiful, haunting music that preceded our main course this evening. And you talked during its playing."

"Is that bad then?" I asked in all innocence.

"Is it bad? Man, you just broke hundreds of years of Black Watch tradition. No one ever talks during the playing of the piobreoch."

"I'm terribly sorry," I said, "but until you just told me, frankly, I had never heard the word piobreoch before."

"You may return to the function. I must warn you, however, that if you ever wish to use my mess again, you will first be required to explain your unacceptable behaviour to the president. I suggest you make an appointment to see the RSM at the earliest opportunity," he stated firmly.

It spoilt my night somewhat, but not enough to stop me drinking a few more at the Black Watch's expense. Next morning I arranged an audience with the RSM. He was a decent man, with whom I had come into contact often enough in the mess and at the Kirk. Managing a reasonable march in and halt, I came face to face with the kilted RSM.

"Good morrow sir, I'm Staff Sergeant Payne of the Royal Military Police and last night, whilst a guest in your mess, I inadvertently broke hundreds of years of your noble regiment's tradition by talking during the piobreoch. I regret my action sir, but by way of mitigation would point out that, until last night, I didn't know what a piobreoch was."

"I cannae pretend that it's not a serious offence staff, but you are English and that explains a lot. And you do attend the Kirk, which means ye cannae be all bad, but talking during the piobreoch is a most serious crime."

I smiled my humble smile.

"Ye cannae get aff with a crime of that magnitude. If you ever want to use my mess again, you'll have tae accept my punishment."

"Very well sir," I said, trusting that he wasn't about to order me to listen to an extended rendering of the piobreoch by the Regimental Pipes and Drums.

"Right then staff, you will parade in my mess at twelve twenty-five hours. You have my permission to approach the bar, where you will order a bottle of the Glenmorangie. At precisely twelve thirty hours I shall arrive, whereupon you and I will drink it."

I carried out my instructions and was quite incapable of working that afternoon. I was however, always welcome in the Sergeant's Mess of the 42nd of Foot.

7

The new OC looked like a male model out of *Vogue*. He was outrageously handsome and his suits were obviously not off the peg. Without ever appearing to be arrogant or superior, he exuded an air of confidence and control that couldn't fail to impress. His office desk was covered in green baize, like a snooker table, and apart from an empty in-tray, it was always devoid of clutter. It may have all been a bluff and perhaps his drawers were stuffed with work he couldn't understand, but one's first impression was that the new boss was a man out of the top drawer.

Every new boss believes that he is going to change the world, or at least his unit. Experience has taught me that within two months, during which time a few cosmetic changes will be attempted, things almost always revert to the status quo. The job of OC of an RMP unit is just too complex to alter everything that's not to your fancy, and the sensible ones merely amend a couple of procedures they find particularly irritating and take things steadily thereafter. Major M had a host of new ideas, the main one being to ensure that the company would be more operationally efficient. This was no surprise, since he was a former infantryman who knew fuck all about military police matters. Within a few days of assuming command, he decided upon an early morning crash out of the unit. This involved packing our kit as if for war and deploying to our survival location, sited a dozen miles from our barracks. The platoon commanders were out to impress, and what better way of scoring points than by starring during the crash out. Each platoon had five vehicles, which had to carry all the platoon's kit and personnel into the field. It made a pleasant change to discover that all of our vehicles were in running order, although one of them did need towing around the barracks a few times before it reluctantly sprang into life. Leaving Landrovers out in the open during the cold and damp German winters is hardly conducive to their well-being. At least the officer's polo ponies were covered up during inclement weather. It was gratifying to know that the Army had its priorities right.

Each of my vehicle commanders had a map, every single one of the men had been out to the location and knew their way there blindfolded, they knew their defensive positions and everyone had his full compliment of kit. All the platoon stores were loaded, so what could conceivably go wrong? Supremely confident that my guys would put in a really professional performance and show the new OC that Tiger Platoon was on the ball, I felt like Monty as we set off in the direction of Soest.

Alighting at the location, I was dismayed to discover that only one of my vehicles was behind me. After twenty minutes, when I was considering retracing our route to find out what was holding my guys up, the OC and RSM arrived in their vehicle. The new man strode over to me. He didn't appear best pleased.

"Are you the Commander of 29 Platoon staff?" he enquired.

"That's me sir, Staff Sergeant Payne," I replied confidently.

"In twenty minutes time, Staff Sergeant Payne, you will come to my vehicle and explain three things to me. Firstly, why one of your vehicles, driven by a Pole, didn't have in inflated spare tyre when it punctured; and furthermore, why the driver of that vehicle had neither a map, nor any notion where he was going."

I would kill Krzeszewski at the first opportunity!

"Secondly, you will explain why one of your vehicles, driven by a Ukranian, ran out of petrol and didn't have a spare jerry can of fuel with him."

Demitriuk must die!

"Thirdly, why the camouflage net affixed to the roof of another of your vehicles flew off as it was driving along and, but for the expert driving of the RSM, would have caused a serious, if not fatal, accident when it landed on the bonnet of our Landrover."

You're a dead man, Godley!

How does one prepare a defence for such a catalogue of disasters? I decided upon telling the truth for a change and conceded that my blokes were guilty of perpetrating a series of unmitigated disasters. I further confessed that they were, in military parlance, a load of crap and then threw in the bit about making a silk purse out of a sow's ear, along with the rest of my well-rehearsed bullshit. I delivered the whole speech with the air of a man who had suffered badly and, guess what, it worked.

Displaying an alarming lack of confidence in his sergeants following the crash out fiasco, the OC insisted that platoon commanders should be present in the duty room whenever their men were on duty. It ensured that the staff sergeants in Werl knew just what was going on and probably improved efficiency a little, but it was a bit of an imposition on blokes with so much service. Being back on the front line again was right down my street, though, and I was involved in several incidents that were worthy of note.

If no official interpreter were available when the German police requested our assistance, I would usually accompany the patrol in order to translate. One particular Saturday evening they called us down to the police station in Werl to assist in dealing with an American serviceman who was in custody. Under normal circumstances, British MPs have no authority over Americans, but the Yanks in Werl came under our jurisdiction by special arrangement. The nearest USMP unit was more than a hundred miles away, at Bremerhaven, and because the incidence of offences involving Americans in Werl had reached epidemic proportions, we had been given disciplinary powers over them. This American soldier turned out to be a Peurto Rican sergeant and he had been apprehended for drunken driving. He spoke no German and the police were bemused by his Hispanic enunciation. The station officer asked me to explain the charges to him and to point out that giving a blood sample was a mandatory requirement under German law. He was less than enthusiastic about donating an armful of his life's blood and made a great song and dance about the violation of his civil rights. His reluctance to give a sample was duly noted by the station officer, who then informed him that he would give blood whether he liked it or not, by force, if necessary. When the Peurto Rican declared that it would take more than one German and a greying Englishman to overpower him, the station officer merely shrugged his shoulders. The American's reluctance to give his gore for analysis was easy to understand in retrospect—this was his third arrest for the same offence and it would mean the end of his career if he were to be found guilty. A fear of needles, or a fight for his civil rights, never really entered into the equation. I took him to one side and informed him that I had seen people severely manhandled by the German police when they refused to give blood. He thought about it for a while, before declaring that he was willing to give a sample.

"You gonna have to take it out of my cock though," he declared.

I translated this to the station officer, who assured the Peurto Rican that they would be happy to comply, even with this strangest of requests.

"Oh yea! Well, just you two old bastards try it, man. You couldn't do it."

"Und I zink zat ve kan," said the policeman.

"Okay. You and whose Army man?" said the irate American, who was losing his composure somewhat by this time.

The old German policeman, who had remained very professional and perfectly calm throughout the proceedings, opened the door to the charge office and called down the corridor.

"Adolf, Werner, Juergen, Dieter, Willi. *Hierher bitte.*"

Five large Germans, looking positively enormous by virtue of the huge, green, leather overcoats they were wearing, entered the office. The station officer explained that the Puerto Rican wished to give a blood sample from his male member, the police surgeon appeared as if by magic, the green leather coats made a forward move and the accused had a sudden change of heart. He rolled up his right sleeve and Adolf, Werner, Juergen, Dieter and Willi went back to their coffee.

On the direct orders of the Brigade Commander, I went to Salamanca Barracks to investigate the strange case of the severely battered Ordnance Corps sergeant. The brigadier had initially spotted the man walking through barracks sporting some pretty horrendous facial injuries. Suspecting him to have been involved in a traffic accident, he had his driver stop the car whilst he talked to him. The brigadier had not been satisfied by the sergeant's explanation of just how he had sustained a cracked jaw and a broken nose and had therefore contacted the OC of our unit. This was the first information we had received regarding the incident.

Despite his great reluctance to talk to the RMP, the sergeant finally told me that he had been beaten up whilst attending a function in the sergeant's mess. It didn't take me long to unearth several witnesses, all of whom confirmed that the injuries had been sustained as a result of a fight between the sergeant and his own CSM. A long-standing feud between the pair had finally come to a head in the early hours of the morning and the junior man had taken a good hammering. I had all the evidence necessary to interview the warrant officer and knock him off; no matter what the provocation, nothing condones kicking a man in the face hard enough to break his jaw, nose and teeth. Within a few minutes of starting the interview, the black warrant officer had admitted kicking his adversary three times in the face. There was nothing remarkable about the case, the interview or the knock off. What was remarkable was the statement under caution that I recorded from Warrant Officer

Class Two (Company Sergeant Major) Winston Cleveland Gumley. This arrogant and thoroughly objectionable man must have included *Roget's Thesaurus* in his list of obligatory bedside reading.

A statement often includes great tracts of reported speech, which invariably goes along the lines of, "I said, he said, I said, he said," with the odd "he replied" thrown in to break the monotony. Gumley was different and his statement was one that I shall never forget. According to his statement, the sergeant had 'said' things throughout the course of the incident; Gumley, however, was too superior to merely 'say' things. In a three-page statement of evidence, he managed to assert, remark, reply, declare, pronounce, reciprocate, mention, articulate, respond and retort. None of his eloquence did him any good though, because upon receipt of my damning report, the brigadier gave him just forty-eight hours to get out of the garrison. The case never went to disciplinary action. Had the sergeant reported the assault immediately after the event, then the SIB would have dealt with the case and Winston Cleveland Gumley would most certainly have been subjected to a court martial. What a pity that he wasn't.

In the early hours of the morning, a telephone call came through from the all night Pizzeria in nearby Wickede. The owner's wife reported seeing two soldiers talking to a known drug dealer in the restaurant and stated that some objects had changed hands. The squaddies were apparently making their way back to barracks.

"Leave this one to me, boss," said Hughie Graham.

He was one of my sergeants, a big bruiser from Leicester. He departed in the police van, only to reappear a couple of minutes later with two Jocks from the adjacent barracks in tow. Hughie began his investigation.

"What's your name, haggis?"

"Private Smith, sergeant."

"I thought all you Jocks were called Mac something or other," he said and without waiting for a reply, turned to the other Scot.

"And you will be Private bloody Jones I suppose?"

"That's right sergeant," replied the second Jock.

The popular TV programme 'Alias Smith and Jones' was being shown on Forces Television at the time and Hughie was convinced they were pulling his leg.

"Trying to take the piss out of me are you? Get in there, you two," said Hughie, as he directed them into a back room.

He took of his jacket, rolled up his sleeves and prepared to conduct the investigation in his own inimitable style.

"Smith and fucking Jones, they've been watching too much fucking telly," he mumbled to himself as he prepared for battle.

Big Hughie favoured a direct style of investigation and the sounds of positive action being taken drifted through from the back room. He emerged a few minutes later.

"I don't know. Can't find any drugs on them and I've looked everywhere, even up their arses. And the buggers still insist that they're Smith and Jones."

I took the precaution of calling up the duty clerk of their unit, gave him their regimental numbers and asked him to call me back with their names. Hughie went back in for another try with them, but emerged to admit failure. Meanwhile, the duty clerk phoned back.

"With reference to the two soldiers staff, the first one is Private Smith of Alpha Company and the other Private Jones of Charlie Company."

"Haven't you got any Macs in your battalion?"

"Aye staff, hunners."

We gave both the soldiers a cup of coffee and Hughie treated them to a talk about the perils of drug taking as if he had nothing but their welfare at heart. They left the duty room content in the knowledge that the RMP really cared for them.

Scottish soldiers stick together like shit to a blanket! Trying to obtain information from a Jock when you are investigating an offence committed by one of his mates is a thankless task. Such *esprit de corps* may be a commendable characteristic, but it doesn't help much if you are a military policeman. A German taxi driver came in to the duty room to complain that the two soldiers he had conveyed from Hemer to Albuhera Barracks had run off without paying the fare. Just to rub it in, they had slashed the rear taxi seats. He drove me down to the Jock's guardroom in his cab and I got straight on with my investigation.

"Let me see your booking in and out book," I said to the soldier on duty.

This is a book that is to be found in every guardroom in the British Army.

"We dinnae hae one staff."

"Who were the last people to come into camp?"

"Dinnae mind staff."

"Who is your guard commander?"

"Cannae mind his name staff."

"Do you know your own name, you ignorant little shit?"

"Depends on who is asking staff."

This was standard patter for an infantryman protecting his own, bordering on the insolent, totally unhelpful, but pseudo polite at the same time. Still, if he had assisted the RMP and his mates had found out, he would have been in for a hiding. It was a waste of time asking questions at the guardroom, so I took the details from the taxi driver and vowed to take it up with the battalion RSM next day.

An audience with the RSM wasn't easy to achieve, especially as he was aware that I wanted to talk about his soldiers' misdemeanours. The RSM wasn't keen to see me, but since we had recently shared a bottle of the Glenmorangie, he afforded me the honour. I gave him the rundown on the previous night's incident, although I was certain that he already knew the full details.

"What makes you think that they were my Jocks?"

"Why else would they have run off into your barracks?"

"Perhaps they were MPs trying to throw you off the trail."

"More likely to have been Jocks scurrying back to their rooms."

"Well, you're the policeman, you tell me."

"I'm certain that they were members of your battalion and that the boy on the gate was trying to protect them, a praiseworthy show of camaraderie to be sure, but not appreciated by the taxi driver whose cab has slashed seats."

"Aye, slashing taxi seats, don't much care for that. What time is it, Wally?"

"Smack on ten sir."

"Well awa' and hae your NAAFI break. Come back here in thirty minutes and I'll hae the guilty bastards here fae ye. Incidentally, the taxi driver needs his eyes testing—there were three o' them, not twa."

"Thank you sir. By the way, the taxi driver will accept restitution without making a formal complaint, provided the Jocks will cough up for the repairs."

"You can rest assured they will Wally. See you in half an hour."

The Black Watch held their Watchnight service in the Kirk at 2300 hrs on the night of twenty-fourth of December and I was dressed a little early. I called into the corporal's mess on the way, to wish the boys well and to have a Coke before walking through to the adjacent barracks. At the bar were seven or eight lost souls; they were the lads who would be on duty on Christmas Day and in a couple of cases, those who were so unpopular that they hadn't managed an invitation to anyone's home for the holiday. I was offered any amount of drink, but decided to wait until the service was over. There would be plenty of people at the Kirk with drink on their breath without me adding to the number. I spotted one of my sergeants in the bar and he appeared to be very much the worse for drink.

Following the church service, I returned to the mess and found the same crowd propping up the bar. The sergeant was giving a rendering of his masterpiece, 'Singing the Blues', which he performed best of all just before he fell down dead drunk. Following this evening's performance, he decided to call it a night and bought a bottle of wine to sustain him on the five-minute journey home. I never saw him again until Boxing Day, when he and his wife asked me down to their quarter for the day. It was a particularly pleasant day out, the company was excellent and there was lots of delicious food prepared by my host's charming wife. I didn't stay over late just the same, as I was on duty for a twenty-four hour stint starting next morning. As was the norm at holiday times, I had a composite shift made up of all the company's platoons. There were two girls on the shift, Susanna the not so secret drinker, who sat in the corner reading and looking pretty, and Val, a tough old boiler from Liverpool. During the course of the morning, Val asked for a private chat in the back room. Perhaps she could no longer control her carnal desire for me and was about to make a move. It wasn't as simple as that, unfortunately, and what she had to say took me back more than a little.

"What are you going to do about the sergeant who raped Susanna on Christmas morning?" she demanded.

"Say that again slowly, Val," I said.

She went on to explain that a sergeant had visited Susanna in her room in the female accommodation block during the early hours of Christmas morning. He had woken her up and offered her a glass of wine, before climbing into bed and forcing his attention on her. I went to speak to Susanna, who confirmed the sordid facts.

"Why the hell didn't you do something at the time, Susanna?"

"I wanted to wait and see you. You're his friend and you would know what to do," said Susanna, the little girl lost.

"This is a terribly serious accusation, you know. Are you absolutely sure that he had sexual intercourse with you against your will?"

"Yes, I'm very sure," she replied.

"You really ought to have reported it, you know?"

"You know as well as I do, staff, that I'm a drunk and that I have a reputation for being an easy lay. Who would believe my word against that of a sergeant?"

"Well, I believe you, for one. Will you trust me to sort this business out?"

"Yes, of course I will," she replied.

I drove straight down to see the OC at his married quarter and broke the news to him. There were most certainly grounds for calling the SIB straight in and having them carry out a rape investigation. They would have enjoyed that. What would that achieve, though, a broken marriage for sure, a ruined career for certain, kids without a father and nothing but trauma for poor Susanna at the court martial when defence lawyer set about her. With Susanna's absolute agreement, the brave and humane OC put his neck on the block and made an eminently sensible decision. He decided to deal with the matter summarily. The sergeant was severely punished and posted away to a detachment, with the instruction never to return to Werl under any circumstances.

He came to see me in my room next day, half in shame and half in thanks for getting him out of the deepest shit. He was wasting his tears and pathetic pleas for forgiveness on me, though; I'm immune to such snivelling. He was left in no doubts about my intentions. If he ever repeated this type of behaviour again, I'd spill the beans and ruin him. He never did and went on to do very well in the RMP. Susanna was a happy, pretty, temperate, married lady the last time I saw her. The OC's decision was vindicated.

Considering that a soldier was likely to spend at least a third of his service in Germany, it's astonishing how few of them bother to learn the language. That's easy for me to say, because I had a head start with German being a compulsory subject at City Boy's School in Leicester. The RMP were in contact with the local population every day in the course of our duties and interpreters were a crucial requirement if the job was to be done properly. Our interpreters worked from the duty room and gave a round the clock service—well, almost.

Joe Deppe was the senior interpreter employed by the unit in Werl. He was a gentle, quiet man, with a wealth of terrific World War Two stories to relate, provided you could encourage him to talk about them. Most of Joe's income went on keeping his daughter Ulrike performing at the very highest level in white water canoeing, in the days before massive sponsorship was commonplace. Keeping her in equipment must have been a real drain on Joe's finances and he was the only German I knew who didn't own a car. His financial sacrifice and her talent brought them the success that they worked towards and the record books for the 70s will show the name of Ulrike Deppe listed as German, European, World and Olympic Champion. He was rightly proud of his daughter's achievements, but modest about the part he played in them. Ulrike remains the only German whom I have ever willed to win in any sporting competition whatsoever.

When things were quiet, I would encourage Joe to walk up to the mess with me, buy him a coke and ask him to tell me a few war stories. My very favourite tale explained why this man, who would eat anything that was set before him, had such a loathing for carrots.

"All the captured prisoners of war were herded onto the football pitch at Herford. After several hours, a loudspeaker announcement ordered all carpenters to exit through Gate A, the plumbers through Gate B and the builders through Gate C. They went on like that until every single trade had been called. That left the odds and sods and, as I had been a clerk before the war, I apparently came under this classification. We were then marched away to the railway sidings, where it soon became apparent that your trade didn't matter, as we were all put aboard the train in any old order. The trade ruse had just been a method of achieving an orderly exit from the stadium. After two days on the train, we alighted somewhere in France and made our way to another football stadium, which was rather grander than the one in Herford. I never had an interest for the game, had never been into a stadium before, and now I had visited two in as many days. We were in St Etienne. This time it didn't matter what trade you were, the first three hundred of us were marched away to coal mine number one, the next to mine number two and so on. Our group marched across the flat countryside for several miles and our target appeared to be an orange coloured mountain that stood out vividly against the verdant green of the surrounding countryside. It was an unusual mountain, not just because of its colour, but because it had a perfectly regular conical shape. Finally we reached the hill, where everyone made an involuntary 'eyes left'. It was difficult for my brain to assimilate exactly what I was seeing. It was the biggest heap of carrots in the world! We marched on to our quarters and I claimed a bed space, before lying down to contemplate the prospect of becoming a miner. As I rested, my mind kept returning to the peculiar heap of carrots that we had seen on the way in. Little did we know that during the next eighteen months, we would become even more intimate with the mountain. We would eat it! It's debatable just how many ways there are to cook carrots, but I've eaten them raw, boiled, fried, steamed, baked, sautéed, in a pie, in a flan, chipped, grated, diced...*Ach Du Liebe*! Now perhaps you realise why I never touch carrots."

Joe also told the story of how he and a comrade, tired of the menu at the mine, made an attempt to escape from captivity by making look-a-like French uniforms out of blankets and odds bits of material. The attempt failed miserably at the first hurdle, when they were unable to respond in French when challenged by the guard. Joe was given a severe hiding and spent a long time in hospital, before returning to the mine and a diet of carrots.

The favourite interpreter by far was the German wife of a warrant officer who worked in our barracks. She was an intelligent, talented and efficient woman, whose stunning good looks and elegant dress sense made her a pleasure to be on duty with. Although she would never see thirty-five again, she could easily have passed for a woman some ten years younger. She had the ability to turn men's heads and she thoroughly enjoyed doing so. Surrounded by randy corporals, she revelled in her working environment and always had time for the younger lads. Her provocative style of dress and a particularly suggestive line of patter excited the youngsters and clearly had the effect of stimulating her too. Her particular fancy was for the fresh-faced teenagers in our outfit, which unfortunately let me out. Whenever the youngsters came into the duty room for a chat with her when I was on duty, I would wreak my wicked, ageist revenge and shoo them away out of spite. Her husband was the tall, dark and handsome type, who was blessed with a wicked sense of humour and a wicked temper to match. He, of course, had no conception of what went on behind his back whenever he was working and she wasn't. It was by no means unusual to see her driving away in her car with a crowd of off-duty corporals in attendance. Presumably they weren't driving out to look at the scenery! I believe that she was indulging herself in her favourite sexual pastime of teasing the young boys and maybe things extended beyond teasing. It soon became obvious to everyone in the barracks, with the exception of her husband, that she was entertaining her band of willing admirers to rather more than coffee and cakes. One lucky young devil in particular was reported to be receiving advanced lessons in sexual technique from the infinitely more experienced lady.

The whole matter came to a head on the night of the Wives' Club party held in the corporal's mess. The ladies had all arrived by bus from the married quarters and this enabled them to get tucked into a few gin and tonics without worrying about who was going to drive home. As far as I was aware, the bus back to Werl departed at midnight with a full complement of women aboard.

I can vouch for the fact that the bus left at midnight precisely, because it was me who opened the gate to let it out. Shortly afterwards, the mess barman brought down his cash box to be locked away and so the bar was definitely shut.

The warrant officer's first call came at 0100 hrs. He wanted to know if the Wives' Club function was still in progress, since his spouse still wasn't back home. I assured him that everything was over by midnight, but offered to walk up to the mess to ensure that she wasn't engaged in a late night conversation. The place was in darkness; Gitte certainly wasn't in there. An hour later the irate Lancastrian called again. He had telephoned some other wives who had been at the function and they had confirmed that Gitte hadn't been on the bus home. I suggested a search of the barracks; perhaps she had fallen down some- where. I was about to leave the duty room to commence my search, when the unmistakable sound of stiletto heels approaching at high speed could be heard. It was the flushed and embarrassed Gitte. It could have been the drink or the cold night air that was responsible for her rosy complexion, I suppose, but to my experienced eye, she wore the look of a woman that had recently been in the company of a gentleman. Her badly applied lipstick, dishevelled clothing and stocking seams running down the sides of her legs were all signs of her having left a bed in haste. The patrol took her home and I called the furious warrant officer, to explain that his spouse was en route for his location.

Before we stood down from duty next morning, Gitte made what was to be her final appearance in the barracks. She went straight into the interpreters' office without a word to anyone, took all her belongings and returned home. She never set foot inside the place again, not even for her husband's farewell function. The couple departed for England a couple of weeks after the fateful evening and left the Army altogether. It was never the same in the duty room after that, for it no longer had the benefit of naughty Gitte to add glamour to proceedings.

Our platoon had certainly struck it lucky this time. We were on nights and would be snugly tucked up in our beds when the general arrived next morning to carry out his inspection of the unit. The barracks had been swept, re-swept, cleaned, painted and polished and only the final bits of bullshit needed to be applied. The unit CSM was a bullshitter in every respect and in his element. He was still flapping around the unit long after everyone else had called it a night. His last port of call was the duty room, where he decided to add his personal touch. Armed with a Dynotape machine, he set about sprucing up the notice board and we soon had red plastic tape all over it. His inspirational offerings included 'Stolen Cars', 'Missing Persons' and 'Absentees and Deserters'. How had we functioned so long without such imaginative leadership? The consensus of opinion amongst the members of Tiger Platoon was that he had overdone it more than a little. Hughie Graham was particularly scathing of his efforts and when the CSM gave him the Dynotape machine, with the instruction to make any further improvements he saw fit, he was simply begging for trouble. The evening was particularly quiet and whenever Hughie was on duty, I would usually have a couple of hours in my bed anyway. He was a capable man. I returned to the duty room early next morning to ensure that everything was in order before the hand-over to the day shift, only to discover that Hughie had taken the CSM's invitation to add a little Dynotape wherever necessary a mite too literally. Everything that was worthy of a name had a red plastic sticker on it: clock, typewriter, ruler, rubber, book, another book, desk, chair, wall, another wall, floor, ceiling, window, lavatory pan, seat, brush, toilet paper holder, chain, kitchen sink, draining board, cupboard, fridge, cooker, kettle, saucepan, larger saucepan and frying pan. Even his boots were lettered left and right, back and front, sole and heel. Hughie was fulfilled. As we left for our beds, a less than enthusiastic CSM was setting about prising little plastic tags off everything.

Three of us from Tiger Platoon set off on what promised to be a good value holiday. A company from Widnes were offering a sixteen-day cruise of the Mediterranean, including a coach trip from London to Venice and then on the *SS Castalia* to Dubrovnik, Heraklion, Alexandria, Haifa, Limassol, Mykannos, Athens, Corfu and back to Venice, all for less than four hundred quid. It was out of season, admittedly, the ship was Italian and crewed by Greeks, which didn't bode too well for the service or quality of the food, but for four hundred quid, it sounded a fair bet.

I had been to Venice several times, but had never seen the waves breaking over San Marco before and the weather looked really rough out at sea. It transpired that the *SS Castalia* was a car ferry that plied the route between Italy and Greece for the majority of the year and that this cruise was a way of keeping the crew in wages during the off season. Being a car ferry and with no vehicles garaged down below, it was hopelessly top heavy and it heaved and rolled with every wave. Within two days of setting sail, everyone was wondering about the wisdom of taking a holiday cruise on the *SS Castalia*. The majority of folks were horribly seasick and the purser had long since run out of seasick tablets. Veteran traveller Payne had an abundant supply, however, and I became rather popular amongst those who would have given an arm and a leg for a Dramamine. Mercifully, the weather improved after Crete and the trip thereafter was excellent. The three of us had a truly memorable holiday, right to the end.

On board the ship was a lady who was travelling with her father and two teenage children. She had recently been bereaved and the trip was her way of trying to get back to normality. This woman was ten years older than me, was two stones overweight, had false teeth and smoked like a Turk, not exactly my type. Nevertheless, she needed a shoulder to cry on and so I bought her the odd Martini and took to the dance floor with her one night, when I'd had an ouzo or two. Not a single comment was ever made to suggest that I might have had an interest in this lady, there was never any physical contact and our final goodbye consisted of nothing more than a peck on the cheek. A couple of weeks after the cruise, however, I received a letter from her. She had clearly got the wrong end of the stick. She swore her undying love and indicated that if I agreed to go and live with her, there would never be a need for me to work again. As tempting as the offer might have sounded, I couldn't even contemplate the idea and wrote to explain my feelings. That didn't put her off one little bit and I was inundated with letters and parcels postmarked Leeds. The content of some of her letters led me to doubt the woman's sanity, especially when she bought an aeroplane, in order to fly over to Belfast at weekends and fly me back to Leeds to do the business. I flatly refused her permission to do any such thing and wrote one final 'fuck off' letter, to convince her that she ought to direct her passion elsewhere. It did the trick and she never wrote again. Instead, she handed the task over to her male company secretary, who proceeded to write to me some very nasty letters. He overdid it when he wrote a particularly abusive note, questioning my right to spurn the lady who loved me. He even went as far as to suggest that I would be held responsible for her impending nervous breakdown. I telephoned the presumptuous bastard and threatened to board the next plane to Leeds and inflict serious bodily harm on his person should he ever be impertinent enough to contact me again. That was the end of the matter, but it taught me a lesson and I never dance at all now, not even when I'm pissed.

My last game of rugby had been several years previously when, at an age when most people have already hung up their boots, I bowed out playing for the Army against the RAF in Cyprus. It didn't prove to be an auspicious swan song—the referee spoilt things by inviting me to take an early bath just after half time. It was the only sending off in my rugby career and my savage treatment at the hands of the disciplinary committee, a three-month suspension, merely accelerated my retirement from the game. Having sworn an irrevocable vow never to play again, I foolishly agreed to make a comeback following much lobbying from members of the RMP Werl side. Presumably some of them remembered my halcyon days and thought that giving me a run out in the first match of the new season was worth the gamble. RMP Werl versus the Black Watch Sergeant's Mess side wasn't a fixture designed to pull in the crowds, but it was just the right standard for my reluctant comeback.

Into the second half and I hadn't done anything wrong, indeed, my trusty right foot had knocked over the two penalties that accounted for our six points. The Jocks meantime had been less than sporting, running in several tries and with ten minutes to play, the result had long since been decided. The referee, being an eminently sensible fellow, had allowed most of the minor infringements to go unpunished, probably to save the pea in his whistle from unnecessary wear and tear. I rather wish that he had blown up for the multiple knock on in the seventy-third minute just the same, but he allowed play to continue. Discovering myself all alone on the left wing, the ball clutched to my bosom and their try line a mere sixty yards distant, I was consumed with that old 'David Duckham' feeling. Beating the first two defenders with a searing burst of pace, I handed off the fullback firmly and was cruising towards the line that was by now a mere ten yards distant. Nothing could stop me from scoring a magnificent try. It was then that it happened and I was afflicted by the malady that befalls all players who go on for too long. My legs went. Those ten yards may as well have been ten miles for all the chance there was of me reaching the try line. I looked inside for non-existent support, but then who could have kept up with such blistering pace? Closing in rapidly, though, were several Jocks, some of who were actually drooling at the mouth at the prospect of maiming a military police staff sergeant.

"Kill the bassa!" screamed their number eight.

"Stott his heed!" suggested the hooker.

I could think of no suitable comment, but as a gesture of appeasement and abject cowardice, I threw the ball to them. They were too preoccupied with getting on with the game to bother about the ball and they stotted ma' heed, just for the pure fun of it.

With the match over and the beer drunk, I set off wearily for an early night. As my alarm clock rang to herald a new dawn, I was so stiff that I couldn't move. It took me an hour to wash, dress and hobble across to the medical centre. The MO, himself an ageing rugby player, was able to diagnose my ailment without an examination. It was premature rigor mortis, a common complaint in older players. He prescribed a tube of Algipan, aspirin and a six-inch nail, to hang my boots on.

To be any good at orienteering, you need to be able to read a map, understand how to work a compass and be able to run like hell over countryside better suited to mountain goats than humans. That would be something like an official definition of the sport, but it leaves out an ingredient without which you can never be successful—pure unadulterated luck. My orienteering assets consisted of a modicum of ability and huge slices of good fortune, which proved sufficient to win several Army events. Despite being comfortable with a map, my cross-country running was always a bit suspect and compass bearings remain a mystery. Perhaps the standard of orienteering was low in the Army, regardless of the great interest in the sport?

The 1980 RMP BAOR Championships were a fine example of just how pure good fortune can overcome ability, skill and orienteering know-how. There were many runners entered in the competition who were better than me, but to my good fortune, the guy who set the course was a PTI with a soft spot for the ladies. He set the women's course in the same area as the main event and placed three of their checkpoints in the same general area as the men's, although a different punch needed to be used naturally. In their haste to get onto the next location, half the male competitors used the wrong punch at one of these three checkpoints and a wrong punch mark on a card meant disqualification. There were no excuses, as the ladies punches were clearly marked, but in the heat of the battle not many bothered to check. To be frank, it never entered my head to check them either, but my amazing orienteering luck held firm and I punched the correct one each time. For me the run seemed to go well right from the start, the checkpoints were either easy to locate, or I was having an exceptionally lucky day. As I ran towards the finish, the course setter congratulated me on a good time. Perhaps there was a chance of a medal for me in the veteran's section? I was keen to win the veteran's prize on this my first attempt in the BAOR Championship, if only to silence the cocky warrant officer who had won it for the last four years. And win it I did, along with the Open Competition. My effort had only been fourth quickest, but the first three home had been disqualified for punching in at the women's checkpoint. I was the champ and not many would have bet on that before the event.

The Unna Fussballfest was organised each year by the police from the small Westfalian town near Dortmund. Participation was by invitation only and the competing teams were predominantly German police sides from the surrounding towns, with Belgian, American and British Military Police teams asked along to add a little international flavour. We had been well beaten in the previous two years of competition, never progressing beyond the preliminary round, but this was to be my last Fussballfest and I was determined to go out in a blaze of glory. The RMP side was going to win, by fair means or foul. We had six good players in our team, the rest were mediocre and we were not good enough to bother the better German's outfits. With a little honest British cheating, however, I was convinced that the gold medals were as good as in the bag. Our RSM was a painfully honest individual, who had great difficulty in accepting my 'Plan for Victory' and referred me to the OC for his approval, or otherwise. The major had no such qualms, beating the Germans was of paramount importance in his view and he gave me permission to recruit a few quality players from elsewhere. I didn't need to look far as the Black Watch were stationed next door and they had a first class team. The QM of the Jocks ran their side and he made five of his players available, all of them approaching six feet tall and therefore big enough to pass off as MPs. They were all Army players and two of them—brothers, in fact—were about to leave the Army to play professionally. We had our team. As the tournament progressed, it became obvious that I had over-compensated for our perceived weaknesses. We waltzed through the preliminary rounds and finally met up with our hosts, the Unna police, in the final. We lashed them six-nil in a particularly one-sided affair. As we didn't know the names of our guest players, we had merely shouted 'Jock!' at pertinent moments throughout the games, and with five Black Watch and two Jocks of our own, we were undeniably a little top heavy, Caledonianwise. It hadn't gone unnoticed. After the presentation of the prizes, the organiser of the competition came to offer his half-hearted congratulations. He was still smarting from the thumping his boys had taken in the final. He was smarting even more from the fact that he knew that we had cheated, but couldn't prove it. He couldn't even say too much, in case he was accused of sour grapes.

"Walter, this year you have many players what is calling Jock," he said in English. "Are not the regiment near to you made of people who are called Jock?"

I didn't like his insinuation and embarked on an explanation as to how Scotland was a deprived area and that many Scots joined the Army because there were no jobs in their homeland. In short, I gave him a load of bluff. It failed to convince him, but I didn't care a damn. We had the winner's trophy—mission accomplished.

The award of the Long Service and Good Conduct medal is made to a soldier who has completed fifteen years of service, without having his crimes detected. In days of yore, the medal was presented after eighteen years and those proud recipients delighted in looking down their noses at us latecomers. If the truth were known, nobody other than an out-and-out creep would ever be entitled to the medal, since everyone drops a clanger at some time or another within those fifteen years. Once an entry of any description had been made on a soldier's Regimental Conduct Sheet, however, he was automatically debarred from ever receiving the award. Although a method of redress exists, it involves much begging and pleading, and soldiers with backbone refuse to demean themselves by submitting an application.

Thanks to a bevy of guardian angels watching over my career, my blue sheet was still a virgin after fifteen years and I was about to receive my LS & GC. It was just as well that they were giving it to me, because there was no way that I would have begged for it. The medal meant nothing to me then, or now. The presentation of the gong is normally made whenever a high-ranking officer happens to be visiting your unit. There is a parade, someone reads out a load of crap about your service record and the bumbling senior officer pins the thing on your chest. Following a weak handshake, the dignitary will then say something patronising about you and the value of the medal. I was determined to avoid such a parade at all costs. The RSM, however, was adamant that my medal would be presented in the proper fashion. One of us was going to be disappointed. My medal arrived from the UK one morning by registered post, Her Majesty presumably being unable to spare a personal courier that day. The chief clerk tipped me the wink that it had arrived and we kept the news secret—until the RSM disappeared to Moenchengladbach for a long weekend. My plan to escape the embarrassment of a parade was then set in motion. Our OC was a very pleasant man, but being a transferee, he was not streetwise as to the ways of the Corps and therefore malleable. The chief clerk gave me the medal on Friday morning and with the RSM a comfortable hundred miles away, I moved in for the kill.

"May I come in for a moment, sir?"

"Ah Superwal, what can I do for you this fine day?"

"Sir, I'm not sure whether you are aware of the ancient Corps tradition first granted during the reign of King Charles the Second? It gives an officer commanding the right to grant a boon to a platoon commander who is about to leave his command. With your kind permission, I would like to invoke the terms of that tradition and request that you grant me a boon forthwith."

I was secure in the knowledge that he hadn't a clue what I was talking about, since it was all a figment of my imagination.

"Well of course Superwal. I must admit that I know nothing about such a tradition, but what is it that you want?"

"I'm about to receive my LS & GC, sir, and my request is that you present the medal to me personally and without fuss. This will negate the requirement for a parade and you will have exercised your powers to grant a boon, as laid down in the charter signed, sealed and delivered by King Charles the Second himself."

"Isn't a parade mandatory under the terms of Provost Marshal's Instructions?" he asked awkwardly.

"Under normal circumstances that would be the case, sir, but those instructions are superseded by the directive of King Charles the Second in this matter."

"Well, in that case, as soon as the medal arrives..."

"Actually, it has already arrived and I have it here in my pocket."

"Are you sure it's acceptable to do it this way, Superwal?"

"No problems, sir, there are a number of precedents," I said, as I handed the brown envelope over the table.

"Well, in that case. Congratulations Superwal, here's your medal."

"Thank you very kindly sire."

I zoomed out of his office and down to the Black Watch tailor's shop, had my medals court mounted, the ribbons sewn onto my service dress and was back in the mess in time for NAAFI break. There was no way now that I could be lumbered with a parade; all that remained was to try and appease the RSM. He called me into his office on Tuesday morning, as soon as the news of the underhand medal presentation had reached his ears. He coughed before he spoke, a sure indicator that a bollocking was imminent.

"You are a devious bastard, Wally, without any doubt. I resent your latest unprincipled performance and I must tell you that I won't be sorry to see the back of you when you leave," he said, manifesting uncharacteristic passion.

It wasn't the first time he'd told me that he would be pleased to see me go either. That was the extent of his ire, however.

It was said that once the news that Wally Payne had received the LS & GC reached the ears of Corps members around the world, several medals were returned to the Army Medal Office, in protest that the medal had been devalued.

Every military unit employs a number of civilian staff and they are usually recruited from within the Army community. In most parts of BAOR, it provided the only opportunity for dependants to find work and competition for vacancies was intense. One of our typists in Werl was a charming, quiet and elegant lady, whose husband was attached to the Black Watch. So pleasant was this lady that, whenever I went into the HQ, I made a point of calling into the typing pool to pass the time of day. Shortly before disappearing for a couple of weeks on a major exercise, I was surprised to find a letter from the quiet typist amongst my mail. The letter thanked me for my friendship and wished me well for the future; it appeared that she had left at short notice. It didn't take me long to ascertain the facts surrounding her brisk departure: her husband had been naughty with the wife of another member of his battalion. Our typist had informed him that the marriage was over and of her plan to return to her parent's home in London. The news came as something of a surprise, as they had seemed such a well suited couple and were always seen together, even at the Kirk on Sunday mornings. The last part of her letter surprised me most of all, however: she asked me to keep in touch and gave her address and telephone number, in case I should feel inclined to contact her.

I disappeared to endure a fortnight's misery in the field and during the course of the exercise, I actually saw her husband. He was stone drunk! That indicated that there was something sadly amiss, since he was normally the most temperate of men. It seems that his failure to toe the abstemious line didn't pass unnoticed and he was quickly sent back to barracks, for being drunk in the field. This disgrace, combined with his admission of inter-unit adultery, was enough to have him removed from the battalion with the rudest of haste.

My leave came up directly after the exercise and I returned to Leicester prior to flying out to the USA the following week. With a few days to kill, I decided to call the lovely Jane. She confirmed that her marriage was on the rocks, before stunning me by accepting my offer of a few days together down in Devon—just to give her a break, you understand. It was very wicked of me, but what kind of man would stand idly by without coming to the aid of a lady in distress? I trust that she enjoyed those few days in Torquay, I certainly did. Her parents lived close to Heathrow Airport and their garage provided me with a convenient parking place for my car when I jetted off to the USA. Returning a fortnight later, they surprised me with the news that their daughter had left home for an unknown destination. I thanked them for looking after my car and returned back to Germany that weekend. Two weeks of fun in the USA had pushed the memory of Jane, and our brief fling, to the back of my mind.

A week after starting work again, I drove down to the NAAFI in Werl on Saturday morning to pick up my necessaries. Turning the corner at the washing powder section, I was suddenly stopped in my tracks. There, right in front of the baked beans, stood Jane and her errant husband. I waved a cheery greeting before departing at top speed for the checkout and exit. Her husband was a PT Corps instructor and a good deal bigger than I was and, although I don't suppose she had said anything about her short break in Torbay, there was no sense in chancing my arm. It appears they had returned to Werl to pack up their house before getting on with their lives elsewhere. I never heard from her again.

Our washer-up in the sergeant's mess was a lady from Hartlepool, who possessed only one more brain cell than the minimum required for sustaining life. Her marriage to a soldier in the Black Watch was on the rocks and as I had recently undergone the trauma of an Army divorce, she had come to me for advice. Her husband's battalion had moved him into barracks and, contrary to regulations, they had ordered her to vacate her married quarter within two weeks. Furthermore, they had denied her access to legal advice. They were badly out of order on both counts, but close-knit infantry battalions seldom see the necessity in conforming to rules and regulations when it doesn't suit them to do so. This girl was so dim they would have considered her no threat; how would she ever get to know her rights? Once they had shipped her to the Army hostel in Wiltshire, she would no longer be their responsibility and they could wash their hands of the whole affair. They really couldn't be allowed to get away with treating her so shabbily, so I decided to fight her corner.

I went to see the Regimental Families Officer on her behalf, to find out what they intended to do for her. He threw me out of his office within thirty seconds.

"Keep your nose oot o' Black Watch business," was the advice of the dour, old Jock officer.

He was quite right, of course, but who was going to help this lady if I didn't? My next move was to contact the Army Legal Services, but they told me they were unable to assist because they were already representing her husband in divorce proceedings. They were helpful enough to suggest I called the RAF Legal Department down in Rheindahlen, however, and before long, Belinda had legal representatives to advise her. I'm not sure that she really understood what was going on, but I tried to explain as we journeyed down to see the RAF Legal Services solicitor. They couldn't have been more helpful and they informed her of her rights and the course of action she should take. They even told the Black Watch that she would be staying in her married quarter for the maximum period allowed. Belinda was most grateful and it pleased me to have helped a very lame dog over a style.

Belinda's final departure from Werl coincided with my shooting away on some more leave, which needed to be taken prior to my imminent posting. For no specific reason, I had decided on Sardinia. On her last day at work I asked her, in all innocence, just what she planned to do now that she was a free agent? Hartlepool didn't sound too exciting a destination and as she was in no particular rush to get there, I suggested she might like to accompany me on my holiday to the sun. She had no idea where Sardinia was, of course, only that it wasn't within a bus ride of Hartlepool, but willingly agreed to come along as my navigator. Not for the first time in my life, I was taking advantage of a damsel in distress.

This female turned out to be the most dull, ill informed and dim person that I have ever encountered. Were it not for the fact that she was a proficient bed partner, she would have been driven to the nearest airport within two days. Had she made a single unsolicited comment, however banal, I would have been satisfied. Even a comment to the effect that a field was full of sheep would have been acceptable. As it was, she never made an attempt to engage me in conversation.

After a week in Alghero, in northern Sardinia, I had tired of our one-way conversations. Her good looks and nocturnal excellence weren't sufficient; a guy needs a modicum of mental stimulation too. Following an irrelevant and instantly forgotten comment over dinner one evening, she finally showed some fighting spirit. She became enraged at whatever it was I had said and being run through with a steak knife seemed a distinct possibility. My assurance that the comment, whatever it was, was in no way meant to be demeaning, wasn't accepted, although she did accept my offer to drive her to the airport the next day. I drove the length of Sardinia and finally arrived at Cagliari airport, only to discover that bloody Alitalia were on strike. There was nothing for it but to drive all the way back to Alghero and have some dinner at the Il Pavone. During the journey back she decided to forgive me for my sins. Il Pavone was a splendid restaurant and we ate there often. The owner was particularly friendly, especially when he discovered that I came from Leicester. He had actually worked in the city and we spent much time reminiscing. On the night of the abortive trip to the airport, however, a thief broke into my car that was parked directly outside the restaurant and in my full view, making off with all my stuff. Should my travels ever take me back to that part of the world, I shall be on the lookout for a small Italian wearing a well-cut suit with a forty-four inch chest and a pair of size eleven Cheney shoes.

I decided to move up to Corsica for the next leg of what was proving to be a disappointing trip, but not before leaving my second suit and another pair of shoes in the hotel room where we spent the night before catching a ship for the French island. Waiting for the ferry at the dockside, I warmed up some Heinz soup inside the car on a small stove and served the first ladleful to her. The plastic plate conducted heat rather too efficiently and she held onto it for only two seconds.

"Eee, it's burning my hands!" she exclaimed, as she threw the plate and contents all over the car seat and me.

I was now down to one pair of trousers and owned a car that stank of Heinz Cream of Tomato ever thereafter. Corsica was closed. It was a Sunday and out of season and so I drove all the way up to Bastia, the splendid colonial town in the north east of the island. We parked up, watched a game of boules and went into a café that was the encapsulation of Colonial France. It had the rich aroma of good coffee, the all-pervading smell of Galloises and was full of Frogs dressed in blue and white-hooped shirts and blue berets. Following a suitable comment about the ambience of the place, Belinda responded with a comment that just about summed her up.

"It seems just like the Wimpy bar in Hartlepool to me."

That was all I needed, this lady was going back to bloody Hartlepool just as fast as I could get her to Calais. Instead of looking for a hotel, I booked a cabin on the overnight ferry to Toulouse. We slept the night away and arrived at the French coast next morning. During the car journey north, I made two further attempts to engage personality girl in conversation. Firstly, at St Tropez, I asked if she knew which film star had made the resort famous? She didn't. Then, at Montelimar, a place whose town sign even has the word 'Nougat' in brackets after its name, I asked her if she knew why the town was famous. She didn't. At that, I gave up and we drove the rest of the way to Calais in silence.

Rick Daley was one of the most miserable-faced shits in the RMP. Mind you, had I had been unfortunate enough to marry a woman as ugly as his wife, I may well have been a miserable-faced shit too. With six platoons at 115, a certain amount of rivalry was inevitable and the fact that Rick and his men were perennial runners up to the mighty Tiger Platoon must have proved irksome to him. There were no real grounds for his aggressive and offensive attitude towards my men, though, other than jealousy. We had a few minor bouts of verbal sparring before our first serious contretemps, which came about when he accused my men of stealing items from one of his platoon's trailers that had been parked on the barrack square overnight. That was an outrageous indictment. Then to accuse me, within earshot of the other platoon commanders, of orchestrating the theft…well, that was just not acceptable behaviour. As a point of honour, I was forced to challenge him to a 'fists at dawn' duel. No one was going to accuse me of inciting my men to steal, even if it was true. He wisely declined my offer. We had several more verbal battles after that and my impending promotion to warrant officer must really have made his gall rise, although the fact that I was to be posted almost immediately might have been of some consolation to him.

Due to leave Werl on Tuesday morning, I arranged to take my platoon out for dinner on the proceeding Saturday evening. We met to wet our whistles in the corporal's mess, before descending upon Massimo's Italian Restaurant to eat our fill. It was a cracking evening, despite the fact that the bill landed up in front of me and we returned to the mess to continue the fun. The bar was in its temporary location above the gymnasium changing rooms and I had just placed the final order of the night, when Daley strode into the bar in his capacity as orderly sergeant. It was a little after the official closing time, admittedly, but the day that an RMP mess closes on time, hell will freeze over. Resplendent in his service dress and red hat, he was determined to be awkward. He was armed with Company Standing Orders, opened at the page dealing with bar opening hours.

"You two visitors leave the bar now," he said to two corporals from another unit. "You other corporals, drink up and leave the bar within five minutes. Staff Sergeant Payne, you will accompany me outside now," said the officious Daley.

The famous Payne temper was instantaneously activated: "You two visitors stay exactly where you are; in fact, have another beer on me. Sort that out please, barman. Tiger Platoon, stand fast. Staff Sergeant Daley, if I accompany you outside, you will be a very sore and sorry man. Fuck off."

"You will come outside now staff," he repeated, mentally recording my comments for the statement of evidence that he would assuredly submit.

I acceded to his request and with two left hooks, knocked him down the stairs. We then finished off our drinks and awaited the repercussions. Daley would certainly have made straight for the orderly officer's bunk to tell his tale. Within fifteen minutes the orderly officer arrived at the mess. He was a friend of mine of many years standing.

"About finished, Wal?" he enquired quietly.

"Just leaving actually," I replied.

On Monday morning I was called into the RSM's office for my final bollocking in Werl. He coughed before he began.

"Wally, Staff Sergeant Daley has made a statement of complaint against you," he said. "A seventeen page statement of complaint, in fact. It's with the OC. Perhaps you should go and discuss it with him?"

Seventeen pages! He must have described every bump he felt on his way down the stairs in graphic detail. The new OC had been my boss on no less than four occasions. I liked him and believe that the feeling was mutual. I knocked on the open door, saluted and entered.

"I understand that my arch enemy has been complaining about me, sir?" I said by way of an opening gambit. "He's a mental defective, you know."

"Seventeen pages of complaint, Wally—anything worth reading in it?"

"It will be unmitigated drivel, sir. He's a perverted arsehole who needs a smack around the ear now and again to make him toe the line."

"Shall I tear it up?"

"It's the best thing for it. May I have the honour?"

I tore the thing up and consigned it to the waste bin.

"Thank you, Wally. How's your mum?" he said, resurrecting an old line of patter that we had between us.

"Fine, thank you sir. How's the mother-in-law?"

I served three tours in the area of Werl, spanning some eight years, and now it was time for the last farewell. Having driven through the barracks gate three years earlier as a married sergeant, I was about to leave as a single warrant officer. I had achieved considerable success, both on the career and marital fronts. A farewell function in the form of a ladies' dinner night was held in my honour on the Friday evening prior to my departure—not a bright idea, on reflection, given that the Guest of Honour was single. Following a splendid meal, it was time for the shallow speeches and the presentation of my gift.

Farewell presentations were nonsensical in Werl, because you effectively paid for the present yourself by a monthly deduction to your mess bill. In fact, you even purchased your own present and the Treasurer reimbursed you later. Already the proud owner of half a dozen pewter tankards, the standard farewell gift, I elected to buy something useful this time—an electric toothbrush.

My farewell speech had evolved over several days and had taken many hours to prepare. It had been well practised and I was confident that there would be a few laughs. Firstly though, the RSM would say a few words. He was a talented man in many ways, but speech making was not one of his strong points.

"Well-Ladies-and-Gentlemen," he said, with a distinct pause between each word, "It-is-time-to-say-goodbye-to-Wally-Payne. Wally-has-been-in-the-unit-for…"

He interrupted his masterpiece to ask me a question.

"Is-it-two-and-a-half-or-three-years?"

"Three years, sir."

"Wally-has-been-in-the-unit-for-three-years-and-has-had-some-marital-problems. He-has-also-run-the-unit-football-team, thank-you-for-running-the-football-team-Wally."

He continued for a while, the audience captivated by his power of oratory. With several people cringing in their seats, he stumbled through to the last sentence.

"Wally-has-decided-on-an-electric-toothbrush. Come-up-and-accept-your-gift."

He gave me the present and sat down, exhausted. Even such a puny effort was an ordeal for him. Meanwhile, I had become aware of rumblings in the crowd. It was clear that some people considered an electric toothbrush to be an inappropriate farewell gift, but since I had paid for the thing myself, I couldn't see what it had to do with them. Perhaps they had drunk too much wine and were expressing their true feelings towards me. I decided not to waste my speech on this rabble, pocketed my notes and spoke off the cuff instead.

"Mr President, my heartfelt thanks for your glowing testimonial to my three years in the company. Running the football team and getting divorced both gave me a great deal of pleasure. I can say, quite categorically, that my time in Werl has been immensely enjoyable. As for those of you who have mocked my choice of farewell gift, let me assure you that it will serve to remind me of you all. Each morning, as I clean my teeth and spit in the sink, you will be on my mind. Goodnight."

I sat down to muted applause, finished my wine and went to bed. A few days later I was off to Hohne, as a Warrant Officer. I'd become a sir.

8

Hohne wasn't the simplest of places to get to, lying in the middle of nowhere as it did. One of our lads had previously served with 111 Provost Company and was able to give me precise instructions about where to change autobahns and what road to take to reach Bergen-Belsen. Having confirmed that I understood his explicit directions, he shook my hand firmly.

"But if I were you," he added, "when I reached Hohne, I'd keep on bloody driving."

This was pertinent advice.

Just before reaching Bergen, the road takes you directly past the remains of the dreadful Belsen Concentration Camp and that sets the mood perfectly for Hohne and the surrounding area. The vast monstrosity that is Hohne Camp was the brainchild of a pre-war German general, who constructed a camp large enough to accommodate an entire brigade of men within a single perimeter fence. The British had moved into the place at the end of the war and we were still there.

Having found the sergeant's mess amongst the rows and rows of identical looking barrack blocks, I went to the Company HQ to tip my hat to my new Officer Commanding. Then I ran into an old chum who was serving in the unit and he invited me for dinner and a few drinks at his home that evening. Driving the few miles from the barracks to the married quarter area in the nearby town of Bergen, I was surprised by the solitude. Apart from the odd British or NATO vehicle travelling the same route, the place was deserted. It was very naughty of me, but it did cross my mind that if I had a glass of wine too many, the chances of coming to grief at the hands of the police were slim. I was made very welcome at my old pal's house and despite my good intentions, the wine, beer and brandy got the better of me. I was in no condition to drive, but if a four-mile walk was to be avoided, then there was no alternative but to get behind the wheel. It was time for an appreciation of the situation. It was two in the morning, the weather was vile, the road was straight and the police would be in front of the fire with their feet up if they had any sense. I would take the chance. The short journey was completely uneventful and I didn't see a vehicle travelling in either direction, until I reached the village of Belsen. An unsuspecting squaddie had been pulled over by a keen RMP patrol and the NCOs appeared to be giving him the works. Despite my condition, I had the sense to adhere to the speed limit through the village, my headlights were dipped and I had indicated correctly whilst overtaking the parked car and the attendant RMP Landrover. Fifty yards from the front gate to the barracks, however, the RMP vehicle swung violently in front of me, causing me to brake sharply. A brand new and exceedingly keen lance corporal approached.

"You were speeding as you passed through the village sir," he asserted.

"Considering that you and your partner were standing outside the Landrover when I overtook you, how come you were able to ascertain my speed? Do you have a Vascar device secreted under your hat?" I said, trying not to slur my speech too badly.

Although the lance corporal was a fibber for sure, he was keen and it must have been obvious to him that I was three sheets to the wind. He probably thought that it was his birthday when he got a whiff of my breath and his hand went for his breathalyser with a speed comparable to that of Wyatt Earp going for his pistol at the OK Corral. The patrol commander made his way to the side of my car. I hoped in desperation that it was somebody I knew; otherwise this inexperienced little lance corporal was about to ruin someone's very promising career. Drunk in charge within eight hours of arriving in my new unit!

"Hello sir, I heard that you'd been posted in," said a familiar voice. "It's great to have you in the company."

It was one of the good guys. We had served together a couple of times and had always got on well. What an opportune time to renew our friendship. To the obvious disappointment of the lance corporal, the big Jugoslav took charge of the situation and drove my car back to the mess. I owed him one.

Four days after arriving in Hohne and I was on my way back to Werl, to play soccer against the team that I had played with for the previous three years. This was an important match, the semi final of the Stanley Cup, which was sure to be a viciously contested affair. Hohne were a good side by all accounts, but because they hardly knew me except by reputation, I only made the subs bench. The ignominy of it, Wally Payne a substitute! By half time Hohne had done enough to be five goals clear, but were trailing by a goal to nil. The ball just didn't want to go in the net. Our skipper decided on a change in the second half and brought on the ageing superstar, to see if he could find the net. It was a successful ploy and midway through the second period, I smacked home a direct free kick to level the scores. The match went into extra time and we were awarded a penalty near the end. I slotted that home as well and that gave us passage into the final. I don't suppose I would have won any popularity contests in Werl that evening. The Werl side, however, were magnanimous in defeat, which was something they must have learnt after my departure!

The final was played on the Army Stadium in Hohne a week later, against 247 from Berlin, the winners of the competition for the last two seasons. There was little doubt that we were rated rank outsiders. The Berlin players had been given time off for training, the players had been written off from duties for weeks, and they were able to approach the final in the sure knowledge that their officers and warrant officers cared about the result. Apathy summed up the attitude of our OC and RSM and some members of our team were still on duty an hour before the match started. At least we were wearing a new strip, obtained that very morning after the second-in-command finally succumbed to my impassioned plea for funds. Mind you, we didn't have any numbers on our backs and the kit was made for giants. Our smaller guys had to run two strides before their shorts caught up with them. We only had two balls; one of them being the match ball and the referee needed that. Is there anything less impressive than a whole side kicking around with only one ball? Berlin, on the other hand, carried a ball apiece as they ran onto the pitch, resplendent in their personalised tracksuits. They undoubtedly won the initial encounter, for sartorial excellence, but the whistle hadn't gone yet. Underdogs we might have been, for they had many of the Corp's better players in their side, but we had some decent lads in our line up too and we weren't about to give them the Stanley Cup on a plate.

We scored straight from the whistle, a free kick was awarded and I chipped it into the penalty area to where Phil Tyne was lurking to head it home. He confessed in later years that the ball actually hit his head rather than him heading it, but it was a goal and we had started well. For me it was to be one of those days that soccer players dream about and after they had equalised, I restored our lead by scoring from the spot. We led 2-1 at the break. They equalised again in the second half, but another free kick allowed me to find Jock

Brogan's head and he made no mistake. At 3-2 in our favour and with twenty minutes left to play, we were subjected to the severest pressure. Stout defending, brilliant goalkeeping, some glaring misses by their forwards and huge slices of good fortune meant that we hung on until five minutes from time. Then the buggers equalised again. The last five minutes saw us besieged in our penalty area until, with only seconds remaining on the clock, I went up field for one last effort. Our keeper thumped the ball forward towards our right-winger, who had been anonymous throughout the game. He chose an opportune moment to shine, however; he flicked the ball onto me with his head and gave me the chance to run at their defence. Why no one came out to challenge me will remain a mystery. My legs were so tired that I would have gladly picked the ball up and given it to them if they had, but the entire defence backed off and allowed me to advance to the edge of the area. Perhaps it was my reputation that made them hesitate, but even at thirty-eight, there was no way I would scorn a chance like this. I blasted it into the bottom left-hand corner for a 4-3 lead. The game lasted for only twenty seconds after the re-start before the referee brought proceedings to a conclusion. We had done it! My boots should have been hung up there and then, for there was no chance of repeating a performance like that. The fact is that I played on for donkey's years. The award ceremony was unique. Our skipper had broken his leg during the game and needed to hobble up on crutches to lift the trophy from the Provost Marshal. In a rare display of sportsmanship, not a quality that many people associate with me, I gave my trophy away to a lad whose place I'd taken in the final. Berlin proved to be lousy losers and declined our after-match hospitality. We didn't care—it left more free beer for us and we drank copiously in celebration of a famous victory.

Alas, there were other things to do in Hohne apart from playing soccer. It would be impossible for anyone to comprehend just how much I hated exercises. In the perverse way of things in the Army, therefore, I was subjected to far more than my fair share. As the commander of the exercise support platoon in Werl, I had taken part in every exercise during the last three years and was considered something of an expert on the subject of provost operations. With promotion and posting to Hohne as Training Warrant Officer, however, exercises would now be a thing of the past. Perhaps it would be necessary for me to write the odd operations order, but someone else could go out and get cold and wet on Lueneburg Heath. At the prospect of becoming office bound, I had gleefully given away all my exercise comforts, prematurely as it transpired, as Major Wallace had other ideas. He believed that he as OC and me as TWO should deploy on every exercise. There was method in his madness. He was yet another transferee from the infantry and he knew sweet bugger all about running an RMP unit, whereas his knowledge of operations was considerable. By spending as much time as possible in the field, he could better hide his inadequacies from his masters. Within a fortnight of arriving in Hohne, therefore, I was back in combats and out for a week in beautiful Niedersachsen. A second exercise followed shortly afterwards and by the time six weeks had elapsed, exercise number three was underway. Newly promoted WO2 Payne was feeling very pissed off with his new posting.

Major Wallace wasn't playing on this exercise, he was returning to the UK to attend his initial RMP Officer's Course. How very astute of the RMP to put a man who had not even attended a basic RMP course in charge of a hundred and fifty men in the busiest police duties unit in the world. As if that wasn't bad enough, they saw fit to post in an RSM who had been a clerk his entire career and who didn't know his arse from his elbow either. It's hardly surprising that morale stank at Hohne.

We were as comfortable as it is possible to be whilst living in a shitty farmyard and we had set our operations tent up inside a barn. I liked being in a barn—it doesn't rain or blow and you don't need to cam up. As the exercise was taking place only a few dozen miles from our barracks, the OC couldn't resist the urge to drive out and visit us on the Wednesday morning. He would then fly back to the UK that evening. He arrived as the second in command, the RSM, two corporals and myself were huddling together for warmth in the tent, breathing in and out rapidly in the vain attempt to make the mercury rise above freezing point. After his initial greeting, he came out with the best comment I'd heard him make in six weeks.

"Let's pop over to the village guesthouse for a glass of beer and an 'O' group."

"Great idea," said I, anticipating the chance to thaw out.

"The invitation doesn't extend to you, sergeant major—you will stay here," he announced to my considerable disappointment, adding: "Your job for the next two years, Mr Payne, is to eat, breathe and sleep exercises."

After three days without a proper sleep, wash, warm or shit, I'm prone to blow my top rather quickly. This was one such occasion.

"If you are looking for someone to do every bloody exercise during the next two years, then you can find some other mug. I've done nothing but bloody exercises for the last three years and I'm pissed off with them," I advised him, ruining my chances of his recommendation for a transfer to the Diplomatic Corps.

"How dare you talk to me like that!"

"It's perfectly easy and you might be surprised at what else I have to say."

"Get outside the barn—I want to talk to you in private," he said, following me outside into the bitter cold.

Officers always like to give out bollockings in private; they don't like witnesses to the crap they spout.

"Sergeant major, I'm not used to being talked to like that and I won't have it. You know what's expected of you regarding exercises and if you don't like it, you can jolly well transfer to another unit," he asserted.

Before I had the opportunity to say my piece, he looked at his watch and continued his prattle.

"It's now 1140 hrs, you have until midday to decide whether you wish to remain in my unit or not."

"Who the fuck needs until midday? I'll tell you now. You can stuff your unit up your arse." In this manner I demonstrated my high breeding.

"Pack your kit and get off my exercise now!"

"Gladly," I said, delighted at the prospect of escaping from the field two days early.

I rushed back to my tent to pack my suitcase, but was stopped by the RSM. The miserable Jock bastard insisted I stay out until Friday. They say that the major wasn't in the best of moods when he departed.

By early Friday afternoon we were back in Hohne and I hadn't been in my office five minutes before the phone rang. It was the first of many calls I was to receive that afternoon, from officers and mates who had heard the disquieting rumours about a Wallace/Payne feud. Wallace, it seemed, had wasted no time in telling the world about our verbal set-to and my acquaintances were merely trying to get my side of the story. In the absence of the OC on his course, I imagined that someone in a position of power would have had me transferred to another unit before he returned. The decision of the spoilsport colonel at Corps HQ, though, was that Payne should stay in Hohne. He presumed that six weeks of separation would serve to cool both our tempers. When Major Wallace finally returned, we had our long awaited head to head. He elected to bury the hatchet and it was noticeable that the majority of exercises thereafter were conducted without my participation.

It was common knowledge within 111 Provost Company that the RSM disliked the TWO with a passion and that the feeling was mutual. Basically he was jealous of me, for not only was I better looking, fitter, stronger and younger than he was, but academically, mentally and intellectually I was his master too. Being a West Coast Scot, he was devoid of a sense of humour and he despised me particularly for my sharply honed wit. The clincher, though, was that although he spoke fine German, my grasp of the language was superior and I had the qualifications to prove the fact In an effort to demonstrate his intellect he had managed to complete the application form of a dodgy management association and, for the payment of a substantial fee, this bogus outfit provided him with a phoney group of post nominal letters to display after his name. He proudly screwed his new brass nameplate onto his door and people flocked from yards around to view it. Now, as it happens, I do hold a qualification that entitles me to use post nominal letters, only mine didn't come through the mail; instead, they took me three years of study to achieve. The appearance of the RSM's sign spurred me on to make something similar to adorn my office door. It was made of thick paper and read, 'WO2 Payne W. RMP, AIB, LS&GC, GSM, scorer of important goals, cricketing sensation, squash player extraordinaire, all round nice guy, GCEs in Maths, Science, English, Human Biology, French and German, A Levels in German and Geography, Leicester City supporter, Member of Leicestershire CCC, Member of Newfoundpool Working Men's Club etc.etc'. It stretched all the way down the corridor, over the top of the RSM's door, over the chief clerk's office and half way down the stairs. With one notable exception, it was considered to be an amusing effort. The RSM came into my office after lunch to display his legendary sharp wit.

"Tak' it doon," he said.

Oh, how I loved his subtle West Coast sense of humour.

There was absolutely nothing for single soldiers to do in Hohne and nobody in a position of authority gave a damn about their welfare. The cinema had closed down because of poor attendances and the bowling alley had gone the same way, although it never occurred to those in positions of power to investigate why. Soldiers don't want to see Bambi and Dumbo the Flying Bloody Elephant, they want blood and guts and sex. That's why they stopped going to the pictures and invested in video players instead. The equipment at the bowling alley broke down every other frame, so it was no wonder that the boys gave that place the heave-ho as well. The Roundhouse in the middle of the camp housed both the NAAFI and YMCA and had so many unused rooms within its immense walls that it could easily have been turned into a place of entertainment. As it was, at 1800 hrs when the coffee bar in the YMCA put its shutters down, there was absolutely nowhere for the boys to go. This former Wehrmacht officer's mess was simply crying out for a McDonald's or Pizza Hut, but the NAAFI have a monopoly in British barracks and wouldn't let an efficient organisation anywhere near them.

Not even an unmarried warrant officer was immune from the boredom that settled on this enormous camp once the sun went down and, without my car, I would have been lost. I took to exploring the surrounding area. Bergen was a one-horse town and it took all of ten minutes to see everything of interest. The fact that it boasted two establishments that sold sausage and chips in the evenings was its sole redeeming feature. Picturesque Celle was down the road and a good place for espying pretty ladies on a Saturday morning. Other than those two small towns, the search for excitement meant a drive along the autobahn to the big cities of Bremen, Hannover or Hamburg. Hansastadt Hamburg was my favourite spot for a little culture and I wandered up there most every week. To keep from going mad inside the camp I took up golf again, without worrying the handicapper, and kept up my soccer, squash and cricket. I may have been bored, but I was fit with it! Walking over the Lueneburg Heath was a joy and most weekends saw me tramping off with a pack on my back. One Saturday morning, imagining that I had stumbled across a murder, I followed fresh blood tracks into the woods and to a copse, where blood and innards lay strewn around. The adrenaline really pumped for a while, until a closer inspection of the remains revealed a quantity of fur. Someone would be eating venison for tea. Lueneburg Heath was rather like Scotland, but without the hills and it came as no surprise that the German conservationists subsequently chose this area to launch their 'No More Military Exercises' campaign.

What was really missing from Hohne, of course, was fanny—the lads simply weren't getting their nookies. What would have been wrong with a discreet little brothel tucked away around the back of the Roundhouse? That's what the Wehrmacht used the building for by all accounts. Being a brothel keeper would have been right down my street and I'd have been happy to take on the job of running the establishment, even on an honorary basis. The pseudo puritanical officers who run the Army wouldn't allow anything like that, of course—they were too concerned with kissing the general's arse to consider the needs of the boys. There are no medals to be won for looking after the welfare of the troops, you see. In fact, the horses in Hohne were better looked after than the squaddies and they got their oats regularly too. At least the entrepreneurial ladies of the area were aware of the shortfall. They set up at the side of roads that ran through the sparsely populated training area and provided a service from the back of a mini bus or car.

My answer to the boredom of Hohne was to enrol myself for an Army course. The prospect of spending six weeks on Humberside learning about motor vehicles and how to account for fuel didn't exactly excite me, but the Motor Transport Officer's Course at Leconfield would serve its purpose, by allowing me to escape from the OC, RSM and 111 Provost Company for a while.

Our thick Jock RSM couldn't get out of bed early enough in the morning to catch me out and he resorted to some pretty outrageous discrimination. Calling a senior ranks conference before departing on his leave, he announced that the stand-in for the period of his absence would be one of the staff sergeants. Now I quite liked the Liverpudlian Jew he had nominated, but there was no way he could be appointed acting RSM when there was a warrant officer sitting in the next office. I ordered all of the senior ranks out of the room and went for the Caledonian bastard's throat.

"Explain to me why a staff sergeant is preferred to me as acting RSM," I hissed, looking him straight in his snakelike eyes.

"As you are going on a course in three weeks' time, I thought you might be too busy," he replied lamely.

"Why didn't you ask me then, rather than assuming?" I demanded and without waiting for another watery response, I added, "Since I'm so clearly indispensable in this rotten unit, I'll save you the bother of changing things around again. I'm fucking off on three weeks' leave, now."

And I did, making an unplanned trip by car to Cyprus and Israel.

A word of warning to anyone with the urge to visit Leconfield—it's the coldest place in the UK during October and late holidays should be taken much further south. The course was tedious, although it unravelled certain conundrums that had always puzzled me. At least I now have a vague idea about what happens when a clutch pedal is depressed and the number of things that move when you turn a steering wheel was a revelation. Most of the other warrant officers on the course were the sort of people who serviced their own cars, or who could change a spare wheel or sparking plugs. That was all way over my head, me being strictly a petrol, oil and lubricants man. I was in awe of their knowledge and was confident only of the fact that my position after the final examination would be plum last. What I hadn't considered was that these mechanical geniuses considered course literature such as *An ABC of Steering* and the *XYZ of the Carburettor* to be beneath their dignity. Consequently, the only person in the whole class who read the booklets upon which the final tests were based was yours truly. To my own and everyone else's amazement, I came top and achieved a 'B' grading for my efforts. For the next dozen years in the Army, I never needed to use a single scrap of the knowledge gleaned at Leconfield.

A strange thing happened when I was on the course. I took to using the same breakfast table each morning and usually had a huge guy from the RCT sitting opposite me. Our conversation was restricted to a good morning grunt apiece, partially because he was always occupied in downing a huge breakfast, but mainly because I'm a tetchy sod for the first hour of the day. On the third Friday we sat across from each other as usual and as I was tucking into my Sugar Puffs and reading the sports page, someone at the table spoke.

"You're an ugly bastard Wally Payne," said an anonymous voice.

I put my *Telegraph* down to see who could have uttered such a scandalous remark, but saw only my breakfast chum and it couldn't have been him, because he didn't know me from Adam. Thinking that I must have been hearing things, I returned to the football page.

"You're blind as well as ugly you old bastard," said the voice.

It was the RCT warrant officer sitting opposite.

"How the hell do you know my name?" I enquired.

"Don't you recognise me, Wally? It's me, Ken Hollins."

The last time I had seen Ken was back in 1967, when we used to run together at the back of Aldershot Barracks in Iserlohn. In those days he could beat me, provided I wore boots and he was in trainers. There was no way he could beat me over three miles now, even if I were to wear diver's boots and gave him a mile start. Ken had put on stones in weight and was unrecognisable from the beanpole teenager I had known and liked so well. Presumably my features had changed considerably with the years too; it had taken him three weeks to recognise me, after all. We swapped compliments, reminiscences and addresses and that was the last time I ever saw him. Despite exchanging the odd letter and Christmas cards, our paths never crossed again. A couple of years later I had a call from a mutual friend, who passed on the distressing news of Ken's premature death.

Firing guns has never excited me. They are noisy, always need cleaning and, whenever it was my turn to fire on the ranges, it either rained or snowed. Range days are only allocated to RMP if a trough of low pressure is imminent in the area, thereby ensuring a truly miserable day for the participants. My arrival in Hohne coincided with the order for RMP to carry loaded firearms on duty, a decision made following the cowardly murder of a British Army colonel in Dortmund. This meant that all NCOs needed to test fire their weapons once a week, or was it once a month? The bottom line was that I spent two or three days of every week down at those bloody ranges at Celle. It was a real pain in the backside, especially trying to teach timid women how to shoot. Don't anyone ever tell me that women make equally good soldiers as men. It may be the politically correct thing to say, but everyone in their right mind knows that it's a load of cobblers.

What finished me as a weapons man was Exercise Cop Shoot. This was a social shooting event hosted by the RMP in Hohne that had become an organisational and safety nightmare. An officer in 111 had dreamt up the idea for Cop Shoot years previously, for the sole purpose of getting himself out of the shit. He had placed an order for bar stock with the NAAFI that wasn't very precise and therefore open to interpretation. Afforded the opportunity of mucking something up, the NAAFI did exactly that and when the stock was delivered, single bottles of wines and spirits had become cases and crates of beer, container loads. When the fleet of delivery trucks pulled away, 111 Provost Company had enough booze to last for years. A method of disposing of this excess stock needed to be found and what better way of shifting a load of drink is there than gathering several dozen military policemen together for a weekend? It was under these circumstances that the plan to hold a shooting competition amongst RMP units in Germany was hatched. Then the German police got wind of the fact that a major piss up was in the offing; so they invited themselves along and Cop Shoot was born.

By the time running the event landed on my shoulders, the whole thing had become much too complex. Participants included not only RMP and German police teams from all over Niedersachsen, but also police teams from the UK as well as, Yanks, Belgians, Frogs, Dutch, Danes and Norwegians. The whole thing was an organisational nightmare. The fact that everything went off without a mishap was down to pure luck and the fact that all my aides were RMP NCOs with plenty of common sense. A diplomatic dilemma did brew for a while, when one of the range commanders saw fit to disqualify the German CID team from Soltau. This gallant band of law enforcers was so drunk by the time they reached the pistol range that none of them could see the targets. They were the first team into the control tent on the second morning, to crave an audience with me. Disqualification for drunkenness would do little to further their careers, it seemed, and they were much relieved when I agreed to let them continue, after placing them last in the pistol-shooting event. It was my misfortune to be responsible for this event for two years running, and it came as a relief to see the back of a competition that actively encouraged shooting and drinking, a deadly combination.

Instead of taking part in the senseless morning fitness runs that our RSM found so compelling, I began to take the footballers away for soccer training. Very soon I had more footballers than the slimy RSM had runners, which had the effect of putting him off soccer for all time. One morning I was approached by one of the WRAC girls.

"Can I come and play soccer with the lads, sir?"

"Certainly not!" I barked. "No place for women in a soccer team."

"I can play, sir," she replied in her distinct Northumbrian accent.

Always a sucker for the Geordie accent and a pretty face, I grudgingly allowed her to accompany us, but only on the understanding that she played for the opposition in the training match. (There would never be a woman in my team!) During the first half of that morning's practice game, a corner came in from the right. Anticipating an easy header to clear our lines, I was just about to make contact when someone rose higher than I did and won the ball. Turning to see whom the aerial artist was, I was astonished to discover that it was Paula Maynard. How could a woman jump that high and win a ball in the air, even against a mediocre header of the ball like me? It transpired that this girl could do more than head a ball; she also had terrific ball control, vision, passing ability and a shot in both feet. Had she been butch, it would have gone some way to explaining her talent in the male preserve of soccer, but this was a pretty, feminine lady. Later I asked her where she had learnt to play.

"I've got six brothers, all of them footballers and two of them professional," she explained. "If I wanted to play with them when I was a bairn, it was always football."

She went on to tell me she had won several England Ladies' caps and that she had played in many of the big stadiums in Europe. Inter-Milan had even approached her to play on the ladies' professional circuit in Italy, but she had fallen in love and got married instead. She wasn't allowed to play in Army league matches, but she was always in my team for friendly fixtures. She surprised many a hard guy with her own toughness on the field and she could swear with the best of us, but it was her silky skills that made the jaws gape in amazement. I recall walking off the pitch alongside Paula and her husband after one particular game.

"Do you know what's really embarrassing, sir?" she asked.

"What's that, Paula?"

"Playing in the same football team as your husband and knowing that you're a better player than him."

Rumour was sweeping the Corps. Could it be that the hardiest of the hardy perennial bachelors, Bones Kitchenbrand, had pledged his troth to a lady from Bognor Regis? To add flavour to the rumour, the woman in question was reported to possess only one leg! The Boneman and I were in regular contact and since he had made no mention of a fiancée, I had placed little credence in the stories circulating about him and the mystery woman.

I was lying in my bed in the Hohne Station mess late one Saturday morning, soundly cursing the refiners and blenders at the Asbach distillery, when a knock came on my door. The Boneman popped his head around the corner.

"Hello mate," he said.

What made his appearance so surprising was the fact that he was serving in Aldershot—at least six hundred miles of driving and a twenty-five mile cross-channel ferry passage away.

"What the fuck are you doing here? Posted? Exercise? Absent?"

"Language please, Timothy, ladies present," said Bones. "No mate, I've come to ask you to be best man for me and Heather. She's outside the door."

"Bloody Hell! Give me a minute while I put some clothes on and we'll go over to the mess for some coffee."

Sure enough, Heather was outside the door and a comely wench she was too. As we walked over to the mess, I took a shufti at her gait. She was walking perfectly normally, not the hint of a limp, and although she was wearing trousers, my educated guess was that this bird was in possession of both of her pins. We drank our coffee and swapped the latest scandal before getting down to the real reason for their visit. They were to be married in Aldershot three months hence and to me they afforded the honour of being best man. I was delighted to accept. There was one question crying out to be answered, of course, but just how does one broach a subject as delicate as an allegedly missing limb? It was imperative to scotch the rumour about my mate's intended just the same, so I decided on a direct approach.

"Bones, there's a silly rumour circulating that must be put to bed at the first opportunity. It's daft I know, but some evil minded buggers have been saying that Heather here only has one leg."

She burst out laughing.

"Wally," she said, "Listen."

She rapped her lower limb with her knuckles and it resounded like a knock on the door. Hillary's leg had been amputated below the knee.

My arrival at the RMP sergeant's mess in Aldershot coincided with the traditional 'Friday at Four', although the Boneman was conspicuous by his absence. Bones, a man who isn't averse to a glass or two, had last been seen walking unsteadily away from the unit lines after a lunchtime session. His current whereabouts was anyone's guess. I was on my fifth pint of lager before he finally graced the gathering with his presence. Bones had clearly not wasted the afternoon, for he was very much the worse for wear and could manage only one tipple before he was led away upstairs to sleep it off. Ten minutes later Heather arrived. I was surprised to see her, believing that tradition demanded that the happy couple spend the night before the big event apart.

"Where is he, Wal?"

"Up in his room, changing."

She joined me for a drink, but was growing increasingly agitated. Her irritation turned to anger when he hadn't appeared within half an hour.

"Where the hell is the man? He knows full well that we have a wedding rehearsal at seven thirty."

Rehearsal! He hadn't told me about any rehearsal. I rushed upstairs and dragged him down to face the music. Heather didn't spare the rod. A thoroughly chastened groom and his tiddly best man were rushed off to the church in the bride's car.

The run through for the big event turned out to be something of an ordeal. The bride and groom weren't talking, although the groom was so sloshed he didn't care much anyway and the best man was definitely the worse for drink. Fortunately for us, another rehearsal was overrunning and it gave us a little time to pull ourselves together a bit before the padre put us through our paces. As an Army padre he was probably conditioned to folks arriving in a drink-affected condition, although we must have been perilously close to the point where we ought to have been sent packing. He would certainly expect us to be in better shape next morning. Heather was still in the hump and she drove us back to the mess in silence. Then she left for her overnight accommodation. Bones and I took another drink to aid our recovery from the bride's vicious tongue and his father Sid joined us. We spent the evening in Aldershot, but by 2300 hrs, Sid had fallen asleep over his curry and both Bones and I were so full of Indian food and beer that we decided to retire for the evening. Tomorrow was going to be a long day.

I awoke early, desperate for a drink of water to reverse the effects of dehydration brought on by the combination of the previous night's beer and Johnny Gurkha's vicious vindaloo. By 0900 hrs Sid, the Boneman and myself were fit to be seen and we went into town for a decent breakfast, with masses of coffee and orange juice. A handful of Panadol apiece and by half ten, we were almost human. Kick off was at noon. We soldiers changed into our No.1 dress uniforms, Sid into his best whistle and we set off for the church. Bones was too nervous to drive; his blood alcohol would never have passed scrutiny anyway, and so I drove his Volkswagen to the famous Garrison church. My firm belief is that it's never too late to call off a wedding and as best man, I considered it my duty to attempt to talk the Boneman out of the folly he was about to commit. A hundred yards from the church, I stopped the car and made my supreme effort.

"Bones, do you want me to do you the biggest favour of your life?"

"What favour is that, mate?"

"Instead of turning right here, why don't we drive straight on? We'll all go to Southend and get pissed."

I'm still unsure why I suggested Southend as a destination; there are thousands of pubs and dozens of better places in-between Aldershot and the seaside resort.

"That's the best offer you'll ever get in your life my son," said Sid, awaking from the dead in the back seat.

"No, I've got to go through with it, mate," he replied, not convincing me fully that he was one hundred percent set on the idea.

In the event we turned right, parked in the car park and met the other guests. The two of us then marched into the church to await the inevitable. Heather was late, but the wait was worthwhile, she looked delightful. The service started well enough, but the Church of Ireland padre dropped a real clanger, right at the important bit.

"Dearly beloved, we are gathered here in the eyes of God to join this couple, Heather and Geoffrey in Holy…"

He only got as far as Holy, before a dozen voices corrected him.

"Steven!" they boomed in unison.

Red faced, he turned to me for help.

"Heather and Steven," I said quietly.

The padre carried on gamely, but he had been put off his stride. His performance after that was no better than average and he wisely declined an invitation to the reception. He would have been ribbed unmercifully had he put in an appearance.

From a professional perspective, my first year as a warrant officer in Hohne was a particularly good one. I had passed three courses with good grades, did all the extramural things that get you noticed and captained the cricket, soccer and squash sides that won the RMP championships. Most OC's would have given their eyeteeth to win any of those three sporting competitions; under my leadership we had landed the lot. So, a full year after arriving and with a very solid year's work behind me, the major called me in for my annual confidential report. This four-page document summed up your year's performance and future promotion is totally dependent on its content. I expected nothing less than an 'A' grade for my efforts and would accept nothing less. I sensed that there was mischief afoot when the OC insisted on reading the report to me, despite my assurances that as a former grammar school pupil, I was well capable of reading it for myself. It was a stinker and dealt with precious little other than the shenanigans that occurred during my first six weeks in the unit and was full of errors and misrepresentations.

Following his reading of the text, he declared, "And therefore I have awarded you ninety-three points and a 'C' grade."

It was a travesty of a report, the write up stank, the points awarded stank and so did the grade. To accept this document would be the kiss of death to any career aspirations.

"Well, thank you very fucking much," I said with venom. "I can see now why you insisted on reading it to me."

"What do you mean by that?" he enquired, as he passed the document over for me to initial.

A soldier is bound to initial his report, to confirm that he has read it and any subsequent arguments about content must be conducted in accordance with well defined Army regulations.

"Because if I had read it myself, I'd have done this to it," I said, tearing it into four pieces with a considerable flourish and throwing them at him.

"Rewrite!" I shouted and stormed out of his office, almost slamming his door off its hinges.

I then marched down to my office and tried to slam my door off its hinges, but it was a security door that was a foot thick and weighed a ton. The second-in-command appeared from across the corridor to ascertain the reason for my fury. Once I'd filled him in, he suggested that I take an early lunch. This dependable, experienced guy then set off towards the major's office for a word in his ear. I returned half an hour early from my lunch and went straight into my office for a sulk. There was a knock on the door and the major entered, carrying a yellow report.

"I've had a rethink, sergeant major. Perhaps I was a little harsh. Take a look at this report, will you?"

He handed me the freshly typed report. The write-up had improved dramatically, the grading was now 'B' and the points total had gone up by ten. I refused to initial this report and informed him that I would be submitting a redress of grievance against its content. He then went back to his office to sulk, but stuck to his guns and made a fight of the whole thing. Following some bitter words, my stubborn refusal to initial the document and his refusal to alter it, the matter landed on the desk of the colonel in HQ BAOR for his consideration. The colonel knew me well and was aware of my propensity to cut off my nose to spite my face. He knew that I wouldn't accept anything less than an 'A' grade and would fight to the bitter end so, as was his right in exceptional circumstances, he took his red pen, scratched out the 'B' and inserted a large, red 'A'. It was the only time in my career that I needed to resort to such drastic action over my annual report and although my method may have been a little unorthodox, it achieved its aim.

9

Major Wallace wasted no time in posting me to Fallingbostel when the detachment commander's position became vacant, and we seldom saw each other thereafter. It prevented any further nastiness between us, but best of all, it meant that exercises were now a thing of the past. You would have imagined that moving myself and my belongings from Hohne, situated on one side of the military ranges, to Fallingbostel on the other would have been a piece of cake. It wasn't. The Station Mess in which I was entitled to live in Fally was being renovated and until that work was completed, odds and sods like me were being accommodated by the REME. I went to see their RSM by way of courtesy. He refused point blank to have me in his mess, for the simple reason that he hated my RSM and would do no favours whatsoever for anyone in the RMP. I hated my RSM too, so that made us blood brothers, but it wasn't enough to win me a room at his place. Not being one to grovel to an Irishman in the REME, I called the Coldstream Guards, the Staffords and the Royal Hussars, to see if they had room at the inn for a house trained military police-man. They all claimed to be full. In the end I felt like a whore, prostituting myself around every mess in Fally looking for a place to lay my head. Having spent several nights back in Hohne and commuting to Fallingbostel each morning, the question of just who was responsible for my quartering still hadn't been resolved. As a single man who paid for his food and accommoda-tion, I was entitled to a room somewhere in Fallingbostel. I threw my problem at the Station Commander and went back to Hohne for yet another night.

Next morning he called me, to confirm that the REME would have to take me whether they liked it or not. On the way down to break the glad tidings to the REME RSM, I bumped into the RSM of the Royal Hussars. He had heard about the nonsense regarding my refugee status and offered me a place in his mess after all. It gave me great pleasure to tell the nasty Irishman that he could stuff his hospitality where a leprechaun stuffs its nuts.

I took over the responsibility for the detachment from a man who may well have been the most bungling sergeant major in the history of the Corps. Our handover should have lasted a week, but following the horrors that were disclosed during the first two days, on Wednesday morning I told him to sod off back to Mablethorpe. It appeared to me that the best course of action was to draw a red line under everything that he had done and start again, picking up the pieces as I went along.

He had been proud to show me a cache of weapons that he had secreted away in a locked cellar. It included knives, bayonets, machetes and pistols; all of which had been collected as either found or criminal property, but which had never been recorded anywhere. I had the lot cut up by the REME and thrown onto a scrap pile. He was equally proud of a fleet of eight bicycles that were hidden in the same cellar. These too were items of found property that hadn't quite made it into any ledger and which he actually hired out to people! They were taken down to the German lost property office at the first opportunity. Then, to my astonishment, I discovered that one of the unit's Landrover trailers was missing and that he was unable to recall when he had last seen it! Once he had departed, I ascertained that it had been returned to the Company HQ some two years previously, although he had never got around to processing the paperwork.

He donated his office fridge to me, along with a couple of dozen bottles of Dortmunder Union beer. It seems that his office had been the watering hole for the garrison warrant officers, many of whom had been in the habit of calling in for a beer most mornings. I sent the fridge and its contents down the corridor to the corporal's mess and gave my visitors a cup of coffee instead. The number of callers dropped off dramatically. His accounts were a shambles and he had never succeeded in balancing them. His *pièce de résistance*, though, was a room on the opposite side of the corridor to the offices. He kept the door of what he called the 'glory hole' securely locked and retained the key on his person. I was finally granted access on Wednesday morning, precisely thirty minutes before I told him to bugger off and leave the detachment. The glory hole contained hundreds of packing cases and cardboard boxes along with old rubber tyres, jerry cans, ropes, old machinery and other items that he imagined might come in useful one day. He was one of those people who never threw anything away. At the end of the thirty metre long room that had served as an indoor rifle range at some time, was what remained of the butts. That included so many tons of fine sand that it's a miracle the floor had never given way. I wondered how he had kept this disaster area from the prying eyes of inspecting officers and just how he had covered up such gross inefficiency for so long.

The detachment's staff sergeants had both remained loyal to this old buffoon, but were clearly delighted to see him on his way. They responded to my rather more positive way of going about things and we set about sorting the place out as quickly as possible. Most of the administrative horrors I could sort out myself, but the glory hole was left to the two platoon commanders. There was frantic activity in and around the place whenever I put my nose around the door. The dross was quickly disposed of until all that remained were several tons of fine sand. How do you dispose of several tons of sand from the second floor of an Army block? The three of us came up with a plan: instead of extra duties for defaulters; we would sentence them to remove a trailer full of sand.

The easiest method was to shovel the sand out of the window and into a trailer placed below, whereupon the stuff could be driven out to the ranges and dumped. I confess that I was heavy handed during this period and guilty of sentencing guys to remove a trailer load of sand on the flimsiest of pretexts. It still took weeks to complete the task and the boys soon became weary of sand. Finally, after returning from a weekend away, one of the staff sergeants took me into the room. It was empty. The boys, pissed off with shovelling sand, had voluntarily set about finishing off the job over the weekend. To show my appreciation, a considerable sum of cash was put behind the bar for free beer at the next social gathering.

Berlin won nearly all of the inter RMP sporting events over the years. It wasn't really surprising, since their unit was static, contained only the more experienced NCOs, and was twice the size of other companies. We had fought our way through to the final of the RMP Squash Team Championships and went up to Berlin to defend the trophy we had won by beating them the previous year. Our team of five travelled up by bus early in the morning and having negotiated the convoluted nonsense at the checkpoints on the way up the Berlin corridor, we arrived in time for lunch. Battle was set to commence at 1400 hrs and I met up with their skipper Tom Leeming, my old pal and sporting adversary, to agree our playing order. We had the best two players in BAOR at that time and so I was absolutely confident of taking the top two matches; it was lower down the order where we had a problem. Our female number three wasn't good enough for their third string and my other two guys weren't really up to winning their rubbers either. I would need to appeal to Tom's chauvinism and macho instinct if we were to retain the trophy. I apologised to the big bruiser for needing to field a woman and he agreed that I should play her at the bottom, where she and all women belonged. Tom was sensing victory, but he had merely fallen into my subtle trap. Paula Maynard would beat any number five, male or female, so by sacrificing our numbers three and four; we would win by three matches to two without a problem.

So confident of victory was the home side, though, that they arranged for the team photographs to be taken before the match. Berlin's team were pictured with the winner's trophies and us with the runners up prizes.

"So we don't look all sweaty and bedraggled," said their arrogant OC.

If ever a ploy was designed to undermine team confidence, then this was it. We considered this the ultimate insult and were more determined than ever to beat the bastards. Paula easily accounted for their number five; we then lost matches four and three, before I levelled matters with an easy win in the penultimate match. That left the deciding rubber to be played out between our number one and Tommy. He must have been suffering from delusions of grandeur to pick himself at number one and, although he gave it everything he had, he was taken to the cleaners. The photographer had to be summoned with haste, to take another set of photos. I really enjoyed the wait, although their major seemed to have lost all interest in the proceedings.

Our two-week summer camp was to be held in Mannheim, where we would be guests of the 95th US Military Police Regiment for the second consecutive year. I was reluctant to accept their offer following the previous year's debacle when they had promised the world, but when push came to shove they didn't deliver. Their help had been grudging, material support non-existent, and their hospitality half hearted. They allotted me sleeping quarters in a storeroom adjoining a classroom that, they assured me, would remain unused during my stay. On my first morning in the place I treated thirty USMP students, including several females, to a full frontal on my way through the classroom to the showers. That was a bad enough start and things just got worse from there on. Despite prior written permission, we were refused fuel at the service station, food in their cookhouse and access to the PX shopping complex. The Hispanic warrant officer in charge of discipline in the camp was no ally, either. This anti-British individual accused our guys of lewd and licentious behaviour following a perfectly harmless Zulu Warrior in the American Club. Then he accused us of showing disrespect to the Stars and Stripes, by failing to salute the flagpole at sundown; and then he had the gall to accuse us of chopping down an oak tree within his camp. That last charge was vigorously defended. My men would never chop down an oak, Britain's national tree. It was a sycamore!

Our OC, being a man with an unhealthy fascination for all things transatlantic, vetoed my idea of training elsewhere. So it was back to Mannheim for another fortnight of hamburgers, over easy eggs and watery beer.

Although subject to the Army Act like everyone else, the Guards can be a law unto themselves when it comes to crime and punishment. The RSM of the Coldstreams in Fallingbostel had precious little time for law books, Judges' Rules or rules of evidence, for he was king of his barracks and he liked his discipline to be swift and harsh. He simply didn't understand the requirement for evidence, or the fact that it took time to prepare a case.

The German police apprehended two Coldstream Guards corporals inside a guesthouse during the early hours of the morning. They had already broken open two gaming machines and were prising open the third when they were nabbed. As was the practice in such cases, they were handed over to the RMP, who would in turn hand them over to their own unit representative at the guardroom. In the sweetness of time the German police would produce statements of complaint, which would be translated into English and form the basis of the case against the culprits. Interviews would be arranged, statements obtained under caution and a case file prepared. This would then need to be translated back into German and the whole thing presented to the Police Advisor, who would decide whether the military or the German authorities would have jurisdiction. It is clearly a complicated and time consuming exercise and six weeks was considered a reasonable period of time for a case to come to a disciplinary hearing. The morning after the break-in at the guesthouse, I received a call from WO1 (RSM) Thick of the Coldstream Guards.

"Reference the break in last night, sergeant major, I'd like the report on my desk by 1000 hrs, so that I can have them weighed off by the CO," he explained.

"I'm afraid that's just not possible," I replied and attempted to explain why it would be in the region of six weeks before he would be able to proceed with the case.

"But they were caught on the premises, they must have done it," he pleaded.

"Yes, I know that sir, but there are procedures to follow and evidence to collect. Once our file is completed, I'll have it brought straight round to you," I explained, knowing full well that he wasn't interested in my reasoning, but only in clearing up his disciplinary case at the earliest opportunity.

"Bloody nonsense all this evidence rubbish. I could have them weighed off and in the guardroom by 1030 hrs," he grumbled as he put the phone down.

Next morning RSM Thick called again.

"Regarding the case of the two corporals who broke into the guesthouse, take your time with the report if you must. I had them weighed off by the CO this morning."

"Is that so, sir? Would you mind telling me what you used for evidence when you framed the charges against them?"

"Well, I went to bed last night and discussed the matter with the wife. We both agreed that they must have been pissed to do such a stupid thing, so I had them reduced to the ranks and gave them each twenty-eight days for drunkenness."

Outrageous! I really couldn't believe what he had just told me. Although the unit would probably have its knuckles rapped at a later date for bucking the system, RSM Thick had achieved his aim. Discipline that was rapid, guards like, but above all, swift.

Two guardsmen, who were tired of life in the Army, returned to barracks after a night on the town. The drink had served to stiffen their resolve that service with the colours was not really for them and that they wanted throwing out at all costs. Standing outside the guardroom, they drunkenly abused the soldiers on duty, until the sergeant of the guard was forced to intervene. To him they declared their desire to be arrested, charged and thrown out of the Army. The sergeant, being an experienced individual, gave them short shrift and threatened violence if they didn't vacate the area of his guardroom with all haste. Undeterred, the guardsmen marched off to the RMP duty room and abused the NCOs on duty there, casting doubt on the parentage of members of the RMP in general. The RMP sergeant that night was a former Rugby League professional. He weighed in at some twenty stone and was a man possessed of a very short fuse. The soldiers quickly achieved their aim to be arrested.

RSM Thick was delighted that I was able to produce the evidence by 1000 hrs next morning and was quite unable to comprehend why it wasn't possible in every case. Reports of incidents involving only soldiers and the RMP can, of course, be produced immediately, since no outside agencies are involved. He jailed his men for twenty-eight days, their period of confinement to be followed by their discharge from the Army. The following evening two more guardsmen who were equally keen to leave the battalion, and who considered twenty-eight days a small price to pay, decided on the same course of action. These soldiers too were sent packing when they started performing outside the guardroom and the obliging ex-Doncaster Rugby League RMP Sergeant was only too pleased to arrest them. Early next morning, I called RSM Thick to inform him of this latest occurrence. He was keen to have the men weighed off as usual, until I pointed out something that he was clearly overlooking.

"I think we may be setting a dangerous precedent here, sir," I said. "That's four guardsmen in two days. If you discharge all the men who pull this trick, you'll only have half a battalion by the end of the month." I wondered if he knew what the word precedent meant.

"Yes, yes, I see your point. You're quite right, of course. Do you happen to have the statements there?"

"Of course, would you like me to give you a précis?" I enquired and read the relevant portions of the statements of evidence to him.

"Now let me get this right. They want to leave the Guards, do they? And they don't mind doing twenty-eight days, don't they? Well, let me see now. Twenty-eight days, they can have that all right, but with regards to being discharged, I don't think so. I'll keep them in instead and subject them to certain inconveniences."

"As long as it's all done in accordance to the Judges' Rules, sir."

"Stuff your bloody rules," he said and slammed down the phone.

Another guardsman had been stopped by one of our patrols and it was established that he was driving his private car without a driving licence, insurance or registration document. My telephone rang at precisely 0900 hrs, as it always did when a guardsman was in trouble.

"Guards sergeant major here, sergeant major. About the driver without the necessary last night, can I have the report by 1000 hrs? I want to have him weighed off by the CO as quickly as possible."

"It's not quite as simple as that, sir. First a statement must be obtained from the licensing authority, to ensure that he doesn't in fact have a licence, then we must..."

"Don't tell, don't tell me, it's that bloody judge nonsense again, eh?"

"That's right sir, we must have evidence."

"Well, I don't think we need any evidence; this man has confessed to me that he has no documents. He has bloody well admitted it to me. What other evidence do you need?"

"He may well have admitted it to you, but what if he should tell the CO that he does have documents?"

"Tell the CO that he has? He wouldn't bloody well dare!"

With that the phone went dead. Once I had all the evidence the report was submitted, although I imagine that the soldier had been dealt with long before our file ever reached RSM Thick's desk.

There was something that didn't smell quite right about our OC's fawning admiration for the US Military Police Regiment down in Mannheim. Even more peculiar was the esteem, bordering on hero worship, in which he held the Commanding Officer of the American unit. Our company had already suffered two summer camps with the Yanks down in Mannheim and now he had arranged for a crowd of us to travel all the way down south, just to attend a parade to mark the departure of the Texan CO. The man was only a lieutenant colonel, for goodness sake, and sending twenty NCOs all that way just to march past a saluting dais, could hardly be considered a cost-effective undertaking. We arrived in the evening to discover that our efforts next day would be confined to marching twice around the outside of a grassed area and performing an 'eyes right' at the saluting dais on the second circuit. Even for a man as useless and disinterested in drill as me, that wouldn't be too difficult. We didn't have much to beat in any case. The other troops on the parade were sloppy Americans, scruffy Belgians and shuffling Germans from the Feldjaeger. Against that lot, we would look like the Brigade of Guards. We did a quick practice—just to make sure we knew left from right and the lads were confident that they could do it with their eyes closed. It was just as well that they felt they could do it with their eyes closed, because that's exactly what the majority of them did. After a night on the town, the buggers all turned up on time and smartly attired, but with each of them suffering from a gruesome hangover. Half of them were still drunk! Impressing upon them that a painful and certain death awaited anyone who let the side down, we formed up for the parade. I was convinced that someone would vomit before the fifteen-minute ceremony was over, but these guys were made of sterner stuff. I called them to attention and waited to hear a noise like cannon fire, but for once, they all came to attention together. Left turn, quick march, left-right-left-right. The boys were going well, especially since some of them were grey faced and all of them red eyed. On the second circuit we had to do the dreaded 'eyes right', a drill movement that is invariably cocked up, especially by the RMP. This time, though, the boys moved as one. I couldn't believe my eyes. The halt was followed by the fall out, whereupon there was a headlong rush for the toilets where the heroes of 111 performed an array of bodily functions. The colonel of the Americans sought me out in the mess after the parade and offered his congratulations on our performance.

"Command Sergeant Major," he said, getting my rank wrong once again, "Your men were sharp today, really sharp. Many congratulations."

I thanked him for his kind sentiments and assured him that the boys would be chuffed to hear his comments.

"But most of all Command Sergeant Major, you were sharp, so very sharp," he added.

Now that disappointed me. For years I had been the whipping boy of the parade square and I quite enjoyed being a sloppy soldier and drill illiterate. Now this clown was telling me that I was sharp. It was enough to confuse a lad.

There were few tears shed when Major Wallace departed for pastures new. His replacement was an officer whose enthusiasm for living in the field was as lukewarm as mine was and that pleased me considerably. Actually, I hadn't done an exercise for ages, not since the unit shipped me off across the ranges to Fally, but as the new TWO hadn't arrived yet, someone had to go out to show the new OC the ropes. The new major wasn't awfully proficient in the field if the truth were known: he was lousy at map reading and possessed an uncanny knack of turning the wrong way at junctions. Nevertheless, we did reach the exercise location.

We didn't see much of each other for the next week as he did the day shift, leaving me to suffer long nights of abject boredom. On the penultimate night shift I dropped the ultimate clanger and this brought the OC and me back into contact. In the wee small hours of the morning a restricted signal arrived at the RMP cell, requesting some grid references from our map. I carefully copied down the grids, translated them into code and sent them back to the originator of the signal. Now, whenever I sent a signal in the Army, I always copied the bumph regarding security classification from the incoming signal. That was because I didn't really understand security classifications properly and copying the effort of an expert had never let me down. This particular signal seemed to have been of so little consequence that I didn't even mention it to the OC when he took over from me at 0800 hrs. I rushed away to my sleeping bag. By the time I woke up, the rotten exercise would be eight hours nearer to its conclusion. There had scarcely been time for me to fall into a deep sleep, before the soft tones of the OC aroused me. The reason for him waking me registered before he had uttered a word. Guess who had sent 'top secret' information out on a signal marked only 'restricted'? My crime reached the ears of the Chief of Staff, who demanded my head on a silver platter. The bastard kept me waiting all day before he finally saw me. Then he delivered a bollocking that wouldn't have bothered a schoolgirl. God, how I hated exercises! Understandably, my new OC wasn't too impressed, but promised to say nothing about my howler provided I didn't divulge the truth about his map reading, or the fact that he didn't know how to put up a 9x9 tent.

There are more than a few folk in the Army who have expressed their reservations about the Army Medical Services. During a weekend soccer match I managed to land rather heavily on my head and despite a sluicing with the magic sponge, spent the remainder of the match in a concussed haze. The referee actually stopped the game midway through the second half, following my vicious tackle on one of my own teammates and had me taken to the medical centre. Following an initial examination, they shipped me off to the military hospital for an x-ray on my head and told me that bed was the best place for me for the next few days. With a headache of the severest proportions, I was only too willing to oblige. A week later I was given a message asking me to contact the Dental Centre at my earliest convenience. The message appeared a little odd, since I had just completed a course of dental treatment and wasn't due back in the dreaded chair for another six months. I called and spoke to the chief orthodontist.

"It's about the x-ray that you had taken recently at Hannover," he explained.

"That was an x-ray on my head, sir. Are the medics subcontracting brain surgery to the Dental Corps these days?"

"No! The x-ray was fine as far as your brain goes, no problems at all. They have passed them on to me because they reveal that you have two impacted wisdom teeth."

"Two impacted wisdom teeth that I've always been blithely unaware of, that don't hurt and are staying exactly where they are, thank you."

He was unable to coerce me into his chair. Years later, I had both of my bottom back molars removed and guess what? My wisdom teeth grew through to replace them.

You could never grumble about the amount of leave you got in the Army. This time I took a cruise liner out of Miami that called in at Cuba, Jamaica, the Cayman Islands and Mexico, before returning to its homeport. Cuba wasn't on the itinerary, but a passenger had a heart attack and needed to be put ashore with all haste. It gave me great joy to impart this snippet of information to the Intelligence Corps when I returned; they don't like people going to Cuba. A single cabin was beyond my budget and I needed to share with one Selwyn Goldblatt, a shy Jew, who was a stressed concrete expert back home in Cincinnati, Ohio. I certainly know how to pick them! He turned out to be a reasonable roommate in actual fact and he possessed a great sense of humour. By the time we reached Grand Cayman he had developed a stinking cold.

"Don't you dare give me that cold, Hebrew," I chided.

"Listen Gentile, I'm a Jew and I don't give away nothing for free. You want this cold, you gotta pay for it."

I thought it was funny anyway.

At mealtimes we were joined by a motley collection of individuals. There was Andrej, a Romanian Jew from Bucharest, his Hungarian grandparents, also Jewish, and Bernice, the all Illinois eating champion. She was Jewish too. I ate an awful lot of bagels on this trip. Andrej and I made it to the bar on the first night and pulled a couple of birds straight away. That was some achievement, really, since Andrej couldn't speak a word of English and we were blundering through in something like Yiddish. My lady was called Kitty Mercado and she hailed from Reno, Nevada. Kitty wasn't the retiring type and as soon as she had a couple of Jim Beams under her belt, she made her play.

"Where I come from we don't care much for marriage and divorce, nor for standing on ceremony. An introduction is enough for a couple to hit the sack. My name is Kitty," she announced.

Using my Sunday name, which I considered the right thing to do under the circumstances, I told her my name was Walter—and that was me fixed up for the rest of the trip. Grand Cayman was nice, as was San Antonio in Jamaica and Cozumel in Mexico too, until I went for lunch there. Pat Boone's song about Speedy Gonzales referred to tortillas and chilli peppers so, on my first visit to a Mexican restaurant, I ordered chicken tortillas, chilli peppers, chips and a beer. The first mouthful was so unbelievably hot that I drained my glass of beer in record time, before turning to attract the waiter's attention. He had obviously seen Gringos before, because he stood there with a second beer at the ready. His anticipation was much appreciated and he was tipped accordingly.

Back in Miami the trip operators offered me an extra couple of days in the hotel, provided I would agree to fly home at a later date. That gave me the opportunity to achieve two aims, to travel on a Greyhound bus and to visit Disneyworld. The theme park was a smashing place, but better was to come for me. On the way back to Miami an extra couple of passengers boarded the coach and I had to sit next to a cracking looking lady. Her name was Kirsten and she came from Narvik in Norway. Poor Kirsten had spent all her money, her plane had been delayed until the next evening and she was at her wit's end wondering where she would spend the night. How satisfying it was to be able to help a maiden in distress.

In the continued absence of a TWO, the job of organising the next annual summer camp fell upon the shoulders of Billy Muggins. I was responsible for all aspects of the camp, including the choice of venue. With regards to the venue, the only place that was definitely off the list was Mannheim, despite the USMPs invitation to spend a third consecutive year with them. It gave me great pleasure to phone the Yanks and tell them they could stuff their rotten accommodation and over easy fried eggs up their fannies, we were going somewhere else. (Come to think, it's no wonder they are such a mixed up bunch, referring to a backside as a fanny!)

Whilst serving with 115 Provost Company some years previously, we had enjoyed a splendid summer camp at the RMP ski hut down in Sonthofen. It was seldom used out of season and seemed an ideal location to me, especially as it would cost us nothing to stay there. At least it hadn't cost us anything when we went down with 115, although the fact that our RSM had been the ski hut custodian before coming to us may well have had something to do with that. With everything organised down to the last detail, come July we were ready to roll.

The long journey south was completed without a hitch, the training went well, the food was excellent and the weather superb. A couple of days before we set off back to Hohne, the OC took me to one side to congratulate me on a well-organised and smoothly run camp. On the final morning I saw the majority of the boys away and returned to the dining room to sort out the remaining administrative matters with the resident staff sergeant. I had a fistful of Deutschmarks to pay a few bills and once that had been resolved, the long drag back to Niedersachsen could begin. I coughed up for the bread, milk, electricity and laundry charges with pleasure; we had been looked after reasonably well. As I was about to shake the staff sergeant's hand and thank him for his efforts on our behalf, he gave a nervous cough and handed me a folded piece of paper. It was a bill for accommodation charges and amounted to many thousands of marks. His boss back in Duesseldorf had obviously seen the opportunity of making up some of the ski hut's financial deficit, by screwing us! We were members of the same Corps, for goodness sake, how could he do such a thing? Especially as he was my namesake! The new OC asked the one question I didn't want him to ask.

"Did you check previously to see if there would be any charge for accommodation?"

I hadn't. The question of being charged to stay in our own ski hut hadn't crossed my mind. Suddenly the OC wasn't so impressed with me any more, all my good work ruined at a stroke. We didn't have enough funds to pay the bill anyway and so the battle as to whether we paid or not was taken up when we arrived back in Hohne. Following some rather acrimonious exchanges between the OC and the captain in Duesseldorf, who had the ultimate responsibility for the rotten ski hut, the matter went to the Provost Marshal for arbitration. He decided upon a settlement that satisfied both parties and we made a donation to the Ski Hut Fund that worked out at fifty per cent of the original bill. I had left the unit by the time the next summer camp came around, but I rather fancy the company never returned to Sonthofen either.

By now, the mutual dislike that the RSM and I harboured for each other had developed into outright hatred. It was as well for both of us that twenty kilometres of ranges separated Hohne and Fallingbostel, otherwise there might have easily been more than words exchanged. He was determined to demonstrate his authority over me, but failed dismally in the attempt. This man was inferior to me in every aspect except rank and he knew it. Aware that trying to catch me out was a futile gesture, he now resorted to bullying my staff sergeants in an attempt to score points over me. With only a few weeks left to serve in this rotten unit, he would need to look sharp if he wanted to register a much-desired victory over me.

He made his last attempt one Thursday afternoon, the day when the company's six platoon commanders were required to meet the RSM and the police office staff to discuss outstanding police reports. This week it was the turn of my staff sergeants to be the first to bare their souls at the conference. I called the RSM to ask if they might be allowed to go into bat last, as the three of us were attending a working lunch at Fally that might conceivably run on a little. Because of an upsurge in crime committed by the resident infantry battalions, I had arranged a get-together of the military police management, local police and infantry warrant officers, to discuss the problem over egg and chips and a bottle of Vimto. It seemed an eminently sensible course of action to me and the Garrison Commander later commended me on my forethought. The RSM would have none of it. Despite the fact that is accepted that Army lunches invariably go on longer than scheduled, he would not allow the two staff sergeants permission to arrive any later than 1400 hrs, the time the conference was scheduled to begin. Needless to say, they were late and the RSM blew his top with them when they finally arrived. I didn't see them again that night and next morning I left early for a meeting at the Divisional HQ in Verden. Two very forlorn platoon commanders met me on my return to the detachment. During the course of that Friday morning, the RSM had ordered them to parade at the Company HQ, where they were charged with disobeying a direct order and marched in front of the OC. They had both been found guilty and given a severe reprimand. That was outrageous! If anyone was to have been charged, then it should have been me. These men, by following my orders, had been given a punishment that would prevent them from ever receiving their LS & GC medals! I was furious and called the RSM's number. There was no reply. It was 1500 hrs by now, so I still had time to make it across to Hohne and have it out with the bastard before he slithered away to his quarter for the weekend. I drove over, determined to close the door on the Scottish deviate and punch his lights out. He was a more devious character than I imagined, though—the dirty bastard had returned to the UK for a fortnight! By the time he returned, I would be posted. The sly swine! Seething with anger, I picked up a leave pass from the orderly room, filled it in effective from after duties that day and stormed into the OC's office.

"Sign that!" I demanded.

"Hello sergeant major. Problem?"

"Problems, actually, sir. Firstly, I have lost confidence in you as an Officer Commanding and, secondly, I believe that your RSM is in need of psychiatric help. I am leaving this unit today. Please sign my leave pass."

"But you aren't due to leave for another two weeks."

"My replacement doesn't arrive for another month, so there will be a period without a warrant officer in any case. My stand-in has already been nominated by me and agreed by you. He would be taking over in the interim in any case, so he can assume command today instead. Following your disgusting treatment of my two staff sergeants today, I just want to get out of your bloody rotten unit. Just sign this and let me go."

"Please sit down, sergeant major, and let's discuss things," said the mild mannered major.

I did sit down and we discussed many things that needed redressing in the company. He was clearly surprised by some of my revelations. He signed my leave pass and I returned to Fally, packed my kit, handed over and left first thing the next morning, still spitting blood.

For me, the real measure of this RSM had been revealed when he summoned me to his quarter one evening. His ginger haired son answered the door and without asking me inside, called his father.

"Ah Wally," he said, "I've been instructed to tell you that your father's dead. Let me know if you want to go on leave."

The message delivered, he closed the door on me. I'd like to think that my handling of such a delicate matter would have been performed with rather more humanity.

Having left 111 in the huff a couple of weeks early, I now had time on my hands before I was due to report to Northern Ireland for my next tour. An aunt was staying with my mum, so I took a train down to London and boarded a bus at Victoria Coach Station. It was going to the south of Spain. Algerciras sounded like a good place to visit, especially because of its close proximity to Gibraltar. The border had just re-opened after years of negotiation and I fancied a couple of days on the Rock. That idea was soon torpedoed, however, as the border crossing was open for indigenous Gibraltarians only; tourists like me still had to journey via Tangier. Following a miserable sixty-hour journey through France and Spain, I alighted in the ugly town of Algerciras and booked into the nearest hotel. It was very much out of season and the management appeared happy to welcome a customer. My bedroom window gave a great view of the rock and I vowed to make a trip to the British bit of Spain, my number one holiday objective. My plans were postponed for twenty-four hours, following an arm bending session with the odd couple that occupied the room above mine. They were a rare pair, whose lifestyle was dedicated to travelling the world and drinking themselves into an early grave. By the third morning of my holiday I was clear headed and set off for Gibraltar, via Tangier. Arriving around lunchtime, I made my way to the RMP Detachment to visit the warrant officer in charge, but missed him by a whisker. According to his local clerk, he would be down in the Fortress Mess. A narrow corridor off the main road led to the mess foyer and it was as I was walking down that corridor that I heard footsteps that were instantly recognisable. Impossible as it seemed, those were the unmistakable footsteps of my former wife. By the time I reached the foyer, she was standing there. For the first time in my life, I was struck dumb.

How long had it been? What had made me visit the mess on this particular day? Was that Mantovani's orchestra I could hear playing in the background? Or that of his wife, Womantovani? Perhaps divine providence had conspired to bring us back together again? Then she opened her big mouth.

"What the hell are you doing here?" she enquired, in her grating Scots accent.

"I'm on my holidays, and you?"

"I'm the PA to the Governor."

She quickly put paid to my suggestion that we ought to go somewhere cosy for a meal and a chat.

"I have someone waiting for me upstairs," she announced.

At the top of the stairs stood a geezer in Royal Navy attire. It was her beau.

"Hello Catherine," said another Jock accent.

"Hello Alistair," she replied, fluttering her eyelashes.

I left them to it, found my chum and together we attempted the mess record for drinking Heineken at lunchtime. It was too much to hope that Alistair might come over for a chat. He had the good sense to keep his distance, having undoubtedly been warned about my temper by my former spouse. Given the frame of mind I was in, he would have finished up flying through the window if he had taken me to task. She came over as she was leaving, to say her final goodbyes and any hopes that I may have harboured regarding reconciliation went out of the door with her. What a strange series of events just the same! A chance trip to the south of Spain, the selection of that particular day to go to Gibraltar, the fact that my mate should already have left his office, that he should have gone to the mess and that she should happen to be there. It surely transcended the realms of probability.

Drinking beer proved such a time-consuming business that I didn't even take the mandatory trip up the Rock before catching the hydrofoil back to Tangiers. I wonder if she ever married Alistair? From my brief meeting with him he appeared to be eminently suitable for her—weedy and subservient.

So it was back to Leicester, a couple of weeks of doing nothing in particular and off to my next posting in Northern Ireland.

10

I had left Northern Ireland in 1976, convinced that the whole sorry affair would be over long before I was required to return for another tour. Seven years had elapsed, things hadn't improved and now the Province was beckoning me back. Reading through the *Newsletter* newspaper on my first morning in the mess, I was struck by the fact that the content was exactly the same as it had been seven years previously—only the date was different. There were still an abundance of murders, bombings and maiming. Outrages were still being condemned by the politicians as barbaric and by the church leaders as crimes against God and humanity. Leaders of both sides were still spouting bigoted rhetoric and spitting hatred of anything decent. Nothing had changed. Distillery were still bottom of the Irish League—nothing had changed at all.

The fact that I was back in Northern Ireland was rammed home to me on my first Sunday morning back in the place, at Seymour Street Methodist Church of all places. For what are probably understandable reasons, I was treated with suspicion when I entered the church that morning. The congregation's welcome was non-existent and I was even moved on from the first two pews I tried to park my bottom in. 'Tommy Curry sits there' and 'That's been Davie Thompson's seat these past forty years' being the reasons for my summary ejection. Sensing my embarrassment, a rather friendlier old gentleman directed me to an empty area.

"You can sit there in Owen Cartwright's pew if you want. He's dead."

Despite thinking of the late Mr Cartwright throughout the service, it was a pleasant hour and I resolved to come again, until several burly members of the choir waylaid me in the church car park on the way out. They demanded every personal detail with the exception of my hat size. It's a crying shame that the situation was so desperate in Northern Ireland that the appearance of a new face in a place of worship necessitates a grilling by the tenors and baritones.

I wasn't wildly enthusiastic about returning to Ulster but at least this time I would be sitting in an office, shining the seat of my pants. The younger element could do the running around up and down the Falls and the Shankhill. Although there was a designated RMP sergeant's mess in Lisburn, my particular appointment made me a member of the HQ staff and entitled me to live in the rather more grandly appointed Garrison Mess. The only other RMP member was the WO1 Staff Assistant, who was to become a good pal during my stay in the Province. He worked in the HQ building across the road from me and appeared to do very little, apart from framing pictures for a fee and playing me at squash. A year later, I took over his job on promotion and discovered that my assumption had been correct. He did precisely nothing.

My job was to investigate complaints against the British Forces, hardly a job that I would have wished to undertake given the choice. The department was commanded by a major who had seen decades of service and was merely ticking off the days to his retirement. His staff consisted of a warrant officer, who was also leaving the Army and who had not put pen to paper for many months, and a female corporal, who did all that was necessary to keep the show on the road. As soon as I arrived on the scene the warrant officer disappeared, the female was promoted and posted and the major took to propping up the bar in the officer's mess.

It was several months before the new major arrived, whereupon we started to put the department in order. By the end of the year, we had an organisation that functioned effectively. Major Paddy Hurley and the Legal Process Office could hold its head up in any company. We were inundated with complaints and claims against the Forces, all of which needed to be investigated. In some cases there were grounds for complaint and compensation, but the majority of the stuff was spurious nonsense. Some of the complaints were bordering on the bizarre.

During the early days of the troubles, a showband was returning to the south of Ireland following a gig in Londonderry, and the border crossing point that Liam O'Casey and his Sons of Shamrock selected to use early that morning was manned by soldiers from a Scottish infantry battalion. Having performed well, the musicians were in good heart and all that the tired entertainers needed to do now was negotiate the crossing point and it was home to bed. Their minibus, which was chock-a-block with musicians and instruments, was signalled to halt by the corporal in charge of the checkpoint.

"Who are you lot?" he demanded.

"O'Casey's Showband sir, we're just coming back from a ceilidh in Derry."

"Is that anywhere near Londonderry?" asked the corporal.

There was no reply.

"Everybody oot o' yon van!" snapped the Scots corporal.

"But sir, the lads are all asleep and it's very late."

"Everybody oot!" the corporal repeated, leaving O'Casey in no doubt.

The strolling players emerged sleepily from the minibus and were subjected to body searches. This was a part of everyday life in Ulster.

"Noo get your gear oot o' the van. All of it," was the next order.

"But it took us hours to pack it."

"Couldn'ae gie a shite. Get it oot."

Realising that argument was futile, O'Casey supervised the unpacking of the instruments and electrical gear and the soldiers made a search. There were no arms, ammunition or explosives on this occasion.

"Now open up your instrument cases."

"But there's nothing in them but instruments; your men have just searched them all, for the love of Mary."

"Open them up again anyway."

The members of the band opened up the cases for the personal inspection of the Scottish corporal.

"Right there the noo, get every man to pick up his individual instrument."

They complied.

"Now, gie the lads a tune."

O'Casey considered the corporal's actions to be rather less humorous than did the platoon of Jocks and he made a complaint on behalf of himself and the Sons of Shamrock. They were awarded compensation for their inconvenience and received a sum that amounted to rather more than the fee they had picked up in Londonderry.

A fat lady from Andersonstown claimed compensation for loss of dignity at the hands of the same battalion. This old cow was a known baddie and she had been arrested, not for the first time, for terrorist related offences. At Castlereagh Police Station she was subjected to the usual screening process, which included being weighed. Unfortunately, the scales in the police station only went round as far as twenty stones before the needle hit a plastic stopper. It was obvious that this particular lady would need a weighbridge rather than bathroom scales to ascertain her fighting weight. The boys all gathered round as she stepped on and they roared with laughter when the needle stuck at the top. Her feelings were so badly hurt that she needed the sum of three hundred pounds to make her feel better again. That was, as near as damn it, one-pound Sterling for every pound of her weight. This was a case so frivolous that we fought it with some vim. To our satisfaction, the plaintive withdrew the claim before it reached the ears of the magistrates.

Then there was the farmer from Fermanagh. He maintained that one of his prize dairy herd had aborted a calf when an RAF jet broke through the sound barrier whilst passing over his farm in the middle of the night. Since he admitted that he was in bed at the time, he had difficulty in proving it was one of ours, especially since they never flew anywhere near the area. We chalked up a win there too.

At 0200 hrs one chilly morning, a known criminal was stopped by an infantry patrol as he was returning home to the Ardoyne. The soldiers then carried out a 'personnel check' on him, a standard operating procedure. The 'P' check didn't hurt, it didn't cost anything, and the subject was usually on his way after ten minutes. This felon didn't object to being stopped; the soldiers were friendly and even gave him a cigarette. What formed the basis of his complaint was that the soldiers, allegedly aware that he was in possession of a Chinese carry out, held him longer than they ought at the roadside, just to ensure that his food went cold. This was the sort of crap that we were supposed to take seriously and wasted our time investigating.

The amazing thing about these politically inspired complaints was the fact that they were invariably witnessed. If you believed the complainants, then every person ever hit by a rubber bullet in Belfast was an innocent bystander. Furthermore, they could produce witnesses that invariably included a lawyer specialising in personal injury claims, a couple of priests and a flock of passing nuns. The more antisocial the hour, the thicker the number of clerics on the ground!

Major Paddy wasn't the easiest man in the world to work for. He was a vile tempered old buffer and he was known to take a drop of the hard stuff whenever he saw fit. He was also a man whose mood was difficult to assess. A comment that he considered rib tickling funny one day could cause him to propel an ashtray in your direction twenty-four hours later. For all his foibles, however, he was a true gentleman, generous to a fault and blessed with a most wicked sense of humour. Most of all, I admired him for his brilliant penmanship. He was a wordsmith of the highest calibre and his ability to sweet talk people was simply world class. Not only could Major Paddy charm the birds down from the trees, he could sell them an insurance policy whilst he was doing so. I recall the occasion when an MOD manpower cutting team descended on the Regiment and left gloom and despondency all around, except in the Legal Process Office, that is. Silver-tongued Paddy managed to convince them that a manpower increase was imperative if our department was to function to the best effect. What a player!

It was the twelfth of July and I wasn't talking to him. He had been in one of his awkward moods the day before and owed me an apology.

"Shall we take a drive down to Belfast and watch the parade?" he enquired, shouting through from his office.

"No thank you, sir. If I do decide to go, I shall go on my own."

"What the Hell's the matter with you then?" he asked, walking into my office and appearing truly taken aback at my rejection of his offer.

"I'm pissed off with you and your bad temper, that's what's wrong with me."

The previous day, a report compiled by one of the corporals had failed to meet the standard he demanded and, because there had been no corporals around to berate, I had been the whipping boy.

"Jesus, is that all? Come on, I'll drive," he replied with a smile.

That was the nearest thing to an apology that you were ever likely to get out of Paddy, so we went to Belfast. We parked the car and walked over to take up a good vantage point in Royal Avenue. From here we could watch all the 'Kick the Pope' bands playing their flutes and drums as they marched along to the 'Field', upsetting the opposition mightily as they did so. As soldiers in Belfast, one was always aware of the fact that we stuck out like a sore thumbs. This time Paddy and I were even easier to spot than usual, since we were the only people in the whole of Royal Avenue dressed in suits. It was a baking hot day and everyone was in casual attire, with the exception of the two blokes dressed in blue pinstripes, striped shirts and RMP Corps ties. We may just as well have been in service dress and waving the Union Jack. The fact that we were attired conspicuously was really brought home when a passing police superintendent saluted us.

"Do you think we might just stand out a bit in this garb, sergeant major?"

"Just a touch, sir."

"Right. It's time for remedial action. We'll change our strategy and adopt a more casual approach. Sergeant major, take your tie off."

Once a month, each member of our office was allowed a long weekend back on the mainland. We were free from the finish of duties on Thursday evening, until the start of work the next Tuesday morning. It certainly kept me sane and my monthly trip home to Leicester was sacrosanct. My fabled fear of flying meant that I usually drove from Lisburn to Larne, took the ferry over to Stranraer and then drove the three hundred or so miles down to home. It was a balls aching trip, but worth the effort to escape Northern Ireland for a few days. In preparation for his imminent retirement, Major Paddy had bought a house at Broughton Astley in Leicestershire, despite the fact that neither he nor his wife had any connections with the county. During the course of the previous weekend, he had made a round trip from Lisburn to Leicester and had found the experience a bit much. This weekend was my turn and I appeared on Thursday morning dressed in civvies, in readiness for a Le Mans-style getaway after work.

"Would it be your long weekend then, sergeant major?"

"It is indeed, sir, to be sure, to be sure," I replied, mocking him slightly.

That was something only to be done if you were departing for a few days, for fear of him devising a way of repaying your impertinence. I was on safe ground, given that I was going away for four days; his memory span was only twenty-four hours at the outside.

"What time is your boat?" he asked, as he did every month.

He could never quite grasp exactly what a long weekend meant, since he was a law unto himself and came and went as he pleased.

"It leaves at 1900 hrs sir."

"Is there not an earlier sailing than that?"

"Well yes, there is, but that's at 1100 hrs this morning."

"Away and catch it then. It's bloody miles to Leicester, you know?"

"Yes, I do know how far it is sir. Thank you, I'm on my way."

"Think nothing of it. Hell, it's miles to Leicester."

I was almost out of the door.

"And when will you be back?" he asked, unable presumably to calculate how many days there were in ninety-six hours.

"On Tuesday morning as usual, sir."

"Agh! That's too soon. Leicester is too far to drive for a miserable couple of days. I should know. I've driven it. Can you make it back for Thursday morning?"

"Well yes, of course I can. Thank you very much, sir."

This time I'd actually turned the corner before Paddy called me back. Obviously he had changed his mind; his offer was too generous anyway.

"Did I say come back for Thursday morning, sergeant major?"

"You did sir," said I, resigned for the worst.

"Jesus, the week's all but over on a Thursday, hardly worth all the rush. Come back a week on Monday."

I could hardly believe my luck and not being one to look a gift horse in the mouth, I was half way down the corridor before Paddy could speak again. This time he wasn't talking to me, but addressing the rest of the staff in the office.

"It's miles to Leicester," he said. "And I should know, I've driven it."

My job in the LPO was hardly stimulating and my presence was barely necessary most of the time. Major Paddy was able to convince those in high places that we were performing a job of national importance and, apart from him and me, no bugger had a clue what we did anyway. Paddy's job didn't get in the way of his socialising at the bar, or his preparation for the big move into Civvy Street and mine didn't stop me socialising and playing sport. Only once was my presence ever missed and that was by one of the thrusting young captains from the HQ who, strictly speaking, was my boss whenever Paddy was over in England. It was the morning of the start of the first Ashes test and what better way to pass a morning than taking in the few overs on the TV? Returning to the office shortly before lunch, my corporal informed me that Captain Fantastic had telephoned and wished to talk with me urgently. I returned his call and was subjected to a fusillade of insults.

"Where were you when I called?"

"In my room in the mess."

"And what the Hell where you doing in the mess during office hours?"

"As one of this nation's haemorrhoid sufferers, I was washing a certain part of my anatomy prior to shoving a suppository into the same orifice. Once it was up my arse, I lay down for a sufficient period to allow the medication to act upon the affected area, before readjusting my dress; squeezing the cheeks of my arse together and walking slowly back to the office. Do you require any further details, sir?"

"I'm really awfully sorry Mr Payne. I wonder if you would be gracious enough to check up on the details of a case for me, please?"

The old haemorrhoid ruse—it works every time! I made sure Paddy knew all about the incident upon his return. He didn't allow anyone to discipline his charges; that was his preserve. He went straight over to the HQ to take on the young captain and the snotty nosed little infantryman never bothered me again.

Our set-up had a command structure of just three. The major was in command, with me in charge of the LPO and Roger Gammie running the Court's Witness section. Roger was an unusual character, loved only by his wife and dog and disliked by a good many people. He belonged to the old school of RSM, a dying breed, who would lay down the law by the book and accept no deviation. His men hated the sight of him and, unfortunately for him, Paddy wasn't enamoured with him either. He managed to impress those that mattered in the HQ just the same, those people he only saw for a couple of minutes each day. He was most proficient at saying "Good Morning sir" in a fashion subservient enough to please the General and, to Paddy's absolute horror, he was told to write the man up for a MBE. When the General asks, the rest comply and on the next New Year's Honours List, there was the name Roger Gammie MBE. That award made him fairly unique in RMP circles, probably in Army circles too, come to that. Here was a warrant officer, who had both the BEM and the MBE, and yet had been refused his LS & GC because of some minor crime committed years previously.

Roger's primary claim to fame was the fact that he could outdo both Mrs Mallaprop and the Reverend Spooner when it came to desecrating the English language. His mistakes amused Paddy so much that the Irishman occasionally turned purple with mirth when Gammie was on the phone. I recall hearing Roger urging one of his men to be more careful when writing a statement of evidence.

"It's all right here in the office corporal, but what happens when you get into the cool, clear light of the courtroom?" he asked.

At Dungannon Court, he once told a group of soldiers who were waiting to give evidence that they weren't required for an hour and that, in the meantime, they might "wish to miranda over to the coffee shop".

One of his corporals was querying the less than glowing annual report that Roger had written about him. He embarked on a lengthy monologue in an attempt to justify the fact that he had marked the individual down and finished with a sentence that he imagined summarised his verbal outpouring.

"You're a good solid cake corporal, but there's no icing," he said.

Later he confided that the corporal had no grounds for complaint.

"I had him over a cleft stick, you see."

It was a pity that he was never commissioned; he would have gone down a treat in the officer's mess.

A former Scots Guards warrant officer, a man who had found the transition from the guards to the real world difficult, was president of our mess. He maintained his guard's style, authoritarian air whilst striding around the place and was guilty of bullying those weak enough to be dominated. This hard line approach was impossible to sustain, however—certainly not in a mess full of clerks, drivers and assorted odds and sods that had long since forgotten the meaning of military discipline. Mad Jock didn't like many people and had a particular dislike for military policemen. His real loathing, though, was reserved for those of us born south of the River Tweed, the majority of mess members as it transpired.

In view of Mad Jock's sworn hatred of Sassenachs, it was a mystery as to how so many of us came to be seated at the Burns Supper Night. Perhaps the chef had over ordered on the haggis? Resplendent in his clan tartan, he sat proudly at the head of the table as the evening's festivities progressed. The welcome, toasts, recitations and even the playing of the pipes were all of the highest order. Mind you, the piping ought to have been good, as the piper was no less a personage than the current world champion, a personal friend of Mad Jock. His performance waned towards the end of the evening just the same, as the whisky began to effect his drone. Even world champions can get pissed. We all drank lots of whisky, the only beverage allowed, someone stabbed the haggis and spoke in medieval lowland Scots and then we all drank some more whisky. As the evening was drawing to a close, Mad Jock rose to his feet, a touch unsteadily it must be said. He demanded hush and addressed the congregation.

"Gentlemen and Englishmen! Before we repair to the bar to continue the motion, we'll hae a few songs and recitations. Aroond the table, anti-clockwise, starting wi' you, Hamish."

As a fellow Scots guardsman, Hamish sprang automatically to his feet and burst forth with 'Flower of Scotland'. He received rapturous applause for his performance.

"Brilliant, big man," said Mad Jock. "Now Alexander, what will ye gie us?"

Alexander was a Rabbie Burns aficionado and he gave us the 'wee sleekit, timorous beastie' thing, which was equally well received. Further songs from Jock, Billy, another Jock and finally Bannockburn Bobby were all rendered in that slow, ponderous, dramatic style, so beloved of Scots in drink. On the express orders of Mad Jock, we Englishmen were not permitted to sing or recite. As our turn arrived, we merely bowed our heads with shame and contemplated the fact that our mothers had chosen to bear us south of the border. With all the participants having completed their efforts, the president made one final offer to the floor. Anyone, regardless of nationality, who had not sung or recited, could now do so before we went into the bar. Sid stood up. He would have been wiser to remain seated.

Sid Khan was a humorous Pakistani Ordnance Corps sergeant whose English was nigh on perfect, although he delighted in playing the part of the subservient sort from the subcontinent.

"What the hell do you want Khan? In fact, what the hell are you doing at a Burns Supper Night? You're not Scots, you're not even English—you're a bloody Paki."

"To answer your questions in the order in which you are honourably asking them, Sahib. I would like to make a recitation, I am here to enjoy your renowned Scottish hospitality and I must disagree, for I am a British passport holder you see."

"Don't bloody well get cocky with me Khan. Is your recitation Scottish?"

"I cannot vouch for its country of origin honourable Sahib, but it's a jolly little ditty, taught to me by my five-year-old daughter. I think that you have seen my daughter Sahib, she is starring in this year's infant school pantomime and she is…"

"For Christ's sake, get on with it Khan and it had better be good."

"But RSM Sahib, I am a Moslem. Should you not have said for Allah's sake?"

"Get on with it Khan," he replied, shaking a fist in Sid's direction.

In a highly affected Indian accent, Sid recited the poem taught to him by his precious daughter.

"Twinkle, twinkle little star, how I am wondering what you are."

He never got any further. Mad Jock went crimson and ordered that Sid be locked away for the night. With so many fervent Scots on hand, the plucky Paki had no option but to accede to being led away to spend the rest of the night in the jail.

It was a good mess to live in. Everyone was in the same boat, bored to tears with our jobs and counting off the days to our next postings. That's not absolutely true—the bomb disposal wallahs weren't counting off the days; those silly sods actually *liked* the place. Nothing thrilled them more than to be called out to deal with an explosive device, even when they were half way through their dinners. Funny people!

Our chef was a star and should really have been working at the Savoy. Our food was *cordon bleu* stuff and this was the only place in the Army where I saw *lobster thermador* on the lunch menu.

The mess manager appeared to be a decent sort too, right up to the time that he absconded with all the takings.

The WRAC girls that lived in the place were a particularly poor looking bunch. That was the reason they were in the Army in the first place, of course—at least they had some chance of finding a bloke, considering they were outnumbered thirty-to-one by the males of the species. If you wanted a decent looking bird, however, then you had to chance your arm and journey down to Lisburn or Belfast. I had my work cut out keeping a female ACC cook at arm's length. She was a pleasant enough person to talk to, but one of those you couldn't fancy bedding if your life depended upon it. It was the crack around the bar that kept many of us sane and I'm grateful to all the other lost souls who kept me company in that wretched part of the country.

The RMP had a decent cricket side and we had been good enough to win the Belfast division of the Army Northern Ireland cricket league. Perhaps two or three of our team were of genuine Army standard and the rest of us could do a bit on our day. The final of the NI championship brought us up against the Cheshire Regiment, the winners of the other division. The side representing the 22nd of Foot was packed with Combined Services and Army players and included one officer who had played at county level before joining the Army. If Ladbrokes had been required to make a book on the outcome of the final, then the Cheshire's would have been red-hot favourites and the RMP long odds outsiders. It was impossible not to be impressed by our opponents' turnout that day in Lisburn—they were all attired identically, with the Roman numerals for twenty-two emblazoned on the smart sweaters. We, on the other hand, looked shabby by comparison. We could all boast a pair of flannels and a white or whitish shirt, although our twelfth man looked less than elegant in his jeans and Castlemain XXXX sweatshirt.

They won the toss and elected to bat, the standard ploy in Army limited over cricket. Their openers looked as if they would be in for the day and they scored steadily from the first few overs, but once our opening bowlers found their length, runs became harder to come by. It turned out to be one of those great days for us as the fielding side; every catch was taken, every shot fielded smartly, and the bowlers found their best form. The mighty 22nd were humbled and returned to the pavilion with just seventy-eight runs on the scoreboard. Even with the reputation of their quick men, this wasn't much of a total to better. Our opening batsmen didn't give their bowlers a chance of keeping the run rate down, as they smashed their way to fifty before the first wicket fell. With only two runs needed to secure a famous victory and with six wickets still in hand, our skipper generously allowed himself to be bowled out, thus affording me the honour of marching out to strike the winning runs. I stunned the crowd by playing two consecutive defensive shots, something not seen from me for many seasons, before reverting to my normal 'hit out or get out' style and putting the ball back over the bowler's head for a match winning four. The Cheshire's may have looked the part, but were found wanting on the day. It was their first defeat for two seasons and it couldn't have come at a better time.

It's often said that one man doesn't make a team, but Harry Furness did. Harry was a good hockey player, although he wasn't much good at anything else, as I recall. Dismayed to see the RMP hockey side propping up the league when he first arrived in the Province, and without a single point at that, he vowed that things would change the following season. Hockey really wasn't my game and although I was willing to support the side, I really had no intention of taking up the sport. By the time the new season began, Harry had convinced me that somewhere inside me lurked a hockey goalkeeper, simply waiting to be let out. They were seriously short in this department and absolutely no one volunteers to be a hockey goalkeeper—unless he is mentally unhinged, that is

"All you have to do is kick anything that comes into the area and I'm talking ball, player, referee or spectator. I've watched you playing soccer over the years—you're perfectly suited for the job," Harry assured me.

So that was how, at the age of forty something, I made my hockey debut. It wasn't an auspicious start; we lost the first match 3-0 and I was responsible for all three goals. The team grew stronger under Furness' leadership, however, and my performances improved beyond recognition. The finer points of the game were lost on me, of course, and I simply kicked anything that came into the semicircle, as coach had instructed. Up to the last match of the season, by which time we were up amongst the top teams in the league, we had conceded only a handful of goals. There was even talk about me representing the Army team, but I declined the offer. The climax of the season was a match at Londonderry where we took on the Queens. They were already champions and had won every single fixture in a long season. It turned out to be a hopelessly one-sided game, although we hung on until the dying moments without conceding a goal. With the referee poised to blow his whistle and bring the game to an end, their star player decided to show his pedigree. He beat four of our players, rounded me and was just about to score, when I lashed his legs away with my stick and fell on him to make sure he didn't put the ball into the net. The referee blew a loud blast on his whistle and raced in to sort out the mêlée. I was ready to accept my marching orders; it had been a diabolical foul, after all. To the astonishment of all the players, especially the aggrieved officer, the referee waved a card at him and awarded us a free hit! We hung on to steal a fortuitous goalless draw. That was the end of the season for the RMP side and the end of my hockey career. It had been fun.

Major Paddy was well aware that my next annual report was a crucial one. Unless I had a strong recommendation for promotion to WO1 this time, I would be barred by age from being promoted the following year. Every time I broached the subject of my report, he would merely wink at me.

"Rest assured, my dear fellow, rest assured," he would say.

He returned from a few days back in Leicester and called me into his office.

"Cast your eyes over that," he said, sliding the all-important yellow form over the desk in my direction. "I should point out that regulations forbid me giving you more than three points out of five for instructional ability because you aren't at the Training Centre, but you'll see that I've given you full marks for everything else," he added.

The old bugger had given me the highest possible marks and a write-up that qualified me to sit alongside the Archangel Gabriel. I was promoted very shortly afterwards and nominated to move over the road into the HQ building, where I would take up the position of Staff Assistant.

11

Before moving over to the HQ, I went on leave. The next stamp in my passport was to be Indian and it was thumped in at Delhi airport at some objectionable hour of a June morning. It was already unbearably hot. A long queue had developed in the arrival hall, despite the fact that it was only four o'clock in the morning. After twenty minutes our queue had inched forward a full yard and a policeman arrived to sort things out, by moving us all into a different channel. The queue may have been a different one, but the speed at which it progressed forward wasn't. Ten minutes later the policeman reappeared and, amidst much mumbling and grumbling, he moved us back to the original channel. Tired and cheesed off after a long flight in economy, I let rip with a few choice Anglo-Saxon phrases. The only person who could have overheard me was the young lady standing immediately in front of me and since she was clutching a green German passport, I presumed she wouldn't have understood my few words of soldierspeak. I was wrong. She turned and gave me the severest of dirty looks, whereupon I embarked on a sincere apology in German.

"It's no good speaking to me in German, I only speak English and Afrikaans," she said in her clipped, South African accent.

The translation of my apology into English was accepted and we engaged in conversation to while away the time. The queue moved forward, imperceptibly slowly. It transpired that she was the Johannesburg born daughter of a South African father and a German mother, that she lived and worked in England and that she was on the same tour as me. Entitled to two passports, she used the German document for ease of travel. She was a pretty creature, tall, strikingly dressed and some twenty years younger than me. Neither of us was aware that this chance meeting was about to affect both our lives considerably.

There were twenty of us on the tour that was to take us on the well-trodden tourist triangle between Delhi, Jaipur and Agra. The eight married couples made up the majority of the group, with us four singlies bringing up the rear. We boarded the bus that took us to the splendid 'Old Oberoi Hotel', where we had breakfast and were allocated our rooms. The complement of singlies consisted of me, a young man from Leeds who made battle tanks for a living, a lovely nurse from London and the South African. I was the eldest by a long way and assumed the role of leader, although not with the absolute acquiescence of the Yorkshireman. The girls didn't seem to mind, or didn't say anything if they did. We were keen to explore and agreed to have a few hours shuteye before meeting up at noon for a preliminary excursion to Delhi.

We assembled in the foyer and decided upon a taxi ride around the city rather than walking, mainly because the temperature was around forty degrees centigrade. At the side of the hotel stood an old Morris taxi, its Sikh driver simply itching to do some business. He was the Oberoi's officially appointed number one taxi driver, or so he claimed and he agreed to show us the sights for what seemed to be a very reasonable number of rupees. As befits a person of my status, I took up the front seat and we set off for some sightseeing. The driver spoke just like Peter Sellers.

"I think it is perfectly charming Sahib, that you would want to bring all your children on holiday with you," he said, putting his tip in severe jeopardy.

Once the error was pointed out to him, he was at pains to butter me up pretty quickly and we enjoyed a grand couple of hours in his charge. It was searing hot and we didn't dare leave the air-conditioned comfort of his cab for many minutes, contenting ourselves instead with looking at the sights through the windows.

I took to calling round to the taxi stand to chat with Mr Singh whenever he wasn't ferrying tourists around. He was a decent and highly intelligent man, who invariably had something wise to impart. The subject of death cropped up on one occasion and I confessed to a certain anxiety at the prospect of popping my clogs.

"You are a perfectly stupid man," chided Mr Singh. "And to think that I gave you credence for being intelligent. How can you be frightened of something that is inevitable? I can positively guarantee that you will die one day—accept the fact and prepare yourself accordingly."

He sounded like Dr Billy Graham with a turban on, but made reasonable sense, I suppose. Mr Singh turned out to be a bit of a dark horse. A seemingly devout Sikh and loyal family man, his annual fortnight's leave wasn't taken up in Amritsar for the purpose of refreshing his spirituality, as Mrs Singh thought, but in Srinigar up in the Kashmir and for an altogether different reason. Ten years previously, he confided in me, he had met a Finnish lady in the hotel. She had fallen for the taxi driver's charms and had returned to India every year since, to spend a couple of naughty weeks together on a lakeside boat.

One of the free tours provided in our package holiday was a visit to a Hindu temple somewhere outside of Delhi, but not far enough outside to prevent us coming back to the hotel for lunch. In the temple courtyard stood a tall, metal column, which was reputed to be several thousand years old and yet showed no signs of decay. I didn't doubt its age, but couldn't accept the miracle bit that was attributed to it. I rather fancy that the lack of rain in the area, rather than any divine intervention, was the reason it had never rusted. The custodian maintained that the pillar possessed magical powers and, for a small consideration, he was willing to divulge its secrets to us. Should a man, no female equality nonsense here I was pleased to note, be able to make his fingertips touch whilst embracing the pillar backwards, his wish would be granted. You clearly needed to be a biggish fellow to achieve the aim, although a small contortionist might conceivably have been successful. The custodian considered me sufficiently large and gullible to offer me the first try and, five rupees lighter, I flexed my backward muscle group and gave it my best shot. My fingertips just touched and he whispered that I should make my wish immediately. What a dilemma! Torn between winning a first dividend on the pools and getting inside the South African girl's knickers, I opted for the latter. Had I gone with the alternative choice, I may well have been a rich man today.

On a trip to Delhi a few days later, I noticed in Indian Army officer wearing a belt with the cross kukri emblem embossed onto the buckle. My inability to conceal my curiosity resulted in a friendship with Balbir Singh, the Adjutant of an Indian Gurkha Battalion. Unlike the adjutants of British Army regiments, who are always run off their feet, Balbir didn't appear to have a very time consuming job and we met most afternoons to drink lime cordials at the Gaylord, his favourite watering hole in the capital. His English was exceptional and although we discussed many topics, he always brought the subject around to his seemingly insoluble problem—a problem he could discuss with a European, but not with any of his own. He had fallen in love with a Moslem girl, a state of affairs that was simply unacceptable to his Sikh family, or indeed to his brother officers in his regiment. I offered my best advice, but to heed my council would mean losing his true love and he wasn't willing to face that prospect.

One afternoon at the Gaylord, he presented me with an invitation card to dinner that evening at his Regimental Officer's Mess. Apparently he had mentioned our meeting to his CO and the colonel had expressed a wish to meet the mad Englishman. I was quite chuffed. Balbir explained that he had arranged for transport to pick me up outside my hotel at 2000 hrs. Punctuality isn't an Indian strong point, not even in their forces it seems, because half an hour after the prescribed time, I was still waiting for my lift. It was time to abort the mission. Walking away with the intention of finding a bar some-where, a sounding horn attracted my attention. There was Balbir, sitting astride a motorbike.

"Your transport awaits you Walter my dear friend," he said, indicating that I was expected to climb onto the pillion seat.

I hadn't expected the colonel's staff car, but the prospect of crossing Delhi on the back of a Tiger Cub 125 didn't instil any confidence. Nevertheless, despite the horrendous amount of traffic and appalling driving, Balbir man-aged to get us there in one piece. The mess was less than opulent. In fact, it was positively shabby and reminded me of the NAAFI coffee bar in Cyprus. The welcome was warm, nevertheless, and Gurkha waiters scurried around with ice cold drinks and pre-dinner tit-bits. It promised to be an interesting evening. The drinks went on and on, as did the time. As midnight approached we were still waiting for dinner and I wondered if the rest of them were as rav-enous as I was.

Eventually Balbir took me to one side and whispered in my ear.

"Walter, the colonel is wondering when you might wish to give the order for dinner to be served."

Shit! There was me suffering from malnutrition and all the time they were waiting for *me* to give the nod for the nosebags to be served!

"Gentlemen, shall we dine?" I said, in my very best BBC accent and was almost killed in the stampede for the dining room.

It's not everyday that you eat dinner in an officer's mess with your fingers and off tin plates, but the food was excellent and the wine plentiful. It was get-ting really late before the coffee and liqueurs were finished and the stifled yawns began. A good time to take my leave, I decided. As I was bidding fare-well to my new friends and thanking the colonel for a memorable evening, Balbir was warming up the Tiger Cub for the return journey. There was no way on God's earth I was submitting to another torturous hour on *that* pillion, especially since the driver was now totally pissed. On the pretext that two trips across Delhi at this time of night was too much to ask of a friend, I had him take me to a taxi stand to arrange a cab back to the Oberoi. Balbir approached a driver, gave him instructions and then pulled out his service revolver and put it to the driver's head.

"Is there something wrong, Balbir?" I enquired.

"No, there is no problem whatsoever, Walter. I am merely impressing upon this rascal the requirement for him to drive you back to your hotel by the most direct route and to charge the fare that he would charge a fellow countryman. He now fully understands that if he is not back here within one and a half hours, having firstly deposited you safely at the Oberoi, then I shall shoot him."

The driver was speedy, direct and cheap.

The Oberoi was a good, Colonial style hotel. The staff was attentive and nothing was too much trouble. Well, they were until the World Cup cricket came on the radio, whereupon they swarmed around the nearest crystal set and nothing was done at all. India won the cup that year and the whole country came to a standstill. The restaurant served two menus; there was the local fare, which was usually my choice, and a European menu that almost everyone else selected. They lived to regret their decision. The Tuesday evening 'Chicken Maryland Punjab Style' and 'Rajastani Scotch Broth' both contained Delhi-Belly-bearing microbes that attacked our group with a vengeance. Many became rather poorly and the hotel doctor was kept fit by running up and down the stairs at all hours. Two people became so ill that they had to be hospitalised and everyone vowed to stick to the local menu on any subsequent visits to the Sub-continent. Despite the ravages of the runs, the entire group were fit to move on when the Delhi part of our holiday was over.

A rather aged bus took us along the Grand Trunk Road to the city of Jaipur. The Grand Trunk Road set me thinking of Rudyard Kipling and I couldn't get the tune of 'Road to Mandalay' out of my head for the remainder of the day. Once settled into our new hotel, it was time to explore. I was loath to join the organised trips to the brass-beating factory and the dhoti weaving sheds and set off around the back streets instead. It was raging hot and the 7-Up sellers saw plenty of trade from the mad Englishman out in the midday sun. I tried the *cha wallah* too, but was gravely disappointed. He produced a stewed concoction so full of condensed milk that it set my teeth on edge. It was remiss of me not to have learnt the Hindi for 'no milk or sugar thanks'. The main street of the city boasted two water stops for the use of the locals, at which holy men of both persuasions dispensed blessed water to their faithful. I was offered a cup at both establishments, but declined with as much grace as I could muster.

I happened upon the local police station, which doubled as a jail, and took the opportunity of introducing myself. The head gaoler took great delight in showing a British military policeman around his pigsty and his style of gaining the attention of his slumbering inmates impressed me greatly. He hit them firmly on the head with his truncheon through the bars. No Police Complaints Board to worry about in Jaipur, whereas the Howard League for Penal Reform was too busy pampering the already pampered prisoners in our own country to venture to a place where they might conceivably do some good.

From Jaipur, it was on to Agra and the Taj Mahal. I thought the Taj was just magnificent and simply tailor-made for a photographic dunce with an ordinary 35mm camera. The place overwhelmed me and I spent several hours sitting there in the shade, simply admiring the construction. Gaining entry to the Taj was amusing and designed to give employment to as many locals as possible. One man directed you to the ticket kiosk, a second took the money and a third issued the ticket. Five yards away, another man took your ticket from you again, whilst his mate tore the ticket in half and put the both halves in a bag held by yet another employee. All this occupational therapy was presided over by a supervisor, naturally.

Many of the world's supposedly great tourist attractions have failed to come up to my expectations; Stonehenge and the Sphinx spring to mind, but the Taj Mahal was everything I expected it to be—and more besides.

We went back to Delhi for our last night and everyone prepared for the second phase of the tour. The majority of the group headed for Bangkok, a few went up to Kashmir, the nurse from London stayed put and a couple from Harpenden and me were bound for Kathmandu. My first visit to Delhi airport had made me wonder about the appalling lack of order in the place and three hours in the departure lounge waiting to be called forward for the plane to Nepal confirmed that organisation was nonexistent. It was a truly rotten airport. The chaos in departures proved too much for me—not even the Valium could calm me down. I concluded that if the incompetence prevalent around the Royal Nepal Airlines desk was indicative of what one might expect from the aircrew, then they could fly over the Himalayas without me. My suitcase had already been booked in and I caused some consternation amongst airport staff, as I climbed over trailers full of cases until I located mine. Then the crazy Englishman made his exit from the airport, via the entrance, and took a taxi to the Oberoi. My reappearance surprised the nurse considerably. Over dinner she managed to convince me that it was foolhardy to throw away so much money and that I should fly up to Kathmandu next day. The hotel fixed things with the airline and next morning I returned to the airport, only to funk getting onto the aeroplane once again. I considered another four days in Delhi too long, even with the prospect of trapping the nurse, so I consulted Mr Singh the taxi driver. He assured me that Amritsar was an ideal spot for a short visit. He was so keen for me to visit his beloved city that he went to the railway station and booked me a seat on the Star of the Punjab.

Next morning I set off for the city of the Golden Temple. At Delhi station there were so many people crowding down the stairs that it would have been possible to take one's feet off the ground and still have been carried down to the platform. The Star of the Punjab was already there. Pasted on the side of first class, air conditioned coaches, was a list, which informed the entire Subcontinent of the name, age, sex, seat number and inside leg measurement of all the posh passengers. My travelling companion for the first part of the journey was a bank inspector, on his way to make a surprise visit to the Hariana branch of the Bank of India. He was a charming chap. Not only did he buy me a vegetarian cutlet on the train and a bag of plums at one of the stops along the way, but he also presented me with the hard-back book that he had been intending to read on the trip.

It was mid-afternoon when I arrived in Amritsar and, despite having occupied an air-conditioned, first-class compartment, I was absolutely filthy. I wondered what state the travellers in third class would be in, following eight hours of being cooped up with the sheep and chickens. A hotel was my first priority and as taxis appeared nonexistent, I set off walking up a long street looking for a likely hostelry. A friendly local spotted me and, taking compassion upon a sweaty European who was heading away from all the hotels, he gave me a lift in his car to the best place in town. It was a splendid establishment in every aspect, except that it didn't serve alcohol. Following a shower and the ritual consigning of the shirt I'd travelled up in to the bin, I wandered down to reception to enquire just where one might obtain a cold bottle of beer. The desk clerk knew of a stall near the Delhi Gate. A trishaw was the recommend mode of transport and right outside the hotel stood such a contraption, along with its aged trishaw wallah. This old man declared that he would be honoured to peddle me to the stall and back for two rupees. That seemed to be an awful lot of peddling for precious little reward, but I had no desire to haggle. In any case, he was probably still ripping me off in his modest way. As we were about to depart, a well-groomed Indian in a smart suit approached.

"Excuse me Sahib."

"Yes?"

"Would you kindly tell me your destination?"

"The Delhi Gate and back; do you want to hop in?"

"Thank you kindly, but no. I merely want to ensure that this unworthy creature is not overcharging you. How much is he demanding for the trip?"

"Two rupees."

"Two rupees is excessive—he is cheating you."

The friendly gentleman then set about the trishaw driver and after a couple of minutes of berating him, he announced that the driver would make the journey for one rupee. He then strode away, presuming to have done me a favour, I suppose. The old boy peddled me to the beer stand as fast as his scrawny legs could manage. I bought three bottles of Pink Pelican Lager for thirty-nine rupees and had him take me back. At the hotel, he put his skinny hand out for his pay and was rewarded with five rupees and a bottle of beer. He was delighted. He would sell the beer no doubt and hopefully buy some much-needed food.

Next morning I took another trishaw trip down to the Delhi Gate and had a wander around the old part of the city. I gave this driver five rupees too, five times the going rate, but still exceptional value. On the way down to the Delhi Gate there was a bridge over the railway line that was steeper than it needed to be. The trishaw drivers couldn't make it up the slope, so they would alight and push the tricycle up the hill with the passengers still sitting in the back. I got out of my trishaw and helped the poor bugger push it up to the top. My target that morning was the Golden Temple of the Sikhs, the focal point of their religion. Apparently two people had been shot dead outside the place the previous day and the Temple wasn't really a good place to be, but ignorance being bliss, I wandered around oblivious of the tension that existed. The fact that many of the men were carrying small arms didn't really register either. I presumed that this was the normal way of things in this volatile land. A kindly Sikh showed me around the area, but I was reluctant to cross the water and into the Temple proper, in case it disturbed people at worship. It didn't compare with the Taj Mahal as a place of beauty, but at least I can say I've been there, which is more than many Sikhs in Leicester can. On the way back I saw something that would have upset the RSPCA had it happened in our green and pleasant land. A bullock, tethered to a lamppost, with its owner merrily engaged in sawing its horns off with a hacksaw! The bullock seemed remarkably unperturbed about the whole thing.

The only problem with my hotel was the fact that it was dry. Enquiring at reception whether there was a method of obtaining a beer without resorting to a trishaw journey, the charming hospitality girl directed me to the English Beer Bar. An ideal spot and within easy walking distance, she assured me. The grandly named establishment turned out to be little more than a small hut, with a couple of tables and chairs placed underneath an awning. Nevertheless, it had a fridge and cold beer. I approached the smiling barman.

"Hello, can you serve me with a cold beer, please?"

"Of course, Sahib, we are the English Beer Bar. That is our business."

"What kind of beer do you have?"

"Two brands, Sahib. One retails for eleven rupees a bottle and the other at thirteen."

"I'll have a bottle of the thirteen rupee beer please."

"You have made a very wise choice if I may be permitted to say so, Sahib. You have selected the Pink Pelican Brand, which is highly recommended."

I downed three large bottles of the very decent brew and was feeling much better for the effort, when an Indian approached. It was Prem, a member of the Amritsar City Council and a man who spoke very passable English. He merely wanted me to squeeze over a few feet, whilst he extricated his motor scooter from underneath some awning. He accepted my invitation to join me in a bottle of beer, but only on the proviso that he bought his own. What objection can there be to a man buying his own ale? Prem sat down and we saw off three bottles each. Six pints of beer at lunchtime is excessive for me, but my thirst was such that I still didn't need to visit the lavatory. We decided on one for the road and, as we were tucking in, Prem offered a little belated advice.

"Keep your eyes peeled for the police, Walter. It is illegal to consume alcohol in a public place in the Punjab."

No sooner had he finished saying it and there was a squeal of brakes. A police Landrover disgorged half a battalion of blue turbaned policemen and a scribe. I was taken to the front of the vehicle, where a self-important inspector sat in the passenger's seat.

"What are you doing here at the beer bar?" he asked.

I would have thought that was perfectly obvious, but having seen the inside of Jaipur jail and having no desire to be an inmate in an Indian nick, I chose to answer politely.

"Just having a bottle of beer, inspector."

"Are you aware that it is illegal to consume alcohol in public in the Punjab?"

"No, I wasn't aware of that fact, inspector."

"What are you doing in Amritsar?"

"I am merely a humble tourist, enjoying the hospitality of the welcoming citizens of this splendid city and taking the opportunity of visiting one of the world's most important religious sites," I said, bullshitting magnificently.

It worked.

"Take your beer back to your hotel and enjoy your holiday."

Then it was Prem's turn. I sat at the table and waited for him. He reappeared several minutes later, looking a little pale.

"Goodness gracious me, what a close shaving," he exclaimed. "I was almost losing my liberty. I needed to use some quick thinking in my replies to that terrible inspector and I hope you will forgive me for using your name in vain. I told him that you were a personal friend and a high-ranking member of the British Embassy in New Delhi. Otherwise, I'm sure that this bounder what have clapped me in irons."

After our brush with the law, we finished our beers with haste. As brothers in crime, Prem considered it only right to invite me back to his place for lunch. I was happy to accept. Travelling through the busy streets of Amritsar isn't recommended for the faint of heart, especially when you happen to be on the back of an old Vespa motor scooter. After fifteen minutes we arrived at Chateau Prem, a humble establishment by British standards, but it had an air conditioner and Prem appeared to be very proud of his family seat. Lunch was served almost immediately, on a large table that was pushed right up against the dining room wall. Prem and I occupied the only two chairs available and his two sons sat cross-legged on the table, their backs against the wall. The remaining members of the family were Prem's wife and a daughter of about twelve years of age, both of whom were outside in the yard preparing the food for the men. Lunch was vegetarian, curried, served on tin plates and eaten without cutlery. It was also delicious and I tucked in with relish. The young boys found something highly amusing about their visitor and giggled incessantly during the meal. I thought it might have been the white skin or blue eyes that was causing the mirth, until the host, unable to remain silent a moment longer, felt compelled to speak.

"Tell me, Walter, is it normal in your country to eat with your left hand?"

Oops! No wonder his two lads were laughing. The Englishman was tucking into his chappattis with the hand reserved for washing one's backside. I had tried hard to conform, by removing my shoes and refraining from blowing my nose in a hankie, but had dropped the biggest bollock of all by eating with my dirty hand.

"Prem, my actions have brought dishonour on your household. What steps may be taken to make amends?"

"You could kindly wash your hand," he replied and led me out to a tap in the yard, where he supervised the ritual washing of my left hand.

After the meal he took me back to my hotel on his Vespa. It had been a marvellous experience and to reciprocate, I invited him and his wife to the hotel for dinner the following evening. They failed to appear. Perhaps my serious breach of etiquette had been too much for him.

At a loss for something to do next morning, the friendly girl at reception came up with a suggestion that took my fancy—a trip to Lahore in Pakistan. She arranged for a ridiculously cheap taxi to take me the twenty miles to the border crossing point at Wagga, to wait for me to return from Pakistan no matter how long it took, and then to drive me back to Amritsar. I arrived at Wagga, unaware of the farcical series of events that crossing into Pakistan would entail. Passport Control and the customs shed were situated inside a large covered area and the queue at the passport desk looked ominously long. A clerk sat behind a desk with fifty or so customers forming a reasonably orderly queue in front of him. Another clerk sitting alongside him appeared to be redundant. He had a sign on his desk that read 'Foreigners'. I was a foreigner, so I gave him my passport. He disappeared without a word and returned to a different desk some twenty minutes later. He gave me my passport, which now boasted an exit stamp and waved me in a westerly direction, towards a sign depicting a fist with an extended forefinger that pointed me towards a high desk. Behind this desk, with his head almost in the clouds, sat a blue turbaned policeman. He subjected my passport to the severest examination, before leaning over the desk to scrutinise the holder.

"How much money are you taking out of the country?" he enquired.

I did a quick bit of mental arithmetic and announced that the sum was 2420 rupees, give or take the odd anna.

"Aha! I have trapped you. You are only permitted to export two hundred rupees," he announced in triumph.

"Oh goodness gracious me," I replied. "What do you suggest that I do?"

"I must notate the facts in the rear of your passport."

"Be my guest."

"Aha! You are a sharp one. You clearly have nothing to hide; otherwise you would never make such a comment. You may take the money with you."

"My gratitude knows no bounds."

"What is that around your neck?"

"An Olympus OM 10 single lens reflex camera."

"Aha! You are not permitted to export such an object."

"Why don't you notate it in the rear of my passport?" I suggested.

"Aha! You are simply too sharp for me, Sahib, there is no catching you out. Proceed."

My passport was stamped yet again and I walked towards the exit of the covered area. Another official confronted me and handed me a chit. Ten strides further on stood another chit wallah, who took the chit back from me before I'd had a chance to read it. I was now on the road that led from India into Pakistan. It appeared to be half a mile long and was lined on either side by offices and stalls selling food and drink. Halfway along, I crossed a thick white line that was painted on the tarmac. On one side, in large letters, it read INDIA, and on the other, not surprisingly, PAKISTAN. I stepped over into Pakistan. Another sign with a fist and extended forefinger directed me to the office of the Pakistan Medical Authority. Inside the office sat two bored medics, one of whom demanded sight of my cholera certificate.

"It's back in my hotel room in Amritsar," I pleaded.

"In that case you are not permitted to enter Pakistan," he replied.

"But I have just crossed a white line on the road that says I'm already in Pakistan."

"Do you know you have a very good point? But you will still have to produce your certificate, or have a further injection and that will cost you ten thousand US dollars."

"Oh you're just being silly, how can I pay such a large amount?"

"Can you swear to me that you are in possession of a cholera certificate?"

"May Leicester City be relegated if I'm telling a lie."

"Pardon me!"

"Yes, I swear it."

"In that case, I will allow you to proceed. Please report to the man sitting under the white tree," he said mysteriously, stamping my passport yet again.

I sat for ten minutes on a chair in the shade of a tree that had its trunk painted white, until a hissing sound attracted my attention. A man beckoned me towards an office building. I walked over to him.

"Hello, Sahib. I am the man that is normally to be found sitting under the white tree, but it so overwhelmingly warm today that I have retreated to this office. It has an air conditioner, you see."

We went into the office where he asked me several inane questions that didn't give me any clue as to his purpose in life. Whatever he was there for really didn't matter, as he gave me the all clear, stamped my passport and set me free to march up to the customs area at the other end of the road. One more examination of the passport, another stamp and I was in Pakistan proper. This episode had taken so long that I decided against travelling on to Lahore. Prem was coming to the hotel for dinner at 1900 hrs, after all. I picked up a pebble to give to a Pakistani mate and headed back.

The return journey started well enough and it took me only ten minutes to reach a uniformed official. He stamped my passport, wished me well and pointed me in the direction of India. Fifty yards on and a chit wallah stopped me.

"Chit please."

"I haven't got a chit."

"Go back to desk for chit please."

I returned to the same queue, where the official apologised profusely for his oversight. He shut up shop, leaving all those behind me to stew and led me up two flights of stairs to the chit issuing office. Ten minutes later my chit appeared. At the foot of the stairs he apologised once again, shook my hand and left me to go on my way rejoicing. The supreme confidence with which I approached the chit wallah evaporated when he examined it.

He shook his head slowly.

"No good chit," he announced. "Chit not signed."

Back to the customs office, where I queued again. The official apologised again, we went upstairs again and my chit was signed. This time the chit wallah was satisfied.

Trudging towards the Indian border was a line of bearers, each carrying a heavy sack on his head. As I overtook them, one young man spoke to me.

"Ay up mate, are you'm all right?" he said, in a broad Brummie accent.

"Bloody hell! What are you doing here, aren't you from Brum?"

"Born and bred mate."

"Then why are you carrying a sack of rice to Wagga?"

"Simple really. I'm wanted for armed robbery back in Brum. This ain't much fun, but I prefer it to spending ten years in Winson Green."

The people you meet!

I made it back to the car park on the Indian side and was immediately surrounded by taxi drivers, all trying to undercut each other in an attempt to get my business. Fortunately, my man was still waiting for me and he came to my rescue.

In the sparsely populated hotel restaurant that evening, I encountered the only other Englishman in Amritsar. He was an objectionable little Londoner who persisted in being so very rude to the waiters that he angered me. It seemed that the chicken korma wasn't to his liking, the dish prepared at the Taj Mahal take-away in Hackney being altogether spicier, apparently. He bleated on for so long that someone English really had to do something about his lack of courtesy. I unilaterally elected myself to perform the task and as soon as the waiters moved away from his table, I went over for a quiet word in the Londoner's ear. He was cautioned that, unless he moderated his tone and stopped letting the side down, I would be forced to break his fucking nose. That did the trick.

Next day it was back to Delhi on the Star of the Punjab. Here I met up with the majority of our Kuoni Group and spent a final evening at the Oberoi. Next morning we went to Delhi airport and boarded the Japan Airlines flight back to London. Already aboard were those in our group who had spent their time in Bangkok and, even before the plane was airborne, the tank maker from Leeds came back to have a chat with me. The South African girl hadn't stopped talking about me all week, he declared. He sportingly offered to swap seats and I smoothed in next to her, despite the protestations of a slant-eyed stewardess. Was the wish made at the Hindu temple about to come true? She agreed to put her journey back to Yorkshire on hold and experience the wonders of a weekend at the Holiday Inn in Leicester.

The next time my arms meet around an iron column in a Hindu temple, I shall definitely wish for a jackpot on the pools.

12

Before departing on leave I had spoken on the phone to one of our RMP officers. He was a man with whom I had served many years previously, when we were both corporals. He had confided that his career had reached its ceiling and that the prospects of him ever making major were nonexistent. For this reason, he was about to leave the Army. To be frank, as an officer he was an unmitigated disaster. Devoid of any man management skills, he compounded his unpopularity by being arrogant, self centred and rude. The men had so little respect for him that he was known throughout the Corps as TCB—'That Clot Burlock'—although the middle word of those three was often changed to give the phrase a more emphatic ring.

I had recently left the Legal Process Office and taken over the appointment of Staff Assistant in the nearby HQ. I was a WOI now and feeling pretty content with life. Until the arrival of my successor in the LPO, though, it was necessary for me to keep an eye on the running of that department too, especially since Major Paddy had left for pastures new. The fact that this organisation could function perfectly well without its officer and WO is perhaps indicative of its importance to the war effort. My replacement would be my old chum Bones Kitchenbrand and the new officer, the pleasant Dick Plummer, who would be promoted to major on assuming the post. Dick was a bachelor, who was by no means as reserved as he appeared at first sight. In a conversation once with Major Paddy, I suggested that Plummer was quiet to the point of being shy, especially when women were around.

"You couldn't be further from the mark," confided Paddy. "If there's a woman around, Dick is the human equivalent of a stag in the rutting season."

Paddy must have been blessed with second sight, for Dick never made it to the LPO. A few days before his promotion, a female lance corporal found her way into his room in the mess and the story leaked out. Senior Army officers become ridiculously puritanical in circumstances such as these and the gallant Captain Plummer was hauled up in front of the General, a man celebrated for his Methodist viewpoint. Dick incurred his severe displeasure. In plain English, that meant that his promotion was on hold for a while.

The dearth of majors in the RMP meant that they would need to promote an alternative captain to fill Dick's vacancy. Unbelievably, the only person available in the whole wide world was TCB.

The awful TCB arrived on a rainy Friday evening. As an old acquaintance and because no one else in Headquarters Northern Ireland would accept the task, I picked him up from Aldergrove airport and conveyed him to his quarter. He didn't like the quarter. I would have been extremely surprised if he had.

TCB had worked with the Special Investigation Branch at one time, until they kicked him out and it was these guys who had given him his fitting nickname. The Legal Process Office occupied part of the SIB block and on Monday morning, I was required to show him around and introduce him to the personalities. His infamy had clearly preceded him, because every single office was either empty or locked.

My brief on the workings of the LPO was cut short by TCB, who announced that he would find his own feet. It wasn't beneath him to ask the way to the pay office in order to submit his travel claims just the same. He spent the rest of Monday, Tuesday and Wednesday attending to his personal administration and appeared totally disinterested in any advice I had to impart. This being his attitude, I retreated back to my office. If he wanted my assistance, he could bloody well ask for it. On Wednesday evening he deemed to call me, to ask if he could borrow my Army car next morning. Our two departments possessed only one car apiece and there was a reciprocal agreement about borrowing each other's wheels. On Thursday afternoon he called me again.

"Mr Payne, the car I borrowed from you yesterday was in a disgusting condition; in fact, it was filthy. You will send someone over here now to have it cleaned."

"Since the car is mine, the decision as to if and when it is cleaned will be mine. You are not in BAOR now, major. Over here, a clean car indicates an Army car. For security reasons, therefore, I shall leave my car dirty."

"Mr Payne, I'm not discussing this matter with you. The car is filthy. You will have it cleaned now. That's a direct order."

"Did I hear you say that it was a direct order?"

"Yes, you did."

"Well, Major Burlock, I'll tell you what to do with your direct order. Shove it up your fucking arse."

I put the phone down on this most arrogant of individuals. It rang again almost immediately.

"Provost Branch, WOI Payne speaking," I said, knowing full well who was at the other end of the line.

"Mr Payne, how dare you talk to me like that! How dare you put the phone down on me!"

"It's very simple in your case."

"How dare you! Report to my office at once."

"Is that a direct order?"

"Yes it is."

"Well, if there's any room, you can shove it up your arse with the other one."

I put the phone down again on the Prince of Arrogance.

My colonel was a pleasant man who liked to run a smooth ship. I telephoned him at once.

"It's your faithful staff assistant here, sir; the plans for tomorrow are as follows."

I gave him a rundown on the next day's business, including dress, transport arrangements, timing and whom he would be meeting—all the stuff necessary to make sure his day went smoothly.

"Thank you Mr Payne, efficiency incarnate as usual," said the colonel.

"By the way sir, I've just had a run-in with the new major," I confessed and gave him the SP before TCB had the opportunity. He would bubble me to the boss for sure. That's the sort of bloke he was.

"Was the car dirty, Wally?"

"Absolutely honking, sir."

"Would you have it cleaned if I asked you?"

"Naturally, sir."

What a creep I can be when necessary. I had no intention whatsoever of visiting TCB's office to pick up the car keys, so I sent my Corporal over to fetch them. He returned empty handed.

"He wouldn't give them to me sir; he says you have to fetch them yourself."

At that I saw red and sped over to his office.

"Give me those keys now, you shit," I said, snatching the fob off his desk.

"Now listen here, Payne, I know all about your reputation. If you think you can try this kind of thing with me, you are very much mistaken. You'll come off second best, I can assure you." He stood up, clenching his fists and adopting a boxing stance.

I was delighted—the arsehole was going to have a crack at me! I slammed his office door shut and advanced towards him. Faced by someone who wasn't the least bit scared off him, he quickly sat down.

"No, no, you've got me wrong—I'm not offering violence," he blubbered.

"Well, it looks very much like it from where I'm standing. The fact is you have put me in fear. I feel that you have the capability of carrying out an assault and I intend to defend myself." I dredged up a few bits of the definition of assault for added effect. I let rip with two swift straight lefts, both aimed to miss his ear by a fraction. He would have felt the wind. I snarled at him and left him sitting wide-eyed in his swing chair. As I was heading back to my office with the car keys, I spotted TCB racing of in the direction of the colonel's office. Pausing to ponder my position, I told the corporal to clean the car and decided that making myself scarce for the rest of the day might be the prudent thing to do. It's not acceptable to treat an officer with such disdain, even one as worthless as TCB. There were bound to be repercussions.

Next morning I went into work earlier than usual and was ready to face the music. The adjutant was already waiting for me outside my office. He approached me, although not with the Sword of Damocles held aloft, but with his hand outstretched ready to shake mine.

"Put it there, mate," he said. "You beat the bastard hands down. TCB got a real bollocking from the colonel and if ever there was a man who needed taking down a peg, then it's that bugger."

The colonel never mentioned the incident again in all the years we knew each other. Some weeks later, though, TCB had the brass neck to call me and ask to borrow my car. Needless to say, he didn't get it. He called the second-in-command to lay a complaint, but he still didn't get it. Later on, an unimpeachable source told me I was by no means the only warrant officer with whom TCB had locked horns. Several of those had gone further than I had done, apparently, by actually whacking the dunderhead.

One of the RMP officers had a beezer idea. If he were to organise a sporting event for the special schools in the district, schools from both sides of the religious divide, there might be a decent chance of an MBE in it for him. It was a good idea all right—for him. Since everyone knew that the officer in question was merely trying to feather his own nest, the response for helpers was embarrassingly weak. Come the Saturday morning of the event, desperation had set in and he came around the offices personally, looking for willing hands. I volunteered, not for his sake, but to ensure that the mentally subnormal kids didn't have their day out spoilt. Clearly there were many that felt the same way, because by the time I reached the stadium, it was awash with helpers—so many, in fact, that every athlete was afforded the assistance of an individual chaperone. My little girl was about thirteen years old and suffered from Down's syndrome. She was a chatty little thing, nevertheless, with a broad Belfast accent that suggested she hailed from the west of the city. In other words, she was a Catholic.

The 'girl's under fifteen fifty-yard dash' was about to begin and Bernadette, my charge, was drawn in lane one. I stationed myself at the finish as she readied herself for the start. A whistle blast, rather than a shot from a starter's pistol, was considered the best method of signalling the start. We didn't want everyone scurrying for cover. Bernadette was a little slow out of the blocks; she was slow over the first thirty yards and, moving at a snail's pace by the time she crossed the line, came plumb last.

Before I could offer my congratulations on a plucky effort, she spoke.

"See me? I'm fucking knackered!" she shouted loudly and promptly disappeared into the ladies' changing rooms.

The sports meeting was voted a success and was marred only by a small amount of sectarian sand throwing in the long jump pit. Not even in the world of the mentally subnormal can you escape the nonsense that prevails in Ulster.

It was time for another ninety-six hour long weekend and this time I was travelling by train from Stranraer. One of the corporals kindly offered to drive me to Larne port and we set out from Lisburn in plenty of time for me to catch the ferry. In front of us at the traffic island near Ballyclare was a car that was travelling slowly in the left-hand lane and indicating a left turn in the direction of Larne. My driver moved out to overtake, on the assumption that the other guy would be travelling in the direction that he was indicating. He was wrong. This was an Irish driver, to whom travelling in the left-hand lane and indicating a left turn is by no means binding. Just as we were overtaking, he switched to the right-hand lane and proceeded in the direction of Belfast. The corporal braked our car to avoid a collision and there was a fair amount of horn blaring and fist shaking before we continued on our way. Paddy, though, had been outraged by our actions and decided to press the point. He drove after us and drew level. He shook his fist and mouthed something unintelligible, before my driver put his foot down and accelerated away. Paddy wasn't about to let the matter drop. He continued in pursuit, flashing his lights. Despite driving at 90mph, we still couldn't shake the man off and rather than race him all the way to Larne, we pulled over onto the hard shoulder. He drove thirty yards further on and pulled onto the hard shoulder too. We met in the no man's land between our vehicles. Paddy was a small, grey haired chap and the wrong side of fifty-five, just the kind of opponent for me. It was he who broke the deadlock.

"See you, you're a fucking terrible driver so you are."

"No I'm not."

"You are so, you're a fucking terrible driver."

"What makes you say that?"

"What makes me say that? Your fucking terrible piece of driving back at the traffic island, that's what makes me say that."

"You're wrong to say I drove badly back there."

"I'm not fucking wrong. You're a terrible driver and you should never have been given a licence. You're not fit to hold a fucking licence."

"I don't think you should have a licence either—you don't possess the basic physical requirements."

"What do you mean by that?"

"You have defective eyesight."

"There's nothing wrong with my eyesight mister, I can tell you that for nothing."

"I think that there must be, especially if you think that I was driving back there at the island. I was the passenger, you see. The driver is back in my car, with his finger on the trigger of a gun that's pointing right at your head should you care to take a wee peek."

"Are you Army?"

"Yes."

"I'm going to make a complaint."

"Be my guest."

Since I was the person who dealt with complaints against the Forces, I don't think there was any need for undue concern. He never complained anyway.

Neil had been in my platoon in Werl and I sometimes saw him hanging around the HQ in Lisburn. Not that he was easily recognisable. The smart soldier of yesteryear had transformed—his attire comprised of all the scruffiest gear he possessed and his hair would have done credit to a Rolling Stone. Whenever he came into my room for a coffee, he would first divest himself of body armour and weaponry and, although I never asked, his current occupation was obviously clandestine. Neil was the easiest of men to get along with and a perfect guy to have as a travelling companion. We were both about to depart on three weeks' leave and I suggested that we do one of the Payne favourites together, a tour around Turkey.

We took the train from London to Istanbul, first class naturally, and a pleasant trip it was too. When you travel first class on the German Bundesbahn, they give you a gift pack that includes various bits and pieces to keep you smelling sweetly on your journey. Just before Istanbul, we both pulled out our Eau de Cologne face wipes to get the sleep out of our eyes. Neil used his first and immediately let out his special squeak, which indicated that something was amiss.

"I've gone blind," he whined.

The malady afflicting his eyes seemed to be contagious, because I went blind shortly afterwards. Only after we had prised our eyes open and inspected the sachets did we discover that we had washed our faces with shoeshine lacquer.

After a grand tour of Istanbul, we took a ship along the Black Sea coast as far as Trabzon, almost the same route as the route Jason and the Argonauts took. After Trabzon, we ventured around Eastern Anatolia visiting, Erzurum, Van, Diyarbakir and Dogubayazit, climbed around the foothills of Mt. Ararat and took a boat across the outstandingly beautiful Lake Van. Finally, from Van, we jumped aboard a bus for the three-day trip back to Istanbul. It took a lot to upset Niel, but something irritated him during the long bus journey.

"How come it's always you that gets to speak the foreign language?" he enquired.

"Bloody hell, Neil, I only know two dozen words of Turkish and they were all learnt from the glossary at the back of my guide book."

"Well, at the next bus stop, I'm going to order my own nosebag and I'm going to do it in Turkish," he asserted.

We pulled in at a roadside cafe shortly afterwards and I went to the kitchen and pointed out my fancy, which is the accepted procedure in these parts. Neil meanwhile announced that soup would be sufficient for him and he asked the waiter for a bowl. I was on my second course and his soup was still to make an appearance.

"Hey garcon, where's my bloody soup?" Neil enquired.

The waiter returned with a glass of water. I went on to my pudding and still the soup of the day hadn't appeared. The hungry Mancunian asked once again about his soup and, once again, the waiter brought him a glass of water. He never did get served and we were back on the bus before we discovered where Neil had gone wrong. A peek at the glossary in my book revealed that the Turkish for water is 'sou'; the waiter had thought he was asking for water. Shrugging off his failure, he decided to try his hand again as soon as we reached Istanbul. This time he decided that some peanuts would complement his glass of beer nicely. We were on our fourth bottle of beer and the nuts still hadn't materialised. He made a last attempt.

"Garcon, for fuck's sake, bring me my bloody peanuts!"

The waiter went away and returned with a tray that was bound for our table. On it was a silver dish, full of strawberries and ice cream. Thereafter, foreign languages were left to me.

Mess rugby is a perfectly stupid game, but the traditional way to round off an evening's entertainment in the sergeant's mess. With the participants attired in their expensive mess kit, the principal aim of the contest is to rip the uniform off the back of your opposing number or, better still, maim him. Two sides, never numerically equal, play something akin to rugby, but without the benefit of a referee or rules and often without a ball. It's never possible to discover which team is victorious, since no one is sober enough to count the scores. Broken limbs often outnumber the tries in any case. The game does present a splendid opportunity for people to settle old scores, though.

The match in the RMP Sergeant's Mess followed a pretty lousy dinner, which had been held to bid farewell to a pretty lousy senior officer. The scene was set for a spirited game, to make up for the shabby meal. With a mere six weeks left to serve before Northern Ireland could kiss my bum forever, I was feeling mellow and didn't think I had any scores to settle. Nevertheless, one had to get stuck into someone and since that cocky bugger Horrobin was in the opposition ranks, he would do as my target man. During a particularly spirited period of play, I found myself in a furious mêlée and as it cleared a little, there was Horrobin's head, conveniently placed only two feet from my right boot. It would have been wasteful not to take the opportunity of damaging him, so I gave him a decent kick in the ear. He proved to be a poor sport and took umbrage at this playful nudge, vowing revenge. Unfortunately for him, someone's arm was broken and the game was stopped before he could crack me back. Although it had been declared that we had seen enough sport for one night, Horrobin wasn't content. He was bent on revenge and hurled a few threats in my direction. Then he went below the belt.

"If you weren't so old, I'd ask you outside," he declared.

"Please don't let my age be any impediment to your aspirations, but I must warn you that, in your drunken condition, you are seriously confusing your ambition and ability," I replied.

I was rather pleased with that pithy retort, especially since I was badly pissed myself. Thereafter, we contented ourselves with swapping a few snarls and nasty looks.

There was precious little to do as a staff assistant and I didn't earn my pay. The colonel, who was also the CO of the Regiment when he wore his other hat, made all the important decisions on the one morning a week that he graced our office with his presence. The major made all the day-to-day decisions, an RAOC sergeant did all the clerical work, a corporal did the running around and the typist typed. I filled in the odd return, wrote a few pages for the Corps historical record each month and made the odd trip out with the colonel. For some inexplicable reason, NCOs who wished to extend their service in Northern Ireland beyond the two-year mark had to be interviewed by me. Apart from me telling them that they needed their bumps reading, they all got the nod. The rest of my working day consisted of chatting up Grace the typist, playing squash until I sickened myself of the game, and talking to the tiresome major, one of the Corps' supreme bores. He specialised in regaling anyone who would listen with his tedious tales of free fall parachuting, simultaneously packing and re-packing his sports parachute. Sadly, the poor fellow was killed a year later, when something went wrong on a free fall jump.

And that's about it for Northern Ireland. Except that my car broke down in the centre of Belfast on St Patrick's Day; the RMP colonel who worked in the HQ was required to resign for putting his senior officer's male member of generation in the wrong place, and I scored the only century of my illustrious cricket-playing career the day before I left. Returning to Belfast along the MI motorway on my very last morning in the Province, a lorry threw up a stone that smashed my windscreen and made me think that my end had come. That would have been wretched luck, copping your lot on your last day in the place. I took my last lunch in the mess, took my leave of the colonel and left Thiepval Barracks for the last time.

Some months previously I had approached the colonel at the Records Office, to discuss my final posting in the Army. After twenty years of service, the Corps had never seen fit to post me to England and I was keen to keep it that way. Eleven years of my time had been spent in Germany; I spoke fluent German and had all the attributes necessary to be an asset to the Corps as an RSM in BAOR. So where did they post me? Colchester. My protestations fell on deaf ears. So, for my last tour in the Army, I was to become an Essex boy. I left Northern Ireland without any regrets; in fact, wild horses would not have been able to drag me back to the place.

13

I just had time to take in the first match of the season at Filbert Street before travelling down to Essex to take over as RSM at Colchester. The Blues hosted Newcastle United in this opening fixture and we got off to an inauspicious start, losing by the odd goal in five. As if defeat wasn't bad enough, I discovered my friend Geordie Lampton, a died-in-the-wool Magpie, sitting a few rows further back in the stand. Our paths hadn't crossed for a few years and on the understanding that he didn't gloat about his team's victory, I invited him home for tea before he embarked on the long journey back up north. Except that he wasn't going back to the Northeast, but rather to the Southeast, where he was a member of my new unit. That was good news. It meant there would be at least one other person in Colchester who was as football daft as me.

The CSM met me first thing on Monday morning and we had a working breakfast together in the mess. The two of us had suffered the excesses of the RSM of 111 Provost Company when we were together in Fallingbostel and it was a relief to discover his career had not been adversely affected by the antics of that spiteful man. The CSM was a good Yorkshire lad, as loyal as they come, albeit just a little khaki-brained. He had gone to the trouble of acquiring a pace stick for his new RSM, in the erroneous assumption that I would, firstly, appreciate the gesture and, secondly, know what to do with the bloody thing. He must have been mightily disappointed to see me throw it in the corner of my office, where it would stand gathering dust for the rest of my time in Colly. Pace sticks and the like just weren't my style. He had arranged for the entire unit to be formed up on parade for my initial inspection and probably expected me to launch into a barrage of threats and promises of changes to come. He would have been disappointed to discover that I used the time solely for the purpose of introducing myself. I much prefer to find my feet before starting to scream and shout. In my own mind, however, I was confident we were going to get along together and that we would make a sound management team.

The OC and I were old pals, from way back in our Iserlohn days, and the fact that I was in Colchester at all was down to him pulling a few strings. We didn't need to stand on ceremony with each other and his opening address indicated that he knew me all too well.

"Only three rules here, Wally. No shagging the WRAC girls, no shagging the wives, and you and I have dinner together every Monday night at the Four Horseshoes at Fordham, to discuss how best to run the unit."

Spoken like the experienced and eminently sensible man that he was, except that he had the number of horseshoes wrong. The pub in Fordham, in which we were to enjoy so many Monday evenings, was actually the Three Horseshoes. His directive seemed fair enough to me and I didn't break his trust—not too frequently, anyway. Major Roy and I had always got along well together and our time in Colchester was to be no different. He took me to meet the Administration Officer and the Operations Officer, both good sorts. Life in this company promised to be fun.

Cavalry Barracks was our home. The self contained little camp had been built a couple of hundred years previously and boasted walls two feet thick, making my office impregnable against musket fire, grapeshot and RPG 7. The splendid copperplate graffiti chiselled into the rear wall of the building by long forgotten soldiers, confirming that 'Arthur and Fred were here—1845', gave us something unique to show our visitors. It may have been a humble little barracks, but it was paid for and all mine.

I had applied for a commission and couldn't be certain whether my stay in Colly would be measured in weeks, months, or years. For that reason, I elected to hire a TV set for my rooms in the mess, rather than buy one. During my first weekend in the south of England, therefore, I wandered into Colchester and happened upon the showrooms of a famous TV rental company. Since this organisation had a branch in Leicester, I considered them a worthy company with whom to do business and marched in to give them my custom. As a lightning fast shopper, I had selected my top of the range model, paid the mandatory three months deposit and arranged delivery, all within minutes. Match of the Day in the comfort of my own room was in prospect for that very evening, until the smiling lady assistant noticed my address.

"Oh! I'm sorry sir, but we don't do business with servicemen," she announced.

That, in my opinion, was a policy doomed to failure in a city awash with soldiers. I demanded an audience with the manager of the establishment, but he was absent from the shop and thus escaped my verbal assault. At my insistence, the shop assistant confirmed that her employer's policy was to refuse the business of military personnel and I left the shop feeling something like Tommy Atkins. Over the years there would undoubtedly have been some soldiers who had proved to be bad financial risks, but I was a WO in the RMP, for goodness sake! I felt more than a little aggrieved and wrote a tersely worded letter of complaint to the manager of the shop. He phoned to offer a watery apology that just wasn't acceptable. Someone had to grovel. In any case, the manager blamed everything on his shop girl and that was poor management technique. My next attack was on the Managing Director of the company, who was given the opportunity of commenting on his company's discriminatory policy before the matter was brought to the attention of Jimmy Young, my MP, the Consumer's Association and Esther Rantzen. His response was swift and the big cheese himself arrived from Basingstoke only forty-eight hours after I had posted my letter. He was armed with smiles, apologies and an armful of statistics, which, he purported, proved that his company was only too pleased to deal with gentlemen clad in khaki. I accepted his apology and explanation, but had no intention of forgetting. The chance to take my revenge arrived a few months later, when I saw one of this organisation's vans parked outside the duty room. The deliveryman explained that he was about to deliver two TV sets to rooms within the accommodation block. It gave me considerable pleasure to kick him and his van out of my barracks.

Having taken over as RSM, I knew that there would be certain aspects of the day-to-day running of the unit that I would wish to change. It never occurred to me that I would want to change almost everything. My predecessor clearly had a totally different concept of how a company should be run than I did, although to be fair to him, we never had the benefit of an official handover at which questions could have been raised. In my opinion the value of a handover is debatable, in any case; most of what you are told goes in one ear and comes undiluted out of the other. Changing things for the sake of change was never my style, but much would need to be altered in Colchester if the place was to function in the way I was determined it would. There were two areas of concern I was determined to address immediately, the lot of the single men and the unit soccer team, both of which had been sadly neglected. One has to get one's priorities right.

As a bachelor for most of my career, I always resented the fact that the Army condoned a policy of discrimination against the single man. Did a married man have to dress for dinner in his married quarter? Did a married man have his quarter and his wardrobes inspected? Did the married man have to book out when he went into town for a beer? Of course he bloody well didn't! Why then should single men be subjected to such impositions? Who were the first to be called out in the case of an emergency? Who stood in for the married men when their wives or children fell ill? Who had to clean up the unit for the visit of a senior officer next day? The single men, of course!

Officers and warrant officers are responsible for laying down unit policy; they are invariably married and, quite naturally, see everything from the married man's perspective. As an RSM, I was now in a position to ensure that the bachelors and spinsters of my company got a square deal. Their lifestyle was about to take a marked turn for the better. I banned booking out and dressing for dinner and encouraged them to invite girlfriends and boyfriends into their rooms. After all, they paid accommodation charges for their rooms in the same way as a married guy paid for his quarter, and there was no prohibition on who he could invite into his home.

Food and accommodation charges in the Army are very reasonable and there could be no complaints about paying full whack. What I always objected to was that a married man, who elected to serve apart from his spouse for whatever reason, slept and ate free of charge. These people, the beanstealers, were totally devoid of shame. A beanstealer is instantly recognisable in a queue for food—he is always to be found at the front, waiting for the chef to signal the off. If for any reason they didn't make the front of the queue, then they stood out because they took twice as much food as they could possibly eat. It was free, you see. Another giveaway was at a messing meeting, where complaints about the menu and the quality of food were aired. The person making the loudest noise and complaining more bitterly than the rest, usually over a trivial matter, would most probably be a beanstealer. I despised them with a passion.

On my second morning in the unit I elected to take my morning coffee break in the sergeant's mess dining room. As there were only two livers-in, I expected either to be in the company of the single sergeant, or to be sipping my Kaiser's Kaffee on my own. Imagine my surprise when I discovered I was sharing my rations of tea, coffee, cake, jam, marmalade, honey, toast, butter and anything else they had been able to bully out of the chef, with the entire complement of company senior ranks. So many people were troughing, in fact; that the CSM needed to shift someone over to ensure that the RSM had a seat. I enquired how much each individual paid for such lavish mid-morning fare, knowing full well what the answer would be. They were graciously permitted to continue this particular banquet without passing the hat around, but thereafter, a charge for feasts of this nature would be levied. Under sufferance, I would authorise the consumption of as much tea and coffee as they wanted at NAAFI break, but if they wanted as much as a slice of toast, then they would pay for it. Never again did I have company at my mid-morning tea break.

The chef's good nature was being further abused, however. At normal meal times I noted that the married personnel made excellent use of the unit's dining facilities, although a glance at the chef's ledgers revealed that no one ever paid for the pleasure. The standard procedure was for the married men to mill around the kitchen until the cook sergeant announced that all the single men had been fed, whereupon they would rush the hotplates like the Gaderine Swine rushing down to the water.

"The food would only go to waste if we didn't eat it, sir," was the totally unacceptable justification proffered by one particular staff sergeant.

These parasites were informed that once the single men began to form queues outside their kitchens at home, waiting to see if anything was going for nothing, then they would be at liberty to do the same thing at the boy's cookhouse. With immediate effect, competitively priced pre-paid meal tickets became available from my office for those wishing to take advantage of the cook's culinary excellence. Those with hearty appetites occasionally bought a ticket, but in general, business was slack. The incurable scavengers still made the odd compulsive foray to the cookhouse to see if they could grab any leftovers, but my regular visits to the kitchen made that a risky business. In fact, I would have spat in the food rather than let these buggers have it for nothing. If a married man wanted to eat in my cookhouse, then he would bloody well pay for it. That was my creed. Just the same, it would be naïve to imagine that they wouldn't have been back in the kitchen making hay the moment my back was turned.

Someone in the HQ was intent on giving me a baptism by fire. On only my second week in the unit, they sprang the Annual Physical Fitness Test upon us. The whole of the company's establishment, with the exception of those on duty and the sick, lame and lazy, were required to run. The test consisted of two runs, each of one and a half miles. Fifteen minutes were allotted for the first run that was completed as a squad; the second run was an individual effort and needed to be completed in a time calculated on age and sex. You couldn't dawdle on the second run, but it didn't require an Olympian effort to gain a pass either. As a member of the over forty age group, my time allowance was most generous, although I could still skip around in the eleven and a half minutes allotted to the under thirties. Failures by those under the age of thirty were quite unacceptable, therefore.

Nevertheless, there were no fewer than eight of my new charges who didn't make it in time. They were invited to my office immediately after their showers, for a little chat. Judging by their times, the majority wouldn't have lost much sweat during the test and oughtn't to have needed to tarry overlong in the ablution block. The married men amongst them were granted rather longer to shower, since they needed to go home to their quarters for the purpose. They had been denied the use of the showers in the single accommodation, as I couldn't see why we bachelors should subsidise their hot water. Once the motley band was cowering in front of my desk, I questioned them individually to ascertain the reason for their failure. They tried all the usual lame excuses on the new RSM, but were unable to elicit any sympathy. They were either overweight, bone-idle or had been on the booze the night before. No problem at all, they were cordially invited to run next morning at 0600 hrs and every morning thereafter, until they all passed. Within a week they had all managed to battle their way around the circuit, with the exception of a nineteen-year old Londoner, an Arsenal supporter. I excused him from running for two days and then ordered him to parade at 0600 hrs the next morning, with his small pack packed with all the necessary items for a stay in the guardroom. Before he started, I presented him with a committal receipt made out in his name. My instructions were that should he fail again this time, he was to carry on jogging as far as the guardroom where he was to lock himself away in a cell. It was a drastic measure and possibly a teeny-weeny bit in contravention of his human rights, but he didn't need to jog as far as the jail as it transpired. He stormed round in a very decent time.

My predecessor's method of working out a forecast of duties was different to say the least and didn't conform to any system I'd seen before. It appeared that if your name was Aardvaark, Arkwright or Booth, you were never short of a reason to bull your boots, whereas if your name was Xerxes, Yarnold or Zloty, then life was pretty cushy. He worked out his master system on a huge piece of stiff paper attached to a giant sized wooden board. The method was hopelessly inefficient and the board looked ridiculous. It was swiftly consigned to the rubbish skip and 156 Provost Company adopted a system that gave everyone a fair crack of the whip. It won the grateful thanks of those guys whose surnames began with the first few letters of the alphabet at least. I also introduced a platoon system, which had been standard policy within RMP for donkey's years, but was something with which my predecessor hadn't concerned himself.

Each day, the senior person on duty would report the fact that the morning parade was ready for my inspection. Usually I was too busy, tired or disinterested to bother myself and invariably instructed the sergeant to carry on without me. Thanks to the CSM, the guys were always impeccably turned out anyway and because I have never looked particularly dapper in uniform, the whole idea of me inspecting them was somewhat embarrassing. During my third week in the hot seat however, in a moment of military fanaticism, I elected to take the parade. This decision clearly came as an unwelcome surprise to the sergeant and despite his attestation to the contrary, I discovered that four men were absent from the parade. Whilst secretly admiring his efforts to cover up for his comrades, I had to chastise him soundly for telling me porky pies and he lived to regret his action. The four defaulters were in my office within five minutes, whereupon I invited them to explain their unwillingness to grace the morning parade. They were all single men who had been to a party the previous evening and they were all suffering horribly from hangovers. I explained to them that the enormity of a hangover had never prevented me from getting on parade and consequently, they could expect no sympathy from me. They paraded ten minutes later in their walking gear and I drove them out into the countryside for a distance of twenty-five miles. Having dropped them all off at different spots and having divested them of maps and money, they were then told to find their way home. They all made it back and, as if by magic, absentees from parade became a rarity thereafter.

The Company soccer team was in the doldrums and it didn't take an Alf Ramsey to realise that none of the senior management had been even remotely interested in the side. Things changed and suddenly the players found themselves with time off for training and they never needed to work the night before a game. Soon we had the semblance of a side. I recall particularly an amusing incident that occurred shortly after my first team selection was published. A staff sergeant came into my office and informed me that one of his corporals, a man that I had selected for the side, was on duty at the time of the match and therefore unavailable for selection. He maintained that manpower shortages prevented him for releasing the corporal. How droll! I was able to solve his manning problems in a trice and still have my full back for next day's match. The staff sergeant discovered that his white belt and armband still fitted, provided they were taken out a notch or two and he volunteered to perform the corporal's duty for him. Despite my best efforts, alas, the soccer team remained mediocre. We were probably the fittest, best trained, best turned out duffers in the whole of the south of England.

Still finding my feet, I returned to the unit lines in the early hours of Monday morning following a weekend up in darkest Leicester. To my surprise, the normally blazing lights of the duty room had been replaced by a subdued glow. I went to investigate and discovered the duty NCO sitting behind the reception desk in an armchair with his boots off, a book in his hand and a table lamp plugged into a socket. It was good to see that he was making himself at home, although what surprised me more was the fact that he remained seated as I addressed him.

"Do you normally perform your duty like this, corporal?"

"Yes sir," he had the gall to reply.

"Well, you don't any longer. Boots on! Light on! Armchair away! Report to me in the morning at 0830 hrs, along with the orderly sergeant!"

This was yet another indication of the sloppy way in which the place had been run. Once I had them in my office I scared the life out of the sergeant and, since the corporal appeared so content behind the desk, I gave him the opportunity of spending the next seven nights in the place.

A couple of weeks later I set my alarm for 0400 hrs and wandered down to the duty room, just to ensure that the lads were carrying out their duties in the way I had prescribed. This time the light was on, but the duty NCO was lying fast asleep on the floor behind the desk, oblivious to everything. The other members of the duty shift were down in the rest room, all of them in the Land of Nod too. I retraced my steps to the duty room without stirring a soul and made an entry in the desk diary, detailing my findings and ordering the entire shift to parade outside my office later that morning. The noisy slamming of the door served to rouse the slumbering oaf behind the desk and I trust that they all had a fraught night once they had read my comments in the desk diary. I wasn't at my most charming next morning and I made the message very plain. The men of 156 Provost Company would either do their job professionally, or they could scour the situations vacant columns for alternative employment.

It's traditional to 'dine in' a new RSM and during my second week at Colchester the mess members honoured me thus. Regimental dinners are great fun and this one ought to have been the very best in my career, it being my first as an RSM. Making a good speech at this dinner I judged to be imperative and so I put in a great deal of time and effort to ensure it would be up to standard. Speaking in public has never been a problem to me, but this inaugural speech proved most difficult to deliver, thanks to a stream of interruptions from one particular staff sergeant. The man had either drunk too much pop, or had a death wish. Halfway through my address and in mid-sentence, I suddenly stopped talking, put down my notes and walked down the table to where the loud-mouthed Londoner was sitting.

"Make one more squeak whilst I'm talking, mister, and I'll break your fucking nose," I whispered in his ear.

That did the trick. He remained mute for the remainder of my monologue. Perhaps it was from this moment on that the senior ranks realised that the new RSM wasn't as soft a touch as his predecessor had been.

There are people in positions of importance in the Army who have the notion that falling leaves must be swept up instantly. Each autumn, soldiers all over the world parade with brooms and rakes to do the necessary. By next morning they have to parade again, to sweep up the leaves that descended overnight. I am of the persuasion that if you wait until December, then all the leaves will have fallen and you can sweep them all up at one go. I know that sweeping leaves gives the boys something to do, but even the most lacklustre RSM ought to be able to find something a little less mundane to occupy his men. Finding a worthy undertaking for your NCOs whilst serving in the UK is certainly a brainteaser. Occupational therapy becomes a skill that needs to be mastered if your men are to remain anything like contented. Rather than issue my men with a bass broom apiece, or to make them clean Landrovers that were already clean, I tried to introduce more interesting methods of filling in the time. Rather than have them run around and around the barracks to keep fit, I introduced a derivative of orienteering that we did in the countryside of Essex and the bordering county of Suffolk. It was orienteering with a difference, in that the participants walked rather than ran and that the last checkpoint was invariably alongside a friendly hostelry—a pub that would accept sweaty, muddy soldiers, that is. I believed that these weekly walks were popular; the boys told me that they were and my confidante told me that the lads were much happier doing that than the boring alternatives. In any case, the RSM liked them, so we did them.

The last of these jaunts for a considerable period of time took place on the Essex/Suffolk border, in an area dissected by a deep, wide stream. The sections of maps that were issued to the lads actually showed two bridges crossing the stream, but I knew from my recce that the northernmost bridge no longer existed. With half the checkpoints situated on either side of the watercourse, it was logical that everyone would need to cross the lower bridge at some time during the morning—either that, or get very damp. Being in my sneaky mode that day, I concealed my car up a track and hid myself in some bushes by the bridge to await the arrival of the competitors. After an hour and a half I was beginning to get confused—not one individual had used the footbridge, although a dozen or more had approached the bridge from the north only to turn right up a farm track. Since the track led nowhere and there were no checkpoints along its length, I became suspicious that there was mischief afoot. My suspicions were heightened when an exceedingly wet lance corporal squelched his way over the footbridge, the only person to cross all morning. It's amazing how quickly a new lance corporal will spill the beans when the RSM suddenly jumps out of a bush and grabs him by the front of his shirt. The poor lad had been ordered to swim over the stream by his wicked staff sergeant, the mouthy individual from the Mess Dinner Night, and obtain all the clues from the far side of the water. Once he had completed that task, he was to rendezvous at a given location. That location was only a hundred yards distant, along the track that I had seen the lads swarming up, like bees on a nuptial flight. The wet lance corporal and I walked up the track together and it soon became obvious that we were approaching the rest of the guys. The sound of music and the clinking of glasses were a dead give-away. Under a large oak tree, in a pretty meadow, a party was in full swing. Whilst the poor lad had been scurrying around the countryside, this lot had been tucking into chicken legs, supping beer and generally making merry. Like Queen Victoria, we were not amused and I declined the staff sergeant's offer of a cold tin of Fosters. My fury at having my good intentions thrown back in my face was monumental.

On Saturday morning the whole unit paraded as I read the Riot Act. This company would work hard and play hard and its leaders would show a sense of responsibility, or else! It was the standard show of strength that an RSM needs to manifest on occasions and it works for a while. Just to prove that I was still far from being a happy man, I ordered them to sweep leaves, pull up weeds and dig gardens for the remainder of the day. It would have been all day too, but the Colchester United game kicked off at 1500 hrs, so I declared an amnesty half an hour before that. Believing myself to have been betrayed by the very people whose lot I was trying to improve, I decided that the buggers could sweep leaves all winter, or until my anger subsided. A few days later I saw the funny side; I'd done many things worse than that in my time. My show of strength certainly worked, though, and visitors to my office were conspicuous by their absence. In the end, life actually became lonely down in my office and so I wandered out to talk to them. Finally several of the lads approached me, to ask when the walks would start again. There were too many of them for it to be contrived, I hope. Anyway, once the cold snap abated, we began again.

Having finally put the unit into the kind of order that satisfied me, it was time to get to know the other warrant officers in the huge garrison and sound them out about their attitude towards dealing with crime. To my way of thinking, the RSM of the unit to which an errant soldier belonged should, whenever feasible, be permitted to deal with any disciplinary incidents internally. Once the civilian police, the HQ or the newspapers were involved, however, then the matter was out of my hands. Then it was usually necessary to prepare a formal report. All the warrant officers were in agreement that a telephone call from me the morning after an incident would be sufficient for them to deal with an incident summarily. They were made aware that, should my facts ever be contested, then a full report would find its way onto their CO's desk. It was never necessary to resort to this course of action.

One of the major units in Colchester was a tough, Scottish infantry battalion that was responsible for far more than its fair share of trouble in the town. Their RSM would vehemently deny that accusation. John Clyde was particularly happy to keep his boy's misdemeanours out of the headlines; a low crime rate would enhance his image as a harsh disciplinarian. Whenever it was necessary for me to call him, he would invariably thank me for my efforts and end the conversation with the same comment.

"Leave it tae me Wullie, I'll peg the bastard."

I always had a picture in my mind's eye of a poor Jock being hauled in front of big John, getting the bollocking of a lifetime and probably a thick ear if he wasn't sufficiently repentant. John was my best customer by far and we talked regularly.

Some months elapsed before a case of a repeat defaulter came along. John listened to the facts as usual, thanked me as usual, but finished our conversation with a variation on his usual theme.

"Leave it tae me Wullie, I'll double peg the bastard," he said.

"Double peg him, John?"

"Aye Wullie. Double defaulter, double pegging! Fifty-six days."

"What's a pegging then?"

"I know you're English Wullie, but surely even an Englishman can divide fifty-six in two. Single pegging, twenty-eight days."

The realisation hit me. Every time I'd called him about one of his lads, he'd jailed the poor sod for a month on my uncorroborated, hearsay evidence. Horror of horrors! I called around to have a coffee immediately and explained my reluctance to have men jailed on inadmissible evidence.

"Ach! We dinnae bother wi' all that Judges' Rules and laws of evidence shite in the battalion Wullie. I have no understanding o' the legal system and I've no inclination tae learn," he said.

I tried once again to explain the rationale behind my calls. The big man smiled.

"Do I try and tell you how to run your unit Wullie?"

"No, of course you don't."

"Well then, dinnae tell me how tae run mine," he said. "You see, there's a great deal of difference between your corporals and my Jocks. Your fellies are all bright lads, some o' mine can hardly read and write. There are some real bad bastards among them as well and if you dinnae rule wi' an iron fist, you'd soon lose control. They'd beat you."

He was probably right, but just the same, I didn't phone him very often after that.

I interviewed all the new NCOs on their first morning in the unit and it was probably a terrifying ordeal for them, especially those who had arrived straight from the Training Centre. Once the CSM had marched the lad in to my office, I would stand him at ease and go through my normal routine. No military nonsense for me, though; I could confidently leave all the khaki-brained stuff to the CSM. My first question was always the same and an interview normally went thus.

"Which football team do you support, son?"

"I'm not interested in football, sir."

"Oh yes you bloody well are. Sergeant major!"

The CSM would be waiting for his cue and would make a mighty entrance.
"Sir?"

"Sergeant major, this man doesn't have a football team. Fix him up with one."

The CSM was as football daft as myself and delighted in playing along. He would march the young man out and instruct him that an interest in soccer wasn't optional in 156, but mandatory. The new lance corporal would be marched back in later, with the name of a football team embossed permanently on his brain. It was always a Yorkshire team, usually Leeds United or Doncaster Rovers. The guys learnt that it paid to be a sportsman in my unit. Word must have filtered down to the Training Centre at Chichester because, as time went on, recruits with not the faintest ability or interest in soccer would arrive claiming to have a passion for the sport. My leg pulling of the new lads came to an end following an interview with one Lance Corporal Tudor.

"Do you play football lad?"

"Yes sir."

"Are you any good?"

"Yes sir."

"Who do you support?"

"Spurs sir."

"Spurs! They're all Nancy boys, aren't they?"

"They are my team, sir. I watch them home and away."

He only supported a London side, but already this lad was an improvement on the non-sporting types that had been arriving in recent times.

"Do you play cricket?"

"Yes sir."

"Any good?"

"I play to a decent standard sir."

"You're a confident young man Tudor, that's for sure."

"Do you play rugby?"

"Yes sir."

Do you play squash?"

"Yes sir."

"Sergeant major! This man is playing squash with me at 1400 hrs, book the court, kit him out and make sure he knows the way there."

I could beat all the alleged squash players in our unit without breaking sweat and was confident that Lance Corporal Tudor would go the same way as the others. He looked the part just the same and hit the ball particularly hard. Perhaps he would give me a decent game. He gave me a decent match all right—he beat me out of sight. He had omitted to inform me during the interview that he had been in the England under eighteen squad.

Bob Tudor turned out to be a very handy sportsman and he excelled in several disciplines. He won the District Squash Championships almost immediately and played for Ardleigh in the English Squash League. He represented the Army at cricket and rugby and was a genuine enough soccer player. I gave him every opportunity to play his games, as I did to all of the sportsmen, with the exception of darts players and fishermen.

There must have been some footballers coming out of the Training Centre, but precious few of them finished up in Colchester. Our team boasted half a dozen assorted strips, we trained two or three times a week, players had time off and yet we remained anchored at the bottom of the Garrison League. Not only were we at the bottom at the halfway stage of the season, but we were also without a single point. Sod's Law dictated that the day that the soccer loving Assistant Provost Marshal arrived for his annual look around the unit, we would be scheduled to play against the Signals Squadron. These buggers had won twelve matches out of twelve and were sure to rattle up a cricket score against our woeful defence. After the OC and I had given our bullshit briefings to the colonel, we trooped over to the pitch, arriving just as the players came off for half time. I slipped over to ascertain the score from our sponge man.

"One—nil," he reported.

"Brilliant," I replied. "We're holding the league leaders to a single goal."

"No sir," said the stupefied sergeant. "We're winning one—nil."

It transpired that we had taken an awful beating in the first half as expected, but the ball simply wouldn't go into our net. The Signals had missed two penalties; hit the bar so many times that it was still wobbling and had missed a cartload of easy chances. On the half-hour, Corporal Menzies had picked up a hopeful downfield punt, run a full forty yards and swung his leg at the ball. It had scorched into the net. The second half was an embarrassment. Our players were camped on their own goal line, yet somehow managed to stop everything that was thrown at them. If the Signals had scored once, they would surely have scored a dozen. Just as it appeared that we must cave in, a miracle occurred. Another long punt, another chase and swing of the leg by Menzies and we were two up. To a man the opposition sank to the ground in total disbelief and we ran out 2–0 winners. The colonel was mightily impressed by our performance; perhaps he didn't know as much about the game as I thought. I was pleased for the lads, though. It was their only victory of the season.

Colin Lampton had two tickets for the midweek match at White Hart Lane, where Spurs were entertaining Newcastle. We sat high in the stand, surrounded by a sea of black and white and watched the Toon take a 4–1 drubbing. By the time we reached Liverpool Street station to catch the train back to Colchester, Colin was beginning to emerge from his post match depression and suggested we take a bite to eat before boarding the 2230. As he bagged a table at Casey Jones' Burger Emporium, I joined the queue to place an order for two double Caseyburgers and two giant portions of chips. As the queue inched towards the counter, I became aware of the guy behind me. He was delighting in bumping himself into my backside each time we moved forward. After four or five thrusts of his male member in my direction, it became pretty obvious it wasn't happening by accident.

"Watch yourself as you move forward, squire," I advised.

"What yer talkin' abart chief?" he replied.

"Every time we move forward, you're banging into my arse. Pack it in."

"Fink yer 'ard enough to do somefink abart it?"

"I'm convinced of the fact."

"Go on then chief, let's see yer do somefink abart it," he invited.

Well, the chief did do 'somefink abart' the state of affairs and smote the scoundrel down. When he regained his feet, he began to bleat on about the fact that he was registered as partially sighted and that I had hit a blind man. Visually impaired he may have been, but vocally he was in great shape and he persisted in pressing home his point about being persecuted for his disability. My order was ready by this time and rather than have my evening repast ruined by this London windbag, I gave him a further 'fump in the north and south' to silence him for good.

I hadn't seen my old pal John Kellard for years, not since the great centre forward and surely the only cricket player ever to have clean bowled five batsmen in five balls, had left the Army to return to his native Northeast. A call from out of the blue revealed that John was in London, attending a course. He explained that he would be delighted if I could turn up for his end of course booze up, being held at the RMP Mess in London the next evening.

Within a couple of minutes of my arrival at the mess, we were swapping stories as if we had seen each other only the day before. The evening was still in full swing at midnight and the prospects of me making the last train back to Colchester had disappeared. Adopting my RSM's voice, I called the unit and ordered a car to come and pick me up. With the drink flowing in torrents, the question of my transport back was quite forgotten until the arrival of Corporal H. He was a big, amiable Londoner, to whom had fallen the unenviable task of picking up the drunken RSM and driving him back to Colly.

My recollection of the homeward journey was sketchy, except that Hyde Park seemed to stick in my mind. Next morning I felt like death warmed up, but dragged myself out of bed just the same and donned my RSM's garb. Regardless of the size of the hangover, it was imperative that the RSM be at his desk at the prescribed hour. Once the important decisions of the day had been taken, it was time to put my bluffing programme into action, by making a lot of noise, creating mayhem amongst the boys and ensuring that the officers knew the RSM was around and in fierce form. Then I could sneak back to bed on the pretext that there was a meeting to attend. Before I could manage an escape on this particular morning, however, Corporal H knocked on my door.

"Mornin' sir," he said, rather too cheerily for my liking.

"What do you want, you vile man?"

"Just thought I'd check to see if you were all right like, sir."

"Of course I'm all right. Why shouldn't I be all right? How dare you come into my office and ask such an impertinent question?"

"I was the geezer what picked you up from the Smoke last night sir, that's all."

"Oh. It was you, was it, Corporal H? Was I out of order? Did I misbehave?"

"Nah! You was on great form, sir. It's only that I ain't never seen nobody pewk up four times in the length of Hyde Park before, that's all. I thought I'd see if you was okay."

"Very magnanimous of you young man," I said. "Now piss of."

The man was keeping me out of my bed.

Next morning, having sworn total abstinence until the next time, I received a call from John Kellard.

"Grand neet the other neet la'," he said. "How was your heed?"

"Grim, Mr Kellard, grim," I replied.

"Me as weel. It wasn't the twelve pints of beer that done wa' the knaws?"

"Wasn't it?"

"Na! It was the twelve double Tia Maria chasers," he explained.

The unit boasted both a sergeant's and corporal's mess that were open for six days a week, but closed on Mondays. It was me that insisted on keeping our place open, although in truth, it was pitifully poorly patronised. If there were no customers by 2030 hrs, the barman was instructed to pack up and spend his evening in the corporal's bar next door. I took a glass or two most evenings, just to show my face, but seldom had anyone to talk to. The only other liver-in was a man who seldom used the mess, for which I was thankful since he was a world standard bore. As a consequence of our place being so quiet, the corporals saw rather more of me than they ought. This wasn't really acceptable militarily, but I was the RSM and no one would labour the point. At least there was a chance of some local ladies in the lad's bar and I don't think my welcome ever wore thin. Hopefully they even had a modicum of respect for their single RSM whom, probably unknown to them, regularly put his neck on the block in their cause.

If ever I fancied a beer on a Monday evening when the messes were closed, then the Drury Arms over on Layer Road was handy. It wasn't a soldier's bar by any means, but the landlord made the RMP very welcome. At the bar one evening stood an old man of some eighty summers, who was wearing a RMP cravat. These things hadn't been in vogue for decades and I'd only ever seen one before. I went over to speak to the old fellow and to investigate his line of neckwear.

"Hello sir," I said. "I see that you are an old Corps man?"

"Am indeed, young man, one of the original SIB men I was," he replied with pride.

Our conversation blossomed as we downed a couple of pints and he positively jumped at my invitation to attend the forthcoming Summer Ball. I decided that I liked old Fred. Confessing that he was no longer a man of the night, he beat an early retreat.

"Got to get home to the old ball and chain before she sends out a search party," he declared.

"Well RSM, it's been a great pleasure to make your acquaintance and I look forward to seeing you again," said Fred.

"Likewise Fred," I declared and put out my hand to shake his. Fred crooked a finger into my palm as our hands met.

"Sorry Fred, I'm not a freemason," I said, presuming this to be some kind of ritualistic handshake.

"Me neither son," he replied. "I've got a bloody arthritic finger."

Each year, military police units were subjected to a technical inspection carried out by the senior RMP officer in the area, a man who really ought to know the score but who seldom did. The normal procedure was for the colonel's staff to sniff around the lines looking for cock-ups, leaving him to drink tea, or something stronger, with the unit management. Our colonel decided to adopt a modified approach for his inspection at Colchester—he would do everything on his own. I believe that he had actually confused the Technical Inspection with the Annual Inspection of the Unit or a trip to the seaside, three quite distinct things, because instead of arriving to look at the books, he began by crashing out the unit for war. Not only did he crash us out, but he did so at four in the morning! Unbeknown to him, his staff in London had already tipped me the wink and when he arrived at the duty room in the middle of the night, he found the NCOs wide-awake and on the ball. I was summoned to the duty room and arrived two minutes later, dressed in my tracksuit and feigning tiredness and surprise.

"Morning RSM. Surprised?" he asked.

"What the fuck are you doing here at this time of the morning sir? Are we at war?"

"Technical Inspection RSM. Crash out the unit. I shall be inspecting at 0700 hrs."

"Very good sir, you certainly caught us on the hop," I lied.

The guys on duty put the well-rehearsed plan into action and very soon signs of activity were evident. Considering that we had prepared everything the previous day, I was surprised at the cacophony of noise that came from the garages. Meanwhile, the APM had a cup of coffee in my office and we talked about rugby. Once the cooks had surfaced, we had breakfast together and then I dumped him off on the OC. At the prescribed hour, the unit was on parade and ready for war. Everything looked good; the guys were all briefed in their roles and were dressed identically. That was an achievement in itself, as there is invariably one clown who will turn up dressed differently to the rest. I marched up to the colonel in a reasonably smart fashion and uttered the age-old crap.

"156 Provost Company formed up and ready for your inspection sir. Sixty-two men on parade, two sick, six on leave and four detached."

These figures always seemed to delight senior officers and although my figures were bona fide, you could say anything that came into your mind and no one would be any the wiser. The colonel began his inspection and approached the first Landrover.

"Show me your first-aid kit, tyre pressure gauge and your perang," he ordered.

The crew promptly produced the first two items, but didn't know what a perang was.

"Man here doesn't know what a perang is RSM!" the colonel shouted triumphantly.

"He's mentally retarded sir. Leave him to me, a good horse whipping will soon sort him out."

I turned to the CSM and asked if he knew what a perang was. He didn't. By this time the colonel was with the second crew.

"Another man here doesn't know what a perang is RSM!"

"You simply can't get the staff these days sir. Leave him to me, I'll have him horsewhipped too."

Thinking that perang sounded a bit African and knowing that the APM was an old Southern Rhodesia hand, I walked briskly over to a guy who had served in Kenya with the Gordon Highlanders. He read my mind before I reached him.

"It's a machete," he whispered.

Saved by the Gordons! By the time he reached the fourth vehicle, word had got around and each subsequent vehicle commander handed him a brand new machete. In fact, each vehicle commander presented him with the very same machete and the colonel inspected the same one at least eight times without ever realising. We finished up with a glowing inspection report.

The APM was aware of my irreverent sense of humour and I saw no harm in sending him a memorandum shortly afterwards. It read as follows:

The order to 'produce parangs' that you gave during your recent inspection of the unit caused some confusion. A subsequent poll of company personnel produced the following interesting replies to the question, "What is a parang?"

A type of fish—5

An island off the coast of Malaya—I

A minor traffic accident—I

Don't know—43

14

The unit was to be graced by a visit from the General, which meant that the boys were kept busy for a week cleaning every nook and cranny. The bullshit was laid on thickest on the top corridor, where it was down to the officers to convince the important man that we were in good nick. In the event, everything went well and the visit culminated in a lunchtime Christmas drinks party for all ranks in the sergeant's mess. Although we managed to spell the General's name incorrectly in the visitor's book, something that he was at pains to point out to me, the whole affair went particularly well. The boys were stood down, although the majority stayed behind in the mess to wind down after a fraught couple of days. The company thinned out during the course of the afternoon until, at the bitter end, there were only two people left. The OC and me, just as tradition demands it should be. We were still in service dress, but by this time we were sporting paper hats and annoying each other with those curly blower things that have a feather in the end and squeak when you blow them. Our QM arrived at 1800 hrs and grumbled about something or other, but he was boringly sober and so we ignored him. Ten minutes later and he was back, to remind me that the mess had been let out to the Garrison Wives' Club for their Christmas bash and that the ladies would soon be arriving. I vaguely recalled giving them permission, but by this time both the OC and I were in the sort of condition where nothing matters, except where the next beer was coming from. Despite further requests from the Q, followed by pleas and finally a full-blown sulk, we were still dug in at the bar when the ladies began to arrive. Major Roy has few equals when it comes to charming the ladies; they fall at his feet and his patter would charm the birds out of the trees. Roy made flattering remarks about their looks and their bosoms, which they loved, and we soon became the star attractions. It was then that the Q, upset by the fact that we were ruining his meticulously planned evening, played his trump card. He sent his broad shouldered wife over to have a word with us.

"Bugger off and ruin someone else's party," she suggested.

How could anyone refuse such a delicately worded offer? We went next door to visit the corporals and carried on with our outrageous behaviour in their mess. Over the next few hours we put the world to rights, until Major Roy called it a night. To be fair, he was travelling down to Kent next morning. I stayed until there were only three of us left, including the barman. Our numbers increased by one when the wife of one of the unit's senior ranks entered. She declared that she was not yet ready to go home and accepted my offer of a drink. Following a number of nightcaps, I was brazen enough to invite her to my room for coffee and she accepted. A cup of Colombian Blue Mountain, a little risqué chat, a stolen kiss and the rest is a blank. Waking at 0620 hrs, I discovered to my absolute horror that the lady was in my bed. I shook her awake and told her the time.

"Better be going," she said wisely.

"What the hell are you going to say to your husband?" I asked.

"Don't worry, I'll think of something on the way home."

"Were we perhaps a little silly last night?" I suggested, wondering if she had any more recollection of the last few hours than I did.

"You were marvellous. We must do it again sometime."

"We were stupid and it must certainly never happen again," I replied.

It was flattering to have been adjudged marvellous, even if my performance had been alcohol assisted, but it would be the height of folly to get involved with this lady. Clandestine sexual liaisons and ruined careers go hand in hand and furthermore, I knew her husband too well. She walked up the road towards the married quarters at 0640 hrs and I spent a fraught weekend wondering whether she would tell her husband the real reason for her late arrival. He came storming into my office on Monday morning, but just for a good old grumble about his wife's tardy arrival home from the party.

"That's the last time my wife goes to one of those wives' club functions," he declared. "Do you know what time she arrived home on Saturday morning?"

I had a pretty good idea. About fifteen minutes after she left my bed, give or take a few seconds.

"No. When?" I asked.

"Half past two in the bloody morning, that's bloody when."

So, she appeared to be a lady of honour. Just the same, I spent the next twelve months wondering whether she would ever let it slip, but she never told. I received the odd suggestive telephone call from her and she gave me outrageous discounts at the shop where she worked and, tempted as I was on occasions, I tactfully declined her kind offers. It doesn't do to shit on your own doorstep too often.

We had self-contained accommodation for the senior ranks, as well as single rooms for almost all of the corporals, male and female. Since this was the 80s, I had no problems with the corporals inviting visitors of the opposite sex to their rooms. My only stipulation was that if a person was staying overnight, then I wanted to know who it was in case the building should burn down and we had one charred body too many in the morning. In addition, whenever an orgy was taking place, then it was mandatory to send me an invitation. I never inspected the rooms with the purpose of catching anyone out and only ever went into their block if there was a specific reason. Like the day I accompanied the CQMS, who was measuring up for new carpets. There was one young lad who lived in a room on his own and when he failed to acknowledge my knock on the door, I allowed the Q to use his passkey. The NCO lay in his bed, a stunned look on his face and with an extra pair of feet protruding from the bottom of his bed.

"I have no objections to the extra pair of feet in your bed young man," I said, "provided that they belong to a female member of the species."

"Y-yes sir, they d-do," he stuttered in reply.

"Would you mind introducing the lady to me?"

"I can't sir."

"Why, have you killed her?"

"No sir. It's just that it's Sally."

I demanded that the sheets be pulled back to reveal the naughty lady. It was indeed the blushing Sally, the gloriously breasted darling of a girl from Cambridgeshire, the personification of all my dirtiest fantasies and my dream screw. And there she lay, in bed with this young man and, presumably, not the virgin I'd always presumed her to be. That boy went up mightily in my estimation.

The RMP Corps Benevolent Fund was badly named, for benevolent was the last thing it was. It was a fund with similarities to Topsy; in that it just growed and growed and prising money out of it was a bugger's own job. Each year, the Corps Secretary would give details of just how clever he and his fellow administrators had been in prudently investing the large sum of money and just how mean they had been in giving as little as possible away to deserving causes. A person applying for a handout from the fund was subjected to a means test of the severest nature.

After he had left the Corps, Inky Davis found himself in a position where he needed alms. It befell me to travel to East Anglia, armed with a copy of his case history and a multi-page questionnaire, to see whether he merited the fund's grudging charity. All that the guy wanted was a measly two hundred quid to prevent the Electricity Board from cutting off his supply. Had anyone stopped to consider just how much it would cost to investigate this case? It would have been cheaper to send him a cheque by return of post. Who, after all, would belittle himself for such a piddling amount, were he not really desperate? Inky hadn't done particularly well since leaving the Army and he really wasn't in a very sound financial position. He had ditched his first wife, he was supporting his kids and now he had a new spouse, a new kid and another on the way. He was also father to four Boxer puppies, one of which deposited shit on my shoe as soon as I sat down.

It was impossible to miss the new Peugeot 504 standing outside his house and it was with the mixed emotions of embarrassment and confusion that I began to fill in the questionnaire. Perhaps he wasn't in such a financial plight?

"Can't you sell that bloody big car and buy a smaller one?" I asked.

"A 504 is about the only car a guy of 6 foot 8 can get into in comfort and I can't sell it anyway, because the bloke that re-sprayed it after the accident buggered the job up and I'm suing him through the Small Claims Court. Then I need a big car for the dogs."

This was classic Inky. Whatever he did degenerated into confusion and complication.

"Why do you need four dogs, Inky?"

"We're going to breed from them."

"I hate to tell you this, but they're all males."

"Yes, but their mother's not."

"Isn't that incestuous?"

"Not in dogs."

"What happened to your gratuity?"

"I bought a van and a hot potato oven."

"Where did you do your business? Isn't this a rural area?"

"Fakenham Races, Hunstanton and at the market," he replied.

I knew that Fakenham Races only operated for a few days each year and that Hunstanton was hardly awash with holidaymakers in winter. I began to doubt his business plan, but he winked at me as if he knew something I didn't.

"The van was no bloody good, though, and it broke down after a couple of weeks. The bloke who sold it to me had done a runner and I never could find him. Then I fell out with the Paki who had the next pitch to me at the market; he objected to the smell of pork sausage and bacon and he damaged my oven. I gave him a good thumping and finished up in court."

Oh dear! Inky's life continued to be one long disaster story. A leopard never changes its spots, it seems.

"One last question, Inky," I said. "I see that you have seven hundred quid in the Leicester Building Society. Why don't you pay the electricity bill with that?"

"I would, but I owe the landscape gardener nearly all of that."

I didn't ask why he had a landscape gardener's bill; although he would have given a plausible reason for the expenditure, I'm certain. He burst into tears at this point, whether from genuine emotion or as part of an Inky Davis ploy, I wasn't sure. I agreed to give him the cash anyway.

The last time I heard Inky's name mentioned was during a telephone conversation. The Army Recruiting Office in Norwich contacted me to request a reference for one of his sons. He had applied to join the Royal Artillery. Normally I will give anyone a reference with the greatest of pleasure, but in this lad's case, I had to refuse. He simply wasn't a fit person to be at the important end of an artillery piece, not while I was still in the Army anyway. After a period of soul searching, I concluded that the answer was to call the recruiting sergeant personally and explain my reluctance to vouch for the young man. Once I mentioned the name Davis, the sergeant interrupted me.

"It's okay, sir, the application has been withdrawn on the instruction of the recruiting officer. The lad and his father came in here last week and finished up fighting each other on the waiting room floor."

Why didn't that surprise me?

The subject of a person's religious leaning was a matter of supreme indifference to me, until I served in Northern Ireland. The legacy of two tours in the Province was that my attitude towards someone might indeed by coloured by his denomination. Whenever a new NCO was posted into Colchester, my eye would be involuntarily drawn to the religion box on his personal information card and, rightly or wrongly, his initial interview would be conducted according to what I found there. That's not as sinister as it might sound, since his accent, his ability to play sport and his physical size was just as likely to have an effect. This over profound preamble brings me to a perfectly innocent story regarding denomination.

With nothing better to do one morning, I went through the company nominal role to determine exactly how many of each persuasion we had in the unit. There was a majority of C of E as usual, an equal number of Methodists and United Reform Church and only three of the Pope's boys. It was sinful for sure, but it occurred to me that if we could move the three papists before any more guys were posted in, we would have a totally Protestant unit. We could add a 'd' to the 'Pro' and become 156 Prod Coy. Now it just so happened that we had a requirement to send one man to Gibraltar, one to Belize and another to the Falklands, and it was as easy as that. Alas, we remained a 'Prod Coy' for only a brief period of time, before the colonel responsible for RMP postings at the Records Office ruined things. He made me an offer I couldn't refuse, an extra man who was to be supernumerary. This bonus NCO was a man with whom I had served before and he was most certainly a left footer. His arrival may have spoilt our Protestant bloodline, but he bolstered up our squash team a treat.

Life hadn't treated Katie Hill too kindly in recent years. A broken marriage had been the last straw and she had let herself go a little. She was prone to certain excesses, with alcohol, nicotine and men featuring highly among her interests. She had never been a pretty girl, but now she was fat, plain and a little unkempt. Even her personality had taken a turn for the worse. Katie needed a complete change, a fresh start. She had decided to terminate her military service. By way of a resettlement course she had chosen to spend some time in a convent; perhaps a period of spiritual contemplation would be beneficial. Those who knew her were astonished at her decision and even more dumbfounded that there was a religious order that would take her in.

Considering that Katie smoked thirty cigarettes a day, I found it ironic that the religious order had dubbed her Sister Consulator for her trial period. By some miracle, though, Katie actually passed her probation and returned to the unit to complete her discharge documentation. If there were a more unlikely nun in the world than Sister Consulator, I'd have loved to meet her. On the day of her departure, I took her in to see the OC for her final interview and, ten minutes later, she was back with me to hear a few well-chosen words of wisdom. My fervent wish was that this girl would make her mark in her chosen pursuit, but in reality I was hopelessly pessimistic about her chances. At the moment of departure, I did something that was beyond the call of duty and kissed her. As a final flourish, I carried the good sister's suitcases out to the car that would convey her to the railway station, and almost ruptured myself

"What the hell have you got in these cases, Katie?" I asked.

"Carlsberg," she replied.

"Carlsberg?" I repeated, seeking confirmation that my hearing hadn't failed me.

"You can't get a beer in the convent, so I'm taking a couple of crates in with me," she said in all seriousness.

And so Sister Consulator left Her Majesty's service and headed for the convent. Rumour has it that she became Katie Hill again a few days later.

Frew Wingrave was a very decent man and I'd always liked him when we had served together in Hohne. Unfortunately, Frew was bordering on being an alcoholic. He turned up for parade on time, performed his duties well and never imbibed in uniform; but, come opening time, he was always the first through the door and the last out. He had made a pleasing impression in his initial interview in Colchester. He was now married with a couple of kids and, more importantly, he had renounced the drink. He explained that he had been dry for four years and that Alcoholics Anonymous had been his crutch, helping him to make this profound change to his way of life. By the time he arrived in Colchester he was a senior corporal and appeared to be an ideal candidate for the vacancy as NCO in charge of our Thetford Detachment. The training area up in Norfolk was used throughout the year by units from all over the UK and it needed the presence of someone with experience to keep the place running smoothly. He was offered the position and was delighted at the prospect of showing his worth.

Six months later I was congratulating myself on having made such an astute decision. The detachment was in fine shape and the unit had received many letters of congratulation from senior officers, all stating that Wingrave was an exceptional NCO. He was obviously a contender for promotion and I would ensure that he received the strongest recommendation.

Frew's father was a doctor and resident physician to the Mission of Seaman somewhere on the East Coast. Wingrave Senior was well acquainted with the problems of alcoholism and it was the good doctor who had put his son in touch with AA in the first place. Frew came down from Thetford one day and requested a private chat. It transpired that his father was suffering from cancer and had only a short while to live. He was given permission to travel up to Grimsby and was present at his father's bedside when he died. He returned to work once he had settled the affairs of his widower father and it appeared that everything was back to normal. The death of his father, though, had a traumatic effect on Drew and he failed to attend his AA meetings. The result was devastating.

The RMP Duty Officer saw fit to travel up to Thetford, to make a few spot checks and to ensure that the place hadn't burnt down. Whilst there, he decided upon an audit of the little hospitality bar that we ran adjacent to the duty room. He called me by phone.

"I think you might want to come up here and check the hospitality bar, sir. There's something badly wrong with the sums," the staff sergeant informed me.

"How bad is his addition?" I asked.

"There have been two hundred and thirty four quid's worth of sales since the last check ten days ago and there's only eighty-eight pence in the kitty."

I ordered him to bring Wingrave back from the detachment with him; there were a few things he needed to explain to me. He marched into my office, his head hung low.

"Okay, Frew—what's the score, son?" I enquired.

He explained about the trauma of his father's illness, his death and the fact that he had missed his all-important AA meetings and gone off the rails.

"So I told my wife that I was going on exercise, took some kit into the detachment and locked myself into the bar for a few days."

"What did you drink?"

"Everything with the exception of the brasso, sir. I draw the line at brasso."

It would have been amusing if it hadn't been so tragic.

"Bloody hell, Drew, what am I going to do with you?"

"I wonder if you would be good enough to send me to Woolwich Hospital to undergo the Alcoholic Rehabilitation Course? I enjoyed the last one and I'm confident it would put me back on the straight and narrow."

We sent him to London and he emerged a month later with the battle half won. The doctors gave him a good report and were impressed by his will to stay off the booze. He was no longer entrusted with Thetford Detachment, of course. He had let everyone down, primarily himself.

Despite suggesting to a few men that signing off from the Army might be in their best interests and assuring others that I wouldn't stand in their way if they wanted to purchase their discharge, I had never been directly responsible for booting a man out. Cpl Noone was to be the first. He was a pathetic little man who, for reasons only he could explain, had selected an active prostitute to be his partner in life. Perhaps he couldn't find anyone else to have him, for he wasn't much of a catch, that's for sure. Not only did his wife have a record for prostitution down in her native Hampshire, but she wasn't averse to taking soldiers back to her married quarter whenever Noone was away on exercise either. Her misdeeds were well documented, both in the unit and with the Social Services Department in the HQ. How this obese, plain and smelly woman could attract punters in the first place was a matter of some conjecture. Perhaps she possessed qualities that were not immediately obvious. Poor old Corporal Noone was well aware of her indiscretions and the fact that she made trips back to Hampshire to ply her trade whenever she was short of cash, but stoically accepted the taunts of his workmates and the soldiers of the garrison. The silly man loved the woman who had borne him two children, or who had at least borne two children whilst she was married to him. I had counselled him, bullied him and threatened him in a vain attempt to make him see that this woman was dragging him down, but I was wasting my time. Had their peculiar lifestyle not directly affected his performance at work, or had it not besmirched the good name of our unit, then I would have considered his private life to be his own. But it did affect him and it did affect the unit. People were laughing at him and adverse comments were being made about a unit that included an active prostitute among its wives. I was forced into delivering the directive that he didn't want to hear. It's not easy telling a man he has to choose between his wife and his job, both of which he loved. My honest and well-intentioned advice was that he should leave her and start his life over again. That would be tremendously hard, but his wife would be looked after financially and he could have a posting overseas if necessary. He wasn't interested in that proposition, but to give him some time to contemplate his position, I sent him up to Thetford to replace Frew Wingrave. He was left in no doubt that returning to Colchester during the following month, for any reason whatsoever, was expressly forbidden. Similarly, Thetford was declared out of bounds to Mrs Noone. The sad young man had precisely one month to consider his options and come to a decision.

It was never my intention to check on Cpl Noone so quickly, although it's doubtful whether he would ever have been convinced. His first weekend there just happened to coincide with a day's walking I had planned in the area. My car was left in the detachment car park and, since everyone in the unit knew the sight and sound of my bilious green machine, he would have been pretty stupid not to realise that I was in the vicinity. Returning to my car after a long day's walk, I called into the duty room to pass the time of day with the troubled young man. He was notable by his absence, but sitting behind the desk, breast-feeding her baby, was none other than his wife. When he finally deemed to reappear, I subjected him and the lactating trollop to a severe verbal battering that left them in no doubt about the seriousness of my intent. Cpl Noone had defied my direct order and I would get him! He was told that if he stepped out of line one more time within the next month, steps would be taken to discharge him from of the Army.

Making more than one trip a month to Thetford was a rare occurrence for me and it was odd that fate conspired to have me back there again only two days later. The major's hangover was of sufficient severity to render him incapable of attending the monthly officer's conference and I was nominated to stand in for him. Arriving in Thetford in time for a coffee before the boring, daylong conference began, I called into Cpl Noone's office. He wasn't there. The lone Thetford man couldn't be expected to man the duty room for twenty-four hours a day, of course, but in the event of him needing to leave for a substantial period of time, he was required to contact the HQ at Colchester and inform them of his whereabouts. I checked with Colchester, and they were unaware of any reason for his absence. He had not returned by lunchtime, nor was he there at 1700 hrs when I set off back. He had been away from the detachment all day without giving anyone a hint as to where he might be. Next morning the duty sergeant called Thetford on my behalf. Corporal Noone was back, but he refused to tell the sergeant where he had been the previous day. I ordered him to drive down to see me.

"Where were you between 0930 hrs and 1700 hrs yesterday, Corporal Noone?"

"On my way to and coming back from Hull, sir."

"Hull? Is that a village in Norfolk with which I am unfamiliar, or are you referring to Hull as in Hull Kingston Rovers?"

"Yes sir, Kingston upon Hull."

"Might I enquire exactly why you went to this particular city? It's a mile or two outside of your area of responsibility, you know?"

"I was taking my wife up to see her sister, sir."

"Oh, were you indeed? In the firm's transport, I assume?"

"Yes sir."

"We are in the shit, young man."

There was no point in prolonging his agony. He had said enough to hang himself and I derive little pleasure from kicking someone when he's down, unless it's a goalkeeper. After a consultation between the OC and myself, he was marched in front of the major and placed on a three-month warning order. This warns a soldier that, unless his military conduct improves within the next quarter, steps will be taken to have him reduced in rank, or discharged. Corporal Noone wouldn't survive for three months. He'd defied me twice in three days, he was bound to drop another bollock before long and I'd have him packing his bags.

Now it so happened that he had been summoned to appear as a witness at Derby Magistrates Court the following Tuesday. A covering letter to the summons had been explicit. Military witnesses must appear in civilian clothing and this fact was impressed upon Corporal Noone. The Derby Magistrates were over-reacting to the security situation, but if they perceived a threat, then they could have our man dressed in civvies.

Had he not been burdened with the problems of being married to a harlot, Cpl Noone would have been an above average NCO. His work was good and he was always immaculately turned out. He was very proud of being in the Corps and also very proud of his uniform, so proud that he elected to wear it when he appeared before the Derby Magistrates. The Chairman of the Derby Magistrates, however, who just happened to know our District Commander, was furious and called the general to register his complaint. This was the straw that broke the camel's back, the final defiant act that would nail the errant corporal. On Wednesday morning I informed the OC that we had grounds for discharging the man and produced the documentation. All that remained was for the brigadier to sign the discharge papers and our corporal would be a civilian. The OC was the sort of man who, despite the enormity of a defendant's misdemeanours, would still seek to give him one last chance to redeem himself. I insisted that every conceivable avenue had already been explored and that he should simply sign the form and take it to the brigadier for his signature. He signed his section of the form, but dithered at the prospect of consigning one of his charges to the dole queue. One of his few failings was the fact that he never saw ill in anyone. I forced his hand, by taking the form to the boss myself. I had no such qualms. After listening to my argument, the brigadier signed the form and Mr Noone took his leave of Her Majesty.

Major Roy and I didn't want to go and tried our hardest to worm our way out of attending, but along with all the other RSMs and OCs of the regular military police units in the UK, we showed up for the Provost Marshal's conference at Bulford. For a whole day I suffered untold misery, as the Corps' wrongs where put right by various smart arsed officers. As usual, those who had been in the RMP for the shortest period of time were the ones with the most to say, especially the transferees from other arms. Whether they believed that they had something fresh to offer, or whether they were just trying to bullshit the PM is difficult to say, but the eloquence of their argument was invariably in direct proportion to the fatuousness of their idea. Plans that had been tried and discarded, long before any of this lot ever contemplated transferring to my Corps, were proposed as new ideas by some of the clowns. The old sweats just sat back, watched and silently groaned. As the day progressed it became more and more difficult to control one's temper, as officers passionately fond of the sound of their own voices droned on, pontificating on subjects that might have been specifically designed to make my gall rise.

One of my pet hates at that time was the insistence on recruiting ever increasing numbers of women into the Corps and, as if that wasn't bad enough, maintaining that they could perform their task equally as well as men. There may well be legislation that demands equality for females and, as a law abiding citizen, I accept the letter of the law, but recruiting women to prove that you are in line with the craze for political correctness is pathetically naive. High-ranking officers, dispensing wisdom from their lofty towers, are not the ones who have to go out on the streets and fight crime. Try telling a drunken Scots infantryman enjoying his Saturday night out on the tiles, that the pretty little female military police person who is about to remove him from a bar is his equal and you will find out where political correctness and reality diverge. It isn't possible to make people accept what is alien to human nature, no matter how much legislation you care to create. Being a military policeman in a place like the Sennelager Strip on a Saturday night is a difficult enough proposition, without having to keep an ever-watchful eye on your female partner. Believe me, I've been there and I know. Give me another big lad alongside me, not for any chauvinistic reasons, but for self-preservation. It's a case of horses for courses. You don't send women down coalmines, do you?

Another particular loathing was for transferee officers, creatures from other arms who were allowed to come into the RMP, keeping both their rank and seniority. This opened the floodgates to droves of men who were no bloody good. Had they been any use, they would surely have stayed in their own mob and made a success of it there. Sadly, the RMP was full of these individuals, most of who managed to do nothing, other than lower standards.

The majority of senior RMP officers are woefully ignorant about what goes on at grass roots level. A full colonel at this conference spoke at great length and, to be fair to him, with great skill, about the latest advances in computer technology and how it would revolutionise the RMP duty room. Since our duty room in Colchester didn't have a telephone that gave us direct access to the GPO net, I felt that it was time to get on my rear trotters. As much as I applauded the advent of new technology in the fight against crime, I believed that we ought to ensure that the basics were in place first. The Provost Marshal flatly refused to believe that our District Headquarters had turned down my application for a direct dialling system on no less than six occasions. He didn't believe me, either, when I told him that we had to make all of our calls through an Army exchange and, in our case, an exchange where the staff was recruited purely on their ability to be rude, unhelpful and bloody-minded. He promised to take up the crusade on our behalf at the very highest level, which is the senior officer's way of saying that you have stumped him and that he was in a corner. When I left Colchester, we still didn't have direct dialling.

Mercifully, the meeting was brought to an end at teatime and the PM embarked upon his closing address. He tried hard to convince us that the Corps was in good shape and that the future looked bright. We had heard the same crap from a succession of PMs over the years and no one was convinced, apart from the transferee officers who knew no better. He also attempted to convince us that the thousands of pounds spent conveying us from various points of the compass to Bulford, to listen to a day's unexpurgated shit, was money well spent. His parting shot was to ask if there was anyone at the table who wished to make any final comments. He knew he had made a mistake the moment he said it, because Pete Joyner was on his feet in a flash. Pete, who had a thick Birmingham accent and a propensity for blasphemy, was the last man the PM would have wanted to see get up.

"I'd like to say a few words if you don't mind, sir."

"I rather feared you might, RSM," replied the PM.

"As you all know, I'm leaving this man's Army in a few weeks time and I just want to point something out to you regarding these fucking conferences. I've been to loads of these fucking things and they're all the same. You officers all come here with your big fucking ideas and everyone agrees that they're good ideas. Then we all fuck off home and nobody does anything about anything. The day that any of you lot put anything that we discuss into practice will be the first. I'm fucking off. Goodbye."

That was Pete's farewell speech to the Corps. He may not have been hyper eloquent, but he had hit the nail on the head.

I decided on somewhere a little different for my next leave, but couldn't believe that the plane from Gatwick to Rio de Janeiro wasn't going to stop to refuel until it reached Recife, on the northern coast of Brazil. This flight was definitely going to be a ten-milligram of Valium job. My holiday had been booked through Kuoni, a company I'd travelled with a good many times before, but as we were being called together to board the aircraft, I discovered that it was actually *Woman's Own* who were sponsoring this holiday. I fervently hoped that none of my friends would ever discover the truth and the guide was informed, in no uncertain terms, that this company's complimentary name tags would definitely not be adorning my luggage. Lower end of the market trips invariably make use of off peak flights and, having endured a lengthy flight, I found myself eating an unwanted early morning breakfast in the Copacabana Hotel in Rio. Everyone else on the tour was married and that left me alone at my own table, but not for long. A chap who hailed from Burnley sat down beside me. He explained that he had come out on the same *Woman's Own* trip a week earlier than me and that he had prised himself out of bed especially early in order to meet me.

"I hear you're single?" he said.

I nodded in the affirmative.

"I'm sorry to bother you if you're tired," he said, "but I feel it my solemn duty to tell you about this place. You don't have a minute to spare, you see, and I don't want you to make the same mistake as me. I didn't find out until my fifth day and wasted so much time. Rio is packed with gorgeous birds, millions of them, and so you have to get stuck in straight away."

He produced a copy of the previous day's English language newspaper.

"See the little adverts? They are all for twenty-four hour a day agencies. Just pick up the phone and they will send you whatever you want, directly to your room."

I told John that his concern for my sexual welfare was much appreciated, but that if it was all the same to him, I would like to have a shit, shave, shampoo and a couple of hours in bed before I embarked on the chase. He appeared to be a decent bloke, however, and we arranged to meet in the hotel bar that evening.

Having rested for a while, I called the first number listed in the paper. It was Jayne's Agency.

"Hello, this is Jayne's Agency," answered a Portuguese accent.

"Can you send a girl up to my room in the Copacabana Excelsior, please?"

"Of course, we are an agency. What kind of girl would you like?"

"What sort have you got?" I asked, rather warming to the idea.

"We have white girls, light brown, medium brown, dark brown, black, Chinese, Japanese, Swedish," she answered, before I interrupted her.

"I'll have a light brown one please."

"Young or old?"

"She will need to be mature, about eighteen would be okay."

"You want her to have slim figure or big figure?"

"As a confirmed tit man, she had better be one of your big figure jobs."

"She will be with you in twenty minutes, sir," said Jayne.

Just how many girls did she have on tap there at the agency? The number of possible combinations was astronomical. Twenty minutes later there was a ring on my doorbell and an eighteen year old, light brown, large breasted Amazon stood there ready to pleasure me. Apparently there are so many girls plying for hire in Rio that competition for customers is savage. A young lady would try her utmost to please a punter, in the hope that he would remember her name and ask for her again. I spent a pleasurable afternoon, but didn't note her name for future reference.

Dave and I met up in the hotel, went for a moderate meal in an open-air restaurant and then to a classy nightclub for a drink. The Playboy Club reminded me of Rick's Bar in the film 'Casablanca', right down to the piano player. As we sat in a quiet corner, small groups of beautiful, immaculately attired girls would congregate within touching distance and attempt to whet our sexual appetites. After a few minutes they would move on, leaving the next group of lovelies to appear for our examination. I was rather taken by this place and was about to make my selection for the evening, when Dave urged a little patience. There was another place he wanted to show me. We moved on and descended a flight of stairs that led to an underground disco. It was similar in size to the concert room at the Fatfield Working Men's Club in Durham, except that this place was throbbing with lovely girls rather than pissed miners. A couple of dozen customers were sitting around the place, with probably a hundred and fifty young girls touting for their business. On the stage, dancing provocatively, were a further fifty ladies dressed in bikinis, and posted at either end of the stage was a big breasted, naked girl. This was to add a little artistic flavour, I presumed. Dave soon disappeared with a girl he had met the previous evening and this left me alone and totally spoilt for choice. Fortified by a few glasses of the local sugarcane spirit mixed with lemonade, I quickly made my selection for the evening and returned to the hotel with her. Maria de Jesus Santos wasn't as good as the afternoon girl and I left her off my call again list too.

It doesn't take you long to realise that you have to keep your wits about you whilst walking around Rio. Tourists are a main source of income for many of the locals and most are easy prey for the streetwise gangs roaming the streets. Shoeshine boys were a particular hazard and they had an array of tricks in their repertoires to ensure that their services would be required. On my second morning I was walking merrily towards the Copacabana beach, when a shoeshine boy approached toting his homemade box containing brushes and a tin of Kiwi.

"Shoe shine mister?" he enquired.

How did he know I was English? Surely he didn't recognise my Corps' tie?

"No thanks son, I've just cleaned them. Old British Army habit, you know."

"You look at shoes," he advised.

His accomplice had managed to deposit a huge blob of gunge onto my previously shiny toecap. A clever ploy and I hadn't seen or felt a thing. A large leaf served to scrape the muck off, but as it's not unknown for these shoeshine boys to attack people refusing their services, I walked briskly on.

There's always someone ready to rip you off in Brazil. Some of the con men are good and you part with your cash with a smile, but others are just blatant cheats. As a tourist, you are expected to pay over the top for your newspapers, bus fares and medicaments, and even for your entry fee to places of interest. To me, it was the single most annoying thing about Brazil and it quite put me off the place. Despite being ripped off at every turn, there were places in Rio that simply had to be visited, even when the gods are conspiring against you. My luck was out during my holiday: my climb up Sugar Loaf Mountain was made in the fog; I had a rotten viral infection whilst visiting the statue of Jesus Christ and made an excursion to the inland town of Petropolis in the pouring rain.

The hotel arranged trips to the Maracana Stadium and I went along to watch a match. It was rotten, not as a game of football, but because we were sitting in a section of the decaying stadium that positively reeked of urine. Then I discovered that the hotel was ripping us off, too. It was possible to travel to the Maracana by public transport and buy your entrance ticket at the gate for a tenth of the price they were charging. Consequently, I saw five matches in eight days and it would have been six, but one match was postponed when a Vasco de Gama player was killed on the day of the game. On the way back from watching Botafogo play against Fluminense, I became the victim of an accomplished pick-pocketing duo. As I was standing in the aisle of the bus, waiting to alight outside my hotel, the guy in front of me began to play the fool. Just as the bus slowed down to stop, he dropped something on the floor and bent down to retrieve it, ensuring that his backside connected with my groin. My involuntary action at being bashed in the bollocks was to jump backwards, thus giving his accomplice standing directly behind me the opportunity to dip my pockets. It was all done very slickly; I suspected nothing, felt nothing and was relieved of the contents of my pockets in seconds. The bus was pulling away, with the two guys still inside and waving at me, before the realisation hit me. They had stolen the equivalent of one US Dollar and dozens of wet paper hankies. I hope they developed colds as bad as the one from which I was suffering. You have to give respect to experts in any discipline and these two thieves had mine.

Another mammoth mistake was to take a ride on the ancient old train that runs from the centre of Rio to the hilltop suburb of Santa Theresa, one of the poorest areas of a desperately poor city. For the majority of its route, the train ran up the middle of the public road that wound its way to the top of the hill. My 'How to Survive in Rio' book cautioned against travelling on this train. Foolishly, I chose to ignore the advice. The train stopped around twenty times in each direction and as it moved from one stop to the next, hordes of children jumped onto the sides to gain a free ride for a hundred yards or so. They would jump off shortly before each stop, in order to avoid the eagle eye of the conductor. As the train climbed the slope, I became aware of the large police presence at every street corner and presumed that the Pope or some other dignitary was about to visit the area. What I didn't know was that this was one of the roughest parts in all Rio and that the huge complement of lawmen on the streets was just the way things were in Santa Theresa.

For the first and only time in my life, I had elected to wear my camera slung around my neck, like an American tourist at the Tower of London. That was a big mistake. As the train was pulling away from stop sixteen, the freeloaders clambered onto the sides of the carriages as usual, including one black youth that was posted directly by my side. I even edged over a little, to give him a bit more room to hang on as we rattled away towards the next stop. As quick as a flash, he made a cross handed grab at my camera strap, pulled his hands apart and effectively twisted the strap around my neck. He then jumped off the train, expecting the strap to break and thus allow him to escape with my Olympus. The strap didn't break, though, and as he continued to yank it in an effort to make it snap, I finished up hanging on for grim death. Before long my head was bent down outside the train, only inches from the wheels and the pressure of the strap on the back of my neck was choking me. I was unaware until that moment that you could choke from pressure applied to the back of the neck. Believe me, you can. Two equally unattractive choices faced me; I could let go of the side of the train and finish up under the wheels, or hang on and choke to death. Fortunately, the strap finally gave way and left me with no decision to make.

The Santa Theresa Strangler made off with my Olympus OM10, with me in hot pursuit. My sprint didn't last for long, however, as a phalanx of black youths, at least two of them sporting cutthroat razors, blocked my path. At that, I performed a very smart about turn, ran after the train and climbed back into my seat. Everyone in the carriage must have witnessed the attack, but apart from a fat lady in the next seat who shrugged her shoulders and muttered something unintelligible, no one paid the slightest attention to my plight. My camera had gone forever. What a good job they hadn't noticed my Rolex! I remained on the train as far as the upper terminus and then came straight back down again.

Back at my hotel, the receptionist feigned concern at my loss and gave me a card with the address of the Tourist Police Station in nearby Ipenema. The Police Station was the strangest sight to behold. Clearly I wasn't the only person to have been mugged that day, as the place was awash with victims. Flags of all nations were pinned to the walls of a huge waiting room and the procedure was to wait underneath the flag of your nation, until a detective and interpreter was available to hear your complaint. Judging from the throngs of people camped underneath the German and Swedish flags, those nations were having a particularly bad day. To while the time away, I chatted with my near neighbours. Neither of them was British, but they believed that better service was available under the Union Flag. One was a Dutchman, whose false teeth had been stolen from Copacabana Beach. He was worried about the prospect of eating nothing but soup for the remainder of his holiday. The other was a Russian whose attaché case containing everything of value he possessed had been snatched. My detective turned out to be a cheerful soul, who told me what I already knew—the chances of getting my camera back were precisely zero.

The adjacent beaches of Copacabana and Ipenema are immense and are always awash with the most exquisite female forms. The area is a bird watcher's paradise. On Saturdays, however, the beaches were given over to the male population and were transformed into the largest expanse of football pitches in the world. Scores of full sized pitches are marked out in the soft sand, complete with goal posts and nets, corner flags, uniformed officials and all. Beach matches last only an hour, due to the strength sapping quality of the soft sand, but the skills of the barefooted participants was amazing. No wonder the Brazilians have such silky skills when they learn to play on surfaces like these. The place was sheer bliss for a football fanatic like myself.

During one of these beach matches, I witnessed one of the most bizarre incidents I've ever seen on a football pitch. Judging by the number of spectators gathered around the touchline, this was an important game and it was when the red team's centre forward was brought down in the area that the trouble began. The referee missed the incident, but having been jostled to the sideline to consult his linesman, he gave the spot kick. After ten minutes of mayhem, the referee finally managed to pace out twelve yards in the sand and place the ball down for the penalty. The guy who had been fouled in the first place took it, but blazed the ball a mile over the bar, whereupon the opposing players mocked him unmercifully. He went berserk and a full-scale riot ensued, with the player who missed the penalty being one of the main protagonists. After being subjected to much intimidation, the referee showed the centre forward a well deserved red card. This induced a complete brainstorm from the player, who knocked both the referee and a linesman to the ground. Surprisingly, the crowd didn't involve themselves in the fun, although one of them had the gumption to alert the police and soon the sound of sirens could be heard. The police arrived and half a dozen armed officers strode into the fray. The centre forward was beaten unconscious and handcuffed behind his back. When he recovered his senses, he was marched away with a drawn pistol pointing at his temple. I have seen plenty of players receive their marching orders; some of them have needed to be coaxed off the field of play, but never have I seen a gun used to effect an expulsion! The game then continued, with no apparent animosity amongst the players who only minutes before had been on the verge of killing each other.

During my second week in Rio, I became victim to a most debilitating virus. It left me so weak that I couldn't even find the strength to call Jayne's Agency. I wasn't sorry when the time came for me to return to the UK.

15

The Ministry of Defence sends you a letter when your commissioning application is successful. Paragraph one informs you of your good fortune and at paragraph two they remind you that your selection is only provisional and dependent on the successful outcome of a medical examination. My trip to see the MO was a very important matter, therefore, my whole future being dependent upon the result. It was held at the Colchester Medical Centre, where an octogenarian Scottish doctor would do the business for me. Actually, a medical orderly did all the mundane bits like the eye test, blood pressure, height and weight and left the important stuff for the doctor. I was summoned before Dr McNasty, a very old man with a Scottish accent and a very disturbing shake. In front of him was the familiar four-page Army medical form. My personal details and the results of my preliminary tests were recorded on pages one and two and, on pages three and four were listed all the diseases known to mankind. I knew this form well enough. Every soldier goes through the ritual of the Army medical once a year. Usually, the doctor handed you the form and you answered the 'Have you ever suffered from' questions with a tick in the appropriate box. Dr McNasty however, belonged to an age when time was not of such consequence and he insisted on reading all of the questions to me. The inquisition began.

"Mr Payne, have you ever suffered from epistaxis—that's nose bleeding, you understand?" he asked, painfully slowly.

I had suffered from many a nosebleed on the sporting field of combat and once even needed to have my nose cauterised, but answered 'no' to stop him probing any deeper. He scratched a tick onto the page with an ancient Waterman's pen and steadied himself for question two.

"Mr Payne, have you or any of your close relatives, that's your mother, father, brother or sister, you understand, ever suffered from any respiratory diseases?"

I wasn't about to reveal the fact that my poor old Dad suffered from every pulmonary complaint known to man and answered 'no' once again. The immense list of questions went on and on and apart from admitting to jaundice at the age of seven, my answers were all in the negative. Up until question number twenty-two, that is.

"Mr Payne, have you ever suffered from bed-wetting since the age of twelve?"

Despite the importance of the medical and the fact that the doctor appeared to be devoid of a sense of humour, I couldn't resist a flippant retort.

"Not since that terrible night back in 1978, sir, when I drank eighteen pints of McEwan's lager," I replied.

He looked at me over his half moon glasses and scratched another tick. I never discovered whether his tick indicated that I was a bed wetter or not. He moved onto the next question, which was altogether more serious and dealt with conditions of the rear passage. After an absolute age, Dr McNasty announced that my medical examination was complete and told me to bugger off. Since my whole career depended on this medical, I felt justified in asking the old boy whether or not I had passed his examination. He showed emotion for the first time that day, emotion bordering on anger.

"Young man, I'm not at liberty to discuss medical in confidence matters with you," he replied.

I argued the point that medical in confidence meant that the subject was between the physician and his patient and that, for the present, I was his patient. He wasn't buying any of that, though.

"Mr Payne, I have already told you that I am not at liberty to disclose such information to you," he said. "And furthermore Mr Payne, let me refer you back to your inappropriate reply to question number twenty-two."

He turned briefly to page three of the form, before getting a better idea and turning the form over to the front page.

"No, let us consider page one of the document instead. Payne, Walter, forty-four years old, 5 feet 11 inches, 14 stones," he read. "Colour of eyes, blue. I can accede to all of that, Mr Payne, but—colour of hair—dark brown! Mr Payne, who do you think you are kidding?"

With a sweep of his quill, the old codger changed my personal details to read 'colour of hair—grey'. There was a fleck at the temples admittedly, but grey! The old bugger had paid me back for my moment of humour. He was, nevertheless, a man who could display magnanimity in victory.

"By the way, Mr Payne, I think it would be reasonable for you to instruct your tailor to make your new service dress," he said as I left his surgery.

Just prior to commissioning, a lady friend and I decided on a trip to Cyprus. Still a reluctant flyer, I swallowed a couple of Valium and half a bottle of whisky prior to boarding the plane. Once on board, I then drank all the free booze the stewardess would give me. Consequently, my recollection of the flight is a little sketchy; although my lady friend assured me that my conduct was bad enough for the Captain to have been within his rights to clap me in irons. It seems that I conducted a singsong, solicited help from all those sitting in rows 18-22 in completing my *Sunday Express* crossword, ate two British Airways dinners, drank more whisky and finally fell asleep. Had I slumbered on until we reached Cyprus there wouldn't have been any problems, but the combination of Valium, whisky and a surfeit of food didn't lie too comfortably on my stomach. Regurgitation was the answer. Not once, but six times I raced to the toilets to do the business. The first five trips were uneventful, but discovering the toilet locked on my sixth visit, I put my shoulder to the door and gave the old lady sitting on the toilet apoplexy. The steward sat me down and gave me a stern warning about my conduct. My lady friend, meanwhile, looked the other way and pretended she wasn't with me. I fancy that the crew was glad to see the back of me once we landed. To compound my felonies, I managed to lose my wallet containing six hundred quid between the plane and the hotel. My lady friend revealed the whole sorry tale to me next morning. It crossed my mind that should the Army hear about my behaviour, there was a good chance I'd never see the inside of an officer's mess. My gushing apology was penned there and then, on some very nice notepaper supplied by the Amathus Beach Hotel. It did the trick. British Airways wrote me a nice letter, explaining that they had scores of idiots like me on their flights every day of the week and that I should forget the whole thing. They even made me a cut-rate offer—for an air aversion therapy course.

After the holiday, it was back to Colchester for a few days. I handed over the reins to the CSM, who was promoted to replace me once I'd gone and the boys saw me off in style. It was with a modicum of regret that I left Colchester.

Two minutes after stepping out of my Ford Escort at the Training Centre, an officer approached to tell me that an Escort wasn't really an officer's car and that it would be wise for me to move up market. Arrogant swine! Anyway, an Escort Ghia is an up-market car in my part of Leicester. That, however, is the kind of snobbery that's prevalent amongst officers; they say it tongue in cheek, but they mean it really. At least there was an officer behind the wheel of the Ford and I had all the kit and an ID card to prove it. In fact, I had two ID cards, my normal one and a blown up version that a guy in the SIB made for me. This bogus job measured three feet by four and had been sitting on the back seat of my non-officer's car, ready to present to the recruit on duty at the main gate when I drove in. If the young man at the gate was surprised to see a card of such dimensions, he didn't let on. He merely saluted and let me through to the mess.

I spent the first night in the officer's mess with all the other guys; the course would start next morning. As well as us newly commissioned types, there were last year's commissioned grunters who hadn't yet done the course, transferees, brand new Sandhurst types and even some foreign officers. How they planned a syllabus to embrace the required learning for so many different groups remains a mystery.

Our first morning was taken up with administration. The six of us who were newly commissioned grunters went to the HQ immediately after breakfast. Here we sat in a room facing four clerks armed with piles of papers. Within half an hour, we apparently went from being warrant officers to civilians, civilians to second lieutenants and second lieutenants to full lieutenants, all without feeling a thing. The paperwork completed, we wandered back to the mess to change into service dress, before reporting over to the sergeant's mess for the traditional last meal. It was a bit like the Last Supper, only with an RSM in charge. After the meal and a couple of drinks, we paraded outside to be marched over to the officer's mess by the RSM. That was something that none of us was looking forward to particularly. Fortunately it rained so heavily that the parade had to be cancelled and we all crammed into the back of Landrovers for the hundred-yard trip instead. Even then we were late in leaving, as John Askwith was having a spot of bother with his new shoes. Whilst the rest of us had worn our brown shoes to the lunch, John had been resplendent in an aged pair of Hush Puppies and still needed to take his uniform shoes out of their box and lace them up. His new footwear hadn't seen a brush, polish or duster, of course, as one foolish officer saw fit to comment.

"Rather poor show, Askwith," said the snobby sort.

"What's wrong with them? As issued they are."

"No bull on them, old chap, that's what's wrong with them."

"Just like yours, then," said John, stamping on the snob's toecaps and ruining hours of patient spit and polish.

Bulling wasn't something I was likely to spend much time on during the course. Askwith neither, if my initial judgement of the man was anything to go by.

As the colonel officially welcomed us, I couldn't help wondering how many people in the Corps would be retching into galvanised buckets at the thought of Wally Payne standing, in his own right, at the officer's mess bar. Tough shit on them.

The Training Centre changed into summer dress soon after our course started and, as happens every year, a cold snap started the same morning. Askwith was from the SIB and hadn't worn a uniform for years. By lunchtime on the third day, he was feeling decidedly chilly in his shirtsleeves and did what to him was the sensible thing. He put his pullover on. Just his luck to run into the Commandant the moment he set foot outside the mess.

"Why are you wearing a pullover, Lieutenant Askwith?"

"Because I'm cold sir," John replied honestly.

It was a bad start for the Yorkshireman. Actually, what could be sillier than freezing to death, when you have a perfectly serviceable pullover lying in your room?

Glancing through the course syllabus, it appeared that the only thing that I hadn't already done was sword drill. The six feet six inch adjutant was a most unlikely candidate for drill instructor, but he was in charge of our efforts with the Wilkinson swords. The first lesson was a very low-key affair and we were told to wear any form of clothing, provided we had a belt and sword frog. The frog is the bit that the sword slides into. Everyone assumed that the adjutant was referring to a Sam Browne belt, with the exception of Askwith, who arrived wearing a snake belt with a frog attached to that. Amazingly, it worked. It came as no surprise to me to discover that I was as useless at sword drill as I was at foot drill. The negligent discharge of my sword from the frog was a phenomenon never previously observed on a drill square, or so the adjutant assured me. After three lessons, several of us were excused from taking any further part in sword drill. We were declared to be beyond instruction. The adjutant suggested that I spend any spare time bulling my brown shoes. I had no intention of doing any such thing. Instead, I found a sergeant who had been in the infantry who would do your shoes brilliantly for a fiver. Never was five pounds better spent. Thereafter, all my shoes ever needed before a parade was a little humph of breath and the quick flick of a yellow duster. I never bulled that pair of shoes ever again.

The Grand Dinner to officially welcome the course members to the mess was an important occasion and also the first time that most of us had worn our new mess kit. This uniform was designed by a sadist at the turn of the century and although it looks immaculate, it's a bugger to wear and almost impossible to get into. Forgetting also that we now had spurs attached to the back of our boots, several of us attempted to break our necks whilst descending the stairs to the bar. When dinner was called, I took a quick look at the seating plan and made my way to my seat as the music played. Some clown had put the plan the wrong way round and as we bowed our heads in prayer, instead of me standing behind my chair next to the Provost Marshal, I found myself standing behind someone else. There was just time for me to skip around the table as everyone was settling down and for me to smile pleasantly at the PM as I took my seat. The dinner was a splendid affair and the playing of the National Anthems by the Royal Signals band quite moving. After our Anthem, they played the Soldier's Song for Paddy, the Norwegian tune and then something very long and eminently forgettable for an African officer. The last Anthem was to be for Samuel the Israeli, who stood proudly for his turn. Seemingly, the Israeli National Anthem was not a tune the band played with any regularity and they didn't know it, neither did they have the music. Instead, with great improvisation from the bandmaster, the band struck up with 'If I was a Rich Man'. Samuel approved.

I passed the course and was given a super write-up by the officers who ran the show. The only adverse comment was about my service letter writing, although they failed to mention the fact that I was called out of the test on this subject no less than three times. That was to discuss the altogether more important subject of my forthcoming posting. Initially, an administrative officer informed me that I would be posted to Aldershot. That didn't appeal to me at all, since a female officer commanded the unit and putting a woman in charge of a military unit full of men is sheer lunacy in my opinion. On my second trip outside, they told me that I wasn't going to Aldershot after all, because it wasn't Corps policy to post a single man as second-in-command to a unit commanded by a woman. Instead, Edinburgh Castle was to be my new home. Finally, they called me out to cancel Edinburgh Castle, in favour of another plan. They would send me to the territorial unit in Edinburgh, just down the road from the Castle, on Leith Walk.

At the very end of our instruction the news was broken that, for the first time, there would be a final examination on the course. The test would consist of questions taken from the content of the lectures we had endured during our period of misery. This created shock waves. It was announced that the test paper would be in a multi-choice format, which meant you ticked either box A, B, C or D. That gave me a chance of obtaining 25%, just by ticking the same box all the way through. Rumour had it that 65% would be considered a good score, as some of the questions would be purposely obscure. The night before the exam, those commissioned warrant officers who were pals of a certain officer were summoned to his room for a clandestine meeting.

"I've got the answers to tomorrow's test, lads. Anyone want a copy?"

Instead of spending the night swatting like the rest, the old hands repaired to the Old House at Home, the hostelry directly outside the barracks gate and drank to the health of our benefactor. Exactly how he had come by the answer paper was something he didn't care to elaborate upon. By next morning, I had memorised the entire list of one hundred answers.

During the examination, the invigilator left us to get on with the test paper. You can trust officers, you see. Well, you can trust proper officers—I'm not so sure about the commissioned labourers. I set about finishing in record time and within ten minutes, half of my questions had been answered. Time to slow down a little before I gave the game away; after all, fifty answers in ten minutes was a bit 'gildi'.

"How many have you done, Walter?" enquired the real officer sitting on my right.

"Fifty, Donal, just taking a breather," I said cheerily, exuding supreme confidence.

"Gosh! I've only managed eleven and I'm not sure about three of those," he moaned, displaying a lack of confidence for the first time in a month.

"Need any help, Donal?" I shouted, loud enough for everyone to hear.

Then I gave him two correct answers, followed by an incorrect one, just for fun. Within half an hour, all of those who had been privy to the tips were back in the mess, drinking coffee and eating lemon curd sandwiches. The real officers, those ex-warrant officers upon whom good guy status had not been bestowed, three confused foreigners and a permanently confused Irishman, were left behind to scratch their heads.

On the last day the Deputy Commandant announced the results, the look on his face indicating that he was aware that a fiddle had been perpetrated.

"The examination results were surprising to say the least," he said. "Equal first place with a score of 98% were…"

Four of us had tied for first spot; three others were only a mark behind. The highest genuine score went to Donal with 62%. For my part, I'm still wondering how I managed to drop two marks!

16

Sometimes planning in the RMP can be a little hit and miss. The period of time allocated for handovers can be so short that nothing worthwhile can be achieved, or so lengthy that you are sick to death of the guy you're taking over from by the time he finally departs. The latter was the case in Edinburgh. Terry and I had six weeks to do the square root of nothing and we agreed that the time would be better spent if we took three week's leave apiece. He lost the toss, so I took the train down to London, walked along to Victoria Coach Station and hopped on the first bus going south. This particular service was bound for Athens, by way of Rome and Brindisi. It didn't appear to be a very popular route and the bus was all but empty once we had disgorged all the 'Ities' at Rome. The remaining fifteen were all bound for Athens and what a diverse bunch we turned out to be. There was a one-eyed Senegalese gunner in the French Army, who claimed to have sired seventeen children. He was a most interesting character, but needed to be given a particularly wide berth on account of the most violent body odour. There were two Aussie 'shielas' going walkabout, three ladies hairdressers from Reading, a lesbian from Hinckley, John the drug addict, an Italian bible reader, a Hawaiian archaeologist and an Iranian Army officer. The undoubted stars, however, were the three Irish colleens, whom I christened the Vestal Virgins. They kept themselves to themselves and only came to my notice because they were the only ones who never left the bus at the watering holes along the route.

The bus stopped at a motorway service station just short of Brindisi in the south of Italy and we all trooped off for some much-needed refreshment. The Vestal Virgins didn't visit the cafeteria, however, but instead sought the shade of a large tree. I bought an ice cream and a couple of bottles of water and was tucking into my cornetto, when one of the girls plucked up the courage to come and speak to me. She asked whether she and her friends could have a sip of my water. I accompanied the lady, Shiela, back to the girl's shady spot and gave them a bottle of water, which they dispatched with great speed. They explained that they had neither food nor water, nor the wherewithal to buy any. With embarrassment, they accepted my offer to buy them an ice cream apiece and, as our bus pulled away, I took the opportunity of moving to the back to talk to these interesting fish out of water. They came from County Cork and had decided to visit a Greek island, almost on the spur of the moment, after seeing a travel programme on the TV. They had precious little luggage and minimal funds, just sufficient to purchase the bus ticket and a single fare on the first boat out to the nearest of the Greek islands.

"What about food, your return trip and somewhere to sleep?" I asked.

Mary, the largest and most sunburned of the trio, simply fingered the crucifix that hung around her neck.

"We shall trust in the Lord, sir, trust in the Lord."

Having left the bus in the centre of Athens, I took the girls to the docks at Piraeus by way of the cheap underground system and directed them to a park near to the shipping agent's offices. Here they could sleep without fear of being assaulted. It was evening by now, so I arranged to meet them for breakfast next morning and headed off for the cockroach infested, but convenient, Delfini Hotel. Next morning, the girls were in buoyant mood; they had booked passages to the island of Seraphos and were keen to take a look at Athens before steaming away that evening. They were also more than ready for a free breakfast.

"So you're off to Xios this afternoon, Walter? Is it famous for anything?" enquired Shiela, easily the brightest of the trio.

"Precious little apparently, except that Homer is reputed to have been born there." "Who in Jesus' name is Homer?" asked Mary.

"Holy Mary Mother of God, are you thick or what?" said Shiela, disgusted at her friend's ignorance. "Homer was a classical Greek poet and playwright, thousands of years ago."

"Ah yes, I thought he was," said Mary unconvincingly. "Well, I thought he was either that, or a piano player."

Anne was the third of the Vestal Virgins and the quiet one. She asked me about my plans to visit Xios and found it quite beyond her comprehension that I had enough time and money to do whatever and go wherever I wished.

"Walter, does that mean you can go anywhere you want?" she enquired.

I nodded agreement.

"Jesus! The world's your lobster," she said.

Mary decided to say something about the quality of the local milk that was served at breakfast. She was a milkmaid back in Ireland and, as such, felt qualified to offer an opinion on such matters.

"Do you know what I really fancy?" she said to anyone who would listen. "I'd like a nice pint of ice cold milk, straight out of the cow."

Neither of the other two girls commented. Presumably they knew what she meant.

The 'Vestal Virgins' were a quaint threesome and I was sorry to leave them, but there was a ship lying ready in the harbour and this evening for Xios she would sail. Shiela actually wrote to me some months later, to give me the run down on their holiday. Seraphos was virtually uninhabited, it appeared, but they had been befriended by the local police and had spent six pleasurable weeks on the island, before hitching back to England. They swore to come back the following year, but never did. Anne got married, Shiela went to live in Canada and Mary stayed in County Cork, to look after her cows. I would meet Mary again, though!

Xios was nothing to write home about, although the twenty-four year old Canadian girl that I met there made things bearable. She was holidaying alone, in order to ponder the question of marriage to her fiancé. It appeared that he was a man of the soundest morals, who steadfastly refused to sleep with his fiancée until they were married. I trust that my advice and my positive action to relieve her frustrations helped her come to a decision. As my ship departed back to Athens, she stood alone out by the lighthouse, waving her white hankie. It was all terribly moving. After Athens, it was on to Cyprus, before returning to Edinburgh and my new job at McDonald Road.

My new home was the Officer's Mess in Edinburgh Castle, where I was to live in supreme isolation for the best part of eighteen months. There were other single officers in the command, but they were all men of means who owned their own properties within the capital. The only people to interrupt my solitude were a succession of military doctors and dentists, who made the journey north to take their Fellowship examinations. Most of them were rather too arrogant to talk to an old commissioned warrant officer, although having doctors on tap was rather comforting. Not many people, for example, can have had their hernia diagnosed by two newly elevated fellows, whilst lying on the floor in the bar, drinking a very decent champagne.

The place was packed out at lunch times, when everyone and his dog came into the HQ for a subsidised lunch. This was the only justification for keeping the place open, as the presence of one living-in member hardly warranted half a dozen staff and keeping several dozen rooms heated all winter. I seldom made the midday trip up for lunch, my excuse being that working down in Leith made it rather too far to walk—although the real reason was that I couldn't stand the majority of the pompous lunchtime crowd. The HQ appeared to be staffed by a really snotty bunch of officers and a horde of retired officers that couldn't bear to sever the cord and leave the military environment. One of these retired sorts had the gall to corner me in the bar one lunchtime.

"Tell me, old chap, what's a seemingly decent fellow like yourself doing in a shower like the military police?" the ignorant bastard asked.

In deference to his extreme age and because of my inexperience in the ways of the officer's mess, I allowed his ignorance to pass. Had he made such a comment a year or so later, he'd have been sitting on his Scottish arse rather smartly. Had a member of the RMP made a similar comment about any of the Scottish Regiments represented at the bar that lunchtime, he would have been thrown summarily from the castle ramparts. I recall that on my first day in the mess, the president had been at pains to point out that I had been accepted as a member only under sufferance. There appeared to be three reasons why I was so unacceptable to these arrogant sods: the fact that I was a military policeman, the fact that I was a commissioned warrant officer, and the fact that I was English! There was nothing that they could do to stop me living there, however; my appointment entitled me to live in the Castle and that's just where I would stay, just to spite the buggers.

The mess was located in an old building that had once been the residence of the Governor of the Castle. It was a rather spooky place in which to live alone, especially at night. The building creaked and groaned and the windows rattled incessantly in the wind that seemed to blow permanently around the battlements. It really was a breezy spot; a mere zephyr down on Princes Street developed into a full-blown gale by the time it reached top field. I imagine that returning to this ancient building late at night would be a daunting experience for anyone of a nervous disposition.

One of the TA sergeants drove me back to the Castle one evening, when a surfeit of OVD rum had rendered me temporarily incapable of taking the wheel myself.

"Mind the ghosts, sir," he shouted, as he dropped me off at the front door.

Now the spirits that occupied the building and I had an understanding—I never mocked them and they didn't bother me. On this occasion, however, my drunken bravado surfaced and I made a disparaging comment about ghosts. Once inside the building, I made my way through the dining room and into the kitchen, in order to raid the fridge and have a bite of supper. The dining room was a long, thin room that contained a huge oak table that ran down its middle and which was always groaning with silver. It was here that I ate my meals, usually on my own. Breakfast was taken at one end of the table and, from this position, provided the Scotch mist wasn't too thick, I could just make out my dinner place set at the bottom end. Between the dining room and the kitchen were two stout swing doors, the first of which was always chocked open by a solid wooden wedge. Having raided the fridge, I was just negotiating the chocked open door and thinking about the spirit world, when there was a rush of cold air against the back of my neck. The door had swung itself closed for the first time in years. There's probably no official record for the quickest man in the world over thirty yards, carrying a tray of Stilton cheese and cream crackers, but Linford Christie would have been hard pressed to keep up with me that night.

The address never failed to give me a kick. The Castle, Edinburgh—some billet, although the Post Office did its best to spoil things by tacking on a postcode. I even became an address dropper and threw my posh address into the conversation at every opportunity.

"And could I have your address, Mr Payne?"

"Yes, it's the Castle."

"Which castle? *The* Castle?"

"Aye lassie."

I had wandered down for a rare breakfast on my third Thursday in the mess and discovered a fellow human being taking his early morning coffee. My cheerful greeting fell on deaf ears and my efforts to engage the man in conversation met a brick wall. I was determined that my fellow diner would at least acknowledge my presence and so carried on talking. Eventually he laid down his *Times*.

"I don't care to converse over breakfast if you don't mind," he said, before returning to his Arbroath Smokies.

That was bloody rude.

"My profound apologies. I shall make a point of never talking to you again, be it at breakfast or at any other time," I retorted, picking up my *Daily Mail* and returning to my Sugar Puffs.

Once he had gone, I went into the kitchen to enquire whether the staff knew the identity of the ignoramus. He turned out to be one Colonel Tamworth and he commanded the local TA Infantry Battalion. So he was a lieutenant colonel—but that didn't give him the right to be so rude to Captain Payne, Royal Military Police. It transpired that Colonel Tamworth stayed overnight most Wednesdays, when he was usually too full of whisky to make it back to his countryseat in Kelso. The following Wednesday evening, I wandered into the bar to take a lonely brandy, but instead of finding the place dark and empty as usual, I discovered the rude colonel at the counter, tucking into some single malt. He appeared in good form and offered his hand by way of introduction.

"Topper Tamworth," he declared. "Care for a dram?"

"No thank you, colonel," I replied. "And if you don't mind, I don't care to converse when I'm pissing it up in the bar."

He was quick on the uptake, I'll give him that and he apologised for his earlier rudeness. From that day on, we became good pals and often bent our arms together on a Wednesday evening. We even talked at breakfast next morning.

Colonel Tamworth appeared to appreciate the company of a rough diamond; someone who could tell a rude joke and didn't give a shit about anyone's elevated status in life. He came from a particularly well-to-do family and he had married into money, too. His home was in the Borders and his address was almost as impressive as mine—it consisted of the name of the house and the county, Roxburghshire. He even invited me down to stay the odd time. It was some pad and stood in acres of land, with horses running around a huge paddock at the front. My first guided tour of the estate took up the best part of a morning and included getting bogged down up to our knees in a potato field that would have produced enough tatties to feed the five thousand and still leave plenty to spare. The place even had its own reach of river and when the salmon came up, he invited all his rich friends down to flick their flies into the water. It was all somewhat removed from a pit village in County Durham and a rough housing estate in Leicester, but I always felt very much at home at his place.

Leith Walk is a wide thoroughfare that leads all the way down from Edinburgh to the docks at Leith and must be the only street in Great Britain where double parking is the norm and triple parking by no means out of the ordinary. It's full of foreign restaurants, shops selling everything and anything, bookmaker's shops and pubs. There are so many pubs along its length that if you tried to take half a pint in each of them, you would only make it half way down one side before you fell down dead drunk. I really liked the feel of the place, despite having been the victim of a racial attack on its pavements.

Striding up the Walk in uniform one Saturday evening, I saw two ladies who were very much the worse for drink coming down the other way.

"Well, just look who it is," said the first.

"Crivvens, so it is!" said the other. "How are you keeping?"

"I'm afraid that you have me at a disadvantage, ladies," I replied. "I don't think I've ever set eyes on either of you before."

"He's bloody English!" cried the first lady, simultaneously clouting me around the ear with her handbag.

Her friend prodded me in the rude bits with her umbrella and the pair of them chased me as far as the pork butchers, before calling off the hue and cry.

The Territorial Army Centre in McDonald Road was a vast piece of real estate that would have fetched a pretty penny had the Army wished to sell it. We had offices, a drill hall, garages, an indoor range, stores and messes, all in the one huge former dwelling house. It was home to the HQ and two platoons of Scotland's only Territorial Military Police Company. The other two platoons were based in Stranraer and at Glenrothes, in Fife. Drill night was held on Wednesdays and we trained every alternate weekend. My presence and that of the two Regular Army senior ranks was mandatory during those periods, otherwise we were free to come and go as I saw fit. Diligence was my watchword, naturally, but I seldom missed a soccer match, horse race meeting or a trip to Powderhall greyhounds for the two years I was in Scotland. My boss was conveniently stationed in York and he didn't stray north of Hadrian's Wall very gladly, the OC was in the TA and although he attended every session, he was too busy with his civilian business to bother me overmuch. I wasn't even aware of the existence of a TA HQ in Glasgow for the first year and after that, they paid me only a single courtesy visit. As Permanent Staff Officer of 243 Provost Company Royal Military Police (Volunteers), I had found myself a bobby's job.

The men who serve in the RMPTA are generally a decent lot and some of the members of 243 had been with the unit for twenty-five years or more. They had seen so many Permanent Staff Officers come and go that they knew what changes I was likely to make before I made them. An old TA sweat told me that all PSOs went through three distinct phases during their two years with the unit.

"For the first six months, he will try and change everything for what he perceives to be for the best," he told me. "During the second six months, he will gradually realise that he is wasting his time, because the TA soldier will only do what he feels like doing. Then, for the last year, he will put his feet up and wait for his next posting."

He was spot on.

You need to watch your charges like a hawk just the same, and then they still pull the wool over your eyes at every opportunity. We had one sergeant who regularly took a pint of beer with me at the pub in McDonald Road, above which he had a flat. Checking the unit travel claims at the end of the month, I noticed this man had been claiming expenses for the car journey between Dundee and Edinburgh a couple of times a week for several years. There were some anomalies that I dare not commit to print, in case there is no statute of limitations on the offences that some guys committed.

A truly wise PSO would never take leave during his two-year stint with the Terriers; nor would he ever attend a course, or even go away for a weekend. For the moment you turn your back, they take that as a licence to put all their loony ideas into practice and then it can take an age to re-establish the status quo. There was never an occasion that I returned from leave without discovering that someone had been busted or promoted, without any reference to higher authority, naturally. The fact that a military unit is bound by an establishment table, which dictates how many soldiers of each rank may be on its strength, was considered an irrelevance by our TA officers. We functioned with a surplus of two sergeants and a staff sergeant for a considerable period following my return from one particular period of leave. They corrected the anomaly during my next absence, by busting a few guys to even things up.

The civilian staff members at McDonald Road numbered just three, Robby the resident caretaker, Len the chief clerk and professional accordion player—not necessarily in that order—and Norma the typist.

By all accounts, Norma was a difficult lady to get along with. She had seen at least sixty summers and a profusion of guys like me, the majority of whom she had disliked intensely. So, instead of the dolly bird I'd hoped for as a typist, I'd landed a fat, old boiler with a chip on her shoulder that was built like a front row forward. Previous incumbents of my position had forewarned me about her constant moaning, groaning and forecasts of doom and gloom. At first I had to agree with their opinions but, once the façade had been chipped away, underneath I discovered a rather dear old lady—a lady who had every reason to be unhappy with her lot in fact, although she never unburdened her not inconsiderable problems onto others. Provided that one allowed her to have a crack at the *Sun* crossword before throwing any work at her, you were halfway there with Norma. It helped, too, if you made disparaging comments about the person to whom letters were addressed. The fact was that she had done more than enough typing to sate her over the years and she really appreciated a good old moan. Confirmation that I had won her over came when she included me on her coffee-making list, for a cup lovingly prepared by the formidable lady was acceptance indeed. Not that she lowered her guard in any way. When it was time to brew the coffee, she would block the doorway to my office with her hands on her hips.

"Yes? No?" she would enquire.

I always said yes. And that's how I will always remember Norma, standing menacingly in the doorway and defying me to refuse her offer.

With so many years served in the Civil Service, she could have attained a much higher grade had she been prepared to move elsewhere. McDonald Road suited her personal circumstances, however, so there she remained. I had the pleasure of completing her annual report on two occasions and erred hugely on the side of generosity whilst making her assessment. The second time she came in to sign her report, she took me to task about the content of her pen picture.

"You know that most of that is a lie and I know that most of that is a lie, but thank you anyway," she said.

Gratitude from Norma, an honour not afforded to many.

Among the annual round of inspections with which all military units have to contend, one of the most futile must be the visit of the Fire Advisor. He will advise on all matters pertaining to safety and will invariably suggest all manner of rebuilding work, alterations and repairs to the fabric of your real estate. No matter how well intentioned his ideas, they are seldom acted upon, since the Army ran out of money for such niceties years ago. Work service requests submitted on the advice of the Fire Advisor and considered vital to the well being of the troops had been submitted and resubmitted for year after year at McDonald Road, without as much as a gallon of fire retardant paint ever reaching the place. I had been in Scotland only a few weeks and was still trying to find my way around my considerable chunk of real estate, when the Fire Advisor descended on me. Over coffee and chocolate biscuits, I ascertained that he was Cumbrian, that he had recently served in Cyprus and that this was his first inspection since he had arrived in Scotland. As any experienced military man will tell you, the grading of any inspection in the Army is directly influenced by the quality of the coffee, biscuits and small talk. We drank Kaiser's Kaffee, ate Cadbury's biscuits and chatted about Cyprus. After our elevenses we embarked on a walkabout of the unit lines, followed by the building's faithful caretaker, who was clutching an enormous bunch of keys. Through the offices, stores, drill hall, messes and garages we snaked, the advisor taking notes, but seemingly content with what he was seeing. At the bottom of the garage was a door through which I was yet to venture.

"What's in there, Wally?" he enquired.

"Haven't got a clue," I replied in all honesty and turned to ask Robby if he could unlock the mystery door.

He was shaking his head violently, an action that only served to increase the interest of the advisor. With the greatest reluctance, Robby opened the door and revealed a walled area about thirty feet square, which was open to the elements. What was stacked in that small area, referred to by Robby as the 'wee cubby hole', buggered belief. On the floor were hundreds of jerry cans, many of which contained petrol and paraffin, several dozen Calor Gas containers (one of the unit members was the local Calor Gas man) and, where space permitted, cans of paint and thinners. On top of this lot were several dozen old rubber tyres and, to ensure that we would have had a wonderful blaze should this disaster area ever catch fire, hundreds of wooden camouflage poles had been thrown willy-nilly onto the heap.

"I can't believe what I'm seeing," said a shocked Fire Advisor.

"That's because it's not there," replied the quick thinking Payne. "Or, at least, it won't be there this time tomorrow."

"Can I bank on that?" he asked.

"Guaranteed," I said, and took him for some more German coffee and Cadbury's chocolate biscuits.

The Army keeps a close watch on just how you spend public money and anyone attempting to fiddle a few bob from this source is really asking for trouble. I ran a tiny imprest account in Edinburgh that only involved a couple of hundred quid each month, but it was watched over as if it were the Crown Jewels. Regulations required that the account holder attend a course that was held somewhere in Hampshire, but since Hampshire was a million miles away and considering the fact that I had worked in a bank as a lad, I exempted myself. No one ever noticed! My accounts were always balanced on the last day of the month and sent off to the South of England, where they were subjected to the scrutiny of the Pay Corps. The girl who dealt with my account was a charming young thing, who was always on the phone asking me to explain my latest diversion from the accepted method of accounting. There were no real howlers, though, and she always gave me ten out of ten for effort. Should anything stump me, then I was always at liberty to call the girl with the sexiest voice in the whole of Hants. In addition to 243, she was responsible for a load of other TA units in our part of the world and when she mentioned that she would like to visit her units, I was happy to oblige by making the arrangements.

She elected to travel up to Scotland by bus and was scheduled to arrive at the coach station at 0700 hrs. I went to my office early, walking via the coach station, just in case the bus should have arrived early. There was hardly a soul about at that time of the morning, only a fat lady with a suitcase who was waiting for someone. I carried on down to McDonald Road, had some coffee and returned to the coach terminal at the correct time. It was still very quiet and the fat lady was still waiting there alone. Suddenly it dawned on me! I approached this big, big girl and, sure enough, it was my accountant. My hopes of a naughty week with a sexy little thing had gone up in smoke. This bird was immense and I was genuinely disappointed. By the time we had eaten breakfast and I had delivered her at her digs, however, she had convinced me that looks weren't everything. She was just as charming in the flesh as she was on the phone, although I couldn't help wishing that she wasn't so gross.

We went out to an Indian restaurant for a meal that first evening and it was here that she made me feel really guilty for thinking the way I did. As she nibbled at her dinner, she apologised for her appearance and explained that, only a year before, she had weighed many stones less. That was before leukaemia had been diagnosed and she had embarked on steroid treatment. I took the opportunity of calling up all the account holders she was due to visit, just to forewarn them of the poor girl's condition. Our trip around Scotland went off famously and I think she felt much better for having taken the holiday. Her boss was gracious enough to write me a nice letter, thanking me for my efforts on her behalf.

To my intense disappointment, I have never been approached by a gentleman attired in a bespoke apron with a view to joining a lodge of the Freemasons. Unlike King Arthur's knights, no one ever invited me to sit down at a Round Table. I remain unwanted by the Rotarians and neglected by the Royal Antediluvian Order of Water Buffaloes. None of the rebuffs really matter, though, because one of the most exclusive of all organisations elected me to their membership. Yes, I was a Munstermauler! Membership of this elite band was restricted to twelve members of the RMPTA in Scotland, ten men and two women. Entry was restricted to persons who had performed a spontaneously outrageous deed whilst in the unit lines. The watchword here was spontaneity. Many persons attempted to gain election by stage-managing a preposterous act, but they were quickly rumbled and never again considered for membership. My nomination resulted from having taken summary action against a particularly unpopular sergeant whom, when his judgement was adversely affected by drink, flatly refused to give me the keys to the mess. The act of smiting this bounder secured my election to the ranks of the Munstermaulers, whose existence was unknown to me at that time. During the course of a social evening held a couple of weeks later, I was requested to accompany two corporals from the bar and into an adjoining anteroom. Here, eleven Munstermaulers were lying in wait and following a brief initiation ceremony, I was voted in as a member of the august band.

Meetings of the Maulers were infrequent and quite nonsensical, the whole thing being just a bit of harmless fun. The fact that our meetings took place during our TA training weekends, however, irked the non-members intensely. Membership was in no way a reflection of rank or length of service and certain key members of the unit were highly miffed that they weren't allowed to be part of the charade. There were folk who would have given their eyeteeth to be part of the gang of twelve. Our meetings were conducted in a particularly light-hearted fashion and an example of just how frivolously we approached matters can be gauged by the proposal I tabled at a meeting held in the Isle of Man, during our summer camp. My proposal was that Munstermauleress Helen Smith, who was about to enlist in the Regular Army, should present a pair of her knickers, henceforth to be known as the Helen Smith Memorial Knickers, to be displayed in the corporal's mess. The motion was carried by eleven votes to one and the framed garment may still hang somewhere in Edinburgh.

My first year's membership of the clandestine body was made complete at the AGM, when I was awarded the Jock Day Trophy, a cup awarded annually for outrageous behaviour above and beyond the call of duty. I had imagined that the inimitable Willie Wallace would have been a more deserving recipient, but my truly incorrigible behaviour one weekend at Stranraer, when I ejected several locals from the TA Centre bar and threatened to assault the TA second-in-command when he tried to intervene, swung things my way.

Later that year, the question of bullying, initiation ceremonies and secret societies raised its ugly head in the Army. Following an unsavoury incident, where certain Scottish soldiers shoved broom handles up the bums of recruits during an initiation ceremony, a directive was issued banning secret societies. The Munstermaulers were vaguely secret, I suppose, although totally harmless, but we decided to call it a day nevertheless and disbanded with honour.

You do some pretty daft things when you're full of drink, especially when that drink is OVD rum. This strong, dark rum was the favourite tipple at 243 and it outsold the traditional Scottish spirit by a long way. The patriotic nature of the Jocks wasn't compromised, however, as this particular rum was produced in Kilmarnock. Our unit was on exercise in the north of Scotland and, in an effort to escape the mosquitoes[1] that proliferate in this part of the world, the officers and senior ranks were hiding in a large room that served as a bar. These mosquitoes thrive on Army issue insect repellent and a few tots of OVD rum, taken internally or applied externally, are the recommended precautionary measures to be taken against their spiteful bite. On this occasion the rum took a particularly savage beating, with the RSM and I leading the way. As the rest retired unsteadily towards their sleeping bags, the Dundonian RSM and I decided upon an extremely silly game before turning in for the night. The rules were simple. Whoever could throw an empty lager can the furthest, won a pound from the other. It takes considerable effort to hurl and empty aluminium can any distance at all, and although I finished up well in pocket, I hurt myself.

During the course of the next week, I became aware of a swelling in my lower abdomen and my left testicle began to hurt like Hell. I had recently read a *Reader's Digest* article entitled, 'I am John's Testicle', which urged gentlemen of a certain age to consult their doctor should this part of the anatomy be causing concern. I hotfooted to see Jock the Doc, who had a grope around, stood back to admire the view and made me cough several times. Then, after scribbling something unintelligible in my notes, he told me to put my breeks back on and addressed me seriously.

---

1. Very well, as the purists from the Scottish Highlands are almost certain to point out, these are not in fact mosquitoes, but midges, a tinier version of the blood-sucking pest that infests and plagues most of the Highlands. But for the benefit of the uninitiated, we'll just refer to them as mosquitoes, right?

"Do you want the good news or the bad news, Wally?"

"Give me the good news first."

"Well, you hav'nae got cancer."

"And the bad news?" I asked, bracing myself for the worst.

"You've got a hernia."

I had the diagnosis confirmed that very evening, by two Fellows of the Royal College of Surgeons, no less. The pair was celebrating their elevation to the Fellowship in the officer's mess and in-between glasses of Moet & Chandon in the bar, they gave me the once over on the carpet. Two beds in the Chalmer's Hospital were dedicated for the exclusive use of Army officers and two days later, in I went. Next morning, the surgeon repaired five hernias, mine included, all before NAAFI break.

Immediately after the operation, I realised that having a football hit into the middle of your back on a cold day wasn't the worst pain known to man after all. I need to confess that my performance as a recovering patient may have lacked a little in the pluck department. The hard-pressed nurses would undoubtedly have been relieved to see me shuffling sedately out of their ward at the end of my stay. Lying in the mess was no fun either; boredom quickly set in and I simply had to find something to do.

Perhaps it was a little ambitious of me to go off on an excursion quite so soon, but I took a cab to Craigie Hall, to watch the regular RMP unit in Edinburgh take on the cross border raiders from the RMP unit in Catterick at cricket. Adhering to the tradition of high standards and sporting excellence at cricket matches, neither unit could field a full team and the luxury of an official umpire was the sort of thing that dreams are made of. Having declined offers from both teams to grace their starting line-ups, I was approached by the home skipper just before the start.

"Will you umpire for us, sir?"

"I'd love to under normal circumstances, but I've just had my hernia done and can't stand for more than five minutes at a stretch."

"We can give you a chair," he said, knowing full well that I was a sucker for involving myself in any sporting event.

What clinched it for me was the production of a new ball, a thing of beauty and something rarely seen at an RMP match. And so it came to pass that I umpired a cricket match, from both ends, whilst seated on a chair. Was there ever a previous occasion where an umpire has stood, whilst being seated the whole time? That's probably one for Wisden.

As a sporting patriot, I find it hard to conceal my delight when England wins at anything. Victory is sweet when the Germans are the vanquished, but sweetest of all is when the Jocks are the victims. During my two years in Scotland, England triumphed against the auld enemy at everything, even schoolgirl's lacrosse. As one of only three Sassenachs amongst a hundred Jocks at 243, I was able to use these sporting successes to redress the racial abuse meted out to those of us born south of the border.

Every couple of months, our new TA recruits took the overnight train down to London and then onto Chichester, to undergo their basic training. The good souls of 243 always turned out in numbers to bid them farewell in the mess—it was an excellent excuse for a booze up. Fully ten minutes before opening time at this latest farewell bash, the barman phoned in to give a lame excuse as to why he couldn't make it. I wished a thousand curses on the man. Rather than have the night ruined, however, I decided to pull on the barman's apron and pull the pints myself. The PSO in a TA unit needs to be flexible. After a couple of hours of dispensing drinks at break neck speed, the barman eventually showed and that allowed me to return to the proper side of the bar to resume my favourite pastime—Jock baiting. All Scots have short fuses and making them lose their temper is simplicity itself. The slightest hint of an anti-Scottish comment suffices. I was once married to one, so I know this assertion is true.

The bar was full to overflowing and I was standing in the corner, being rude about the Scottish rugby fifteen that had recently been beaten by England and watching Sergeant Petrie's bile rising nicely. He was the most amiable of men under normal circumstances, a keen Terrier, loyal Scot and a person blessed with a level head. In drink and under pressure from a piss taking Englishman, however, his demeanour changed. He put down his drink and turned towards me.

"Sir, you're the best PSO we've ever had here in McDonald Road," he volunteered, "but I cannae tak' any more of your anti-Scottish bias."

And with that, he gave me the classic Glasgow handshake. Fortunately for me, it lacked a little direction and only bruised my lip rather than break my nose. The mess fell into silence. No matter what the provocation, it's a little unseemly for a sergeant to butt an officer in the face. Poor old Petrie, he was set upon by some of the more burly Jocks and bundled unceremoniously towards the exit. Half way across the dance floor, though, he managed to struggle free and ran back to where I was sitting dabbing my sore lip. Without further ado, he launched himself over the table and scored his second handshake of the evening. Quite an athletic feat, I thought, to find his target with both feet off the ground and his body parallel to the floor. The arrest party recaptured their man and he was beaten back over to the far door, before escaping for the second time. This was not a proficient arrest team! His dander was really up by now and he honed in on me yet again. This time, he scooped up a table and hit me on the top of the head with it. Sgt Petrie was beaten senseless by some embarrassed senior ranks and dragged away. He took no further part in proceedings, but this wasn't the end of my troubles. His fiancée was sitting only two chairs along from me and she decided to get in on the act.

"You're laughing at him!" she screeched.

Laughing I most certainly wasn't—grimacing in pain, more like. She elected to continue the assault on the lone Sassenach just the same and advanced to contact. I'm not sure what implement she used to carry out her assault, a nail file, perhaps, but in two separate attacks she succeeded in cutting both my forehead and hand, before finally lacerating my back through my suit and shirt. That was enough passivity for one evening, I reckoned, and as she came in for the third sortie, I gave her a firm dig on the nose. That had the desired effect and she sat down for a good cry.

The CSM was the senior person present and he decided that we had all seen enough excitement for one night. He closed the bar and everyone went home, or dossed down on the floor of the drill hall. As for me, I went off to the medical centre to have my injuries examined by the MO, just in case there should be any repercussions following the evening's frivolities. Although I had been sorely provoked and acted only in self-defence, an officer hitting a female corporal in her own mess is nigh on indefensible. I imagine that the Provost Marshal would have been somewhat lacking in compassion had the matter ever come to his ears. Next morning, I went into the unit suffering from a particularly sore head that was only partially attributable to a surfeit of alcohol; a table crashing down on the top of it hadn't helped. Before there was even time to make a cup of coffee, Sergeant Petrie and his fiancée were knocking on my door. Neither of them looked in peak condition, especially the girl, who was sporting a cage over her nose that was held in place by lots of sticking plaster. Her eyes were badly bruised too. I didn't recall hitting her that hard.

"Can we have a word please, sir?" asked the sergeant.

"Of course, come in and sit down," I replied.

"We'd like the SIB called in to do an investigation about last night. We've been down at the Royal Infirmary half the night. You broke her nose!"

"You are aware that I was head butted twice, hit over the head with a table, stabbed in the hand and the face and sustained a six inch laceration to my back before I retaliated, aren't you?"

"Aye, but you assaulted her and broke her nose. We want the SIB calling in."

"Very well. You realise that you will ruin my career by doing this, but then that's probably your intention. Let me assure you of one thing, however, you can forget any aspirations you may harbour about getting on in the TA."

"We still want an SIB investigation," he insisted.

I asked them to consider the matter for a further half an hour and then to return to my office. If they still felt the same way after a cooling off period, then I would call the SIB and make their day. As soon as the pair left my office, the CSM appeared.

"Excuse me for eavesdropping sir, but did I hear right? That pair want an investigation carried out on last night's wee bit carry on?" he asked.

"Yes, that's what they said. They will be back in half an hour."

"Don't do anything there the noo," said the giant CSM. "I'll hae a wee word wi' the twa o' them."

Within five minutes, the sergeant and his fiancée were back in my office. Their demeanour appeared to have changed considerably.

"Can we hae another wee word sir?" asked Petrie. "We've changed wor minds you see. We just want tae forget the whole thing, if that's all right with you?"

"I can't say that I'm sorry to hear that," I replied, feeling mightily relieved.

"Water under the bridge sir," said Sergeant Petrie and the pair offered their hands.

This wasn't the last time that the big CSM would come to my rescue.

17

Mary O'Brien, one of the Athens 'vestal virgins', called me out of the blue, not from her cowshed in Eire, but from Edinburgh.

"I'm in the Green Cow in the Cornmarket and half full of Guinness," she declared. "Get your arse down here before I get completely full."

The girl worked in a byre every day and then drank in a pub called the Green Cow on her holidays, I ask you! I hurried down to the hostelry and had a glass or two with the big Irish girl, as we reminisced about our trip to Greece. She had consumed rather more than was good for her and on returning from a trip to the lavatory, I discovered her in the arms of an equally drunken Scotsman. My presence was clearly surplus to requirements and I made my way out of the bar. Mary never even noticed.

Despite living nearby, the CSM had never been to Annfield to watch Stirling Albion play, until I coerced him into watching his local side take on Montrose. Payment of a very modest sum gained us access to the ground and we found our way to a dilapidated stand, where a man wearing a red and white hat, scarf and rosette was standing guard. He was clearly one of the team's long-suffering fans, a stalwart supporter since youth, one presumed.

"How much to get into the stand pal?" I enquired.

"A pound for the two of you boyo," he replied in a thick Welsh accent.

"You don't sound very Scottish to me?"

"Born and bred in Llanelli isn't it."

"What the hell are you doing here then?"

"Moved here with the job; love sport, already had a red and white scarf from watching the Scarlets, Stirling play in red, so here I am. On the committee now I am, isn't it."

It was a particularly poor stand and the regulars appeared to have spurned the place, preferring to huddle under a covered standing area on the opposite side of the ground instead. When we sat down, we discovered just why the place was so poorly patronised. The seats had been rescued from some long redundant picture palace and not only were they wet, but with few exceptions, they had a large spring sticking up through the cushion. I made a rude comment about the standard of the seating to Taffy as I left to buy our Scotch Pies and Bovril, mandatory fare at Scottish soccer matches. We stuck it out for the first half, but our backsides couldn't take another forty-five minutes of torture and we made our way behind the goal for the second half. By the next season, they had laid Astroturf at Annfield and had given the old stadium a reasonable facelift.

One of my all time footballing heroes was the Portsmouth, Newcastle and Bradford Park Avenue midfield hard man, Jimmy Scoular, the man with the biggest thighs in the world. 'Thighs like Jimmy Scoular' has long been one of my favourite quips, especially when espying a woman with fleshy thighs wearing a skirt that is patently too short for her. Not too many people remember him now and my comment invariable requires explanation, but it pleases me to say it anyway and it gives me the opportunity to tell youngsters about one of football's real hard men.

Larbert is the home of Stenhousemuir FC and on a foul Thursday evening in February, the local team were taking on Arbroath in a Second Division match. It wasn't an event that was likely to catch the imagination of the residents of Fife. I was the only person to alight from the train at Larbert and finding no evidence of human life on the station, I climbed the steps that led to street level. I put up my coat collar and umbrella and scanned the horizon in the hope of finding someone who could direct me to the football ground. There wasn't a soul to be seen. After five minutes, a solitary male approached, his head bent against the weather.

"Can you point me in the direction of the Stenhousemuir Football Park please?"

"I'm going there myself, I'll walk you down," he replied helpfully.

For a moment I thought that I'd discovered one of nature's most rare creatures, a Stenhousemuir fan, but he was soon to dispel that idea.

"Do you think they'll win?"

"Couldnae gie a shite," he replied. "I'm going fae a couple at the Social Club."

He was going to drink beer in a social club whilst a match was taking place in the adjacent stadium. That was beyond the comprehension of a football fanatic like me. As we walked along, he made an astute observation.

"You're no fae these parts?" he remarked.

"No, I was born near Newcastle," I replied, omitting the fact that I'm a Leicester lad by adoption.

Jocks, whilst having precious little time for the English in general, are surprisingly fond of Geordies. I have discovered that it pays dividends to stress one's northern connection when conversing with them.

"My uncle played for Newcastle," he said.

"Oh really! Who was he then?"

"It was years before your time. I doubt whether you'll mind him."

"Try me."

"Jimmy Scoular," he said, adding, "He came fae Corphorstine."

As if there could have been more than one Jimmy Scoular! I confessed my admiration for his uncle.

"Have you got big thighs?" I enquired, trusting that he wouldn't get the wrong notion.

"That's a funny question," he replied, "but aye, all the family has big thighs."

This could indeed have been the great man's nephew. The match was awful, the Scotch pies gristly and the Bovril watery, but it didn't matter. I'd walked to the match with Jimmy Scoular's nephew.

In the event of hostilities, the role of 243 was to move to Germany and assume responsibility for traffic control in designated areas. Despite the importance of such a task, financial restraints in the Army dictated that the unit never got within three hundred miles of the Fatherland during my two years with the company. For summer camp, the lads had to content themselves with a wet fortnight in Weymouth the first year and an even damper couple of weeks on the Isle of Man the second. Not that the location bothered the lads unduly, as most were only in the TA to get away from the wife for a fortnight each year. The NCOs of 243 surprised me greatly when I first saw them strutting their stuff in the field. Considering that their vehicles were worn out, their kit obsolete and the fact that we were forbidden to switch on our radios in the UK, they were bloody good. Despite restrictions on just about everything, including the number of days they were allowed to train, they were a bunch of guys with whom I was proud to be associated.

A badly devised system of budgetary control had been put into effect in RMPTA units, a system that was particularly hard on us because of our geographical location. Who was the buffoon who decided that each of the four independent RMPTA units should be allocated an equal amount of cash for their annual travel budgets? As all recruits were trained in the Corp's Training Centre on the south coast of England, was I the only person who wasn't surprised when my allocation for railway warrants ran out before those guys who ran units in Stockton, West Bromwich and London?

In addition to the monetary considerations, a restriction was put on the number of days a soldier was permitted to serve each year. This was a brilliantly conceived plan too and the measly number of days allotted made it virtually impossible for us to function. Meanwhile, our TA HQ in Chichester had an abundance of spare man-days and travel funds, but the tight sods wouldn't part with any of it. Having fought the good fight for as long as possible, I gave up the unequal struggle in December of the second year, when my budget was spent and extra man-days were denied me yet again. My solution to the problem was somewhat unorthodox. I picked up the phone and called the Provost Marshal, to wish him a Merry Christmas and Happy Easter, explaining that since we didn't have the wherewithal to function, the unit would be closing down until the beginning of the next financial year. Thanks to his sense of humour, common sense and fax machine, we had an abundance of everything by start of play next day. The parsimonious officer at RMPTA HQ phoned next day, to tell me that I was both disloyal and a conniving bastard. He wasted government money on that call. I knew already.

When the Isle of Man was announced as the venue for our Summer Camp 1987, our OC was most anxious to ensure that we sail from any port other than Helensburgh. He needn't have worried, because the RCT Water Transport unit at that location had closed down many years before. I pressed him as to why he was so reluctant to sail to the Isle of Man from the fair port of Helensburgh. He related the following story:

Our Summer Camp in 1972 was being held on the Isle of Man. Our route was to drive from Edinburgh to Helensburgh and from there, we would sail to the Isle of Man by courtesy of the RCT Water Transport Squadron's LSL. The drive went without a hitch, as did the embarkation procedure. All that remained was to relax, enjoy the trip and await landfall some thirty-six hours hence. Those thirty-six hours came and went, as did our stock of beer, and still there was no sign of terra firma. Another twenty-four hours passed and we still hadn't sighted land, and the LSL skipper, a young lieutenant, was showing signs of strain. Finally the coastline hove into view. As the ship made shore, a man out walking his dog came up to see what was going on.

"Ahoy there," said the skipper. "Are we far from Ramsey?"

"Can't say I've ever heard of the place boyo," replied a Welsh voice. "But Holyhead is only five miles around the headland."

The skipper had managed to miss the Isle of Man altogether and had landed on Anglesey. By steering north west, the ship, containing several dozen seriously pissed off Jocks, reached the Isle of Man next day, but even this only counted as a limited success. Instead of landing at Ramsey, the skipper put the front of the ship down on the main tourist beach at Douglas. I was somewhat embarrassed, as the lads all drove up the beach, scattering children, deck chairs, donkeys and all those assembled for the Punch & Judy show.

Our journey, via the Heysham-Douglas ferry, was tame by comparison.

It was time for some leave and my fiancée and I set out for Malta, by train and ship. The train ride down through northern Italy was memorable for the fact that we were in the same compartment as a most interesting old gentleman. Unlikely to see the age of seventy again, he regaled us with a series of intriguing stories. It seems that whenever he had the inclination, he would walk a section of the ancient pilgrim route between the UK and Rome. This time, he alighted some fifty miles north of the Italian capital and set about walking the final leg. Once he reached St Peter's, he was to have an audience with the Pope, who had been briefed about his exploits.

The holiday must go down as a success, I suppose, if only by virtue of the fact that we didn't fall out until we reached Naples. Here she managed to fuse the lights in the entire hotel with that bloody hair-dryer that she insisted on taking everywhere. After that episode and the argument that followed it, I actually put my escape plan into operation, but only made it as far as Naples railway station. Here, an old fellow with whom I shared a bench whilst awaiting the Paris bound sleeper, talked me out of taking the train. Naples is a lousy place, although Pompeii was worth a look and Mt. Vesuvius awesome. From Naples, it was on to Reggio de Calabria on the tip of Italy's toe, to catch the ship to Malta. A taxi driver at Reggio railway station saw me off beautifully. In my very best Italian, which consists of perhaps ten words and the names of the Italian soccer teams, I asked him to take me to a decent hotel. The drive to the Ritz took him fifteen minutes and cost me a large number of liras for the privilege. Next morning I looked out of the hotel window, only to discover that the Ritz and the railway station were fully fifty yards apart. Nice one, Luigi!

My travels in Turkey interested the old fellow particularly, as the next walk he proposed to undertake was from Rome to Jerusalem. Since he was well travelled in Italy, I reciprocated by asking him whether he knew anything about Reggio de Calabria, our final destination in Italy. He knew the place very well, he declared, but only through the bombsights of his Lancaster bomber during the war.

He took me up on an invitation to dinner at Edinburgh Castle once, when he was travelling up to see his brother in the north of Scotland. He dumbfounded me when he signed the mess visitor's book. The old fellow appeared to hold every medal for gallantry ever awarded during the Second World War and was a Member of the European Parliament. I wonder if he ever made it to Jerusalem?

On leaving Reggio, the ship called into Catania in Sicily and thus afforded the passengers a view of Mt. Etna. It was a freezing cold morning as we pulled alongside and it appeared that I was the only person aboard who considered the view worth getting a cold nose for.

Malta didn't appear to have altered in the twenty years I'd been away and I looked forward to a week of rediscovering the place. My fiancée meanwhile, was engaged in putting the final touches to her plan to spoil my week. My determination to visit the old military areas that had once been part of my life was matched by her determination that she wasn't going to visit them. Consequently, we spent most of the week apart—I explored and she took in the rays at the poolside.

One of my pilgrimages in Malta was to Mosta Fort, where the RMP Dog Section had been based prior to the British withdrawal from the island. A friendly staff sergeant from the Malta Artillery gave me a guided tour of the camp, once he had convinced himself that I represented no danger to the security of his establishment. We talked about the British Army and the Maltese Regiments who had served Her Majesty, before he stunned me with a question I could never have anticipated.

"Do you know Bert Mulpeter?" he asked.

Of course I knew the Maltese with the Irish sounding name—he had served as a corporal in the RMP for many years. Bert was this guy's next-door neighbour and these days, apparently, he was to be found at Pawla prison, as governor on one of the wings. This was a man who had been given his redundancy after eighteen years service with the colours, because he was considered to have reached his ceiling as a corporal. Now he was a governor in the island's only jail! It demanded investigation. Having survived a body search and some damn silly questions at the prison gate, I was escorted through to Bert's office. To be perfectly honest, his face didn't register after so many years, but I was clearly in the right place because, on the wall behind his desk, hung an RMP dress cap. The basic niceties completed and with tea served, it was necessary to ask the burning question.

"Bert, with due deference to you and your abilities, you hardly set the world alight as a military policeman. How the hell did you make it to this heady position when you didn't join the service until you were over forty years of age?"

"I found the prison service in a badly organised state when I first joined," he explained. "So I reorganised everything in line with the teachings of the good book."

How could the Bible help revamp a rundown prison set-up?

"So you found the Bible helpful in your reorganisation plans, did you?"

"No, not *that* good book, the other one," he said, brandishing an ancient copy of the Provost Manual, the RMP guide to provost procedures and a document that had been superseded many years previously.

She didn't enjoy Malta. Just to rub things in, as I was fetching some cold drinks from a kiosk on Naples station on the way back, a flasher jumped into our compartment and exposed his Italian excuse for a male member to her. She had seen bigger!

"The Leith Police dismisseth us," we used to say in the schoolyard. It never occurred to me that I would ever visit the town, let alone visit the Leith Police. One of our TA corporals was a teacher at a Sunday school down in Leith, where he and an older man taught the youngsters from the Methodist Church. Their duties also extended to a Bible study evening once a week, immediately after their normal school lessons. The corporal arrived one evening and asked for a closed-door session with me. He explained that his fellow Sunday school teacher was not all he was made out to be. He had evidence to prove that his fellow teacher had been showing his charges more than the Bible during their Wednesday evening sessions. As well as introducing the older boys to the joys of masturbation, this evil bastard had indecently assaulted three lads under the age of ten.

"Is there anything I can do about him sir?" he asked.

"Bloody right there is," I told him.

I went straight down to the CID at Leith and they came to interview the corporal at once. Thanks to his evidence and a confession from the alleged Bible teacher, the dirty bugger went to prison. Tragically, a few years later, something drove that well-meaning and very decent young corporal to take his own life.

Regulations stipulated that the OC of the regular unit in Edinburgh and the PSO of the TA unit should take turns to be the Chairman of the RMP Association in Scotland. That's what the regulations required, but for various reasons I held the position for the whole two years of my stay in Scotland. The Old Boys Association met about eight times a year, either in the Castle or at the TA Centre, the latter location being the most popular venue. Most of the members were getting on a wee bit and they found the ascent to the Castle a bit much, especially in winter, when the esplanade could be a bit icy. The whole business of keeping the Association functioning at all was an uphill battle. As the older guys died off, there was no interest from the younger people in supporting the RMPA. I can't say that I blame them. Nevertheless, I tried my damnedest to make gatherings interesting and lost count of how many letters I needed to address and stick down, to inform the membership of the next riveting meeting. My secretary was no help in this regard. She refused to have anything to do with the Association, having suffered a perceived slur from a member back in days of yore. She had a long memory.

Should the weather be inclement on the night of a function, or if I should have been unwise in my selection of the evening's entertainment, the numbers attending might be as low as ten. On the other hand, if Highland dancers or a piper were on the menu, we could expect fifty or more. The Jocks are a patriotic lot. One of the old characters that attended would recite the whole of Tam O'Shanter the moment he heard the swirl of the pipes and keeping him quiet was probably my most difficult task. If you haven't heard someone recite the entire poem, then I commend it to you, but only once.

The person that really kept our little organisation going wasn't me, but Maggie MacDonald. Maggie owned a couple of restaurants in Edinburgh and specialised in outside catering. Whenever we had a meeting, therefore, we could be assured of a decent buffet that was invariably provided free of charge. Her association with the RMPA had come about many years previously, when she began to hire RMP NCOs to act as waiters at functions whenever she was pushed to find staff. The whole arrangement was mutually beneficial to all concerned and, as the years went by, she became a keen and valued member of the gang. The good lady was known to be partial to a drop of whisky and whenever a complimentary bottle came my way, I would pop it round to her restaurant. She did have just cause to take me to task once, when I delivered a complimentary bottle of the water of life to her without looking at the label. She announced that she would be unable to do anything with the contents of this particular bottle other than tip it down the sink. It was a bottle of the Glen Campbell, you see.

Arriving back at my office after lunch one Tuesday afternoon, I was surprised to find one of the RMPA members awaiting my return. He was the bearer of the direst news. Fighting to hold back his tears, he explained that Maggie had died suddenly the previous Friday afternoon. Huge numbers turned up at the crematorium for her funeral later in the week—so many, in fact, that there were scores of us who never even saw the coffin. She was only in her late forties and the RMPA in Scotland would never be the same without her.

After eighteen months of living in the mess on my own, Mark arrived to command the regular RMP unit in the Castle and to keep me company in the bar. He was a fellow single man and a decent guy to boot. Mark, being a proper officer rather than a commissioned warrant officer, was rather more acceptable to the toffee nose bunch in the HQ. He hadn't been living in the mess for a week before he broke some news over dinner that really pissed me off. He had been selected to play for the Castle Mess Curling Team in a fixture against the District Mess. In a year and a half, I had never been invited to play anything and his selection irked me more than a little. Admittedly, I had never been on the ice in my life, but there again, neither had he. I had seen the game often enough on the TV and it's only like green bowls on ice after all. He had been asked to fill in because he was a real officer. They would have turned up short-handed rather than ask a commissioned labourer like me to play. Mark was full of himself and performed well enough to become a regular in the side. The Mess President was a snotty officer from a famous Jock regiment; he was also the curling team manager, selector and captain. When I next bumped into him, he was at great pains to point out how well Mark had equipped himself in the team.

"I wanted to talk to you about that Hamish," I said. "How come you invite him to play for your team when you never ask me, a former England under 23 international?"

"You've played to that standard, Wally?"

"Absolutely! I played seventeen times for my country and have an Olympic silver medal to boot. I've not played for some time now of course," I lied.

"Would you turn out for us in the return fixture next week?" he asked.

"Gladly."

Me and my big mouth! They had selected me for a curling match, when the nearest I'd ever been to an ice rink was to watch Durham Wasps play ice hockey when I was a lad.

Dress for the pre-match lunch was tweed suits. I ask you! My wardrobe didn't contain a tweed suit, nor did I have any intention of buying one, so I made up an excuse to miss the lunch and turned up directly at the ice rink. Taking to our lane for a few practice throws before the rest arrived, I quickly discovered that it's nothing like as easy as it looks. The 'stone' flies down at quite a lick and the hard bit is throwing it down, officially called 'laying the stone', gently enough. When the match started, it soon became apparent to my fellow curlers that I was either the biggest liar of all time, or that my touch had deserted me cruelly. We lost the match, but they selected me for the following game just the same. Hamish must have detected some latent ability. I declined their invitation, however; the outlay for a tweed suit for only half a dozen matches a season didn't seem cost-effective to me.

Ray Stratford came up with the idea of a 4 Guards Brigade Group Provost Unit reunion, to be held at his TA Centre at Tulse Hill in London. Twenty years had come and gone since the halcyon days of Rawson's Rangers and it seemed like a sound idea to me. The Man of Kent had already done a lot of the hard work, although as the newly appointed 'Person Finder General' for Scotland and the north of England, I was required to do my bit too. The first person on my list whose address couldn't be confirmed was Geordie Rogers, who lived somewhere in Tyne & Wear.

I remembered that Geordie was a man who wouldn't travel by train under any circumstances. This reluctance came about following a journey he had made several years previously, after his workingmen's club's annual seaside outing to Blackpool. Full of the local Lancashire brew, he made it to Blackpool station and boarded what he believed to be a train bound for Newcastle. He was on the wrong train, of course, and awoke next morning to find his carriage shunted into some deserted sidings, with him the only person aboard. His investigations revealed that, rather than him being in his native northeast, he was actually in King's Lynn, a fair hike from Newcastle by any stretch of the imagination. He attributed his *faux pas* to a 'change of beer', the classic Geordie defence for any mistake.

Many years previously I had been to the Roger's abode in Hetton-le-Hole and could recall his parent's house in Barrington Terrace perfectly well. This time, though, I couldn't find the street at all. There's bugger-all to Hetton-le-Hole, and by the time I'd gone up and down the main street a dozen times in the hope of finding a landmark, people were beginning to get suspicious. A friendly local came to my assistance.

"Have you any idea how I get to Barrington Terrace?" I enquired.

"How long since you were last in Hetton?" asked the local.

"It must be going on ten years I suppose."

"And the rest. They pulled that row down thirteen years since."

"Actually, I'm looking for a lad called Geordie Rogers; he'd be about my age and used to be in the Army."

"Well, that's a big help mind. Half the people in Hetton are called Rogers and the other half answer to Geordie."

I'd picked on the right fellow just the same. He knew the family, he knew Geordie and he knew that he was in the Hetton Comrades Working Men's Club at that very moment. Sure enough, I found him in the bar and the pair of us drank to excess, as befits two former Iserlohn men who hadn't seen each other for so long. All too soon it was time to run the gauntlet of the local constabulary, by driving my trusty Fiat back to my Aunt's home in nearby Penshaw. As I was driving away, however, the Federation Ale suddenly got the better of me and, instead of reversing out of the car park, I shot forward onto the hallowed turf of the club's bowling green. Luckily, I was able to locate reverse and speed away before any of the members saw the carnage. Causing damage to a bowling green is a capital offence in these parts. After all that, Geordie never turned up at the function.

The next lost soul on my list was Tom Robeson, the inimitable Robbo, a man whose presence at the reunion was obligatory. Someone had actually come up with a possible address for the Glaswegian and it was my intention to find him the very next day. I would have sallied forth immediately at the prospect of meeting up with this old comrade, but duty called, in the form of a drive north to Helensburgh to sort out a problem with the booking of a firing range. My route to Helensburgh took me through Glasgow and I was telling my fellow passenger that I needed to come back to the city next day to look for an old friend, when I needed to stop the car at a zebra crossing. Now I know that nobody will believe me, but the person walking over the crossing was none other than Robbo! I sprang from the car a shouted his name.

"What the fuck are *you* doing here?" he demanded.

We greeted each other on the crossing and I explained about the reunion. He was a big fan of the idea. By the time we had finished reminiscing, the traffic was backed up into the city centre and tempers were getting frayed, so we arranged to meet at Queen's Street railway station in Glasgow the following evening. My train was delayed somewhere between Edinburgh and Glasgow and it pulled into the station twenty minutes late. As I bustled my way through the throng on the platform, a voice boomed out from atop a luggage trolley.

"Typical fucking officer, always fucking late!"

We slipped into the nearest pub and caught up on ten years worth of stories. It was a brilliant evening and such a joy to meet up with this guy once again.

All in all, we came up with the names of seventy-two guys who had served with the old unit. Ten had disappeared, several weren't interested and three were pushing up the daisies, but on a filthy November evening, forty of us gathered at the south London TA Centre for the mother of all reunions. Despite the grey hair, receding hairlines and the odd few pounds of overweight, we were all just the same as we had been twenty years before. A person's character, it seems, doesn't alter overmuch with the advancing years. Xavier was still spoiling for a fight once the alcohol set in and Dave's frugal nature was still apparent as he grumbled that a fiver a head for the buffet was a bit steep. Shrubb slipped away without paying and, as was to be expected, it was Robbo who performed with the stripper.

A camp bed had been set up for me in one of the offices and it was very late when I made my unsteady way back for a lie down. Stratford swore that he knew nothing about it, but my camp bed had a leg missing and one of these days, I'll get him back for that miserable night's sleep. When I was finally dozing off, a voice called me. It sounded like Taffy, so I jumped out of my three-legged bed and went out into an empty corridor. It must have been a dream. No sooner was I asleep, than the voice called out again.

"Wally, wake up and let me in boyo," pleaded a Welsh voice.

Again the corridor was empty. Tucking myself in for the third time, I contemplated cutting down on the lager if it was going to make me hallucinate after a mere dozen pints. Just then the voice spoke again.

"Wally, can you hear me boyo?"

"Yes, I can hear you, but where the hell are you?"

"I'm outside your window, freezing my bollocks off. Open the main door and let me back in will you?"

I went to the front door and let the grateful Welshman inside. He had been unable to locate the lavatories when nature had called and had dashed outside in his underpants to relieve himself. The door had slammed shut and left him on Tulse Hill High Street, dressed only in his underpants and in ten degrees of frost.

Next morning, we all sat down to an exercise breakfast and a bottle of Russian Stout, a perfect end to a perfect reunion. Robbo declared the evening's events to have been 'fucking brilliant', which just about summed things up.

The job of running a Territorial Unit is so complex that you need to be able to rely on your fellow regulars without having constantly to check up on them. It was getting on towards the end of my time with the TA before I discovered that my previous Quartermaster, a person that I had trusted unreservedly, had been less than honest. The man had only been out of the unit for a few weeks, when a couple of his howlers were revealed. Perhaps a more diligent PSO would have discovered the anomalies before I did?

Running a TA outfit involves mastering a multitude of skills not normally encountered in a regular unit. One of these unique skills was the purchase of rations from local suppliers for weekend exercises, when you had no idea how many men would show up. Obviously the foodstuffs needed to be ordered in advance, but when all your men are volunteers who have no compulsion to turn up, what do you do? Listen to Michael Fish's weather forecast on a Thursday evening is the answer to that conundrum. If he promises a dry and sunny weekend, then order rations for seventy men. If he forecasts a deep depression over the Azores on the other hand, thirty-five should suffice. For years, a gentleman by the name of Swift had been the unit's flexible and understanding supplier of provisions. He was local, he delivered what we wanted on time and he didn't mind waiting until the end of the month for the Army to cough up his money. The old CQMS swore by the man and assured me that he was perfectly trustworthy. With no reason to doubt either the grocer or the CQMS, once a month I made out a cheque drawn on public funds in favour of the supplier, gave it to the Q and he delivered it. When the long serving QM moved on, Swift was retained and everything carried on as normal. Just before the end of my time in Edinburgh, however, I had reason to visit an optician whose premises just happened to be opposite those of the good Swift. As it was at the end of the month, I decided to save the new CQMS a job and to take the cheque with me. Despite dealing with the man for almost two years, we have never actually set eyes upon each other and so my visit afforded me the opportunity of paying his bill and saying both hello and goodbye at the same time. To my considerable surprise, the grocery store turned out to be a video rental establishment. True, there were sweeties for sale on the counter, but there was a dearth of baked beans, corned beef and those other items necessary for survival during a weekend in the field. The man behind the counter confirmed to me that he was Mr Swift, supplier of foodstuffs to 243 Provost Company for the last decade.

"How long since you stopped selling groceries then, Mr Swift?"

"A couple of years now," he replied. "Ever since the supermarket opened directly over the road."

"How do you supply us then?"

"Perfectly simple, I buy the stuff from the Cash & Carry and add 10% for myself and 10% for your Q."

At least the man wasn't trying to cover up, but there had clearly been a serious fiddle perpetrated here. If I were to push the matter, then questions would have be asked as to why I hadn't discovered the irregularity before. Best to keep stumm and put it down to experience. Fancy the CQMS risking his career, and probably his liberty, for a few paltry quid. Within the hour, Mr Swift was in receipt of a letter thanking him for his unstinting efforts on behalf of the unit, but stating that we would be using an alternative supplier in future.

Our massive chunk of real estate boasted a twenty-five-metre rifle range on its top floor. It had lain unused for many years following a visit from the Health & Safety people, who had declared that the fans that sucked in the air at one end and blew it out at the other, were fitted the wrong way round. Despite monthly applications for funds going back for three years, the TA Authority for Scotland had still to allocate the money to enable contractors to be hired to change the fans around. The range, therefore, remained closed and there was no reason for me to go into the place. It was used sometimes for doing a bit of drill, if the weather outside was typically Scottish, and also for storing a few bits and pieces. I was aware of a large number of ammunition boxes at the butt's end of the range, but had never examined them. There was no reason for me to question the old QM's explanation that they were all empty and that they might just come in handy one day.

The replacement CQMS was a man who considered passing wind in public to be rib tickling funny; he also supported Bristol City, so I sacked him without any further ado. The third CQMS in as many weeks was a different kettle of fish altogether. He was keen, efficient and supported Leeds United, which was altogether more acceptable. He went through the unit like a dose of salts and proved to me that the longstanding QM had been a deceitful, idle, cheating and untrustworthy individual. In short, I had trusted a man who had pulled the wool over my eyes.

The new guy came into my office one morning and dropped three live rounds onto my desk.

"Found them in the first of the ammunition boxes that I opened in the range," he declared.

"But those boxes are all empty, aren't they?" I asked hopefully.

"Those boxes are all full, sir; there must be several tons of brass up there and God knows how many live rounds."

The CQMS took me up for a look. Sure enough, it appeared as if no empty bullet cases had been disposed of in 243 for decades. Over the course of the weekend, I employed a crowd of the TA lads to sieve through every box of empty cases. They found a further twenty-seven lives rounds. A friend in the Ordnance Corps arranged to have them fired off without anything being said and the Navy Ordnance Depot, located somewhere to the north of the Forth, were soon wading knee deep in brass. The whole exercise took three hours. Why had it lain there for so long I wonder?

18

It's a sign that you are getting on a wee bit, when your life assurance policies begin to mature. Mind you, the money comes in handy and allows you to undertake the sort of adventures that you couldn't previously afford. With an appreciative nod in the direction of the man from the Pru for managing my meagre investment so astutely, I rushed off to book passages aboard the QE2. It was to be a holiday in the USA for me and old what's her name, my betrothed at that time. From New York, where the mighty ship would dock, our itinerary would take us to Chicago and thence to Las Vegas, where I would be content to lose my grubstake, before heading back in the opposite direction. The tickets were to hand, leave confirmed and we were ready for what promised to be an exciting holiday, when that ridge of low pressure that caught out Michael Fish and his mates at the Meteorological Office struck the UK. By a stroke of good fortune, I had travelled down from Edinburgh to London a day earlier than necessary and by the time the undetected hurricane had struck the south of England, I was already tucked up in bed in Clapham. We slept through the storm, but awoke to power cuts next morning. Thanks to a battery-operated radio, we were able to tune into the BBC and learn of the havoc that the weather had wreaked in the south of the country. We were due to be in Southampton to board the ship by early evening, but the South Eastern Region of British Rail was non-operational and almost every road in the south east was blocked by fallen trees. The chances of reaching Southampton in time for the departure of the QE2 appeared remote. Nevertheless, Cunard telephoned us to state that we should report to Waterloo Station as previously instructed, explaining that we would travel by coach rather than by the usual train. Despite the chaos that was apparent all around, we managed to make it to the dock and the QE2 sailed for New York a mere thirty minutes later than scheduled.

The ship may have left pretty well on time despite the weather, but the sea was waiting to take over the attack. As soon as we were clear of the protection afforded by the coast and out into the Atlantic proper, the big vessel began to roll and heave. I had never experienced waves of that size before and my mind recalled the old wartime newsreel footage of the Atlantic convoys. Dinner on the first evening was a hoot. Table allocations counted for nothing, as only a handful of passengers could face the prospect of a six-course dinner in the howling gale. The ship's guest concert pianist and her husband partnered us at our table. She was an interesting lady and I went to all of her concerts, out of loyalty rather than because of the content of her programmes should the truth be known. She was much too Mahler, Bartok and Stockhausen for my taste. Even the company of the pianist and the prospect of six *cordon bleu* courses couldn't keep me at the table that first night, however, and I decided to forgo the last two dishes, in favour of a couple of Sea Legs and a glass of water in my cabin. The QE2 was soon awash with seasick passengers and crew. Having suffered from the malady myself on several bumpy crossings between Zeebrugge and Dover, they had my heartfelt sympathy. The ship's infirmary did a roaring trade in anti-seasick injections at $10 a shot and for me, that was ten bucks well spent. The injection made you drowsy and an early night was prescribed immediately afterwards, but the effect was dramatic. By next morning you couldn't have been sick if you wanted to be, no matter how rough the sea.

Why my betrothed and I were betrothed will always remain a mystery, probably to the pair of us, since we were supremely unsuited to make the trip through life together and we fell out constantly. It was inevitable that we would fall out sooner or later on this trip and it turned out to be sooner—on the third afternoon at sea, in fact. She had made a most uncharacteristic choice of afternoon entertainment, by selecting to play Bingo in the Grand Lounge. I had no difficulty in giving that a miss, but at her request, agreed to fetch our washing from the ship's launderette. It was quite the biggest launderette I've ever seen and it was easy to lose one's way amongst the washers and dryers. She had given me precise instructions as to the location of our spin dryer; it was the last machine on the left. Armed with that piece of intelligence my Harrods carrier bag and I went to retrieve whatever it was that she had left spinning. Now the only other person in the place was a very tall American, clearly a passenger from the lower decks, who was reading a paperback book. He ignored my cheery greeting and thus confirmed my opinion of his race. I was merrily stuffing the contents of the last dryer on the left into the Harrods bag, when a large hand grabbed me by the shoulder. It was the tall American, who had a serious look on his face.

"Y'all had better leave my property where it is boy," he drawled.

"No, no, these are my things," I replied, erroneously as it transpired.

"These here are my Fruit of the Loom jockeys," he declared, retrieving a pair of his underpants from our Harrods bag.

"Oh dear, I appear to be at the wrong machine," I stuttered.

"I've heard about guys like y'all, stealing people's undergarments and all. It's a perversion they say."

That was an unacceptable slur. Goodness knows that there are plenty of defects to my character, but stealing underpants certainly isn't one of them. This guy didn't just think that I was a tealeaf, but considered me a Willy Woofter to boot. He was undoubtedly taller than I was, but Wally Payne was younger, heavier, and probably tougher, if push came to shove. My honour needed defending; one couldn't allow an American to talk to Briton thus.

"How dare you cast aspersions on the character of an Englishman?" I declared, pushing him backwards. "Any more insinuations of that nature and I'll be forced to knock your block off."

My bluff worked. He returned to his seat without commenting further. I put his Fruit of the Loom garments back in their rightful place and located our stuff, in an adjacent dryer. That fool woman had given me bad information! In her haste to involve herself with Kelly's Eye, she had almost caused me to get a punch in mine. Back in the Grand Lounge I extracted revenge, by ripping up her bingo tickets for the next game. She in turn called me disgusting and that was the end of the *entente cordiale* for the remainder of the holiday. As if that wasn't bad enough, the Wall Street Stock Exchange suffered a massive crash overnight and I lost a lot of money. The loss depressed me somewhat, although I took comfort from some of those in the first class cabins, who reportedly lost millions. Nobody jumped over the side just the same.

The QE2's onboard entertainment was excellent. From morning until late at night there were organised pursuits to suit every taste. Being a sports buff with an interest in the obscure, I quite fancied my chances in the sports quiz held in the Grand Lounge. To my dismay, however, my thirty-eight points out of a possible forty was only good enough to win me the Parker biro awarded to the runner up. I had been beaten into second place by an old gentleman with an American accent, but who sported a black blazer emblazoned with a REME badge. The conundrum as to how he had managed to achieve one point more than me was only revealed on the return leg of the voyage, when they asked the very same set of sport's questions. It appears that they only had one set! The scoundrel had been doing the same quiz for the second time. I added to my collection of QE2 Parker pens, by taking a surprise second place in the Old Films Quiz. The fact that my lamentable lack of knowledge on this subject was sufficient to secure me the runner's up spot only goes to show the desperate standard of competition.

The trip went off splendidly, especially as my fiancée wasn't speaking to me. We went our own merry ways, meeting only to eat and sleep. This was a perfectly agreeable state of affairs as far as I was concerned. On arrival at the Big Apple, not an attractive city in my view, we deposited our suitcases at Grand Central Station and wandered around on foot. One day was sufficient to confirm that New York is tall, noisy and brash. My breakfast that morning consisted of a couple of bagels, eaten at Hymie's Deli. In the interest of safety, I should point out that swimming ought not to be attempted within two days of eating one of Hymie's bagels. Following an overnight trip on Amtrak, the much-maligned American railway system, we reached Chicago. Despite the disparaging remarks made about Amtrak by American acquaintances, I considered this particular train, and all the others on which we were to ride during the holiday, to be of the highest quality. We had fallen out badly about something else by the time we reached the Windy City and so did the tourist sites independently. It shames me to confess it, but I funked a trip to the top of Sear's Tower. Much too high for me!

In the evening it was back to the railroad terminal, which seemed remarkably like a railway station to me. Here we boarded the long distance train that went from Chicago to Los Angeles. The three-day journey to Flagstaff, Arizona, was to prove a most pleasurable travelling experience. The seats and beds were excellent, the food top quality and reasonably priced and the printed sheets that they gave out, showing you places of interest along the route, a great idea.

I found myself unable to resist the train's bar, which offered a competitively priced cocktail of the day, served by the most gorgeous barmaid. She was forced to suspend her operation for part of Sunday, though, as the train passed through the state of Kansas, whose licensing laws prohibited the sale of alcohol on Sundays, even on trains passing through. We finally arrived at Flagstaff, where it was all change for the Grand Canyon. We were billeted at the Pony Soldier Motel, a splendid hostelry that, fortunately for us, had a very friendly and understanding locksmith on call. How can two people, sleeping in the same room, both lock themselves into the bathroom on the same night?

Just how very small the world can be was confirmed next morning, as we tucked into our giant Pony Soldier breakfasts. A lady at the next table had a sister that had married an Englishman, who lived in the very same Cumbrian village as my betrothed.

After breakfast we took a Greyhound up to the Grand Canyon. The bus trip turned out to be the only bright spot in a hugely disappointing day, as the Canyon was fog bound and I never took my camera out of its case. Our schedule was so tight that we couldn't make an attempt next day, when the sun was shining brightly—naturally. Instead, it was all aboard another 'dog' that would take us on a serpentine route, through Kingman, the place were everyone got their kicks whilst travelling on Route 66 and then to Las Vegas. An archetypal Texan, who occupied the seat across the aisle from me, spoiled my enjoyment of the trip. He never took his ten-gallon hat off during the whole journey and spent the majority of his time spitting the residue of a lump of chewing tobacco that was wedged under his bottom lip, into a Coca Cola bottle. As if that wasn't gross enough, the doddering old fool kept knocking the bottle over and deposited the disgusting black goo onto the floor of the bus. No problem though—he simply rubbed the liquid into the carpet with the soles of his cowboy boots. Considering that the restrictions heaped upon Greyhound travellers—smoking, eating, drinking and playing personal radios loud enough for a fellow passenger to hear—are all punishable by ejection from the coach, I was surprised that spitting goo into a coke bottle escaped the driver's attention. By the end of the day I was fed up with the bus and could have done without diversions to Henderson and Carson City. Eventually, however, the blaze of lights in the distance heralded Las Vegas. Five days in the splendid Pioneer Hotel lay ahead.

It is said that one either loves or hates Las Vegas. I loved it. There are gambling machines everywhere, even in the chemist's shop where I bought my Andrew's Liver Salts and on the railway station. In fact, the opportunity to lose your shirt lurks on every street corner. The whole place is designed to relieve the punter of his cash as quickly and as pleasurably as possible. Free drinks are on offer to gamblers in the hotels, regardless of the stakes for which you play, and they are served to your table or machine by battalions of pretty, busty and scantily clad little things. I heartily supported this method of dispensing drinks and may have drunk rather more than was good for me on occasions. Our room had a king sized bed, which was just as well, as we weren't talking in anything more than monosyllables and it allowed us to sleep in the same bed without coming within yards of each other. One short, but profound conversation resulted in the agreement that our relationship would be over once we arrived back in England. We seemed to get along rather better after that.

With some form of gambling available at every turn, I was in seventh heaven and even gambled on the Keno whilst eating breakfast in the bedroom. Keno was invented for those people who couldn't find enough ways to lose their money; it's a bingo type game that is played around the clock. You could even buy your tickets from the chambermaids, toilet attendants or the waitresses that brought your breakfast.

Each of the larger hotels employs a personality, usually a former boxer who is down on his luck, to supervise the Wheel of Fortune, the obligatory adornment of every hotel foyer. This method of gambling had long since failed to attract the serious punters, but it was traditional and perfectly wonderful for a keen boxing fan like myself. The ex-pug in our hotel was Joey Maxim, the man who had relieved Briton Freddy Mills of his World Light Heavyweight title in the immediate post war years. To the fury of my fiancée, I spent hours talking to him and trying to impress him with my knowledge of the fight game. Actually, Joey Maxim was never a stylish or elegant boxer, more of an effective spoiler and he was never remotely popular outside of his hometown. I liked him just the same.

This being a gambler's paradise, I didn't restrict myself to the Pioneer and was very content lurching from hotel to hotel, leaving my money behind. My favourite method of throwing it away was on a horseracing machine in one of the smaller hotels. This machine took a fair proportion of my cash, although I recouped a fair amount of it and achieved a moral victory, by drinking several crates of their Mexican beer. The larger hotels had stupendous stage shows and it seemed that all the top names were appearing at one place or another. We both wanted to see the Judds at Caesar's Palace, but after waiting for half an hour in a queue that stubbornly refused to budge, I aborted mission and succeeded in infuriating my alleged fiancée once again. She was a woman who never quite came to terms with the old adage, 'Time, tide and Wally Payne wait for no man'.

All too soon it was time to catch the train back from Las Vegas to Chicago, but since all the cash I was willing to lose was already in the hands of the casino owners, perhaps it was just as well. Even the tunnel that led from the last casino to the railway station was lined with slot machines; the greedy buggers wanted to fleece you right to the bitter end. Finally, we were aboard the Amtrak train that was to take us back east. I woke up early next morning to see Salt Lake City and the Temple—both were visible through our sleeper window. Later that day, we passed through the Green Desert of Utah. The conductor urged passengers to keep their eyes peeled for a glimpse of an animal called the 'jackalope', a hybrid cross between an antelope and a jackrabbit that was indigenous only to the Green Desert. And then, beneath a tree, suddenly I saw one! A couple of years later I mentioned this sighting to a group of Americans with whom I was enjoying a Thanksgiving Dinner. Once they had recovered from their mirthful writhing around the floor, they explained the reason for their humorous outburst. The jackalope, it appears, is the midwest's equivalent of the haggis, the legendary Scottish creature that has legs shorter on one side to allow it to run around hilltops.

We were sitting down to lunch as the train reached Denver and a boarding passenger joined our table. This terrible man was to be responsible for one of my worst ever hangovers. To complement his chicken, this hippie type produced a bottle of over proof Bahamian rum, which he offered around the table. It was a palatable tipple, but strong. After lunch, the hippie and I went down to the bar where a few other travellers joined us, all of them intent on giving the rum a try. The card school, which was to last all the way to Chicago, had entered its embryonic stage. In retrospect, the whole thing may have been a hustle, but fair or foul, the result was the same. By the time we arrived in Chicago, I'd lost every last cent of cash and owed a couple of hundred dollars to a retired taxi driver from New York. There were enough traveller's cheques in the cabin to settle my debt of honour and I scurried away to fetch them before he drew his Colt 45. The New Yorker insisted on meeting me in the deserted coffee lounge, a little odd, but perhaps gambling debts were traditionally settled in private in the USA. Armed with my cheques, I was about to put my signature on the things, when the ex-taxi driver's ham sized fist closed over mine.

"I don't want no money from you, Limey. I just wanted to be sure that you were willing to pay up," he said, to my great surprise and considerable relief.

He went on to explain that he harboured a deep-seated affection for the British that went back to his days in Blighty during the war. He declared that he would accept a cup of coffee at New York Central Station in lieu of the cash and I was pleased to honour my side of that particular contract.

From New York Central Station, we took a taxi ride to the Waldorf Astoria in a cab driven by a man from the Ivory Coast. As he was able to converse only in French, it occurred to me that whilst this language might prove advantageous to a cabby in Paris, it wouldn't be much help in the Big Apple. The

Waldorf was part of the Cunard group and we took advantage of the facility that offered a night's accommodation in the hotel at special rates. Having waited ages to register, black mark to the Waldorf, we hurried to our room to look at the menu. A Waldorf salad in the hotel was a must. Once I'd consulted the menu and considered the prices, however, the salad suddenly became a must not. The average guest at this hotel probably doesn't need to count his pennies, but even if money had been no object, there was no way I would ever have paid those over inflated prices. The command decision of those occupying room 708 was to wander out and find the nearest pizza parlour. Armed with what Tom's Pizzeria maintained was a standard sized pizza, but which would have passed in the UK as a cartwheel, we headed back to the hotel. Having become lost attempting to sneak in the back way with our wares and thus avoid prying eyes, we finally discovered the main foyer and crossed over to the lift before anyone saw us. This lift had a pointer at the top, like in the old films, and we were the only customers waiting as it reached the ground floor. Unfortunately, it disgorged a dozen people; the men dressed in tuxedos and the women in gowns, each of who gazed at the pizza and made me feel inferior.

During a recce of the hotel, I spotted that Cunard had a desk in the foyer. It was here that the QE2 travellers, who had stayed in the hotel whilst the ship had cruised the Caribbean, were able to book their bus seats for the journey back to the docks. Following the regulations to the letter, we didn't really qualify for a seat, but since we were travelling on the ship and were resident in the hotel, it didn't seem unreasonable to me to expect a free trip down to the port. The Hispanic staff of one man and two ladies who manned the desk didn't agree and gave a million reasons why we couldn't claim seats. This had the effect of activating my easily activated hot temper and a heated exchange between three touchy spics and an even touchier Brit ensued. Having finally asked for their particulars in order to lodge a complaint with Cunard, one of the ladies tore the identification tag from her ample bosom and hurled it at me. (I refer to the tag, of course, not the bosom.) I didn't consider that the sort of service one would have expected from Cunard. In the end we took a taxi, but not before I'd sought out those spics one more time, to tell them what they could do with their bus.

The trip back from New York to Southampton was pleasant, despite the sea being a little bumpy. One of my old favourites, Guy Mitchell, was the star turn for the trip and, although he had lost a little of his zing, he was still good. We occupied exactly the same cabin on the return journey as on the way out. I was disgusted to discover that the counterpane on the bed still had a hole in it, that the tie rack was still broken and that the curtains were still defying gravity, by hanging onto the rail by the absolute minimum number of hooks. As a result of my shabby treatment at the Waldorf, combined with the multitude of minor disappointments on board, I penned a long letter of complaint to Cunard. They responded with their standard reply to complaints, signed by someone with a German name, and omitted to enclose a voucher for a free trip. Perhaps I expected too much—our cabin was only third class after all. Certainly though, unless I could ever afford one of the better cabins, this ship wouldn't see me again as a passenger.

To cap it all, the special train from Southampton Docks to Waterloo broke down in Kent. We were provided with complimentary British Rail sandwiches and free drinks, it's true, but I wondered what the posh Yanks made of the stop-start fiasco as the train blundered on towards London. If the train journey didn't disappoint them, then the laughable luggage recovery system at Waterloo Station certainly would have. Hundreds of passengers were left to scrimmage in an old goods wagon, into which hundreds of designer suitcases had been unceremoniously tossed, as two harassed West Indians tried their best to sort things out. It was utter chaos. At Waterloo my, by now, ex-betrothed and I queued for separate taxis without talking. She boarded one to Clapham and a burgundy coloured cab took me to St Pancras. Our affair was over. I was a free man again—for six weeks, anyway. Only a few days before I was due to leave Edinburgh, she phoned me on some pretext or other and we arranged to meet again. A week later we were married. As my old daddy used to say, 'Marry in haste, repent at leisure.'

I had only a couple of week's left to serve in Scotland and my replacement arrived shortly after my return from the great American adventure.

It's all too easy to drop a clanger with classified documents and the failure to keep both your register and documents in the specified manner can be injurious to your career. I had held classified documents in several units prior to arriving in Edinburgh and believe that I can claim to have been fastidious in their control. My approach at 243 was no different—all the checks were carried out as required, all the documents were in place and I had no qualms about signing them over to my successor when the time arrived for our handover. There was precious little in the way of classified stuff retained in the unit anyway. As I was soon to discover, however, I had made a serious error by omitting to physically count the pages of the only bound book to grace the security cupboard.

Several days before the official handover of my classified documents, the officer in charge of the local Intelligence Corps unit had called me to ask a favour. He wanted permission to use my premises at Stranraer for a reason that was far too secret to talk about on the phone and, as the place stood empty for the majority of the week, I was only too happy to oblige. This turned out to be one of my better decisions.

My replacement was a tiresome character that had to have everything done by the book. I fancied that his two years with the TA might prove rather difficult, unless he mellowed considerably and quickly. He would find nothing wrong with my classified stuff, though—I'd been so careful. But not careful enough, as it transpired—that single bound volume had a page missing! There is a set procedure to be followed in the event of any anomalies and my replacement insisted on informing the Intelligence Corps at once. His limited brain wouldn't have known how to function in any other way and, in addition, he would thrill at the idea of dropping me in the shit. When they arrived, I was pleased to see that the team was lead by the guy who had borrowed our building in Stranraer. By rights, signals should have gone off to all sorts of formations, to inform them of my foul crime. My replacement was urging me to comply with the regulations, but the Intelligence captain told me to hang fire.

The first thing my intelligence pal did was to read the front sheet of the book with the page missing, only to discover that the whole thing should have been destroyed three years previously. That didn't let me off the hook, because the fact remained that there was a page unaccounted for. The next step was to check with the originator of the document. The formation that had disseminated the book no longer existed, but the telephone number at the top of the covering letter belonged to the colonel who had signed the thing and he was still behind the same desk, albeit with a different department. He turned out to be a really good egg. He sympathised with my problem and assured me that I was, without doubt, the only person in the world with a copy of the document.

"Put the Int Corps wallah onto me, old chap," he said.

I handed him over, but could still hear the conversation.

"Yes, I recall that book particularly well," he fibbed. "It was dispatched with a page missing, don't you know, and caused me all sorts of drama. Since 243's copy is the only one still in existence, you could do me a great favour by having the thing destroyed and then send me the destruction certificate."

What a player! My chum agreed to this course of action and thus repaid my kindness to him. My successor was the only one who wasn't content with the outcome, but there was nothing he could do about it.

After his intransigence during the confidential document saga, I insisted that he count every bullet, empty case, tin of Spam and toilet roll in the place before I handed over to him. If he liked things doing by the book, he could have them that way.

Receiving a farewell gift never fails to embarrass me and I'd really rather do without. With a display cabinet already groaning under the weight of pewter tankards and having a wall full of plaques, there was no requirement for the lads of the TA to present me with anything at all. The TA RSM had already given several oblique hints that the boys wanted to give me something, but I pretended not to understand. He then adopted his altogether more direct, Dundonian approach.

"Whit dae ye want?"

"Nothing Tara, I really don't need anything at all."

"But we always gie the PSO a guid send aff."

"I'm sure you do and I'm sure we'll have a great piss up, but leave the pressy out, there's a good chap."

He asked me numerous times and simply wouldn't take 'no' for an answer. Finally, on the Wednesday evening before my departure, he asked me yet again. I sat him down.

"Look Tara, you're a nice man, your lads are all grand lads and I shall be truly sorry to leave you all. I shall take a lot of happy memories away with me and it won't take a farewell gift for me to remember you all with affection. All I want to do is to ride off into the sunset, like John Wayne."

"That's it then, why didn't you say so before," replied the RSM. "We'll get you a horse."

I didn't get a horse, but something with an equine connection—a very nice carriage clock.

No matter how content I may have been in a unit, a fall out with the management is inevitable before I leave anywhere. Would 243 be any different? Everything appeared to be going well enough on this, my last Wednesday evening in the unit and the last time that I would see the majority of the boys. The corporal's mess had been prepared for my farewell bash and everyone would be there at 2030 hrs to say goodbye. At the prescribed hour everyone was present, with the notable exception of the OC, the second-in-command and the RSM. It was absolutely typical of the TA that these key personalities should go into a conference at the precise time my farewell started. After waiting for what I considered a decent period, the rest of us got on with the party. I resolved that if they didn't show up within an hour, then they could stick their carriage clock up their arses. Someone must have got a message to the trio that was in conference, because just as I was taking my last draught of beer before storming out in a huff, they appeared. Not a word of apology, naturally.

It turned out to be a terrific farewell and several people had very touching things to say about me. I would miss many of these men and wished them well in the hands of my successor, although I'm not sure that he was up to the task.

Only one question remained unanswered in 243. Which of you bastards stole my camouflage jacket?

19

Despite enjoying my time with the Terriers in Edinburgh and having been guaranteed an extension had I cared to apply, my desire to return to the regulars won the day. TA soldiers are genuine enough guys, especially those with a few years service under their belts, but the certain lack of professionalism that is ever present in part-time soldiering tends to grate after a couple of years. I needed to return to the world where a parade scheduled for 1800 hrs meant precisely that and not a time that best suited Jock. TA soldiers invariably have a sound reason for failing to show up on time, but tardiness is simply not conducive with the efficient running of a military unit. For this reason I accepted the appointment of second-in-command at 111 Provost Company and moved to Hohne. It was to prove a particularly poor decision.

You know when you are nearing Hohne—when the number of Volkswagen vans parked in forest glades and from which the rural whores ply their trade, begin to outnumber the dwelling houses. It was late afternoon as I drove past the last of the vans, irreverently parked near to the infamous Bergen-Belsen Concentration Camp and then, five minutes later, into Hohne Camp. My previous tour in Hohne had been pretty awful; things must surely be better this time around, I thought to myself as I drove through the gate. Calling into the duty room to announce my arrival, I was pleasantly surprised to discover a dinner invitation waiting for me. Major and Mrs Jason Lemond 'requested the pleasure'. I had never met Jason Lemond, or his wife Vera, but perhaps such a nice touch augured well. The staff sergeant on duty was an old pal, a blunt Yorkshireman who called a spade a spade and a man whose opinion could be trusted.

"What are the OC and his missus like, Mick?" I asked, putting him on the spot.

"Put it this way, sir," he said, glancing around to ensure that he wasn't being overheard. "The lads call him Coco the Clown and his wife is known as Viper Vera, or alternatively, Acid Mouth."

"Say no more, Michael, forearmed is forewarned," said I.

A lack of punctuality has never been one of my vices and so, at 2000 hrs on the dot and armed with a decent bottle of champagne and a box of chocolates, I rang the doorbell of the Lemond's quarter. A tall, gangly man with exceedingly thick lenses in his glasses answered the door.

"You must be Major Lemond," I said, offering my hand. "I'm Wally Payne, your new second-in-command."

His handshake was weak. We went into the lounge and made small talk with the gaggle of other officers gathered to welcome me. Then, feeling compelled to add something to the conversation, Coco came out with the first of the arrogant, ignorant and ill-informed comments that I was to hear over the next six months. This opening gambit, designed for all to hear, was unnecessary, provocative and downright rude.

"I consider Wally to be a perfectly silly name and I won't have my second-in-command called Wally. I shall call you Walter," he declared.

"You may call me whatsoever you wish, but my name is Wally whether you like it or not and it's the only name to which I answer," I reciprocated.

The die was cast. The evening's dinner was passable, although not *cordon bleu* by any means. Viper Vera imagined herself to be the Mrs Beaton of Lueneburg Heath. Her *piéce de résistance* that night was a moist sort of pudding, which brought patronising compliments from the other diners—tasted like stewed ginger biscuits to me. It didn't begin to compare to one of my mam's steam puddings.

I had the luxury of a two-day handover from my predecessor, an officer well past his sell-by-date. In my view, he ought to have retired many years before. He was pathetically loyal to Coco and led me to believe that the OC was a decent man, when he knew bloody well that he wasn't. If he had known how badly Coco would run him down the moment he left the unit, he might have been more inclined to tell me the truth. Mind you, it would be obvious to anyone spending more than ten minutes in the company of Lemond, half-wits included, that he or she was in the presence of a prick of the highest order. He would have been a psychiatrist's dream patient, since his superiority, persecution and inferiority complexes, as well as his megalomania, all manifested themselves at various times. My dislike for the man was instantaneous and, within a week, I was aware that working with him was going to be extremely difficult. What was to prove most irritating was the way he treated the men. His haughty style of management may have been acceptable in the days of the Raj and may have been tolerated in the infantry regiment where he had seen most of his service, but there was no place for it in my Corps. No officer has the right to keep men waiting for hours on end outside his office, simply for the perverted pleasure that wielding power over subordinates gives him. Both the RSM and I took him to task about this, but talking to a brick wall would have been more rewarding than talking to this buffoon.

Coco had been in the RMP for a whole two years and this was his first command. He transferred from an infantry regiment that must have been astonished to discover that another arm was willing to take such a liability off their hands. The job of Officer Commanding 111 Provost Company was way beyond his capabilities and to entrust the lives and careers of men to this twerp was an act of criminal negligence on the part of the senior management of the Corps.

My failings are legion and I have been accused, often correctly, of a whole host of character defects. Slyness, however, wasn't one of these, until Coco detected the flaw. It all came about when Glasgow Celtic were programmed to play against Werder Bremen in a pre-season friendly soccer match, and with the Weserstadion being within bottle throwing distance of several Scottish units, the German Police requested an RMP presence at the game. With the pair of us both keenly interested in soccer, the RSM and I included our names on the list of men performing duties at the match. This was, in my opinion, a perfectly sensible decision and hardly a matter that needed to be brought to the attention of the OC, especially as the match was being played on a weekday evening. Once the news of my intention to travel to the match reached the major's ears, however, he confronted me in my office. It was clear that he was not best pleased. Closing the office door, he stood in front of my desk with his lip all of a quiver.

"You, second-in-command, are sly," he declared.

"Would you care to repeat that accusation? I fear I must have misheard you."

"You, second-in-command, are sly," he repeated.

"Do you know what, Jason?" I said. "You wouldn't be able to find a single member of the Corps who would agree with that spurious allegation."

"You have arranged to journey to the forthcoming football match at Bremen without consulting me," he said loftily. "In future you will be required to inform me of all your proposed actions."

"Oh really! I attend an awful lot of soccer matches, you know. Why don't I just bring you a programme back and save us both a lot of bother."

"You are being insolent," he chided.

"You're bloody right I'm being insolent. I am forty-six years of age and what I do in my own time is, and will remain, bugger all to do with you, provided that my actions are neither illegal nor immoral. Let me make it perfectly clear to you—I shall be attending the football match this evening, whether you like it or not."

He left my office without further comment and I went to the match.

Coco chose an occasion when the office corridor was full of NCOs waiting to see the chief clerk for his next display of stupidity. He must surely have been suffering from a brainstorm when he was unprofessional enough to shout "Come here you twit!" in my direction over the heads of the men. It certainly made my hackles rise.

I steamed down the corridor, bundled him into his office and informed him that the last person to refer to me thus was still receiving treatment in an intensive care unit. He mumbled a defence of sorts, maintaining that he had said something else. If he imagined that I was gullible enough to swallow that, however, he was badly mistaken.

When I had been in Hohne for a couple of months, he called me into his office for a private chat. This next outburst of nonsense riled me considerably and gave me an insight into a hitherto unseen facet of his character, his inferiority complex.

"I have no proof of any description," he stuttered, "but I believe that you are being over friendly with the RSM."

Considering that the unit management team comprised precisely three persons, Coco, the RSM and me, I was at a loss to understand how I could be too friendly with the man.

"What the hell do you mean by that idiotic comment, Jason? Are you suggesting that we have an unnatural relationship? If that's the case, then I'll feel compelled to punch you on the nose this very moment for making such a slanderous assertion," I shouted.

"No, I'm suggesting no such thing. It's just that I believe you are using the sergeant's mess on a regular basis," he replied.

"Yes, I go there every Friday afternoon at Happy Hour. And on every occasion that I have been there, so have you. Do you have any more nonsensical accusations, or can I get on with administering this unit?" I said, already at the door.

His next classic was to start interfering with the unit accounts. Now, if there was one thing at which I excelled in the Army, it was running accounts. Five years working for Barclays Bank and the fact that I'm a qualified member of the Association of the Institute of Bankers may have had some bearing on that. Coco, on the other hand, was the archetypal accounting dunce; you can spot them a mile off. They are the only people in Germany who consider it worthwhile counting the one and two pfennig coins. His main interest wasn't in ensuring that the accounts were being run correctly, of course; what he really wanted me to do was sell his wife's cottage industry goods through my shop account. There was no way the lads' money was going to be spent filling shelves with her shoddy crap, though, and I told them both so. They were not amused.

The following three months were traumatic and I decided that enough was enough. He refused to accept advice from either the RSM or myself and seemed to believe that he had learnt all that there was to know about the RMP inside a couple of years. Our combined service of more than forty-five years counted for nothing in his eyes and there was every danger that my famously short fuse might erupt if I were subjected to much more of his indifference towards those around him. Conforming to the Army system, I submitted my application requesting an interview with our colonel in Bielefeld, to discuss a matter of a military nature. This certainly put the wind up Coco and he demanded to know the reason for the interview. Even a numbskull like him knew full well that I wasn't required to tell him and so I didn't. He resorted to charm, but I refused to elaborate on my motives and he was obliged to forward my application. Next morning I saw the colonel and gave it to him from the hip and, although he sympathised with my plight, he maintained that he had no option but to make me soldier on in Hohne.

During a second interview with him only a month later, I reiterated my problems and asked him to post me anywhere in the world. He was aware that Coco was in imminent danger of getting a punch on the nose, but he hadn't the courage to post me and merely gave me the following piece of futile advice.

"Go back, do the Corps a favour and punch him on the bloody nose."

And a fat lot of good that would have done me. So it was back to Hohne, grit my teeth, once again, and soldier on.

My first posting to Hohne had been a disaster. This time, as an officer and a married man, I felt that things ought to have been better. My profound dislike of the OC jaundiced my whole outlook at 111, however, and I couldn't find a single redeeming feature about the place. Our married quarter was located within the barracks and was large enough to accommodate a battalion of infantry. It consisted of five rooms, each of which had been home to no less than six private soldiers when the block had been used as single man's accommodation. The central corridor was the length of a cricket pitch and it was difficult to see the far end once the mist had rolled in from the moors. 'Homely' was not a word that springs to mind about the place and we had two rooms, our spare bedroom and our spare, spare bedroom, that I never ventured into. Loads of room for visitors, therefore, but who in their right mind would come to Hohne for a holiday? The quarter was ideally sited for aficionados of the bagpipes, which after two years in Edinburgh Castle I most certainly wasn't. The Scots Guards Officer's Mess was right next-door and they never wasted an opportunity to have a piper wailing away outside. The view from our west facing windows was less than inspiring, overlooking two cemeteries as they did. They contained the remains of those poor souls who had survived Belsen, but died subsequently as a result of their maltreatment in that wretched place. It could, by no stretch of the imagination, be considered a 'des res'.

It was necessary to condition oneself to the fact that we were stuck in the middle of Lueneburg Heath and that wherever we wanted to go, it was always miles away. Driving four miles in each direction to buy half a dozen bread rolls for tea was nothing. It was either that, or eat what passed for fresh bread at the NAAFI, surely the worst purveyors of foodstuffs in the world. Any decent shopping needed to be done in one of the large towns like Hannover, Bremen or Hamburg.

Nobody enjoys attending security conferences and any officer with his buttons on will designate the task further down the batting order. Even Coco wasn't clown enough to get lumbered and he always contrived to be otherwise engaged whenever the Hohne Station Security Meeting came up. That left me to represent the unit more often than not. These days security was top of the agenda in BAOR and the safety of married quarters and barracks concerned everyone. Hohne Camp was a massive piece of real estate and physically securing a barracks with a ten-mile perimeter fence is nigh on impossible. Nevertheless, plans were formulated and at least we went through the motions. Entry and exit were controlled through one main gate, sangars appeared overnight, extra guards were posted and miles of barbed wire sprouted along the outer fence. The new regulations for checking vehicles and personnel entering the barracks certainly had a marked effect and the queue of vehicles waiting to enter in the mornings stretched back miles towards Bergen. Security was now stricter than it had ever been and everyone felt more confident as a result of this positive approach to the problem. People contravening the rules were dealt with harshly and four cavalry troopers who climbed the fence, rather than walk all the way to the main gate, were punished severely by their CO. I was content with the new measures that had been implemented, too—until I took a casual stroll to the back of the barracks one afternoon.

Over in a corner, behind the cricket pitches, was a gaping hole in the fence where a foot gate had once hung. It was possible to walk in and out of the camp unchecked and, because of the isolation of the area, unseen. Surely I wasn't the first person to observe this glaring anomaly? As it transpired, a security meeting was to be held the following day and such was my zeal to bring up the subject of the hole, I could scarcely contain myself. Peregrine, a young Guards officer, chaired the meeting. He gave us a terrorist assessment, told us how splendidly his beezer security plan was progressing and asked for comments from the floor. I had two points for him. Firstly, as we were in the depths of winter and the temperature was falling to minus fifteen degrees in the early hours, what steps were being taken to ensure that the men in the sangars didn't freeze to death? Peregrine assured me that this subject had already been addressed and that they intended to do precisely nothing. The senior officers in the HQ had considered the question of providing heaters, but came to the conclusion that heat might make the soldiers drowsy and so the idea had been shelved. This was a decision made by officers who had obviously never stood in a sangar themselves, otherwise they might have realised that the reactions of a warm, drowsy soldier are rather quicker than those of a man who has just died of hypothermia. All the other commissioned warrant officers who were present backed up my argument. They, at least, understood what I was harping on about. The top brass had spoken, however, and the boys stayed cold. I then broached the subject of the hole in the fence. It afforded easy access to the camp for any aspiring terrorists and, more importantly, it was too near to my married quarter for comfort. Peregrine and his fellow wimps in the HQ apparently knew all about this matter, too.

"Not to worry, Wally, we in HQ know all about it."

"Well then, why is it open and when is it going to be repaired?"

"It isn't going to be repaired in actual fact. There's absolutely no problem, though; it's really not worth worrying about," he stuttered.

"Stop waffling and get to the fucking point, Peregrine," snapped a commissioned warrant officer from the Artillery.

"Well, actually, the General rides through that old gate when he takes his horses for exercise on the ranges," said Peregrine, who then braced himself for the imminent onslaught.

Because the General liked to take his horse out through this hole, the safety of the remaining four or five thousand of us who lived within the barracks was compromised. Bloody outrageous! All those guards freezing their balls off every night in an effort to keep the place safe and all the time there was a bloody big hole in the back fence. Peregrine had his orders from above, however—the General would continue to ride his horses onto the ranges whether we mere mortals liked it or not. It was a disgracefully selfish decision, the sort of thing that should have been brought to the attention of the newspapers back in the UK. That was my last attendance at a security meeting in Hohne; if they were going to condone crap like that, then there were more sensible things to do with my time. The hole still hadn't been repaired when I left the rotten place.

It was now 1988 and the Army was strapped for cash and cuts had to be made. In true British Army tradition, therefore, savings were made in places where they shouldn't have been. This way, money was available for politically correct and public relations related matters and, of course, officer pursuits. The polo ponies in Hohne already had better accommodation than the soldiers did and when winter really set in that year, money was made available to provide better heating in the stables. Provided the polo ponies were as snug as a bug, nobody in authority gave a shit that the boys in the sangars were freezing their bollocks off. It was the money thrown away on the occasion of the visit of our Royal visitor that really took the biscuit, however. She was programmed to stay in the officer's mess just long enough to sup a cup of coffee, twenty minutes at best. Just in case she needed to relieve the Royal bladder, however, a new lavatory was constructed at a cost of thousands of pounds. She never used the place. Meantime, the soldiers in my unit had kit that was falling off their backs.

One of the principal tasks of RMP in the field is traffic control. Consequently, no expense was spared in providing the boys of 111 with the best safety equipment that money could buy. If only that were true! The lads that stood at the side of the road directing exercise traffic in all weathers and for hours on end were issued with a pathetically inadequate fluorescent bib that had the words 'MILITARY POLICE' emblazoned front and rear. This miserable piece of plastic apparel was inadequate when it was issued and had been designed with cheapness, rather than the safety or security of the man wearing it in mind. Now they were worn out and useless, but despite promises going back years, the replacement garments were still to be seen. Some of our bibs were so decrepit by now that I actually saw boys wearing garments proclaiming that they were members of the 'LITARY LICE' and the 'LIAR POLICE'. One man, who was actually of Eastern European extraction, sported a bib suggesting that he was a 'LARY POLE'. He was inordinately proud of this bib and my accusation that he had tampered with the lettering in order to obtain the desired effect met with howls of denial. Meanwhile, a superb, fleecy, yellow reflective jacket was in production. This was the very jacket that had been promised for years, but which had been held back for a variety of reasons. The real reason was, of course, cost. What was the point in spending money on protecting the life of a military policeman, when it could be wasted on erecting a hideously expensive bronze statue of a bloke on a horse at the main gate of the RMP Training Centre?

To the eternal shame of those that ran our Corps, rather than demand the delivery of these jackets, they sat back and watched as one entrepreneurial officer purchased a large supply himself and sold them to the NCOs at a profit. What a disgrace that military policemen needed to buy their own kit in order to perform the job properly. Whoever heard of such a thing? That was like asking a tank commander to buy his own shells, an infantryman his own rifle or a cook his own chip pan. It was an outrage and I brought the subject up every time a senior Corps officer wandered within earshot. Our hierarchy were shameless, though, and, not for the first time in my career, I appeared to be in a minority of one. The RMP is made up of first class men and, because they wanted to be safe and to look presentable, they all put their hands into their own pockets. Our senior officers just looked on and let them do it. Shame on you all! As a matter of principle these jackets weren't on sale through my unit account; anyone wanting one had to shop elsewhere. Coco wasn't happy about it, but I wouldn't compromise my principles for anyone, especially not for an incompetent like him.

In the Army, almost every small corps has difficulty in recruiting young officers, although that's hardly surprising. Having endured the misery of being moulded into an officer and a gentleman at Sandhurst, these thrusting young men seek action. Stacking blankets in the RAOC, telling a driver where to drive a lorry load of those blankets in the RCT, or sleeping under a blanket waiting for nothing to happen in the RMP, can surely have little appeal. Young thrusters want to be leading men over the top in the infantry, commanding a tank like Monty, or sweeping down in a helicopter to bloody the enemy. The RMP have always been short of good quality young officers and a crisis of recruitment in the Corps in the early 70s left the chiefs of our august organisation in a dilemma. There were two possible solutions to this predicament and, naturally, they took the wrong option. Commissioning more warrant officers, men with intelligence, bearing and experience was the option that was discounted. That would have been frowned upon, because it would mean that pukka officers would need to share the same mess, bar and, heaven forbid, shithouse with those nasty, hairy arsed, commissioned labourers. Proper officers, you see, believe that they are mentally, physically and morally superior to other ranks. One of the real reasons for the reluctance to commission too many warrant officers is the fact that they tend to expose real officers for the incompetent, arrogant and self-important prats that many of them are.

The chosen alternative proved to be the catalyst for the decline of the Corps of Royal Military Police. This was the decision to recruit inexperienced officers from other arms. Can you believe that the RMP allowed officers to transfer from other arms and allowed them to keep their rank and seniority? Why didn't we recruit bank managers or coal mine deputies, allowing them to keep their seniority, naturally, for they knew as much about being military policemen as those rejects from the RCT, KOB, RIR and DWR did. The concept was flawed and fraught with problems, but it was preferred because it served to keep the officer bloodline pure. Not surprisingly, there was a rush of officers who were no bloody good in the direction of the RMP; it was an offer that was too good to refuse. Let's face it—if they had been any good, they would have stayed in their own mobs, wouldn't they? Decent RMP officers, those being brought along slowly to gain the experience necessary to perform the demanding task of commanding a military police unit, suddenly found themselves tumbling down the seniority list, as refugees from elsewhere assumed command of units that they were patently incapable of running. The good guys departed in droves, leaving us with companies led, in many cases, by incompetents and failures. Which brings me back to Coco the Clown.

The day of the OC's Annual Planning Conference dawned, a day that would have far reaching consequences for me. The conference was a sound idea in principle; all those with the rank of staff sergeant or above would be in attendance and a lively discussion could be anticipated. Principle and reality diverged once the OC had taken the floor, however, as what ought to have been an open forum degenerated into a dreary monologue of tired old ideas, interspersed with some crazy notions. There was to be no discussion on any topic; Coco laid out his mundane and sometimes crackpot ideas and declared that these would be carried out without discussion. The fact that every single person in that room had a minimum of five times more service in the Corps than this reject from the infantry was of no consequence. Those present at the meeting bore the whole outrageous performance stoically, although the odd gasp of disbelief was audible on occasions and the shaking of heads grew to epidemic proportions as the monologue droned on. The straw that broke this particular camel's back came over the question of leave policy. In a company with the heaviest workload of any RMP unit in the world and where the NCOs willingly gave much of their own time to complete their police case files, he decreed that they had too much free time and leave. With immediate effect, the 'Lemond Plan' would require all men who were not on duty, or coming off night duty to sleep, to submit a leave pass for any day that they were not working, unless it was a public holiday. This, believe it or not, was to include weekends! The Easter grant, he declared, would entitle a man to a two-day grant only—Good Friday and Easter Monday. Should he be off duty on either of the days in between, he would be required to submit a leave pass and have the days taken from his annual privilege leave entitlement. Similarly, Christmas Day and Boxing Day would be classed as a grant, with the remainder of the Yuletide period coming off a guy's leave entitlement. Apart from being an administrative nightmare for me, this was quite the barmiest idea that any of us old hands had ever heard. I could take no more of his crap and, half in anger and half to stop my OC from making an even bigger idiot of himself than he already had, I rose onto my back trotters and told him that his plan was unworkable, vindictive and plain daft. The effect on Coco was dramatic.

"How dare you talk to me like that?" he demanded.

"Quite simple, Jason. Whenever I hear something that is so blatantly unfair to the men, then I feel compelled to fight their corner. It's an involuntary action."

We had something of a slanging match there and then, which in retrospect was a stupid thing to do in front of the men. It was my only mistake. I opened the door and invited him down to the nearest vacant office, where he was required to listen to some home truths. He was left in no doubt that his 2ic[1] and all of his men thought that he was a pompous prick. I didn't return to the meeting, but went home to my quarter to cool off.

Within ten minutes of arriving at work on Monday morning, Coco asked me to come down the corridor to his office. To my considerable surprise, he promptly ordered me to surrender my RMP warrant card. Once the sneering man had the document in his clammy hand, he announced with great satisfaction that I was suspended from duty and that I was required to return to my quarter to await his further instructions. He appeared to find the satisfaction of wielding power over a better man sensual. He was brought back to reality by my suggestion that it would be helpful to whomsoever was replacing me, if I were to balance the books first. He agreed to that and I demanded my warrant card back for the two hours it would take me to complete the task. After handing over to young Ian, I went home and sat with the wife for a couple of weeks. We played a lot of Scrabble, read all those books that we were always going to read one day and had a pleasant break, all on full pay. Following two weeks of rest and recuperation, I was summoned to the office of the world's most inept OC. He handed me a copy of the form that dealt with the removal of an officer from his appointment. Typed on the form were the spurious reasons why he considered my position in the unit untenable. His Pulitzer Prize winning effort read:

> Captain Payne has been 2ic 111 Pro Coy since June 88. He has clearly found life as a Company Officer difficult, with regard to loyalty towards military and civilian staff. Furthermore, he has allowed personal grievances to influence his judgement when dealing with subordinates.
>
> I have had cause to council Captain Payne on 2 particular occasions. In November he failed to carry out a specific duty. In February his treatment of civilian staff was brought to my attention. Finally on 10 March he was disloyal to myself, in front of about 20 SNCOs.
>
> These particular incidents have made it impossible for Capt Payne to continue to serve as my 2ic. By nature of the appointment, it is impossible to have him within the company. It is in the best interest of Capt Payne and the Company to move him to a different appointment.

Anyone who knew me would have taken one look at that tripe and realised that it was a load of bollocks. Coco, presumably, thought that this badly penned rubbish would be sufficient to nail me. He even had the brass neck to ask whether I was willing to accept his written comments, or whether I wished

---

1.   Second in command, for the uninitiated!

to submit an appeal. Surely he didn't believe that Wally Payne would take this kind of treatment without a scrap? He denied me the privilege of taking a Photostat copy of the offending document, so I copied every word written on the form in longhand and at a speed so slow, that he enquired no less than three times whether I was finished. It was obvious that he was very uncomfortable with my presence and beginning to squirm, so I wrote even more slowly. He also required me to sign three copies of a suspension certificate that, according to the regulations pertaining to the suspension of an officer, needed to be processed up the chain of command. I duly signed the forms, but they were never sent anywhere—were they, Coco? What did you do with them? They certainly weren't hidden in your office, because several of the senior personnel of the unit, men who cared rather more for me than for you, searched the place from top to bottom. (A word of advice, by the way—never leave that kind of publication in your desk drawers.)

The terms of my suspension forbade me from entering any barracks, mess or my own unit lines. That one fell at the first hurdle, since my quarter was located inside the barracks. Whoever wrote the regulations hadn't thought too carefully about that possibility and had obviously never served in Hohne. There was another anomaly. What if a suspended person lives outside a barracks and his church is inside? Was he to be prevented from attending his normal place of worship on Sundays?

This was the time for me to consider preparing my appeal against Coco's phony allegations, but how could I refer to the necessary books and documents if I was prevented from visiting my unit? Someone in a position of authority, an officer who had at one time been the subject of an unjust suspension himself, telephoned me at home. He told me that, if I should care to visit a certain RMP unit in Germany next morning, I would be given every assistance in the task of preparing my defence. He had clearly been very busy on my behalf. I called the OC of the unit concerned and he confirmed that he would be delighted to help. My welcome was wholehearted and both the OC and 2ic were primed and ready to start work on my behalf. It came as no surprise to hear that Lemond wasn't beloved in this neck of the woods either. We sat down for a whole day, dissected Coco's puny effort and formulated an appeal that was written and rewritten until a final draft was ready. Next day, we took this draft to the chief of staff of a nearby Divisional HQ. He was an officer well versed in appeals of this nature and he gave mine the once over, suggested a few subtle changes and finally gave it his seal of approval. He also gave Coco's flimsy submission a cursory glance.

"Don't tell me that this is the best he could do?" he said and thereby gave my confidence a considerable boost.

It had taken the best part of two days to get everything just right and my debt to those officers who assisted me is considerable.

When I arrived home at lunchtime on Friday, there was a message awaiting me. The Officer Commanding required a copy of my appeal on his desk by 1700 hrs without fail. Well, hard shit, you're not going to get it! The text of the regulations regarding appeals was well known to me by now and they stated that an officer should have a 'reasonable amount of time' to submit his appeal. Considering that it had taken him ten days to produce less than 150 words, it seemed unreasonable of him to expect me to produce an altogether weightier submission in a mere seventy-two hours. The real reason behind the undue haste to get his grubby paws on my appeal had nothing to do with its content—he wanted it so that he could pass it up the chain of command, without my suspension certificate, before he departed on leave. His leave started from 'After Duties Sunday', although in common with the accepted practice throughout the Army, this was taken to read 'as soon as you can slide off on the preceding Friday'. No, the blighter was trying to sneak off two days early. What price the two-faced bastard's high moral stand on the boys having too much leave now? I resolved that he would be presented with a copy of my appeal on Monday morning and not a minute before. He could follow the rules for once and bloody well wait. Four times that evening he sent a patrol to enquire whether my appeal was ready. Four times they went back empty handed.

The thought of him sitting at home, seething with anger and being forced to endure two further days of the viper's perfectly ordinary cooking, filled my heart with joy. And I'll bet he swallowed hard when he finally saw my appeal. I would have loved to see his face. He may have realised by this time that it might have been an error of judgement of some magnitude to take on Wally Payne and friends. Here's my appeal:

Introduction.
I have been the 2ic of 111 Pro Coy RMP since Jun 88. My duties include the maintenance of Imprest and Service Funds Accounts, the supervision of MT and QM departments, duties as Families Officer, UPO and Signals Officer, as well as the control and recruitment of Civil Labour. I am also required to understudy the Officer Commanding.

Perception of Performance.

My previous commissioned appointment was as PSO to the RMP TA in Scotland in the rank of A/Capt. This diverse and demanding job, not dissimilar to my present appointment, prepared me well for the position of 2ic with a regular company and I was rewarded with CRs graded 'Low Excellent' and 'Middle Excellent' for my endeavours. Notwithstanding the differing aspects of my current job and new skills that need to be mastered, I consider that my performance as 2ic has been no less effective than were my efforts with the RMP TA.

OC's Briefing 10 Mar 89.

During a conference briefing by the OC to Company Officers, WOs and SNCOs on 10 Mar 89, the subject of leave was considered. A Forecast of Events was produced, which indicated that the grant for the Easter Stand Down (24-28 Mar 89) was Good Friday and Easter Sunday and that the remainder of the period was to be taken as Privilege Leave. In addition, NCOs were to be required to submit leave passes for one day's privilege leave to cover the Corps holiday on 22 Sep 89. I pointed out to Major Lemond that it had never been the practice within any of the numerous Provost Units in which I had served, to require NCOs to take Privilege Leave over a holiday period, nor was it the normal practice to require the submission of leave passes for Corps holidays. In retrospect, I can see that my comments may have been construed at the time as lacking diplomacy. I sincerely felt, however, that it was my duty to point out to the Officer Commanding his breach of accepted practice concerning the taking of Privilege Leave and to speak on behalf of the Coy personnel. This was a management meeting where ideas and comments from the 'shop floor' should normally be welcome.

Suspension from Duty.

On Mon 13 Mar 89 at 0915 hrs, I was called to the OC's office. He required me to read and sign 3 copies of a certificate suspending me from duty, withdrew my RMP Warrant Card and ordered me to my quarter to await further orders.

AFB 9926.

On Wed 22 Mar 89 at 1640 hrs I was summoned to the OC's office, where I was allowed to read and sign a copy of AFB 9926. I made a note of the text and indicated that I would be submitting an appeal against the content. In several cases the comments are vague and preclude specific rebuttal, however, Maj Lemond gave a fuller explanation of one particular allegation at the time. This allegation is explained in detail at para 6d. On Thursday 23 Mar 89 at 1040 hrs, I telephoned

Maj Lemond and requested further clarification of the comments made on the AFB 9926. He stated that he was 'not prepared to enter into lengthy discourse'.

<u>*Specific comments of appeal*</u>

    a.   *Loyalty towards Military and Civilian Staff*
<u>*Comment:*</u> *At no time during 25 years service in the Corps has my loyalty been brought into question. There are always times when unpopular decisions must be made and these I make without reticence. I have been approached by unit personnel who have expressed certain misgivings about the Officer Commanding. These persons were firmly dealt with. I raise this matter with reluctance, but feel that the time has come to defend myself. It would have been inappropriate to tell Maj Lemond for obvious reasons, although had he been aware of my actions, the question of loyalty might never have been raised. I am unaware of any singular occasion when I may have been guilty of disloyalty to those with whom I serve.*

    b.   *Personal grievances influencing judgement*
<u>*Comment.*</u> *Due to the vague nature of the allegation I can only assume that this refers to the time when WO2 Murray, the Fallingbostel Detachment Commander, failed to invite me to a function. This matter became the subject of longstanding, good-natured banter between WO2 Murray and myself, with no indication of ill will on either side. The OC has misjudged the situation. I resent the insinuation that my rank or position would ever be used to settle a grievance.*

    c.   *Counselling*
<u>*Comment.*</u> *In October 1988 the OC called me into his office and stated that,* <u>*although he had no evidence to support his assertions,*</u> *he believed that I was frequenting the WO's and Sgt's Mess on a regular basis. I informed Maj Lemond that this was not the case and that my rare visits to the Mess had only ever been on the personal invitation of the President. The sum total of my visits to this point did not exceed 6 and, on most of these occasions, Maj Lemond was himself present. The OC further suggested that the RSM and I were too friendly and suggested that we socialised together on a regular basis. Up to that time I had visited the RSM's quarter only once, he had never been invited to mine. Apart from attending 2 German Police functions to which we had both received official invitations and travelling to watch a soccer match at Lueneburg, our social paths never crossed. I do*

not consider these allegations worthy of the title 'counselling'. I can recall no other occasion on which I have been counselled by the OC.

d. *Failure to carry out a specific duty.*
    Comment: Maj Lemond stated on 22 Mar 89 that, on an unspecified date during Nov 88, he ordered me to procure a photostat machine for Falling-bostel Det. I have no record or recollection of this alleged order. At that time, the question of obtaining a photostat machine for the Det was ongoing and progress was being made with various staff departments. Had I failed to carry out a specific duty, I consider that Maj Lemond ought to have made further reference to this matter within the 4-month period, which has since elapsed.

e. *Treatment of Civilian Staff.*
    Comment: In February 1989 Maj Lemond received a verbal complaint from Mrs Robinson, a locally employed clerk/typist, regarding my response to her complaint. During the course of the morning in question, Mrs Robinson had complained that her back was aching because the table at which she worked was firstly too high and later too low. I took steps through the CQMS to obtain a table suitable for Mrs Robinson from ASU and the matter was satisfactorily resolved. Mrs Robinson is known as a disruptive woman, who continually complains for spurious reasons. Her dismissal has been discussed with me by the OC on more than one occasion, but because of pregnancy and the fact that she indicated her intention to resign mid-year, she was allowed to continue. My treatment of civilian staff invariably errs on the side of benevolence and is never less than proper and professional.

f. *Disloyalty to OC.*
    Comment: The matter that has been construed as disloyalty has been explained in Para 3.

Summary.

It is undeniable that I have found Maj Lemond difficult to work for. I have been unable to come to terms with his inability to communicate and relate to those within his command. My advice, based on 25 years of service within RMP, is seldom heeded and the style of management adopted by Maj Lemond is not conducive to harmony within a close-knit, independent RMP unit. My style of management is forceful and my comments may sometimes lack a sense of timing. Those traits, however, could never to construed as manifestations of disloyalty or ineptitude. During the last 9 months, my force of character has been used to positive effect to protect the position and name of my Officer Commanding when I have found it necessary to refute certain disparaging comments directed to me by officers and soldiers within the Division with regard to Maj Lemond. During my last 4 years as a Warrant Officer, the gradings on my CRs were 'O', my grading on my 2 CRs to date as an officer have both been excellent; clearly someone is assessing my character incorrectly. I maintain that the nebulous case outlined in the AFB 9926 does not warrant the drastic action being taken against me.

<u>*Conclusion.*</u>
I respectfully request that the AFB 9926 be withdrawn and the attack on my character expunged, that my RMP Warrant Card be re-issued, that my suspension be lifted and that I be re-instated as 2ic, 111 Pro Coy RMP.

Perhaps the senior officers in the HQ were flummoxed by this case and unsure about what course of action to take, because a further two months of sitting on my arse at home followed my submission. It was a frustrating time for sure, although I did manage to travel around Niedersachsen extensively and, in retrospect, rather enjoyed my extended holiday on full pay. Jason didn't see fit to let the affair affect his holiday plans, so I saw no reason why we shouldn't take a couple of weeks down in the south of France. Someone in the HQ gave my cheeky leave application the green light and it was off for two weeks in the Grand Hotel at Sete. All that fine seafood and magnificent scenery helped me to forget the pantomime that was being played out back in Hohne. This period also served to show me exactly who my real pals were. Actually, all the guys from whom I would have expected support turned up trumps and from those whose friendship I suspected to be superficial, there was silence. At this time, however, not one person in a position of authority in the RMP called up in an official capacity to offer support, advice or information. Apart from one man, they all left me to rot. The one glowing exception was the officer who arranged for me to visit the unit where I prepared my defence; he put his neck on the block several times and kept me informed of exactly what was going on. With his help, I didn't need the rest of the spineless bunch anyway.

Almost three months after the Training and Planning Conference, I was summoned to the Brigade HQ for an interview with the Commander. Easter had come and gone by now and as I walked towards the HQ, I wondered if the lads had been forced to put in their leave passes. That, after all, was what had started all this nonsense in the first place. I marched into the brigadier's office and was surprised that he came towards me and offered his hand. He sat me down at his casual table, offered me coffee and biscuits and started to chat. This wasn't the dreaded 'interview without coffee' that awaits those with whom the brigadier is not best pleased. It was the production of Cadbury's chocolate biscuits that finally convinced me that I was on a winner. He came to the point and was direct.

"This whole affair is nonsense and should never have gone this far," he said.

Tell me something new, brigadier! He went on to say that he wanted the whole thing dropped and suggested that my career might be adversely affected if I were to continue with my appeal.

"Sir, you must be aware that Major Lemond initiated all this nonsense," I replied. "Why don't you have him withdraw his allegations? With regards to my career, sir, I don't give a hoot about promotion quite frankly, and further-more, it's my intention to contest my OC's lies by taking the matter to the highest authority."

This didn't please the important man one little bit, so he played his ace card.

"I have already spoken to your colonel at Corps HQ. You will be moved to Detmold with immediate effect. I will not back your appeal and it will there-fore be academic whether you pursue it further or not."

There is an old Army adage about not pissing against the wind and to con-tinue would have been just that. On the brigadier's advice, my appeal was reduced to a 'representation not amounting to an appeal', which would go up the chain of command just the same. That satisfied me, although not some of my fellow officers, who urged me to push it all the way. They hadn't heard what the Brigade Commander had said to me and it was my pension, not theirs, that was on the line here. My bags were packed without a moment's hesitation and I left Hohne without so much as a backward glance.

There were two officers in Hohne who showed me true support during the period of my suspension; one was the lieutenant who replaced me, the other, a major in the RAOC. This pair visited me regularly in my quarter and we shared a glass or two down in Bergen whenever the mood took us. They did this primarily out of friendship, but also to demonstrate disdain for Coco and their disregard for stupid regulations. They were friends indeed.

20

Both the town of Detmold and 114 Provost Company were like a breath of fresh air following my period of purgatory up on the Lueneburg Heath. The OC was a decent man and it was a joy to be working with a rational human being once again. My sugar coating was back on and my phone started ringing as if nothing had ever happened. What short memories some people have. Detmold—'Wet Mould' in soldier parlance—is a charming old town, although the natives were beginning to tire of playing host to Tommy. What really poked them off was the fact that the area was the base for our nasty tanks and that we had been knocking chunks out of their streets, pavements and buildings since the end of the war.

Our unit lines were in Hobart Barracks, on the outskirts of the town. In the days of the Third Reich it had been the Fliegerhorstkaserne and we shared it with the Brigade HQ, the Air Corps, a cavalry regiment and all the other odds and sods. The RSM turned out to be none other than my old pal and religious adversary, Shaky Will Beatty, Hamilton's best-known catholic. That indicated that things would be fairly noisy along the top corridor.

Having taken over the administrative reins from a hyper correct officer, there were no fears of finding any skeletons in the cupboards that might come back to haunt me at a later date. The fact that John left everything in good shape was just as well, since my drive and determination, considered by those who wrote my confidential reports over the years to be the soul redeeming feature of an otherwise notorious character, were in terminal decline. My interest in the Corps of Royal Military Police had been irreparably damaged by the Coco Lemond affair and I had no intention of forgetting the way that the Corps turned its back on me. Perhaps I had been in the Army too long, anyway. This was no longer the fun organisation I had joined so many years before. Financial restraints and cost effectiveness appeared to rule everything these days. I might well be that monetary considerations always did effect every decision made in the Forces and that, as a fun loving corporal, I simply didn't see life through the jaundiced eyes of the old administrator I'd now become. I had no gripe with the Army being cost effective, but moratoria and expressions like 'lean and mean' and 'smaller but better' were merely synonyms for less money and a poorer quality of life for soldiers, especially those down at the bottom end of the pecking order. Government Ministers with responsibility for the Armed Forces and senior officers in the MOD were always at pains to assure the public that the troops were happy with their lot and that morale was high. The only reason they peddled such crap was the fact that the Commanding Officers whose units they visited hadn't the guts to tell them what life was really like. To tell the truth and admit that the men were thoroughly pissed off with all the cutbacks wasn't what the bigwigs wanted to hear, and anyone failing to toe the party line would undoubtedly find his career adversely affected. Officers and soldiers are, of course, their own worst enemies; despite the constant cutting of manpower, equipment and money, they will always make sure that a task is completed, by working until it is. Seeing that the job was still being done, the civil servants would try another little cut each successive year. So it went on, until there was not only no fat left on the bone, but they were paring away at the bone too. And still the soldier would produce the goods, because failure to do so would indicate that you couldn't, or wouldn't do your job—and bang would go another career. Rocking the boat wasn't allowed.

By this stage of my career, I couldn't give a shit about rocking the boat and, for the sake of the NCOs in my charge, I'd have tipped the boat over if necessary. Even here, at the end of the 80s, the single man was still getting a raw deal in the Army. Despite my waning interest, I remained in indefatigable fighter for the rights of the singlie. Half of the single boys in Detmold lived in decent rooms within the main RMP HQ complex. They had every comfort and the mess was within crawling distance for those who needed to seek solace in the fruit of the vine. A bed in this single man's Hilton wasn't easy to come by, however, and before a person was elevated to top field, he needed to spend a period living on the lower floor of the dreaded Block 54. As an occupant of the Hilton was posted or, more drastically, he got married, then the longest serving inmate of the British Army's most disgraceful accommodation block would gleefully gather together those of his possessions that hadn't mildewed and move over.

My first sight of Block 54 shocked me. It hadn't seen a lick of paint since the German Army's lease ran out in 1945. The toilets stank of urine where broken sewage pipes hadn't been repaired and an interesting array of lichen and moulds flourished on the shower walls. The rooms were damp and mildewed, and had insufficient lights and power points. Had this accommodation been within a British prison, the Howard League for Penal Reform would have had plenty to say about it. My immediate reaction was to consult the unit's nervous QM, who produced a sheaf of requisitions for repairs to the dreadful Block 54 going back nine months. Nothing had ever been done. A more diligent CQMS might have stirred the water a little more, but to give him his due, he had followed the procedures to the letter. My next step was to contact the branch of the HQ that dealt with such matters. In fact I contacted them time without number, only to hit the same brick wall. They informed me that nothing other than emergency repairs was being undertaken, because Block 54 was scheduled for complete renovation under the Hobart Barracks Renovation Plan.

For the next two months I noted every telephone call and emergency repair submission, in readiness for the punch-up that was sure to follow when I took the matter to higher authority. Meanwhile, not a single pane of glass was replaced.

Brigade HQ grew weary of my constant grumbling and finally gave me the name of the warrant officer who was supposed to be running the renovation project.

"He's the chappie who is actually wunning the show," said Rodney, a snotty-nosed officer blighted with a pronounced lisp.

"Oh! Somebody is actually in charge of the project then?" I sneered.

"Yes, it's WO2 Smith. He's been away on a long course for several months, but he'll be back on Monday."

"And in all that time fuck all has been done, I suppose?"

The cheeky sod put the phone down on me. I gave Mr Smith a couple of days to settle back in before calling to continue the battle. He turned out to be a decent, helpful Geordie and he confirmed that nothing would ever be done to the block, because it was scheduled for complete renovation. He even appeared at my office with heaps of files, photographs, blueprints and models and convinced me that the modernisation plan was a truly wonderful concept.

"Okay, I agree that the idea is sound in principle, but that doesn't stop the broken pipes in the shit houses from stinking the block out," I said. "What I want to know is exactly when you are going to start work on the Black Hole of Detmold?"

"I had a nasty feeling you'd ask that," he said. "My sheet of paper with the dates on is back in my office. I'll call you in the morning."

"I won't be able to sleep with the suspense."

On 13 April 1989 at 1000 hrs, the answer to the mystery was revealed. My phone rang.

"Hello sir, WO2 Smith here. Work on Block 54 will start in August."

There was a pregnant pause.

"But not this August."

"Go on, tell me. The builders arrive in August 1995," I said sarcastically.

"Not a bad guess actually, sir. They're scheduled for 1997."

So, unless the roof blew off or the place caught fire, by virtue of the fact that we were pencilled in for renovation, they felt no compunction to spend any money on the place for the next eight years! That was disgraceful. As I mentioned before, a toilet and washroom were constructed in the officer's mess in Hohne on the off chance that a certain female might want to powder her nose. The fact that funds can be found to finance such cosmetic projects is difficult to reconcile, given the stupid battle that was going on to prevent the plague from breaking out in Block 54.

Having this building made fit for human habitation became something of an obsession. A new OC arrived, a man still full of thrust and drive and a person who liked to have things done immediately, if not sooner. When he became aware of the extent of the squalor in which our men lived over in the Black Hole, he was all for dragging the officer responsible out of the HQ and sticking his head down one of the lavatory pans. I suggested a little more restraint, but was pleased to receive his blessing to adopt a rather more militant approach. My first opportunity to torpedo them came with the visit of a divisional colonel, who allowed me to discuss matters affecting the efficiency of our unit from my perspective. I invited him to take a tour of the unit lines. He was suitably impressed with the modern and well-maintained appearance of our real estate, until we arrived at Block 54, which I had purposely left until last. He was stunned and asked to see our requisitions for repairs and promised to take the matter up.

The result of the colonel's visit was that my popularity waned considerably over at Brigade HQ, although a few tradesmen arrived to effect minor repairs in the Black Hole. The vile ablutions remained untouched, though, and now smelt like a Turkish lavatory on a summer's day. The Environmental Health officer was the next notable person to be given the unit tour. He declared the infamous block unfit for habitation and laid it on good and thick in his report. It seems that he carried little clout, however, as none of his recommendations were ever taken up.

Our ARU (Annual Inspection of the Unit) was to be carried out by the Brigade Commander on Wednesday and I had prepared a programme that was required to be at the HQ forty-eight hours prior to the inspection. Having given them a sporting chance to enjoy their first cup of coffee, I called them up on Monday morning.

"Good morning Roland. It's Wally Payne, custodian of the Army's most vile piece of real estate. You are aware of the battle I'm waging to have this place made fit for men to live in and you may be pleased to know that this is probably the last time that I shall call you on the subject. As you know, old chap, the brigadier is conducting our ARU on Wednesday. Unless renovation work starts in Block 54 by tomorrow afternoon, then my OC and I will arrange for morning coffee on the day of the inspection to be served in the toilet area of the block." I said this much to the joy of the OC, who was listening in.

Roland muttered something about blackmail, but that same afternoon, heavy plant appeared at the site. They started work on Tuesday morning, but by Wednesday we had a major crisis on our hands. The builders succeeded in fracturing the water main and flooded the entire ground floor. It all turned out splendidly in the end—the whole place was renovated and all the lads were able to submit sizeable claims for spoilt personal items. The war had been won.

114 Provost Company was an administrative nightmare. I offer a brief explanation of the set-up, fearing, however, that it will be Double Dutch to anyone who has never served in the Army. Here goes. With a HQ in Detmold, the unit had detachments at Herford, Minden and Bielefeld, with police posts in Guetersloh and Hamelin. As if that wasn't enough to keep me busy, matters were confused by the fact that the Bielefeld guys were on the strength of another RMP unit and had alternative masters at HQ BAOR. Even more confusing was the detachment at Minden, whose men and equipment were on the strength of a unit that was in a different division. This became something of a conundrum at exercise time. An administrative nightmare it may well have been, but I could reconcile myself with the fact that there were loads of guys from whom to select a winning soccer team.

One of my duties was to see all the new arrivals, to find out if they had any family, financial or sexual problems. Mainly, though, I wanted to find out whether the new guy could play football or cricket. At twenty-three years of age, Lance Corporal Milburn was rather older than the majority of NCOs arriving from the Training Centre on their first posting, but given his outstanding academic qualifications, this was hardly likely to prove an impediment to his swift movement up the promotion ladder. As it was still midseason when he arrived, I enquired only about his soccer skills and no mention was made of the summer game. He played centre forward for us for the rest of the season, and most impressive he was too.

When the cricket season arrived, I arranged net practices in my quest for half decent players. Milburn showed no interest in netting and consequently was never selected for the first half dozen fixtures of what proved to be a most successful season. Included in our team was an excellent fast bowler, a Yorkshireman who had actually played in the Lancashire League. He certainly knew his cricket and, following our seventh consecutive victory, we chatted on the way back to the pavilion.

"Appen I don't know why you don't pick Milburn for th'team sir," he said.

"Can he play? He's never told me he can play."

"Appen he's a better bowler than me sir," said the Yorky.

If this were anything like the truth, then Milburn would need to be seen with all haste. By chance, I happened upon him next morning in the NAAFI Foodhall.

"I'm told that you are something of a cricketer, young man?"

"Well, yes sir, I can play a bit," he replied, his slowness of speech and thick Tyneside accent belying his quick wit and undoubted intelligence.

"Have you played for anyone decent?"

"Well, I turned out for Chester-le-Street in the Durham League and then for Durham in the Minor Counties," he replied.

I tried to keep calm.

"Did you play for Durham long?"

"Just for two seasons, because then Middlesex asked me down for trials and I was on the ground staff..."

I didn't hear any more of what he was saying. Bloody hell, we had a county standard player in the unit—well, as near as damn it, and we weren't playing him!

"What do you do?" I asked, my excitement mounting.

"Well, I bowl mainly," he said, "but I can bat a bit as well."

Then I asked the most obvious question.

"Why the hell haven't you been to the nets?"

"I was going to, sir, as soon as my heel gets better. I've badly bruised it, you see, and can't come off my full run."

Bruised heel or not, he was selected for the next game, which just happened to be a vital RMP Swinden Cup match against the much fancied Osnabrueck eleven. A cocky Australian exchange officer led their side. He talked a decent game, but needed his sails trimming. After consultation with Milburn, he agreed to open the bowling off his short run up. His short run up looked fairly long to me and he soon embarrassed the arrogant Aussie and his team. He was ferocious, even at this supposedly reduced pace and soon decimated their batting. By the end of the innings, he had taken six wickets for next to no runs and our target for victory was very modest. To rub things in, he opened the batting too and was still at the crease when we overtook their total with eight wickets still intact. He was an ever-present thereafter and I soon handed the captaincy over to him.

In the middle of the cricket season, one of the staff sergeants from our Herford detachment, a man whose knowledge of sport was minimal, phoned to ask if I was interested in a soccer match.

"It's the middle of the cricket season staff," I explained.

"I know sir, but they're arranging a pre-season tour and wonder if we would like to play them on August 4th."

"Who are they, staff?"

"Celtic," he replied, the name probably sticking in the craw of this devout Orangeman.

"Which Celtic would that be then staff? Herford? Guetersloh? Stalybridge?"

"None of them, sir," he said. "It's Glasgow Celtic."

"You don't know much about soccer, old chap; someone is pulling your leg."

"There's no joke sir, honestly," he explained. "Their German representative has just been into the duty room. Celtic are playing a match against a regional select team on August 4th and they want a mid-morning kick around with someone easy, followed by a drink and a bite to eat before the evening game."

Two months later we hosted a team that played in green and white hoops and had numbers on their shorts. I drank a glass of orange juice with Paul McStay, Charlie Nicholas, Tommy Craig and several others. The squad surprised me by their good manners, friendliness and sobriety—not a glass of beer was there to be seen. The only person taking alcohol was the manager, who appeared more interested in buying a duty free Mercedes than he was in the forthcoming match. It was no surprise to me that he was replaced during the season. The Assistant Manager was kind enough to compliment me on my knowledge of the game, especially the German scene, but surprised me by asking a question to which I believed he should already have known the answer.

"What like are this lot the neet Wullie?"

It seemed odd to me that a professional outfit of Celtic's standing hadn't done their homework on the opposition, but I assured him that the Germans would be hard pressed to hold a Highland League side.

"Nae problem then Wullie, we'll tank them nae bother," said Tommy.

And they did, at a canter, as we watched from the VIP seats.

Our soccer team at 114 wasn't the best in the Army, but we were keen, fit and certainly good enough to lift the RMP Stanley Cup. As 2ic of the unit, for once in my career I was in a position to ensure that an RMP side was properly looked after. My fanaticism may not have won me friends amongst the detachment commanders, but I could ensure that the best available team turned out each week. We had won through to the final of the Stanley Cup that was to be held at Werl, my old stamping ground. I considered this to be a wonderful achievement, although beating Coco Lemond's team in the second round gave me great satisfaction too. I didn't travel to Hohne to see that second round match; the thought of losing the game with him watching would have been too much to bear.

Our opponents in the final were 247 from Berlin. That unit made it through to the final of almost every sporting competition. Just the same, I had never been on the losing side against them in what must have been a dozen encounters over the years, be it at soccer, cricket, rugby or squash. By fiddling course and leave dates, we had our very best side prepared for the big day, and then it snowed and the match was postponed. The date for the final was put back by two weeks, by which time I had problems. For a start, two thirds of the lads were on exercise and had to be brought back in from the field, hardly the ideal preparation for a final. Then, two days before the game, our outstanding goalkeeper was whisked away to Colombia. He was a Spanish linguist and was needed in Medellin. Surely the drug cartels were aware of the upcoming Stanley Cup Final? On the morning of the match there were pitifully few of us on the coach taking us to Werl—thirteen players, the skipper's wife and me, to be precise. As custodian of the unit's various funds, it was certain that the soccer team wouldn't need to put their hands in their pockets today. We breakfasted in style in a decent restaurant and later took a light lunch, arriving at the ground an hour before kick off. Berlin turned up mob handed as usual and filled one side of the touchline with their supporters. This made the skipper's wife and myself feel a little inferior, considering we were the only two people occupying the opposite side. As usual, 247 were the favourites, but our lads were in buoyant mood and definitely looked sartorially superior in their new Sunderland strips. Just before they trotted out for battle, I announced a win bonus—all they could eat and drink, anywhere they wanted to celebrate, always provided we lifted the Stanley Cup, of course. What's the harm of a little bribery, even if it does ruin one's amateur status?

The teams were evenly matched, but with only ten minutes left to play, we were trailing by the odd goal in three. With our team on the attack and the action in their penalty area, the ball appeared to be handled by one of the Berlin defenders. Now, it's just conceivable that the ball may have been played onto the defender's arm, but that didn't stop me from launching into an appeal for a penalty that could be heard several miles away. It's also conceivable that the volume of my scream and the proximity of the referee to the source of the shriek may have influenced his decision. Be that as it may, the dear fellow gave a loud blast on his Acme Thunderer and indicated a spot kick. Phil Tyne calmly slotted the ball home for the equaliser. The score remained at 2–2 after extra time and it came down to a penalty shoot out. Berlin lost their composure, whereas our gallant lads scored with each of the kicks necessary to lift the Stanley Cup. The Berliners were less than generous in defeat, some of their team and supporters suggesting that I had unfairly influenced the referee. Being a good sport was never my strong hand, but the referee is the man with the whistle; there's nothing to stop a spectator voicing his opinion from the sideline. We celebrated back in the Herford Mess—just lots of beer and pizzas, but what a super night.

Once the barriers came down and the British Military Authorities gave permission for personnel to travel over into what had been East Germany, I was in my car and away. There was no sign whatsoever of mine fields, guard posts or barbed wire as the crossing point approached. Someone had been working desperately quickly to remove any evidence, it seems. There was nothing to even suggest where the border had been and it was only when the road surface began to look patchy and the houses shabby that it occurred to me that I was already in the East. I espied an old man and his grandson walking along the road together, so I stopped to give the lad an apple and enquire of the grandfather whether this was indeed the old DDR. He confirmed that it was. He was delighted to tell me that he was visiting his son's house that day, for the first time in ten years. Previously it had been impossible for him, or any other citizens of the DDR, to travel within six kilometres of the Inner German Barrier without special permission.

My first port of call on my lightning trip to the East was Muelhausen, where they made the awful Trabant cars. Next was Eisleben where Martin Luther preached, then Halle, Leipzig and Colditz. By now Colditz will probably be visited by thousands of tourists every week, but at this time a visitor was a rarity. The place was functioning as a mental hospital and I enlisted the assistance of a Downs Syndrome patient to show me around. My high-speed day trip around the old DDR was spoilt somewhat, by a discovery that I made at Leipzig Railway Station on my journey back. There was no film in my camera! All those wonderful shots and I'd forgotten to load up with Kodak.

There was nothing for it but to make another trip the following weekend. The locals must have wondered mightily about the foreigner who was speeding in and out of towns, tarrying only long enough to bang off a couple of pictures. This time my journey took me into Czechoslovakia as well and I stayed overnight in a town with an unpronounceable name, just over the border. My lodgings were at the Hotel Thermal, which struck me as a most inappropriate name for a hotel that was unable to provide its guests with hot water. I fell foul of the local constabulary on my way out of town—by driving the wrong way down a one-way street. A packet of Rothman's cigarettes, carried for such eventualities, not only secured an exemption from serving my time in the salt mines, but a police escort out of town for good measure. Then it was on to Prague, surely one of the most magnificent cities in the world, before heading back to Germany via Pilsen, of beer fame.

My third trip into the DDR within a month was made in the good company of the unit's WRAC staff sergeant, Di Bawden. We had known each other for years and I was always grateful to her for sound advice and for her good humour when things weren't going too well for me. I mention this little excursion, because this was the last time that we ever socialised; a posting saw me off to Hong Kong shortly afterwards and then the dear girl died, far too soon, before I ever saw her again.

Living in a posh house with no requirement to work, all the money you need, a couple of holidays abroad each year and a good social life...Most women would aspire to such a life, wouldn't they? Not my wife. Having been fully involved and occupied as a WRNS officer, she found the lifestyle that she was forced to endure whilst married to me just too tedious. Her only mental stimulation came from playing badminton on Tuesdays and from running the Church Coffee Swindle. She needed something more challenging than that in her life and was willing to leave me in order to find it. So it was back to the mess and life as a single man. Let's face it, isn't that a man's natural state anyway? I could now take in every soccer match in Germany, bowl whenever inclined and prop up the bar without suffering any pangs of conscience. Our union had been a mistake from the start and my overwhelming emotion when she walked out of the door was one of blessed relief

Following a long and distinguished career, the Provost Marshal was leaving the Army on retirement and was visiting all RMP units on his farewell tour. As the OC was on leave, I was in charge of things down Detmold way and was eagerly anticipating my meeting with the brigadier. He was a very decent man and had my greatest respect, but I felt that he might have taken rather more decisive action on my behalf at the time of the Coco Lemond business. I looked forward eagerly to hearing anything that he might wish to say on the subject. As soon as the date for the visit was confirmed, the Deputy Assistant Provost Marshal called me from Herford. As a senior major, he wished to offer his services in the absence of the OC. The devious sod was either looking to kiss the brigadier's arse, or was scared that I might lose my temper and cause a scene in his Divisional area. I firmly impressed upon the major that, despite the fact that he outranked me, he had sweet bugger all to do with the running of 114 Provost Company. He was assured that I was, and would always remain, better equipped to talk to the Provost Marshal than he was and, for good measure, I enquired whether his phone had been out of order during my suspension. That spelled the end of another beautiful friendship.

Before there was even time to pour the Provost Marshal a cup of coffee, he broached the subject of my suspension. He stated that the matter had been unfortunate and badly handled, but added that he wasn't about to run Coco Lemond down. The brigadier had missed his vocation—he ought to have been a diplomat. Unhampered by the compulsion to approach things in a roundabout fashion, I told him that Coco ought to be run down, preferably by a ten-ton lorry. The brigadier finished off his chat about my recent tribulations by asking me to forget the whole unfortunate incident.

"I trust that you haven't lost your enthusiasm for the Corps?" he asked.

"My enthusiasm is non-existent. I am remaining in the RMP until the 15th April next year, when I will be eligible for my officer's pension. Thereafter, I shall disappear, never to be heard of again," I replied.

He seemed genuinely concerned that my feelings had been so badly wounded. He assured me that the Corps needed me and stated that he wanted me to stay. I reiterated my previous comment, assuring him that the 15th April would see me on my bike.

"What have I got to do to appease you?" was his next effort.

"You could try sending me to Hong Kong," I replied brazenly.

"Will you extend your service if I send you to Hong Kong?" he asked.

"Yes."

"Then it's yours," he said, after which we moved on to other matters.

Shortly afterwards and not entirely out of the blue, I received a posting order to Hong Kong.

My replacement arrived two months early. He had been on secondment to the Canadian Armed Forces and they had sent him back before the completion of his tour of duty. After a few days in his company, my sympathy lay with the Canadians. He proved very hard work indeed and it was agreed that I should hand over to him at the earliest opportunity, before blood was spilled. With my embarkation and privilege leave to take before arriving in Hong Kong, I had two months to kill before my presence was required in the Far East.

21

Having scoured the pages of every maritime brochure produced that year; I finally stumbled across a cruise offered by CTC Lines. Their voyage from Southampton to Australia could have been tailor made for me; it would enable me to alight in Singapore, have a couple of days there and then fly up to Hong Kong to take up my appointment. With the proceeds from the sale of my car, I booked a single cabin on the *MV Belorussia*.

Don't ask me how she found out, but my wife phoned up to have a go.

"I hear that you have sold the car and bought a cruise ticket. Half of that money should be mine," she declared.

"How do you work that out? I bought that car for cash before we were married?"

"My lawyer says I'm entitled to half."

"Tell your lawyer to bugger off."

Suddenly my brain, oft times devoid of original thought but occasionally known to spring into positive action, came up with a brilliant method of escaping from this latest attempt to elicit funds from the Payne estate. Her silver fox fur coat was still hanging in a wardrobe in my house in Leicester.

"Okay, you can have half of the money. That's fifteen hundred—do you want cash or a cheque?" I said, probably much to her surprise.

"A cheque will be fine thank you."

"Okay, I'll send it to you in a parcel."

"I said a cheque would do."

"Yes, I heard you, but it will need to be in a parcel, because it will be wrapped in half of your fur coat. Do you prefer the left or right-hand side?"

"You can't do that!" she wailed. "I bought that coat for cash before we were married."

There was a long pause, as the realisation of what she had just said registered and then she put the phone down.

Before you could say 'shiver me timbers', I was travelling on my first class complimentary rail ticket to join the good ship *Belorussia*. Only one other CTC label was evident on a traveller's suitcase and I only noticed this guy as we pulled into Southampton station. We passed the time of day and shared a taxi to the docks. The taxi ride afforded me ample time to realise that Ken, a chef from Sunderland, was a raving poofter. As it transpired, he was a very decent guy.

I was anxious to get into the departure lounge, to eye up the pretty little things that would be travelling with us on the Love Boat. A stunning sight greeted me as I stepped into the place. It was awash with passengers journeying with Saga, the company that does holidays for pensioners. Those who weren't with Saga were with Saga Plus, who cater for the over eighties. The only time I've ever seen so many wheelchairs gathered in one place was at the start of the London Marathon. Not a bedworthy female was in sight. I went on board with my new chum Ken and we had our pictures taken at the top of the gangplank. Perhaps this was the nearest I'd get to a lady on this trip?

The ship had recently been refitted and my cabin was terrific, as were the dining room and the other public rooms. At mealtimes, we were served by flocks of attractive Ukrainian waitresses, all sworn to a non-fraternisation clause under their contracts it appeared. Even without female company, the next twenty-four days to Singapore would be perfectly bearable. Our second evening aboard saw the Captain's 'Welcome Aboard' evening, which was the only formal event of the trip. Given that the majority of passengers were Australians, it came as something of a surprise to see dinner jackets and ball gowns on show at the 'do'. Not a pair of shorts, vest or pair of thongs in the place. After dinner I wandered along to the ballroom to listen to the band, but tiring quickly of the Valeta and Charleston, I left the dancing to the geriatrics and made for the bar at the back of the ship. I was scarcely half way down my first pint, when a vision in green materialised. The tall, pretty lady of no more than twenty-five summers didn't beat about the bush.

"Care to come back to the front of the ship for a dance?" she asked in a marked Aussie accent.

"Dancing isn't something that I do," I replied, using one of the *Reader's Digest's* 'Ten Ways of Refusing Without Upsetting' that had featured in this month's issue.

It didn't work and she was miffed.

"Are you knocking me back?" she asked.

"If 'knocking back' translates into English as declining your kind offer, then yes madam, I'm knocking you back."

She went off on her own, leaving me to my beer.

Next morning, all those who were capable of making it up to the sports deck without a Zimmer Frame gathered to see what the sporting programme had to offer. Resplendent in my Leicester Tigers rugby jersey, I found myself next to the Australian girl, who was no less pretty for having shed her ball gown in favour of a pair of shorts. My goodness, what a pair of pins! Following a little sporting chatter, I attempted an apology for knocking her back the previous evening and suggested a cup of coffee by way of a peace offering. She accepted.

Over a couple of tinnies in the bar that same evening, we got down to the nitty gritty. She explained that finances had required her to travel steerage on this voyage and that she was occupying a lower deck cabin with three other persons, one who appeared to be suffering from TB, the second who was asthmatic and a third, who suffered from a bladder condition. I felt it my duty to explain to the damsel in distress that my cabin, on the promenade deck, had two bunks and only one occupant, a man whose speciality was giving afternoon cuddling lessons to young Australian ladies. Now that may well be as corny a line as it is possible to cast, but the bait was taken and I had my shipboard romance after all. Andrea was twenty-four and easily young enough to be my daughter, but that's how I like them. We were both otherwise involved and so our arrangement was that we would enjoy each other's company as far as Singapore, whereupon we would shake hands and say goodbye. It worked perfectly and, having played the part of happy tourists in Lisbon, Malta, Port Said and Colombo, our paths diverged early one morning in Singers.

After two perfectly average days in Singapore, which in my view had lost a lot of its character following the drive to create a modern, clean and efficient city, it was time to climb aboard a Singapore Airways flight bound for Hong Kong.

My arrival in Hong Kong was perfectly timed. A quick handover from my predecessor, which was a waste of effort given that he did everything in such a nonconformist fashion and it was time to get on with the Christmas and New Year festivities. Over the holiday period, I was preoccupied with the question of whether I wanted to continue in the Corps or not. Despite surviving the nonsense in Hohne and being given the Corp's plum posting, it didn't take a genius to realise that my career was over. They had given me my Pyrrhic victory by sending me to Hong Kong, but you just don't rock the boat in the Army and get away with it. My conclusion was that it was time to call it a day. I had no interest left, no longer had any confidence in or respect for the upper echelon and, despite all the fun to be had in Hong Kong, I didn't want to wear that red beret for another two years. On my first day back at work after the holiday, I threw my letter of resignation onto the colonel's desk. He was surprised, but as he was leaving the Colony imminently, I don't suppose he cared one way or the other. Nevertheless, he went through the motions of asking me to reconsider. That was a futile gesture—my irrevocable decision had been made and all I wanted to do now was to hand in my warrant card at the earliest opportunity.

The required forms were submitted to the required departments in the required fashion. Now it was only a question of waiting for an acknowledgement and a date for leaving Her Majesty's employment. It was a long time in coming. A letter from Provost Marshal's Branch was hand delivered by the new colonel when he arrived to take over the unit, several weeks later! The letter contained all the paperwork that I had submitted six weeks previously, with a scribbled note attached, directing my attention to a section that had not been filled in to their satisfaction. Had it taken them six weeks to discover the error? My second effort was equally unacceptable for some other piffling reason and this was returned, along with a very snotty letter from a major who was clearly toeing the party line. He suggested that my release date would be delayed unless I filled in the forms correctly next time. Who did he think he was kidding? Since this major was being so bloody childish, I decided to show him what being infantile *really* means. The following note was sent directly to the Provost Marshal. I was well aware that it would win me no plaudits, but it would have the effect of letting him know that I was being fucked around unnecessarily by one of his subordinates. Mind you, my gut feeling was that he was driving the whole nonsense himself anyway. One thing for certain, he wouldn't appreciate my insolence and would be forced to act. The note read:

Tick the box you think most accurately reflects the comments that should be directed to an officer who tenders his resignation after 27 years loyal service in the 'caring' Corps of Royal Military Police.

A.   *Thanks for your loyal service, Wally, and every good wish in Civvy Street.*

B.   *Are you sure you want to leave chum, why not reconsider?*

C. *This application simply isn't good enough! It doesn't conform with AGAI para 38.006! If you don't submit Annex A to Chapter 38 of AGAIs correctly, you may be required to serve a full year's notice.*

It wasn't a very good effort; on reflection, I ought to have been much more caustic. Having popped the letter into the mailbag, I had the good fortune to injure myself playing badminton during the HMS Tamar Mini Olympics, probably the lowest standard of badminton played anywhere in the world. My doubles partner was no badminton man and I ran around in circles covering for him, doing something horrible to my back. Prior to this incident I had always given short shrift to guys who complained of back pain, something that I will never do again. As I lay on my bed in the mess, unable to discover any way of positioning myself that didn't cause me agony, my letter reached the PM. He was so incensed that he called Hong Kong to speak to me. It would have been a one-way conversation, I fancy, but with me lying on my bed board and unable to move, it was the colonel who took his call and the initial flak. The PM ordered that Captain Payne should submit a letter, giving his reasons for wishing to leave the Corps. This letter, he decreed, was to include an apology for the content of the unsolicited note sent by the said captain. My letter, penned whilst still suffering considerably from my bad back, read:

I have been instructed by the Colonel to write to you explaining my reasons for wishing to retire from the Army. One overriding reason has prompted this action, although a combination of minor factors has influenced my decision.

You will be aware of the incident at Hohne in March 1989, which involved Maj Lemond and me and resulted in my suspension and subsequent posting to Detmold. Despite the two years which have since elapsed, I am still angered by that officer's spurious allegations and the fact that he caused me to believe that I was suspended for a three-month period, when in fact he never saw fit to process the suspension certificate up the chain of command. The most hurtful matter, however, is that during those three months when my liberty was taken (QR 6015 prevented me from visiting my Unit, Barracks or Mess), not one person from 111 Pro Coy, HQ RMP 1 (BR) Corps, HQ BAOR (Pro) or HQ PM (A) ever contacted me with advice, council or instruction. Indeed, to this day, I have still to be informed of the outcome of my representation. The treatment of this honest burgher was shabby and the betrayal by a senior officer, whose promise of an investigation into the bizarre episode never materialised, left a sour taste. To me, it will always remain a matter of the utmost incredulity that my Corps allowed what was, by any stretch of the imagination, a minor occurrence, to escalate into a dispute requiring an officer's suspension for 3 months and a representation to the Army Board. I am aware that allowing an incident that is now history to fester is counterproductive, but I have learnt a desultory lesson regarding the value placed on service and loyalty within the RMP. The consequence is that my love of the Corps is dead, without prospect of resurrection, and I feel that I am no longer capable of giving myself wholeheartedly to the job. To continue any longer, even in Hong Kong, would be unfair to my Colonel and to the NCOs in my charge.

Recently I have discovered that petty regulations that I would have shrugged off as part and parcel of Army life not long ago, have become matters of severe irritation. Instructions to 'complete in triplicate', 'annotate in red' or 'submit detailed justification' are simply begging a ribald reply from me. Such rude comments would be manifestations of my impetuosity, a characteristic commented upon by generations of CR compiling OCs and which, despite my headlong plunge towards that awkward age, stubbornly refuses to abate. My recent unfunny submission to your office falls into this category and I apologise for being rude enough to post it.

Unlike the first 25 years of my service, the last 2 years have proved less than fulfilling. For me the Army is no longer fun. I believe Sir that I have given the RMP a good run, but that the time to move on to pastures new is overdue. The last thing I seek is an acrimonious departure and I therefore request that you sanction my retirement at the earliest date convenient to the Corps.

That just about hit the nail on the head and it wasn't too bad an effort considering that I was in acute pain whilst putting pen to paper. What pleased me was the fact that I managed to skirt around an apology for the content of my other letter, merely feigning my remorse for having posted it instead. It was undoubtedly an unconventional way of achieving my aim, but nonconformity has always been my style and this time it worked. Permission was granted for me to draw retired pay with effect from 5 Aug 91.

I wasn't able to rediscover any of the fire that had been a part of my character prior to the Lemond fiasco and this latest battle with PM (A) did nothing to fuel the embers either. It was just a matter of going through the motions after that, which is enough to adequately perform your job in Honkers anyway. In reality, it was all sport, social functions, horse racing and leg over for me from then on.

Life was very swish in the officer's mess, especially for a lad who had grown up on the New Parks Estate, not Leicester's most salubrious district. My suite was on the twenty-fifth floor, which gave me an unrestricted view over Hong Kong harbour and Causeway Bay through one window and the traffic jams in Gloucester Road through the other. Suffering from a lifelong fear of heights, however, I would gladly have forgone the magnificent vistas for a bed down at ground level. The view over the harbour from the dining room was magnificent and I never tired of it. The food was excellent and there were so many waiters that they fell over one another in their efforts to serve us. The only meal that didn't appeal to me was tea, which was nothing like the tea my Mam used to fry up for me. This was the toff's version and was always the same as far as I could make out. Someone in procurement had cornered the market in tuna and cucumber, and wafer thin sandwiches containing those two fillings were there for our delectation each evening. The Mess took up three floors of the inverted gin bottle that was the Prince of Wales Building, inside which you could have spent your entire tour had you been so inclined. Messes, dining facilities, offices, accommodation, the gym, squash courts, tennis courts, car parks, the library and even a church were all to be found inside this one skyscraper, and a small skyscraper at that by Hong Kong standards.

One Sunday morning I decided to give the church a whirl, the first time I've ever gone to church simply by descending in a lift. The vicar was fine, the folk that made up the small congregation were all very pleasant and the curry lunch in the officer's mess following the service was first rate. After a month or so, it suddenly struck me as odd that the post service lunches were always held in the officer's mess. What about the grunters in the vicar's flock? Did they have some special dispensation that allowed them into the officer's mess? That I doubted very much. The vicar provided the answer.

"Considering that the congregation consists predominately of officers, I consider it reasonable that the curry lunch should be held in the mess. I'm afraid the other ranks do not attend the church in sufficient numbers to warrant consideration," he explained, unsatisfactorily in my view.

The arrogant man of the cloth was given the benefit of my opinion on this subject and I defected immediately to the Methodist Church in Queens Road East, where discrimination was not practiced.

One of the drawbacks of living in that lofty tower was the fire alarm system, which had been fitted many years before and was in drastic need of an overhaul. The bells were always going off in the middle of the night and, although everyone knew they heralded a false alarm, it was a brave man that took this risk of staying in his bed on the twenty-fifth floor. Walking down all those stairs during the wee small hours of the morning was something I could have cheerfully done without, along with the rugby scrum for the lift back up once the proceedings had been declared to be a false alarm.

For all the home comforts provided in the mess, my social life was so full that I seldom used the facilities. I heard tell there was a TV lounge and a snooker room somewhere, but I never found the time to locate them.

At least twice a week, my very best Chinese chum, Lin Hung Yee, would invite me to join his friends for dinner. These often lavish affairs were invariably held in an establishment that had never seen a 'gwai lo' customer before. One of the regular venues for these dinner nights was the Pigeon Restaurant in Chai Wan, a huge establishment that specialised in 'Eat and Drink all you can' nights that really drew in the punters. The place was unusually crowded on the evening that a Mandarin singer from the mainland was engaged to belt out a few numbers for the enjoyment of the diners, as they tucked into chicken's feet and sucked on San Miguel bottles. Halfway through that evening, the Master of Ceremonies appeared mysteriously at our table and soon became engaged in a conversation with Cecil Chan. Now my Cantonese isn't up to much, but I do know when someone is talking about me because I can recognise my Chinese name, Ngau Ching Leung. It baffles me as to how my Chinese friends came to select that name for me, since it translates into something like 'Bad Tempered Bull'. The MC began making notes as Cecil spelled out my name in English.

"W-A-L-L-Y, Warry. P-A-Y-N-E, Pay-nee. Warry Paynee."

"Why are you giving that man my name Cecil?" I asked.

"I not give him your name."

"Yes you did. Look, he's written it down in his book."

"He just want know your name, because you only gwai lo in restaurant."

That didn't strike me as particularly plausible, but with large volumes of San Mig and brandy inside me, I gave the matter no more thought. The Mandarin lady came back to do her second spot just then, this time dressed in the scantiest of costumes. After a few songs, the lights went off and the place was thrown into pitch darkness. The MC took the microphone and began to announce what I presumed to be the next song. His voice rose gradually, until he shouted out the only three words I understood.

"Mister Warry Paynee."

At that, there was a drum roll and a one million candlepower spotlight picked me out. That swine Cecil Chan had volunteered me to sing and dance with the entertainer. The rest of our gang pushed me forward and, not wishing to lose face, I climbed onto the stage to join the sequined singer. The embarrassment was almost too much to bear as I was forced to dance with her for an uncomfortable couple of minutes, before she elected to sing the only

Mandarin song to which I know the words. My rendition of 'Rose, Rose, I Love You' was reasonable, presumably, since the drunken audience gave me a tumultuous ovation as I returned, red faced, to my table, the sounds of 'Encore' ringing in my ears.

Another of Lin Hung Yee's dinner nights took place up in China, in a city with a million inhabitants but the name of which I had never heard before. White men were certainly a novelty in town and parents brought their children to the bar where we were drinking our beer, just to witness the phenomenon. Now the boys thought it amusing to order the most outrageous dishes whenever I was present and the restaurant where we dined that evening had enough strange items on the menu to allow them to excel. Before we went in, Lin pointed out an animal locked in a cage outside the restaurant. I had never seen its like before. It looked something like a small beaver and Lin called it a forest fox, although it looked nothing like a fox to my eye. The thing was tame and hungry, so I fed it with some lettuce leaves. Following an appetizer of silk worms, which my Chinese pals insist are good for the eyes, or is it the testicles, we were served with a mild curry. It tasted reasonable and the meat had the taste and texture of beef. I asked Lin if he knew what kind of meat was in the curry.

"You remember nice little animal that you fed with lettuce leaves?" he said.

Oh no! They say that the Cantonese will eat anything with four legs apart from a table and a chair, but surely not tame forest foxes? There wasn't much on that menu to tickle my taste buds and the terrapin soup was particularly nasty. The last dish was Foo Yung, an omelette that the chef fills with anything he has left over. This one was good, a bit salty, certainly, but tasty enough to tempt me into a second helping.

"What's in the Foo Yung, Lin?" I enquired.

"I don't know name in English, but you know when rice get wet and then the fly lay eggs on rice? Then little white things that move about come from eggs—that is what in the foo yung."

Rice maggots!

At the other end of the spectrum, there are a profusion of good restaurants in Hong Kong and one of my favourites was the Bombay Palace, which didn't serve Chinese food, needless to say. I took my fellow officer's mess inmate Chris Hodges to supper there one evening. Although the very best of company, Chris is a self-confessed sporting illiterate, from whom a sagacious sporting snippet would be unlikely. Looking across the tables full of diners, who hailed predominately from the Indian sub-continent, I remarked to Chris that one of the gentlemen sitting on the next table bore a striking resemblance to World Squash Champion, Jahingar Khan.

"Wouldn't know him if I bumped into him," replied Chris. "And what's squash, by the way?"

I called the manager over for a quiet word.

"Hey up Gupta, that bloke sitting opposite me looks the spitting image of Jahingar Khan," I said.

"There is a very good reason for the likeness, Mr. Wally," replied Gupta. "You see, that is Jahingar Khan. And the gentleman sitting with his back to you, that is none other than Jansher Khan."

How dare Jansher Khan sit with his back to me! The highlight of the evening came later, when I was watering the horse. Who should come in and use the urinal next to mine? None other than the great man Jahingar, that's who. I can't imagine why he should have recognised me, but he obviously did because it was he who initiated the conversation.

"Hello," he said.

"Hello," I replied.

Okay, so it wasn't much of a conversation, but have *you* ever talked to him?

It didn't take me long to reacquaint myself with the Wanchai district when I first arrived. It wasn't what it had been in the old days, for sure, but there were still plenty of places to enjoy an evening, at a price. The Old China Hand was still standing and it became my watering hole away from the mess. Sitting in the corner of the place one evening was a guy who looked familiar and our eyes met several times before I decided to wander over and talk to him.

"I'm probably quite mistaken," I said, "but you bear a striking resemblance to an old pal who I haven't set eyes upon for the best part of twenty years."

"Don't tell me I've changed that much Wally, you haven't," replied Gordon Rose, one of my old teammates in the Army soccer side.

We spent a lot of time together after that, drinking beer and talking football. Come to think of it, that's all Gordon and I ever did talk about.

Notwithstanding my activities on the soccer front, playing squash, walking the Hong Kong hills, eating, drinking and generally making merry, there was also the twice-weekly horse racing to contend with. Early in my tour I met up with Alan Kenworthy, a guy that had served with me in RMP Hong Kong the last time I was there. As well as him helping to fill in my social calendar with lunch dates at expensive restaurants and being my snooker opponent every

Friday afternoon, Kenworthy was something of a horse man and always good for a tip. (Sorry about the snooker, colonel. You thought I was holding the fort whilst you were up in Fanling playing golf, didn't you?)

One Saturday morning Kenworthy tipped me the sure-fire winner of the first race on the afternoon card at Sha Tin. I travelled up to the racetrack by train and, as it was a cool day, I wore a jerkin that had a zipped pocket on the upper arm. It was the perfect place to put my identity card and cash. A chap who was as streetwise in Hong Kong as me ought to have known better than carry cash around like that and I certainly should have known better than to unzip the pocket and count my cash whilst on the underground train. Arriving at the racetrack, I opened the pocket to take out $10 for my entrance fee, only to discover that some opportunist had accepted my open invitation and relieved me of $1900. At least he had the decency to replace my identity card and to zip the pocket back up again, a true professional. That left me without the funds necessary to clean up on the first race, my sole remaining object of value being a return rail ticket. I used it to take me as far as Kowloon Tong, where I alighted from the train, ran to our detachment in Osborn Barracks and borrowed money from every NCO in the unit. By running back to the station and catching the first train, I was able to make it back to Sha Tin with just enough time to place a bet on the first race. Kenworthy's tip obliged at 6–1 and I recouped all the stolen cash with one bet.

Alan Kenworthy, tipster extraordinaire, took me to Macau for a weekend's punting. The plan was to bet by telephone on Hong Kong's Sha Tin Saturday afternoon card, visit the Canidrome for a flutter on the dogs that evening, travel across to watch the Macau horses on Sunday afternoon and, finally, go back to the Canidrome again on Sunday night. We were in a punter's paradise. By using Kenworthy's telephone account, we wagered on the races at Sha Tin and, by the end of race four, we were both well in pocket. Race five was an event for new horses—griffins, as they call them in Hong Kong. After an age studying the racing page, Kenworthy gave his considered judgment.

"Anything can win this bloody race."

The betting had been heavily influenced by the fact that three top class British jockeys had been engaged to ride in the race. The punter's money had all gone onto the three horses partnered by the class jockeys, leaving everything else out with the washing. We bet on the two rank outsiders, to come in first or second with the field and then to come in first and second in their own right; that's called a dual forecast in the UK and a quinella in Hong Kong. In truth, we believed that we were throwing our money away.

All fourteen horses crossed the finishing line together. Following a lengthy steward's enquiry and multiple objections against both of our horses, a photo finish placed our two selections first and second, at 58–1 and 47–1. The quinella paid $9876 for a unit and we had thirteen of them. You don't have them come up like that very often.

The officer's mess had a reserved box at Sha Tin and on the first Saturday in May, because I'd had no offers of a place in a better box that afternoon, I elected to go along and suffer a session with the betting duffers. At that time my punting was going through a particularly lean spell and my April salary had pretty well all gone the way of the Jockey Club. At least it was a charitable organisation. I wasn't yet aware that a chance occurrence earlier in the week was about to affect my fortune.

On Thursday, I had gone walking in the hills above Kowloon and had taken a breather on a path, near to a large boulder on the side of Lion Rock. My sandwiches and Mars Bar safely negotiated, I gathered up my rucksack and set off on the second half of my trek. Not five strides had I taken, when a six-foot monster of a white snake emerged from behind the boulder! It scared the daylights out of me, especially considering that I'd just spent the previous twenty minutes sitting just five yards from its hole. I froze and was quite incapable of doing anything except repeat the words, 'Fucking hell', several dozen times. The snake reacted more positively and hurled itself over the path's edge and into the bush. It was a close run thing as to which of us was the most scared, although my money was on the human. When my Chinese friends heard of my adventure, they were convinced that such a sighting heralded huge amounts of good *fung shui*. They advised that I should bet with absolute confidence at the races on Saturday.

Secure in the knowledge that my *fung shui* was about to reach an all-time high and armed with some hot tips from Alan Kenworthy, it was a confident punter that boarded the bus for Sha Tin. My first long shot bet, or 'exotic' as the Chinese call them, was a double quinella. This involved selecting the first and second horses in two nominated races, a tall order. Kenworthy's tip for Race 1 had been for the favourite (No. 8) to win from either horse 1, 2 or 3. They came home in exactly that order and I won $189—all of which went onto the second leg. His tip for Race 2 was horse No. 7 to win from No.5.

"Throw another horse of your own choice in for good measure," he had advised.

Now the day before, I had written a letter to the members of the sergeant's mess, urging them to pay their fees with rather more haste than hitherto. My tongue in cheek circular offered to accept payment by cash, cheque, bearer bond, promissory note or any foreign currency, with the exception of Nigerian Nunga, considered too volatile, or Vietnamese Dong, which were simply too rude. Remembering this letter, my eye was drawn to one of the beasts running in Race 2, a no-hoper by the name of Dong Win. As the horse's name had caught my eye, however, it would have been folly to omit it, so I included it as my personal selection. Dong Win won and horse No. 7 obliged, too, by coming in second. The long odds against the winner meant that I picked up a huge sum for my efforts. At the tote payout window I waited until two other officers arrived to collect their puny winnings before stepping up to drag myself. I wanted to be observed. News of my mammoth draw spread quickly and on the strength of that win, my tips were in demand for the rest of my tour.

Once Roy of the Rovers hung up his boots, it left me as the world's oldest active soccer player. My boots ought to have been consigned to the bin years before in reality, but as I could still do a few things with the ball without making a complete fool of myself, what was the harm in turning out. Hong Kong is a great place for participating and there are soccer leagues to suit all standards and ages. Wong Sui Ming recruited me for two Chinese sides and I turned out regularly for them. My problem was that I could never last a game out. It had nothing to do with my fitness, but rather with the fact that my left calf muscle was knackered. For five years I had strained it in every match and it was in the lap of the gods as to how long I lasted. Several Army doctors had examined my calf and had all come to the same conclusion.

"You're too old, pack it in."

What did *they* know?

Following a particularly bad strain during Saturday's match, I was still limping on Monday morning as Staff Sergeant Roger Ching passed my way. He was a keen local player and offered to take me to see his Chinese doctor friend, a man who specialised in sports injuries. Most Europeans give little credence to the ability of the local bone doctors, but when it comes to the knocks and strains common to soccer players, perhaps they do have something to offer. Roger took me down to Western, not a place where white faces proliferate, and into his pal's surgery. To my amazement, I knew the fellow! Many years previously he had been the team doctor to Jardines FC, when they played in the Hong Kong first division. My photo was even on his surgery wall, as part of the Army FC team that had graced the league at the same time. His examination was swift. After a few pokes, knowledgeable nods and Cantonese cries of dismay, he asked my age.

"Ah so! You already too old! Stop playing now and throw away boots," he advised.

The kindly doctor went on to explain what was causing my problem and convinced me that my playing days were over. He was wrong just the same. Not long afterwards, Gordon Rose put on his sports physiotherapist's hat and cured my long-standing problem in two, five-minute sessions.

I was to meet the Chinese doctor again, rather more quickly than I would ever have expected. This time, though, the roles were reversed and I drove Roger Ching to the surgery for treatment. Our unit side was playing against the Military Hospital team on their pitch when Roger was felled by an awful tackle and lay prone on the ground. As luck would have it, they had a doctor in their side. Following his diagnosis and immediate first aid, he called me onto the pitch to tell me that Roger had a Collis' Fracture of the arm, which involves a fracture and a dislocation in the same place seemingly and is very painful. I took him to reception for treatment and although an X-ray confirmed the soccer-playing physician's diagnosis, Roger refused further treatment. He wanted to be treated by a Chinese doctor, so I drove him over to Western.

The traffic was awful and the journey took an age, much to the consternation of Roger, who was suffering badly by the time we arrived. The injured man explained his problem to his Chinese doctor, who promptly summoned three assistants before setting about our gallant winger. The assistants pinned him to the floor and the doctor replaced his dislocation without giving him as much as an aspirin to numb the pain. It was the only time that I saw a Chinese turn pure white. The doctor then told me to take his friend back to the military hospital for further treatment, leaving me wondering why we had travelled all the way to Western in the first place. The medics at the military hospital were most reasonable, I thought, considering that Roger had spurned their earlier offers of treatment and they soon plastered his arm. If he were to suffer from the same injury again, I wonder whether he would choose to be treated by a Chinese doctor?

It was only to be expected that I should fall out with someone before leaving Hong Kong and, of course, I did.

I have played some rugby and watched a great deal more, but have never really been one of the rugby crowd. I dislike having to drink beer because it's mandatory to do so and I'm not passionately fond of women supporters who wear sheepskin coats and know more about the game than me. My interest in the Hong Kong Sevens, therefore, was minimal and the frantic panic by mess members to obtain tickets for the event left me puzzled. The mess was in turmoil as the event approached. The 'Sevens' were, by all accounts, the highlight of the Hong Kong social calendar and an event definitely not to be missed, always provided you could get a ticket. The mess received a small allocation, although I didn't even bother to put my name down for the scheduled ballot.

Being blithely unaware of the value of tickets, I had actually declined the offer of a Chinese friend, who claimed that he could provide me with as many as I wanted. Realising that I might be in a position to help out those who were unlucky in the ballot, I called up to see if my pal's offer was still extant. Two hours later, forty tickets were in my possession. This acquisition was to make me a villain and a hero, simultaneously. The ballot for the tickets obtained through official sources was made next day, immediately after our tea of thinly cut tuna and cucumber sandwiches. After the draw, one lucky female produced her pair for my inspection and the rest of those on whom fortune had shone were soon flaunting their tickets with glee. Astonished at this reaction, I considered this a pertinent time to produce my collection. In all innocence and with profit making the furthest thing from my mind, I offered my tickets to mess members at face value. Almost immediately an officer from the RTR pounced on me. He was a member of the Sevens Ticket Distribution Committee, apparently. There had been some pretty serious monkey business with ticket distribution in previous years and this man and his committee had been commissioned to sort the problem out. The fact that someone with no connection with the game in the Colony could produce an envelope containing no less than forty of the things indicated that the system was still badly flawed. He flew into a rage, or as much of a rage as is possible for a man with such an appalling stutter.

"W-w-w-were did you g-get those t-t-tickets?" he d-demanded.

"Does it really matter? I'm merely trying to help out those without them," I replied.

"N-n-nobody is allowed to p-purchase m-m-more than t-ten."

"I didn't purchase any; they were obtained for me on sale or return."

"I b-b-believe that these t-tickets were ob-obtained illegally."

"Are you accusing me of having committed an illegal act? In which case, may I remind you of the laws pertaining to defamation of character?"

"N-n-no, I'm n-not accusing you of anything, it's j-j-just that n-nobody may p-p-purchase m-more than t-ten t-tickets."

"Look here chum, anyone may purchase ten tickets, right? Well, four Chinese friends bought ten tickets each and gave them to me. They are not stolen, but purchased from the legal outlet. There is nothing on the tickets to say that they are not transferable and I am selling them at face value and not trying to make a profit. What's your gripe?"

David wasn't a happy ticket distribution committeeman; his plan for fair distribution obviously didn't work. It didn't work because it was devised by Brits, in the assumption that they were dealing with fellow Brits and that fair play would prevail. But this was Hong Kong, the Chinese were in charge of distribution and British rules didn't apply. I wonder what he would have said if he had been privy to the truth? The tickets had come directly from a Chinese pal who was involved with the distribution; they had never come anywhere near to being offered to the public. What's more, getting my hands on a further forty tickets, or a hundred and forty for that matter, could have been done by simply picking up the telephone. Many Army officers live in a world so divorced from reality that they are a liability to themselves and to their men. David was such a man and he wasn't finished with me yet.

"I-I-I must ask you to d-disclose your s-s-source. If y-you d-don't disclose your s-s-source, I shall t-take the m-matter f-f-further."

"Please your bloody self. I shall dispose of these tickets elsewhere. The mess members know who to thank for the fact that they are no longer available to them."

The RTR man was not about to let the matter drop and he approached me several times, to demand that I reveal my supplier's name. He was beginning to make me feel like a criminal. He even went to the extent of informing the police, although quite what he thought they could do for him is beyond me. Some of my tickets went to our corporals, several to a cook at Stanley Fort and others to a policeman in the New Territories. David was finally reconciled to the fact that I was never going to disclose the information he wanted and so he resorted to ignoring me. He refused to speak at breakfast, pretended not to see me when we passed in the corridor and lifted his head haughtily as we passed each other on our training runs. As the weekend of the 'Sevens' approached, he made a last, desperate effort to discover the source of the tickets. It was an agitated David that collared me down in the foyer of the Prince of Wales Building.

"C-C-Captain P-Payne, I shall ask you one m-more t-time to divulge the n-name of the p-p-person who supplied you with those t-t-tickets."

"Give up chum, I won't tell you."

"V-Very well, I shall inform your c-colonel."

"David, be my g-g-guest," I replied.

By the time I'd reached my office that morning, less than five minutes walk from the main building on foot, the colonel was aware of the situation. David had wasted no time in getting on the blower. The colonel invited me into his office.

"I understand that you have a large supply of 'Sevens' tickets?" he stated.

"No sir. I did have, but they're all sold by now. However, if you need a few?"

"No, no, I have some already. It's just that David has been on the phone and I think that you are aware of his dilemma. Couldn't you just inform him of where you obtained such a large supply?"

"No, I couldn't and David can fuck off."

"Would you tell me where you obtained them?"

"No sir, I won't."

I walked out of his office. With my time to do in the Army, both he and David could kiss my arse.

By the time the following year's event came around, David and his committee had changed their method of allocation. This system didn't work either. I was a civvy by this time, but had plenty of tickets if anybody wanted them. And they came from exactly the same source.

You have to be very careful where you dip your wick as an officer, for there is always some sneaky sod willing to drop you in the shit and military history is littered with promising careers cut short by a moment's indiscretion. Of all females, the WRAC must be avoided like the plague. A liaison with a female NCO and you're on your bike before you can say Exemplo Ducemus. With so much spare around in Hong Kong, it's the height of folly to involve yourself with them anyway. Even as a single officer, the thought of a dalliance with a WRAC girl had never entered my mind, until Corporal Lewis asked for a personal interview. She was an attractive young woman whose private life had been scarred by a tragedy beyond her control. Basically, she needed two things, a mature shoulder to cry on and a posting back to the UK with all haste. The posting was easy to fix but, fool that I am, so was a shoulder for her to cry on. She was in my office regularly, on the pretext of me giving her an update on her posting, but we began to enjoy our chats more and more. For fear of gossip, I stopped seeing her in my office and took her out for drinks instead. Then we started jogging together and walking the hills at weekends. It had been a long time since I had felt so comfortable with a lady and the urge to get inside her knickers was considerable. Somehow, however, we managed to keep the relationship platonic. It would have been crazy to get involved; both of our careers would have been in jeopardy. Hell, my pension was only weeks away! Mercifully, her posting order came and she returned to the UK to sort out her life. For my part, I shall never stop kicking myself for not chancing my arm.

"No farewell functions for me, folks—just let me slip off into the sunset, like John Wayne on his horse," I had instructed all and sundry.

The men of RMP Hong Kong had other ideas, however, and my last week in the Army turned into an ordeal by food and alcohol. On Monday, there was a splendid party thrown by my civilian Chinese pals, at a restaurant in Aberdeen. Tuesday saw me bending my arm with the corporals in Hong Kong and, on Wednesday, I was ambushed by the corporals from Kowloon. I felt a little queasy on Thursday morning, but that evening's function promised to be rather more civilised. The colonel had invited me to his house for dinner. A thoroughly enjoyable evening was in prospect, if his previous dinner nights were anything to go by.

Armed with a decent bottle of champagne for the colonel's memsahib, I walked from the mess to the duty room to bum a lift up to the colonel's quarter. During this two-minute walk, I saw several of the unit's senior ranks walking towards the Prince of Wales Building, including several that were stationed up in the New Territories. I gave them a cheery wave. Never for a moment did it register that it was unusual to see men from Sek Kong on the Island during the week. Even at the colonel's house, it never occurred to me that anything was amiss, not even the fact that despite being early, I was the last to arrive. The dining table wasn't set for dinner, but the colonel explained that away when he announced we would be dining in the officer's mess. I had been through the mess dining room only thirty minutes earlier and it hadn't been set for dinner either, yet still nothing clicked. We were all driven to the barracks and it was only when we were in the lift and someone pressed the button for the twenty-second floor that I finally smelled a rat. The officer's mess dining room was on the twenty-fifth floor. The lift stopped and the door opened to reveal the RSM standing directly outside in the sergeant's mess foyer.

"Captain Payne, sir, welcome to the Warrant Officer's and Sergeant's Mess and to your dining out evening," he announced.

The buggers had only organised a full regimental dinner, less mess kit, in my honour. I had been taken in brilliantly, which spoke volumes for my powers of observation. People said gushing things about me, the colonel made a fine speech and the food, drink and company of my comrades were of the highest order. It was a truly memorable occasion and next morning I awoke to my fourth hangover in a row. Friday night promised to be even harder going.

The corporals, desperate to see the back of me presumably, held yet another farewell during Happy Hour. I was saved from tarrying too long in their company by the fact that I had to leave at 1830 hrs and hotfoot it back to the Island for my officer's mess livers-in farewell bash. I was already three parts pissed before sitting down to what was another fabulous do. There were still a few of us in the Mess at 0500 hrs, drinking half pints of Bailey's Irish Cream.

It was Saturday afternoon before a raging thirst brought me out of a drunken slumber. A screeching hangover, combined with the permanent desire to vomit, made me contemplate the wisdom of getting into my current state. I stayed in bed all afternoon, rising only to take a sip of water or to be sick. Teatime came and there was no respite; soon it would be time to get ready for the big one, the Chinese NCOs farewell dinner. In my current condition, there was no prospect of me making it to the Victoria Hotel. At 1800 hrs, though, showing courage beyond the call of duty, I forced my evil body out of bed and performed my ablutions. I would have much preferred to stay put, but such was the importance of this dinner that I needed to make the supreme effort. To fail to turn up would have caused great loss of face, both for me and to the organisers. The queasy feeling wouldn't abate, though, and between the mess and the main gate I needed to divert a couple of times, to wretch in the bushes. I made it only as far as City Hall, before veering left into the building to inspect their porcelain. Four hundred yards further on and I was sick in the harbour. What a disgrace! One of the Chinese guys caught up with me just before the Victoria Hotel and I was able to spin him a load of bullshit about having eaten some bad seafood. The trek to the hotel had been the most miserable one-mile walk of my life.

Edmund Chung, the senior Chinese soldier in our unit, had laid on a classy affair in a superior restaurant; the boys were doing me proud. As usual at Chinese functions, there was a lot of drinking, talking and playing of Mah Jong before getting down to the eating. I walked around like a zombie, attempting to make my frequent trips to the toilet as surreptitiously as possible and trying to create the illusion that the party was fun. My stomach had never been as bad as this before and I tried some Chinese tea with supposedly curative properties, but that only sent me off to the lavatory again. A glass of hot water was prescribed by one of the lads, but that made me sick too. Even the hair of the dog failed. The fact was that there was no way I was going to survive a dozen courses of Chinese banquet. Despite the huge loss of face, there was nothing for it but to get to bed and sleep this awful hangover off. On the pretext of visiting the toilet once again, I slipped away and walked along the harbour front, back to the mess. Edmund Chung gave me my present next day. I apologised wholeheartedly for letting him down and really meant it. He explained that he had covered up for me, by telling everyone that I had been sick for several days, which was right in a way. He saved my face and gained my undying gratitude.

My last official day in the Army was the 5th August 1991, by which time I was already earning a second wage with a civilian company down in Thailand.

END

978-0-595-35110-7
0-595-35110-7

Printed in the United Kingdom
by Lightning Source UK Ltd.
106650UKS00001B/44